The Right Hand of Command

The Right Hand of Command

Use and Disuse of Personal Staffs in the American Civil War

R. Steven Jones

STACKPOLE
BOOKS

Published by
STACKPOLE BOOKS
5067 Ritter Road
Mechanicsburg, PA 17055
www.stackpolebooks.com

Printed in the United States of America

10 9 8 7 6 5 4 3 2 1
First Edition

Jones, R. Steven
    The right hand of command: use and disuse of personal staffs in the Civil
War / R. Steven Jones.—1st ed.
        p.cm.
    Includes bibliographical references (p.) and index.
    ISBN: 0-8117-1451-9
    1. United States—History—Civil War, 1861-1865—Manpower. 2. United
States. Army—History—Civil War, 1861-1865. 3. United States. Army—
Staffs—History—19th century. 4. Generals—United States—History—
19th century. 5. Command of troops—History—19th century. I. Title.

E491 .J66 2000
973.7'41—dc21   99-088554

CONTENTS

Dedicated to the memory of my parents, Bob and Pat.

PREFACE

On July 20, 1861, Union major general Irvin McDowell needed help. Under pressure from Pres. Abraham Lincoln to attack Confederate troops near Washington City and fight the battle that most Northerners thought would end the Southern rebellion, McDowell had 34,000 troops, most of them poorly trained ninety-day volunteers, struggling through the muggy Virginia heat toward a creek known as Bull Run. McDowell's plan to attack Gen. P. G. T. Beauregard's 25,000 Rebels was a sound one, he thought, but it involved feints and flank attacks, and he wondered if his green troops and commanders were up to it. They had already taken four days to march little more than twenty miles, supplies were stretched along the line of march, and the unseasoned soldiers were exhausted before they had even fired a shot. Worse yet, with the enemy now at hand, two artillery batteries were lost. With no aide-de-camp at hand to find them, the beleaguered McDowell rode off to do it himself. British newspaper journalist William Howard Russell, in America to cover the civil conflict, spotted McDowell and commented on the general's menial task. McDowell replied that his staff was so small that he had to do the work himself. Russell reported, "The worst served English general has always a young fellow or two about him who can fly across the country, draw a rough sketch map, ride like a foxhunter, and find something out about the enemy and their position, understand and convey orders, and obey them. I look about for these types in vain."[1]

McDowell's predicament mirrored one that field commanders shared throughout the Civil War—they needed competent assistants to help them with not only the particulars of campaigning but also with the day-to-day routines of running large armies. Military historian John M. Vermillion says that army commanders have so many responsibilities—from handling paperwork at headquarters to fighting—that they cannot be successful without "a close circle of functional assistants." He calls that need for help the "corporate nature of leadership."[2]

On paper, Civil War commanders had the organization at hand to give them the help they sorely needed—the military staff. Civil War historians Herman Hattaway and Archer Jones call the military staff a commander's "management team," assigned to make the general's job easier.[3] Staff systems in both North and South were alike, for the Confederate Army copied the U.S. Army's staff organization. Every general with a field command had a staff, sometimes called a "general staff," sometimes a "field staff." That staff was divided in two: One-half was the special staff, which handled the problems of supply and transportation for the command, be it division, corps, or army; the other was the "personal staff," which kept the records of the army and sent orders to combat units.

Although staffs in the field were sometimes known as general staffs, European armies sometimes called special staffs "general staffs." Consequently, that usage spilled into American army vernacular. To make matters more confusing, by the time of the American Civil War, European armies had developed national "general staffs" to make operational plans and to train staff officers for field duty. Also, during the course of the Civil War, the United States set up what was known as a "general staff "in Washington, but since it coordinated transportation and supply, albeit for all armies in the field, it was in reality a special staff. To avoid unnecessary confusion, this book will avoid the use of the term "general staff" as much as possible, reverting to it only to explain staff developments in Europe that provide context for American staff work. In all other instances, the umbrella term for both staff units operating in the field will be "headquarters staff." Individually, the two halves will be called "personal" and "special" staffs.

The U.S. Army had used special staffs since the days of the Revolution, and by the start of the Civil War their duties were clear. Special staffs included a chief of engineers, chief of ordnance, quartermaster general and assistant quartermaster general, chief and assistant chief of commissaries, provost marshal and assistant provost marshal, chief surgeon, and chaplain. These men did not exercise line authority but did control men in their own department. For example, the chief engineer directed all the engineers attached to the particular army. Likewise the chief of ordnance oversaw soldiers handling artillery pieces and their ammunition, the quartermaster and commissary generals directed those attending to supplies and their transportation. At higher-level headquarters the chief surgeon and medical officers under him established field hospitals and evacuated sick and wounded soldiers. The duties of staff chaplain are equally obvious. As the jobs of special staff officers are self-explanatory, and because officers well understood their usage by 1861, I will not deal with special staff usage. Some special staff officers, however, are sources for other information.[4]

Of particular interest is the second subunit of the headquarters staff — the personal staff. On June 22, 1861, the U.S. Congress passed an act that allowed each brigade commander one assistant adjutant general and two aides-de-camp for his personal staff. The number of staff officers increased at higher command levels, and generals often took as many staffers as the War Department would approve, with the assistant adjutant general acting as the commander's main assistant. As the war progressed, generals commanding independent armies usually had one chief of staff (acting as the main assistant instead of the assistant adjutant general), two military secretaries, up to seven aides-de-camp, two assistant adjutants general, and one inspector general.[5]

A personal staff could be of great help to a commander in carrying out a campaign. An efficient personal staff could collect information, prepare plans, translate decisions and plans into orders, send those orders to lower echelons, see that orders were properly executed, and give opinions to commanders.[6] Yet traditional usage in the army, and perhaps a commander's uncertainty about what to do with his personal staff, often relegated staffers to the roles of office clerks or couriers.

Guidelines for personal staff usage did exist in 1861, and they came from Europe, largely France and Prussia, where the Napoleonic Wars had swelled the size of armies and, necessarily, advanced the duties and the functions of the staff.

Military theorists in France and Prussia wrote about staff duties and organization, and some translations of their work were in the United States and available for Civil War generals to use. Their writings revealed that modern headquarters staffs had three major elements: clearly defined organization and duties; well-educated staff officers; and chiefs of staff who played key roles in the function of the staff. France and Prussia also developed national entities—the Staff Corps in the former, the Great General Staff in the latter—that trained staff officers specifically for assignments with field commanders. Those national staffs also developed wartime strategies and policies that staff officers used as guidelines when assisting army commanders.

With no national general staff to help them, and with few War Department guidelines for staff work beyond the proper form for filling out reports, Civil War personal staff officers were adrift. Rather than reflect a national standard, staffs usually reflected the character of their commanding general and did as much—or as little—as he expected of them. They were often curious mixtures of West Point–trained soldiers and inexperienced civilians. They might be neighbors from the general's hometown, members of his family, or friends of a political sponsor. Some men became excellent staff officers; others never rose above inefficiency.

Because every army, corps, division, brigade, and regimental commander had a staff, no study of limited scope can explore the workings of each headquarters. Instead, I've decided to focus on four generals who, by reputation, might have gone beyond the limited help that officers' manuals offered in composing and using personal staffs. Each man was a West Point graduate and a central player in the war, and each man had a chance to expand the boundaries of American staff work. They are George B. McClellan, Robert E. Lee, Ulysses S. Grant, and William T. Sherman. McClellan, while timid on the battlefield, was a learned soldier and a superb organizer, and had seen firsthand Prussian staff advances as an observer of the Crimean War in 1854. Lee, the South's legendary campaigner, commanded the Army of Northern Virginia for almost three years, racking up victory after victory whether on the offensive or defensive. Even though few staff advances for the United States Army might be expected to come out of a Southern command, Lee's thoughts on staff work reflected ideas of the old American army. Grant was the Union's most victorious general, campaigning in three theaters and ultimately forcing Lee to surrender. With four full years of independent army command, ascending to the rank of lieutenant general in 1864, Grant had the most opportunity to advance staff work. Sherman gained an independent army command only in 1863, but he became known as one of the fathers of modern warfare when he made war on the civilian populace of Georgia and the Carolinas in 1864 and 1865. Becoming general in chief of all United States armies in 1869, Sherman helped set military policy, including that affecting staffs, for thirteen years.

This study will answer a variety of questions about the personal staffs of these four generals. How did the generals select their staff officers? Did they look for military experience that might help with operations or for business experience to guide them around the headquarters office? Did they cater to family or political favorites? What did they expect from their staffs? Did they want help with intelligence and writing orders, or did they simply want someone to keep track of the many boxes of records at the headquarters tent? Did the generals seek a level of professionalization within their staffs? Did they show evidence that they knew of or understood staff developments in Europe? Did they in any way expand staff usage beyond the bounds of their officers' manuals? What factors caused them to use their staffs the way they did: the nature of their theater, exigencies of war, or simply their personalities? Perhaps most importantly, for it could color the work of the entire staff, what was each general's relationship with his chief of staff? Did he trust the man's opinions and welcome his advice, or did he immerse himself in the minutiae of headquarters, lessening his own concentration on operations and negating the value of his chief? Likewise, how did the chief and other staffers feel about their commanding general? The general and his staff were essentially a family in the field, and friendship, loyalty, and confidence in each other could do much to enhance staff work.

This study will also examine the Civil War personal staff work within the larger scope of U.S. Army modernization. Military historians frequently call the American Civil War the first "modern war," citing technological advances, such as weaponry and telegraphy, and the willingness of Union generals to make war on the Southern populace, not just Southern armies. By World War I, the army had a personal staff system that resembled European staffs, but did the Civil War directly influence this development, or, amid advances in other fields, was it a backwater of staff work? Also, in an age of industrialization, did personal staff work borrow any expertise from railroads, the only American industry by 1860 to have begun a rudimentary modernization plan in its administrative staffing?[7]

Army size also may have played a role in staff development. In the early stages of the war a nationalist fervor, and later, a national conscription swelled Union armies; the Army of the Potomac, for instance, boasted 100,000 men or more for most of the war, and Sherman's combined Georgia invasion force numbered 120,000 in 1864. One might expect the same type of personal staff advancements in these armies as in Napoleon's armies fifty years earlier. Conversely, such improvements might be absent in Robert E. Lee's Army of Northern Virginia, which never topped 90,000 men and frequently fought with 60,000 troops or fewer.

Historical writing about Civil War personal staff work is sparse. Writers such as Russell Weigley, in *Towards an American Army* and *History of the United States Army,* and Allan Millett and Peter Maslowski in *For the*

Common Defense: A Military History of the United States of America, have well chronicled the rise of the army's national general staff. Their discussions, however, center on developments in the special staff bureaus, not personal staffs in the field. Likewise Walter Millis, in *American Military Thought,* devotes his discussion of staff work to early-twentieth-century special staff reforms. Edward Hagerman, in *The American Civil War and the Origins of Modern Warfare* devotes some copy to staff development, but he lumps all staff work—both personal and special—together. While he veers at times toward discussing personal staff work, the main thrust of his study (which, indeed, is only a small part of his book) is the coordination of special staff bureau work in Washington and among field commands. The Civil War saw great advances in special staff work, but Hagerman answers no substantial questions about personal staff work. Neither do T. Harry Williams in *Lincoln and His Generals* or Fred Shannon in the two-volume *The Organization and Administration of the Union Army, 1861–1862.* Allan Nevins, in his *Ordeal of the Union* series, gives personal staff work equally short shrift. Indeed, overt mention of any staff developments is hard to find in the final four books of the series, *The Improvised War, 1861–1862; War Becomes Revolution, 1862–1863; The Organized War, 1863–1864;* and *The Organized War to Victory, 1864–1865.*[8]

In the late 1940s, historian James D. Hittle wrote the classic of staff work, *The Military Staff: Its History and Development.* Hittle charted the course of staff work in Europe and the United States throughout World War II. While his book is indispensable to any study of military staffs, Hittle's section on the American Civil War does little more than point out deficiencies in staff work. Civil War historians Herman Hattaway and Archer Jones, in *How the North Won: A Military History of the Civil War,* acknowledge the paucity of research in personal staff work and recommend it as an area of study. Jones later ignores the topic in *Civil War Command and Strategy.*[9]

A spate of other Civil War narratives, micro-histories, and biographies of the four generals in this study give sporadic clues to their personal staff usage, but none specifically deal with the topic. Those include Shelby Foote's three-volume *The Civil War: A Narrative* and Bruce Catton's many narratives, especially *Mr. Lincoln's Army, A Stillness at Appomattox,* and *Grant Moves South.*[10]

Other books biographically chronicle the generals in question or provide specific histories of their campaigns. Grant's biographies include Geoffrey Perret, *Ulysses S. Grant: Soldier and President,* William McFeely, *Grant: A Biography;* Brooks D. Simpson, *Let Us Have Peace: Ulysses S. Grant and the Politics of War and Reconstruction, 1861–1868;* J. F. C. Fuller, *The Generalship of Ulysses S. Grant;* and Albert Richardson, *Personal History of Ulysses S. Grant.*[11]

Many books detail George McClellan's campaigns and military career, but none examines his staff relationships.[12] In a 1975 article, "The Professionalization of George B. McClellan and Early Civil War Command: An Institutional Perspective," Edward Hagerman criticizes Little Mac for failing to adopt a Prussian staff system, even after seeing it firsthand on a tour of Europe, and doing little with the staff he had. "There are no indications . . . [McClellan's] thoughts on staff went beyond his actions," writes Hagerman,[13] but the author makes no full study of McClellan's staff, and he misses instances where McClellan took hesitant steps toward expanded staff work.

Classic works about Sherman, B. H. Liddell Hart's *Sherman: Soldier, Realist, American,* and Lloyd Lewis's *Sherman: Fighting Prophet,* do not examine the general's personal staff system. Neither do recent books, such as John F. Marszalek's *Sherman: A Soldier's Passion for Order,* and Albert Castel's *Decision in the West: The Atlanta Campaign of 1864,* a 665-page study of that campaign. When Castel does mention Sherman's chief of staff, Joseph D. Webster, he incorrectly calls him "John."[14]

Classics about Lee are also largely void of staff consideration. They include Douglas Southall Freeman's *Lee's Lieutenants: A Study in Command* and *R. E. Lee: A Biography,* and Clifford Dowdey's *Lee's Last Campaign: The Story of Lee and His Men against Grant—1864.*[15] Dowdey's 1965 biography *Lee* briefly examines Lee's personal staff. While Dowdey captures the small nature of Lee's staff and criticizes the general for not having an "operations officer,"—someone to "maintain knowledge of the movements of every unit in his own army and, in cooperation with intelligence . . . , [those of] the enemy's forces"—he devotes only a few pages to the topic and does not fully explain Lee's staff expectations.[16] In *Robert E. Lee,* author Emory Thomas provides anecdotes about Lee's staff and uses the officers as primary sources, but he does not venture an in-depth analysis of their headquarters work.[17]

The work that comes closest to the topic with Lee is *Buff Facings and Gilt Buttons,* by J. Boone Bartholomees Jr. As its subtitle suggests, it is an excellent, comprehensive study of staff and headquarters work in the Army of Northern Virginia during the Civil War. Bartholomees looks at the staffs of all the commanders in the army, not just Lee's, and includes a detailed look at the special staff departments as well as the personal staffs. (Indeed, Bartholomees divides headquarters staffs into three parts—a general staff, including the chief of staff, adjutant general, and inspector general; the personal staff, and the special staff—instead of the two-part staff, which has been the traditional structure for previous limited attempts at staff study and which this work uses.) Bartholomees notes, as will this work, that the relationships between Civil War commanders and their staffs were highly personal.[18] "Understanding how commanders and staffs interacted, both personally and organizationally, is a significant issue," he writes.

Bartholomees also regards any attempt to find Prussian General Staff–style advances in American Civil War staffs as futile.[19] To an extent, this work attempts that. But it does not hold up the Prussian staff, which by any reckoning was remarkable, as a level of world perfection. Merely, it is a control model from which to base a comparative study. And *comparative* is a key word. Until now, no writer has attempted a detailed comparative study of the personal staffs of Grant, McClellan, Sherman, and Lee.

Like all historical topics, the information has always existed, waiting for someone to apply the right questions to it and do the required digging. The *War of the Rebellion: A Compilation of the Official Records of the Union and Confederate Armies,* known simply as the *O.R.,* forms the backbone of my research. My methodology was simple, yet time consuming: I first identified every man who served on the staffs of the four generals, then tracked them through each volume of the *O.R.* That revealed the tasks they performed at headquarters and shed light on the generals' expectations of staff officers. Some of the players involved left manuscript collections, but those papers frequently did not deal with their wartime staff experiences. More often the individuals, obscure by any standard, left no papers; the *O.R.* is the only evidence of their staff position. It remained, then, to extrapolate from the pages of the *O.R.* what staff duty was like, filling in gaps with available memoirs and manuscripts.

The results are in some ways surprising. Lee, a former staff officer himself, made the least use of his staff of any of the four men. To achieve so much in his three years of command would almost mandate an efficient staff with clarity of purpose, but Lee actually had few staffers and delegated to them few responsibilities beyond the prewar norms. Lee also made limited and ill-defined use of his chief of staff, Gen. Robert H. Chilton.

Sherman had an economical view of staff work that was almost the antithesis of European staff usage. He believed staffs should be small, and he did not use them in any but the traditional functions of writing and delivering orders. Because Sherman trusted the commanders of armies under his command to execute his general strategies and orders, he would have considered it redundant to send a man from his headquarters to oversee their execution. Though Sherman did not make any staff advances, the traditional role of staffers worked satisfactorily in his command situation.

McClellan showed flashes of insight in his staff usage, and he picked his father-in-law, the capable frontier soldier Randolph B. Marcy, to be his chief of staff. McClellan's tenure in command was brief, though, and he tempered any staff advances he might have made by frequently acting as his own chief of staff.

Grant, renowned as perhaps the greatest general of the war, earns yet another military honor as the most progressive of the four in his conception of staff work. With an able chief, John Aaron Rawlins, and a willingness to listen to his staffers' opinions, Grant molded his staff from a ragged collection of civilians with little military knowledge into a professional body functioning, albeit crudely and briefly, after the fashion of both a Prussian headquarters staff and Prussia's Great General Staff. Grant's staff advances were exigencies of war, which the increasing size of his armies triggered. He did not study staff progress in Prussia or intend to mirror his staff after any foreign army. But, with each of Grant's victories his command grew, and, like commanders in Prussia, he needed a more efficient, professional staff at headquarters to help him manage his armies. Grant saw a need and created a staff to fill it.

In the end, when a general sought personal staff improvements, three factors usually encouraged him to do so. The first factor was army size: Simply, the larger the force under his command, the more a general might seek staff help controlling it. The second factor was cooperative operations—separate columns or armies working toward a mutual objective. That may have involved separating an army for a two- or three-prong thrust in a single battle, or having two or three independent armies work in concert for a single campaign. The last, and most important factor, was the commander's willingness to improve staff work. If a general saw no real benefit in staff work, then neither the presence of a large army nor a plan calling for cooperative operations could encourage him to improve it.

ACKNOWLEDGMENTS

WRITING IS A SOLITARY PURSUIT, YET NO AUTHOR CAN WRITE WITHOUT much help. In the completion of this work, which began as a dissertation, I owe a debt to many people. First, I want to thank my major doctoral advisor, Dr. James L. Huston, associate professor of history at Oklahoma State University. He saw me through both master's and Ph.D. programs and gave me encouragement at just the right times. He helped me mold this work from a skeletal idea into, I hope, a viable historical work. I also want to thank the other members of my Ph.D. committee, Drs. George Jewsbury, Joseph A. Stout, and Elizabeth Williams, all history faculty at OSU, and John B. Phillips, head of OSU's government documents library. I would also like to thank the staff of the OSU documents library for their valuable help.

I would like to thank, as well, Dr. Erwin Sicher, head of the History/Social Science Department at Southwestern Adventist University, for encouraging publication. Thanks also to my student assistants, Matthew Orian and Todd Watts, for helping me with clerical details.

I want to thank two of the men who taught me to write: Wayne Lane, professor emeritus of mass communications at Northwestern Oklahoma State University, Alva; and John Joerschke, former editor of *True West* magazine. They were both excellent mentors who showed me that simple writing is best.

Most of all I want to thank my son, Evan; my daughter, Leslie; and especially my wife, Judi. They have helped more than they know, just by being there. Judi has endured plenty: my pursuit of a bachelor's degree, a master's degree, a Ph.D. I'm sure she thought it was over when the dissertation was completed; now she has patiently stood by while I expanded and edited it. Many times my confidence in the project flagged, but hers did not. As I worked on my manuscript, she did the more honorable and difficult work—making a home for us and our two children. I am proud of her beyond words. This work is for all of my family, but especially Judi.

CHAPTER ONE

Heritage

AMERICAN CIVIL WAR GENERALS WERE UNCERTAIN ABOUT USING THEIR staffs, but French and Prussian generals had a better idea of a personal staff's worth. The Napoleonic Wars in the early nineteenth century saw the advent of mass armies of more than 100,000 troops and a fluid, rapid movement that characterized Napoleon's campaigns. The need to quickly and efficiently move large armies necessitated improvements in both special and personal staffs. After losing to Napoleon at Jena in 1806, Prussian army officers realized that they, too, had to improve their staff systems, and the resulting changes created models of staff professionalism. By the mid–nineteenth century, information on the form and function of those European personal staffs was available to any American army officer who wanted to read it. The U.S. Army, however, failed to recognize the need for personal staff improvement, and by the start of the American Civil War, generals and their staff officers were without official policy or guidance.

European armies had employed rudimentary staffs since the early 1600s,[1] but the French and Prussian headquarters staffs that grew from the Napoleonic era were much advanced. They had three things in common. First, all had clearly organized sections or departments, each with well-defined duties. Second, the staffs consisted of highly educated officers. Third, each had a well-trained and experienced chief of staff assisting the commanding general and overseeing staff functions; the success or failure of a campaign often depended on the relationship between a general and his chief.

1

Napoleon did not set out to advance staff organization, yet progress came from his campaigns. Historian James D. Hittle writes that Napoleon's military genius may have caused him to rely less on a staff than other officers, but "staff functioning . . . [played] an important part in . . . [his] scheme of war." Hittle says that Napoleon did not specifically advance staff developments, but he did create an atmosphere in which they could grow.[2]

Napoleon's "Great General Headquarters Staff" differed from most headquarters staffs in that it served two functions: It was the supreme military staff for all of France, and it was a combat field staff. Still, it shows how Napoleon used his staff to assist him with command. His staff varied from time to time, but the one in place in 1813 appears indicative of his staff throughout the First Empire. It consisted of two groups, the *maison,* which was Napoleon's personal staff, and the Imperial Headquarters, which Napoleon's able chief of staff, Louis Alexandre Berthier, oversaw. The *maison* was a complete staff in itself and answered only to Napoleon. It had three sections: Napoleon's aides, all high-ranking officers who received assignments ranging from diplomatic missions to special commands; *officers d'ordonnance,* lower-ranking officers who issued orders or received special missions that required no command decisions; and Napoleon's "cabinet." The "cabinet" had three bureaus: an intelligence bureau, which consolidated and presented all enemy intelligence to Napoleon; a topographic bureau, which entered information about enemy positions on a topographic map; and a secretarial bureau of three or four men who wrote out Napoleon's orders and directives.[3]

The Imperial Headquarters under Berthier also was divided into two groups. The first group was Berthier's private staff, assistants who helped him carry out his own duties. The second, although called a "general staff," was a special staff, overseeing engineers, artillery, supplies, a military post office, billeting, the evacuation of wounded soldiers, and the furnishing of maps to subordinate officers.[4]

Berthier further broke the special staff's responsibilities into four units. One handled staff records, inspections, and reports and dealt with prisoners of war and deserters; another kept an official journal and supervised artillery, engineers, hospitals, and police; a third oversaw reconnaissance, operational plans, and communications; and the last established and organized the headquarters. An adjutant general, answerable to Berthier, commanded each unit. Berthier outlined this plan of organization in his *Document sur le Service de L'Etat-Major Général à l'Armée des Alpes,* which he wrote in 1796.[5]

Swiss military theorist Antoine-Henri Jomini, who campaigned as a staff officer with Napoleon and spent his later life codifying many of the emperor's techniques of war, provides another view of duties at a French army headquarters. In his 1838 book, *The Art of War,* Jomini gives a lengthy list of staff responsibilities, including preparing orders and itineraries to set an army in motion; drawing up the commanding general's orders; working with the chiefs of engineers and artillery to secure posts and depots; directing reconnaissance of enemy positions; ensuring proper execution of movements and arranging marching orders; providing guidance for advance and rear guards, flankers, and other detached units; providing general instructions for troop deployment before battle; indicating assembly points for advance units in case of attack; keeping supply, baggage, and munitions trains away from marching columns; providing for successive arrival of convoys and supplies; establishing camps and setting regulations for their safety and order; organizing lines of communication and supply and keeping them open for detached bodies; organizing hospitals; keeping accurate records of all detachments; organizing units to round up isolated men or small detachments; organizing and supervising troops in siege trenches; preserving order during retreats; and, in camp, assigning positions to different units and indicating places of assembly in case of attack.[6]

Though much staff work dealt with combat situations, it also covered the mundane clerical routines of the headquarters office. In French armies, staffers kept meticulous records and wrote detailed reports. In 1800 Paul Thiebault, an adjutant general in the French Army, wrote *Manuel des Adjutants Généraux et des Adjoints Employés dans les Etats-Majors Divisionairs des Armées,* which was the first compilation of staff theory and practice. Thiebault outlined staff organization (along Berthier's four-unit plan) and wrote instructions for staff officers. He also penned detailed instructions for writing reports. Thiebault told staff officers how to write reports of various types, whether for inspections or combat engagements, and specifically how to arrange information in each report. He commented that every staff officer should strive to render reports "precise, accurate, and complete."[7]

After Napoleon wrecked their army at the battle of Jena in 1806, Prussian generals began to rethink their command structure as well. Prussian militarists, following generals Gerhard Johann Scharnhorst and August Wilhelm von Gneisenau, began the army's reformation by reorganizing the national general staff. That body dated back to the quartermaster general's staff, which performed technical surveys and made operational plans for King Frederick William in the 1650s. In 1758 Frederick the Great expanded the quartermaster general's staff duties to include laying out camps, building village defenses, and reconnoitering landscape for troop placement. In 1802 Col. Christian von Massenbach recommended to King Frederick William III that the general staff (as the body was simply known by then) function in peacetime to prepare for all possible wartime scenarios. The king ordered it so the next year.[8]

The general staff was ill-prepared, however, to face Napoleon. Before Jena, Scharnhorst, an officer on the general staff, drafted a battle plan that would have massed Prussian forces to meet Napoleon's army at either the Rhine or Main Rivers. Other planners, however, dispersed Prussian forces to cover wide expanses of territory, weakening the army so that Napoleon was able to flank one part of it and cut off the other.[9]

In the post-Jena reorganization, Prussians divided their general staff. Part of it, the Great General Staff, stayed in Berlin to work on operational plans for the entire army. The other part, the *Truppengeneralstab,* or operational general staff, was distributed among field commands. It directly affected personal staffs at headquarters because the officers from the general staff became chiefs of staff to field commanders. They used instructions that Scharnhorst himself had written clarifying the duties of staff officers.[10]

In 1828 the Prussian Army formalized the composition of combat headquarters staffs. A directive divided the staff—perhaps showing a French influence—into four sections: general staff, routine staff, legal staff, and departmental staff. Each section had clear duties. According to Hittle, this definite organization gave the Prussian staff system one of the true markings of a modern staff.[11]

Education was the second characteristic of post-Napoleonic European staffs. Better education systems for both French and Prussian officers had begun in the late eighteenth century, but the Napoleonic Wars again focused the need for a highly educated officer cadre. Both countries had seen the need for better education during the Seven Years War. In France, Pierre de Bourcet, who had proven himself an able staff officer in the war, became director of the Grenoble Staff College in 1764 and personally taught young officers. In Prussia the next year, Frederick the Great opened the *Académie des Nobles,* a military school for young nobles about to become army officers. Frederick tapped some of the knowledge Bourcet was imparting in France by staffing his school with French instructors.[12]

French officer education took another step after Napoleon. Although the emperor did not make any educational advances himself, his campaigns again stirred interest in a more learned officer corps. In 1818 the minister of war, Marshal Gouvion Saint-Cyr, who had witnessed staff officer incompetence on the field, established the *Ecole d'Application d'Etat-Major* in Paris. Eight years later the French army mandated that graduates of the school serve regular tours on the line and that captains on the staff serve in regiments before receiving a promotion. Officers reached a position on the staff corps through a competition that ensured capable officers on the staff.[13]

By the time the Civil War erupted in the United States, the French army had also improved its selection process for staff candidates. Sub-lieutenants interested in applying for the staff corps submitted their names to the war minister, who selected candidates based on their previous educational backgrounds for entry to the school of application of the staff corps. Graduates of the school then had to serve a year in a regiment before they could become an adjutant on a headquarters staff, and then only after an inspector general deemed them ready for the job.[14]

In Prussia, Frederick the Great's educational standards died with him in 1786; that was one reason the general staff was so ill-prepared to fight Napoleon twenty years later. Scharnhorst, however, quickly targeted officer education in the post-Jena reforms. He established three military schools to ensure scientific training for officers, and he created a *Militarakademie* for officers in Berlin. Scharnhorst required a nine-month course of instruction for officer candidates, and he selected officers for a three-year course at the academy in Berlin. Only officers in the top one-third of their class were eligible for a spot on the general staff.[15] The effect of all this was that now field commanders had chiefs of staff, sent from the Great General Staff in Berlin, who were scientifically trained and versed in national policy and war objectives.

The third key element of the post-Napoleonic French and Prussian staffs was the primacy at headquarters of the chief of staff. In *The Art of War,* Jomini explained that, with the geographical scope and rapidly changing battlefield situations characteristic of Napoleonic campaigns, chiefs of staff, who had previously supervised only special staff bureaus, became all important to their commanders. A chief now had to supply his general the proper information he required to make decisions; help him turn his strategic or tactical ideas into orders; draft and deliver them promptly to every commander in the theater; and ensure their proper execution. "To be a good chief of staff . . . a man should be acquainted with all the various branches of the art of war," Jomini wrote. Napoleon's chief, Berthier, called the chief of staff, "the central pivot of all [staff] operations."

What's more, if a general had a keen scientific ability to lay out a campaign but lacked the flash and boldness to execute it, his chief should provide the spark needed for victory. Likewise, if a general was full of blood and thunder but lacked the skill to lay out a sound plan, the chief should be able to fill that deficiency as well. Jomini noted, "the greatness of a commander-in-chief will be always manifested in his plans; but if the general lacks ability, the chief of staff should supply it as far as he can." In effect, the fortunes of a commanding general and his chief were tied together. Jomini understood that and cautioned, "woe to an army where these authorities cease to act in concert!"[16]

In France, Napoleon and Berthier set many precedents for the duties of a chief of staff in combat, but their relationship was often strained. In fact, Napoleon, such a military genius himself that he frequently acted as his own chief, may not have recognized Berthier's value until it was too late. Chiefs of staff at the time were authorized to make troop dispositions if needed, but Berthier did not possess a keen military mind. Historian Hittle says that along with an "unadmirable personality," Berthier had an "incapacity for independent command." Jomini, Marshal Ney's chief in battle against Russians and Prussians at Bautzen in 1813, averted disaster when, with Napoleon's orders delayed, he devised a plan of battle for Ney. But battle plans befuddled Berthier. Once, at Ratisbon, Austria, Berthier positioned forces so strangely that he thoroughly confounded his field marshals. Luckily, Napoleon arrived to fix matters before Austrian troops attacked, but he wrote to Berthier later that "what you have done appears so strange, that if I was not aware of your friendship I should think that you were betraying me."[17]

Nevertheless, Berthier became one of the classic chiefs of staff in history. Thanks to his "methodical mind and . . . administrative genius," Berthier was peculiarly suited to run Napoleon's staff. For years Berthier controlled the staff, oversaw the finances of the army, took care of the emperor's appointments, and saw that Napoleon's orders arrived promptly in the hands of his commanders. In Berthier, writes Hittle, "the chief of staff finally found his true place in military organization."[18] Indeed, Hittle suggests a latent, but often ignored or misunderstood element of staff work—it takes a range of talents to manage an army headquarters. Not every man is suited for every job, and a skilled staff officer might not be a skilled line commander. Berthier's mind belonged in the office, Napoleon's on the battlefield. That Berthier did not have the talent for strategy that his commander had is no denigration of his true clerical talent.

Nevertheless, in his later campaigns Napoleon began to mistrust Berthier. Perhaps the emperor was so confident of his own abilities that he thought he did not need a chief of staff, or perhaps Berthier's ineptitude at making field dispositions soured Napoleon on his chief's other, more valuable, skills. As a result, Napoleon issued orders that all intelligence coming into headquarters bypass Berthier and come directly to him, something that violated Thiebault's recent recommendations. Napoleon began openly rebuking Berthier, and once he referred to his chief as simply a clerk.[19]

Napoleon's treatment of Berthier may have changed history. Perhaps in despair over his commander's disregard, Berthier killed himself on June 1, 1815, as Napoleon's army headed for Waterloo. Napoleon substituted a corps commander, Nicolas Soult, for Berthier. Unaccustomed to the massive job, Soult made several mistakes issuing Napoleon's orders. Napoleon, of course, lost Waterloo, and during the battle he reportedly said, "If only Berthier was here, then my orders would have been carried out."[20] Napoleon had realized the true value of his chief too late.

Prussian militarists, on the other hand, knew the value of a good chief of staff, and military reformer Scharnhorst played a key role in creating the Prussian chief of staff system. Born in Hanover in 1755, Scharnhorst had attended military school, fought in Belgium's revolutionary wars, and served as a chief of staff in the Hanoverian army before he joined the Prussian army in 1801. In the fighting at Jena, Scharnhorst was wounded but joined other troops retreating from the battlefield. On the march Scharnhorst fell in with Fld. Marsh. G. L. von Blücher, whom Prussian historian Walter Goerlitz describes as a "rough, thoroughly ill-educated man, who was nevertheless endowed with an excellent natural intelligence." Blücher recognized Scharnhorst's talent and made him his impromptu chief of staff. Together they regrouped their forces and fought a masterly retrograde action as they crossed the Harz Mountains, diverting several French forces from occupation duty in eastern Prussia. Scharnhorst's and Blücher's cooperation was the first example of what would become the hallmark of Prussian personal staff work—a trained chief of staff advising a field commander.[21]

While Napoleon dealt his chief out of operational matters, the Prussians fully immersed their headquarters chiefs. Scharnhorst had, in effect, been the model for the Prussian system when he aided Blücher. He began to formalize the chief's role at headquarters, setting down instructions for staff operations after the formation of the *Truppengeneralstab*. No longer would a chief simply coordinate activities of subordinate staff departments;

no longer would he be only a conduit for the commanding general's orders. He would, in effect, be a junior partner in command decisions. When Scharnhorst died of blood poisoning during the allied wars against Napoleon in 1813, August Wilhelm von Gneisenau took over the general staff and further cemented the roles of chiefs of staff by making them jointly responsible for their commanders' decisions.[22] Before Jena, such a role for the chief would have been not only impossible but inadvisable; staff officers simply did not have the knowledge or experience to act in such a fashion. The reforms in officer education after the wreck of the army made the new command relationship not only possible, but advantageous for the field commander, as his aide would possess proven scientific knowledge and speak with the authority of the Great General Staff.

The Napoleonic Wars also affected British headquarters staffs, but not like they did those of France and Prussia. Having no staff to work with, Gen. Arthur Wellesley—the duke of Wellington—crafted his own. His success in the Peninsular War, in which England, Spain, and Portugal opposed France, shows that he did an adequate job. But Wellington, primarily concerned with logistics and supply routes, worried most about creating special staff departments to handle those problems. Though he had a personal staff, Wellington did not give primacy to a chief of staff, as did his French and Prussian counterparts. Any advances Great Britain made with headquarters staffs stagnated after Wellington defeated Napoleon at Waterloo in 1815. By 1854, when Great Britain, France, and Turkey allied against Russia in the Black Sea region during the Crimean War, the British army had yet to establish schools for staff officers. Only when that conflict pointed out the need for more efficient staffers did the army create a system of staff education.[23]

American staff work proceeded haltingly after the American army was born in 1775. Soon after taking command of the Continental Army, Gen. George Washington realized that he needed help with administrative duties so he could concentrate on campaigning. Envisioning a type of national staff, largely to help with supply problems, Washington asked Congress in 1776 to create a "war office." Congress responded with a Board of War, but it was not what Washington had wanted. The general had political enemies in Congress, men who thought Washington was doing nothing to win the war. They designed the Board of War to watch over Washington and made it the Continental Army's top military entity, outranking even Washington. Worse yet, when Washington asked for an inspector general to help him establish a training system for his men, Congress complied but gave the job to another of Washington's enemies, Thomas Conway. He was answerable to the War Board, not Washington. Conway, an Irish-Frenchman who had been in Frederick the Great's army, had served briefly with Washington and considered the general a fool for not promoting him. When Washington realized that Congress had ignored his wishes on staff reform and Conway was to be at his headquarters, he became so angry he refused to work with Conway.[24]

Soon, however, Washington had on hand the right man to help him build a headquarters staff. While serving in Paris as American minister to France, Benjamin Franklin became acquainted with Baron Frederick von Steuben, a former Prussian staff officer. Franklin sent Steuben to offer his services to the Continental Army, including a letter of introduction inflating Steuben's rank from captain to general to make him acceptable to the Continental Congress. Regardless of his true rank, Steuben had fought in the Seven Years War and attended one of Frederick the Great's first staff schools. Washington welcomed Steuben and gave him the inspector general's job. In that capacity von Steuben acted as chief of staff for personnel, intelligence, operations, and supply. He became perhaps the only trained staff officer in the Continental Army. Unfortunately, only a few top American generals realized the value of Steuben's headquarters reforms, which lasted only during the war.[25]

Following the Revolution, the American army made no attempt to standardize personal staff usage. As historian Hittle writes, "The wars from 1812 to the Mexican [War] produced some good brush-warfare tacticians and accomplished Indian exterminators," but no body of staff theory or cadre of experienced staff officers. The army based its rudimentary staff systems on the British model, the least progressive of those in Europe. During the Mexican War, Gen. Winfield Scott had an efficient staff, but its composition had nothing to do with War Department guidelines and everything to do with Scott's ability to surround himself with capable men.[26]

In 1862 the United States Army did, in fact, form a general staff, but that was a misnomer. Including the chiefs of the quartermaster, commissary, adjutant general's, engineer, and ordnance departments, and with Maj. Gen. Henry Halleck coordinating them under the title "chief of staff," the body was actually only a special staff. To be sure, the staff was quite effective, tackling the massive supply and transportation job that the North had to master to win the war. Nevertheless, that was only half of what national general staffs in France and Prussia were doing. The staff in Washington did nothing to make operational plans for field generals or supply them with trained, experienced staff officers, such as the Prussian

Great General Staff did in wartime. A staff similar to the Union's also appeared in Richmond, but it lacked a chief to concentrate its efforts.[27]

The United States Military Academy at West Point offered no guidance on personal staff use. Graduates knew little about staff thought—or even of strategy and tactics. When Pres. Thomas Jefferson approved West Point in 1802, he wanted graduates to be more than just soldiers. Like most of his fellow revolutionaries, Jefferson feared large, professional, standing armies, and he saw no reason to educate a class of men with no skill other than war making. Jefferson insisted that West Pointers be civil engineers first, soldiers second. And West Point curricula reflected that desire: Basics included mathematics, heavy on geometry and calculus; and science, which included geology and mineralogy. Although cadets learned army field maneuvers and artillery procedures early in their studies, tactics did not appear until the cadets' last year, and then in a course called "Military and Civil Engineering and the Science of War." Instructor Dennis Hart Mahan, who had graduated first in the class of 1824, based his military lectures on French military thought. Mahan had studied in France for four years after graduating from West Point and, in the wake of the Napoleonic wars, considered France the seat of military knowledge. West Point even emphasized French as a crucial foreign language. Still, the amount of time Mahan devoted to strategy and tactics was brief—only one week out of the one-year course. The rest of the time he discussed civil engineering, architecture, and building fortifications. In short, if any of the West Pointers who would go on to command Civil War armies wanted to know mid–nineteenth century staff theory, they would have to learn it on their own.[28]

If an American officer was inclined to such study, the information was available. Thiebault's staff manual was widely translated, and Prussians had used it in making their own staff reforms. In 1809 Thiebault's compilation crossed the Atlantic and appeared in *The American Military Library.* Jomini's *The Art of War* also was widely circulated. In 1846 Henry Halleck published *Elements of Military Art and Science; or, Course of Instruction in Strategy, Fortification, Tactics of Battles &c; Embracing the Duties of Staff, Infantry, Cavalry, Artillery, and Engineers.* Although he mainly recounted staff developments in Europe rather than recommending staff improvements for the U.S. Army, he did suggest more than twenty books treating staff work. The books on the list, which included those of Thiebault and Jomini, and Scharnhorst's *Handbuch für offiziere,* were all in foreign languages and therefore may have been little help to all but the most linguistically adept of American officers.[29]

Soon after the Civil War began, however, American commanders had available some specific information, in English, about staff function. Cap. G. H. Mendell, of the U.S. Corps of Topographical Engineers, and Lt. William P. Craighill, an assistant professor of engineering at West Point, translated Jomini's *The Art of War* and published it in early 1862. That same year Craighill published *Army Officer's Pocket Companion,* which he intended to perform the same function for American officers as the handbook *Aide-mémoire* did for French officers. Indeed, Craighill based his lengthy section on staff usage entirely on the French model. With the duties of personal staffs uncodified, and with no equivalent to the French Staff Corps or the Prussian Great General Staff to provide guidelines, Craighill included a lengthy chapter detailing the organization and duties of French staffs circa 1860. Craighill listed the duties of chiefs of staff, which varied little from Berthier's day; he included items that required staff attention; and he explained the duties of French staffers in camp and in battle. Emphasizing the clerical side of personal staff work, Craighill explained to American staffers exactly how to keep headquarters records and how to draft orders and correspondence.[30]

By the start of the American Civil War, an alternative existed for personal staff officers who, at the time, were nothing more than office clerks. The French and Prussian armies had expanded the roles of personal staffers decades earlier. In those countries national general staffs trained staff officers in their governments' war-making policy and objectives. Those personal staff officers then became partners in battle with army commanders. The U.S. War Department embraced none of the European personal staff improvements; neither did the Confederate War Department, for that matter, since the South based its staff systems on the North's. Still, all Civil War generals had personal staffs. The information about European staff usage was available to them, if they chose to read it. In truth, though, with no official government guidelines, the character and quality of personal staff work in an American Civil War army depended entirely on its commander.

CHAPTER TWO

McClellan: Hesitation

1861–1862

PERHAPS MORE THAN ANY OTHER AMERICAN CIVIL WAR COMMANDER, Maj. Gen. George B. McClellan was the best prospect for expanding the duties of his personal staff. An able West Point student, McClellan was a bright officer, and he gave the Army of the Potomac, the Union's main Eastern army, the efficient organizational structure that carried it through more than three years of war. Before that, on a tour of Europe during the Crimean War, McClellan saw many of the modern European military staffs in action. Historian James Hittle says that such a background should have made McClellan an American staff innovator, and he blames McClellan, along with his predecessors in high command, for not introducing "a staff system that at least reflected some of the progressive thought of the Prussians." Historian Edward Hagerman also condemns McClellan for the oversight.[1] But they are too hasty, for a glimmer of progressive thought does show through in McClellan's staff usage. Hesitation marks that progressivism, though, much as it marked McClellan's most important campaigns.

George Brinton McClellan was born December 3, 1826, to a prominent Philadelphia doctor, George McClellan, and his wife, Elizabeth. Young George attended private schools, where he became conversant in Latin and French. By the time he was eleven, George entered the University of Pennsylvania's preparatory school, and two years later he entered the university to study law. The boy lost interest in law, however, and George's father secured him an appointment to West Point. He entered the academy in 1842, and at the age of fifteen, was one of the school's youngest cadets. McClellan was an able student, but he was frequently lazy in his studies. One professor described him as "well educated, and, when he chose to be, brilliant." McClellan chose to be just brilliant enough to graduate second in his West Point class of 1846. He habitually studied military topics after his graduation, but the extent to which he read the available literature on staff theory is impossible to know.[2]

After graduation, McClellan served in the Mexican War as an engineer, and in that position, McClellan had the chance to observe a professional staff in action. Winfield Scott used engineers in the double capacity of scouts, and his top engineers, Col. Joseph G. Totten and Capt. Robert E. Lee, made it onto what Scott called his "little cabinet" or advisory staff, which tended to blur the lines between special and personal staff duty.

Maj. Gen. George B. McClellan and some of his staff officers visit the headquarters of Brig. Gen. George W. Morell in the fall of 1861. The balding Morell stands facing McClellan with his hand on the stump. Between Morell and McClellan is one of McClellan's staffers, Albert V. Colburn. To McClellan's left is staff officer N. B. Sweitzer. To Sweitzer's left are the prince de Joinville, son of King Louis-Philippe of France, and his nephew, the comte de Paris. Joinville frequented McClellan's headquarters, and the comte served as one of McClellan's aides. The men on the extreme right and left are unidentified. (NATIONAL ARCHIVES AND RECORDS ADMINISTRATION)

After the war, McClellan accompanied an exploration party searching for the mouth of the Red River, and he served briefly on the West Coast. In April 1855 Secretary of War Jefferson Davis appointed McClellan, now a cavalry captain, to a three-man military commission that would observe European armies fighting in the Crimea. McClellan's traveling companions were Maj. Richard Delafield, of the West Point class of 1818, and Maj. Alfred Mordecai, class of 1823; the party became known as the "Delafield Commission," for the senior major.[3]

By the time the commission left the United States, allied British, French, and Turkish armies were besieging Russian troops at the Black Sea port of Sevastopol. The officers hoped to visit the positions of all the combatants, and British authorities in London readily gave their consent. French officials in Paris, however, fearing that the Americans might divulge information, refused them access to French works unless they promised not to visit the Russian lines. The commission refused and journeyed to St. Petersburg, hoping to get better terms from the Russians. Instead they were delayed, and while waiting for an answer McClellan and his companions traveled through Russia and Prussia, getting a firsthand look at the military organizations of those countries. The Americans finally received word that, as with France, Russia would not allow them access to their lines if they intended to then visit the allies. The Americans gave up and decided to visit only allied works, but by the time they reached Sevastopol the siege was over. Some fighting continued, and the Delafield Commission saw not only the allied troops in action, but the evacuated Russian works as well. Following the war, the commission traveled back across Europe inspecting Austrian, Prussian, French, and British fortifications.[4]

Upon his return in 1856, McClellan wrote his report of the Delafield Commission's trip. It included a detailed account of the siege of Sevastopol, accounts of European army organizations, and a proposal for an American cavalry manual, which McClellan had adapted from a Russian manual. He also included his recommendation for a light cavalry saddle, which the army adopted and used well into the twentieth century.[5] McClellan, however, did not discuss the nature of European staff work. He briefly listed the numbers of officers on the general staffs of the various armies he visited, but he did not comment on staff operations.[6] If McClellan had given any thought to staff usage, he gave no hint of it in his report.

In early 1857 McClellan left the army and accepted an executive position with the Illinois Central Railroad; McClellan apparently used little military organizational expertise in the job, which itself did not affect his later army staff organization. By the late 1850s, the owners and managers of large American railroads were realizing that operations ran better when a central headquarters staff controlled them. But railroads charted their own paths toward staff organization and usually did not borrow expertise from outside organizations. Historian Alfred D. Chandler Jr. notes that, "of the pioneers in the new managerial methods, only two—[George W.] Whistler and McClellan—had military experience, and they were the least innovative of the lot." Chandler reports, though, that centralized staff management did not become standard among railroads until the 1880s, and most small railroads operated effectively until then without it.[7] McClellan might then be excused for not taking staff organizational skills back to the army with him.

When the Civil War began in April 1861, McClellan again joined the army. On April 23 McClellan accepted command of volunteers in Ohio; on May 3 the War Department gave McClellan command of the Department of the Ohio, which included Ohio, Indiana, Illinois, and later, parts of Pennsylvania, western Virginia, and Missouri. Within two weeks McClellan received another honor when his political sponsor, Ohio politician and secretary of the treasury, Salmon P. Chase, secured for him a major generalship in the Regular Army.[8]

One of McClellan's first tasks was building his personal staff. He told Bvt. Lt. Gen. Winfield Scott, general in chief of all United States armies, that he needed "a first rate Adjutant General and two good Aides de Camp." For the first position, McClellan wanted his friend Maj. Fitz-John Porter, who had graduated from West Point a year before McClellan, or, as a second choice, Capt. Seth Williams, a West Point graduate in 1842. For the aide positions, McClellan requested recent West Point graduates 1st Lt. William A. Webb and 2nd Lt. Henry W. Kingsbury.[9]

In an episode that caused McClellan's first disagreement with army high command, Winfield Scott allowed McClellan to have only Seth Williams. McClellan could be satisfied with Williams, however, for they had been friends since serving in the Mexican War together. Williams had made a career for himself in the adjutant general's department of the small peacetime army.[10] A native of Maine, Williams was a devout Yankee Christian who disliked talking about things military on Sunday. He talked with a lisp and added an extra "r" to words in the New England style; he pronounced his general's name "Merklellan." Williams would prove an able adjutant. He remained at the headquarters of the Army of the Potomac long after McClellan left, and he ultimately took a spot on Ulysses S. Grant's special staff late in the war.[11]

McClellan specifically wanted Regular Army colonel Randolph B. Marcy for his chief of staff, and he bypassed Winfield Scott, appealing directly to Pres. Abraham Lincoln to get him. McClellan won his request, and he was quite happy, for he had a special reason for wanting Marcy—he was McClellan's father-in-law. McClellan had met the colonel in early 1852 when Marcy led the Red River expedition. After the expedition McClellan met Marcy's daughter, Mary Ellen (often called Nell), and they began a long courtship. They were married May 22, 1860, in New York; McClellan's future adjutant Seth Williams was a groomsman.[12]

But McClellan's selection of Marcy as his chief was not mere nepotism. Marcy, a West Point graduate in 1832, was a respected and capable officer. After the Red River expedition, Marcy had led other exploratory marches in the West. In 1857 he commanded a column in the so-called "Mormon War." The column had become snowbound in the Rocky Mountains, but Marcy's cool persistence kept his men from freezing to death. By 1859 Marcy had become such an expert on the West that the War Department requested that he write a guidebook for westward travelers. The result, *The Prairie Traveler,* became a classic of the era, not only detailing western routes but describing the hardships of travel in the West.[13]

Historians Hagerman and Hittle say that one of McClellan's true staff improvements was to appoint a chief of staff. Hagerman comments, "McClellan . . . modified prevailing staff procedures with the appointment

Brig. Gen. Randolph B. Marcy in a formal pose. Marcy was both McClellan's father-in-law and chief of staff. He served as an important link between McClellan's headquarters and Washington, and then felt the ire of Lincoln and Stanton as McClellan's fortunes fell. (NATIONAL ARCHIVES AND RECORDS ADMINISTRATION)

of a chief of staff . . . , a concession to continental staff theory not included in his pre-war writing. Whether European precedent or common sense influenced this decision is open to question." Hittle writes that McClellan's actions started "some semblance of staff functioning . . . as all orders were usually issued by the chief of staff."[14] Those writers ignore one thing, however: All Civil War commanders at corps level and above had chiefs of staff; the position was nothing new in 1861. Any improvement would be in how McClellan used Marcy as his chief.

By the time McClellan was ready to take his army into the field in July 1861, he had established his first personal staff. In addition to Marcy—acting as an inspector general, his appointment as chief of staff not yet official—and Seth Williams, McClellan had as aides-de-camp Capt. Lawrence A. Williams, West Point class of 1852 and presently of the 10th U.S. Infantry, and Col. Thomas M. Key. McClellan often referred to Key as "Judge Key," for he was a former Cincinnati commercial court judge.[15]

McClellan first took his army into western Virginia to push Confederate troops from that Unionist area. From the field near Buckhannon, Virginia, on July 7, 1861, McClellan briefly described camp life for his wife. Headquarters was on a hill just outside of town, and "Your father and I share the same tent," McClellan wrote. "Seth has one nearby as an office. Lawrence Williams another as office and mess tent. Marcy, the two Williams, Judge Key, and [Brig. Gen. Frederick W.] Lander [of McClellan's special staff] mess with me. [Lt. Orlando M.] Poe [also of the special staff] and the rest of the youngsters are in tents near by."[16]

McClellan's first engagement of the war was July 11 at Rich Mountain in western Virginia. Trying to flush Confederate general Robert S. Garnett's small army out of that hill country, McClellan sent Brig. Gen. William S. Rosecrans and 2,000 men to smash into a detachment of Garnett's army. Rosecrans succeeded, forcing the surrender of 555 Rebels two days later. Judge Key helped arrange the surrender. McClellan was supposed to follow up with an attack toward Beverly, Virginia, but failed to do so. Nevertheless, he occupied Beverly the next day, and on July 13 detachments of his army killed Garnett and drove Rebels out of the area. McClellan's campaign gave the Union control of western Virginia and its important rivers and rail lines. Even though the combat victories actually belonged to Rosecrans and Brig. Gen. T. A. Morris, another McClellan subaltern, McClellan took all the credit.[17]

After the battle of Rich Mountain, McClellan hinted at one of the ways he intended to use Colonel Marcy—as a liaison who could make sure authorities in Washington understood his wants. McClellan sent Marcy to the capital to deliver captured Confederate battle flags and visit with General in Chief Scott. In a letter of introduction, McClellan explained that Marcy was in "full possession of my views and [can] communicate them better orally than I can on paper." Marcy told Scott that McClellan thought a campaign through Kentucky, western Tennessee, and northern Alabama would be "decisive of the war." Marcy also visited Col. E. D. Townsend, assistant adjutant general, and gave him McClellan's report of operations. Marcy then told Townsend that McClellan wanted another brigade of Regular infantry and some companies of Regular cavalry to continue his operations in the field.[18] In assigning Marcy this liaison role, McClellan realized that he needed a strong communications link with Washington and that Marcy could ably fill the need. The assignment was good; Ulyssess S. Grant would ultimately do the same thing with his chief of staff. Unfortunately, Marcy's relations with Washington officials, including President Lincoln, would deteriorate as his son-in-law's military achievements flagged.

McClellan's victory in western Virginia impressed Abraham Lincoln enough that, within a month, the president brought McClellan to Washington to command the Army of the Potomac. The army had fallen into disorganization and demoralization after Brig. Gen. Irvin McDowell led it to defeat at the battle of Bull Run on July 21. Lincoln supposed McClellan might be the man to whip it into shape.

McClellan took with him personal staff officers Marcy, Seth Williams, Lawrence Williams, and Judge Key. He soon added others. Capt. Albert V. Colburn became McClellan's second assistant adjutant general; and Captain Nelson B. Sweitzer, of the First U.S. Cavalry, and Capt. Edward McKee Hudson, 14th U.S. Infantry, became aides de camp.[19] Hudson, Sweitzer, and Colburn were all West Point graduates from the classes of 1849, 1853, and 1855 respectively.[20]

Even though the war was young, some of the new men on McClellan's staff were experienced. Colburn, an adjutant in the First U.S. Cavalry, had received his first assignment even before the war started. In March 1861 the War Department dispatched the First Cavalry to Forts Cobb, Arbuckle, and Washita in Indian Territory to protect loyal Indians. Colburn had charge of the regiment's records. At Bull Run, by then a captain, Colburn commanded a two-company squadron of cavalry.[21] Hudson had been part of a 200-man relief expedition under former navy captain G. V. Fox, the same expedition that Abraham Lincoln had intended to relieve Fort Sumter in April. In July Hudson commanded a section of artillery that clashed with Rebels near a ford of the Potomac River.[22]

Maj. Gen. Seth Williams. A longtime friend of McClellan, he joined that general's staff as adjutant general in spring 1861. He remained with the Army of the Potomac long after McClellan left, and ultimately took a spot on Ulysses S. Grant's special staff. (NATIONAL ARCHIVES AND RECORDS ADMINISTRATION)

If the men of McClellan's personal staff helped him rebuild the Army of the Potomac, there is little evidence. McClellan's correspondence in neither the *Official Records* nor his papers mentions his personal staff officers in late summer 1861. To be sure, the staffers had jobs to do, and no doubt they dealt with army organization. In September McClellan made Marcy's appointment as chief of staff official, saying that European armies fully recognized the importance of the office, but American militarists virtually ignored it. He noted vaguely that Marcy "entered upon service immediately, discharging the various and important duties with great fidelity, industry, and ability."[23] The bulk of reshaping the Army of the Potomac and establishing Washington's defenses, however, probably proceeded by dint of McClellan's will.

Soon McClellan received another jump in command. Since arriving in Washington, McClellan had clashed with Winfield Scott. McClellan, who coveted Scott's job as general in chief, insisted that the hero of the War of 1812 and the Mexican War was now too old to command. McClellan would not cooperate with Scott, and he refused to update Scott on developments within the Army of the Potomac. When McClellan's opponents insisted that he prosecute the war more vigorously, he replied that

Scott stood in his way. McClellan's own troops came to believe the same, and rumors abounded that the army would turn on Washington if McClellan did not replace Scott. Finally, in October, Scott submitted his resignation; McClellan, not yet thirty-five, became general in chief on November 1, 1861.[24]

If McClellan had intended to copy a European style of staff usage, it would soon have become evident. As general in chief, he commanded not just the Army of the Potomac (of which Lincoln left him in complete command; "I can do it all," McClellan told the president), but also every U.S. land force from Washington to California. In Prussia, staff officers from the Great General Staff, well versed in the policy and wishes of the national army headquarters, were attached to every Prussian army in the field. There they could help field commanders direct concerted operations and bring about unified results. When McClellan took over as general in chief, his headquarters, in effect, became national headquarters. It would have been obvious for a learned commander who had seen first-hand the organization of the Prussian general staff, to familiarize his staff officers with his military theories, expectations, and hopes, and dispatch them to wide-ranging field commands where they could help orchestrate simultaneous campaigns. McClellan did not. The same dearth of information about his staff officers in McClellan's correspondence for late summer 1861 also characterizes his writings as general in chief. Even if he had been inclined to expand his staff's duties, McClellan had little time to do so. In March 1862 Lincoln took the general in chief's job away from McClellan so he could concentrate solely on his Peninsula campaign, an attack on Richmond via a peninsula of land extending east from Richmond to the Chesapeake Bay.

The only thing certain about McClellan's staff during his tenure as general in chief was that it kept growing. Before he was through, McClellan had fashioned a personal staff that resembled a royal court more than an American army headquarters. On November 18, 1861, McClellan wrote to his wife that, after visiting with a number of dignitaries, "I had to see Mr. Astor of New York." Then, almost as an aside, McClellan added, "and [I] appointed him a volunteer aide." Mr. Astor was John Jacob Astor Jr., son of the late fur-trading millionaire. Astor's only apparent qualification to be a staff aide, other than his money, was that early in the war he had chaired a committee that purchased arms and ammunition for the Union. Later, after Lincoln had fired McClellan from command, Astor was one of a group of men who gave the McClellans a house in New York City. Accepting the house, McClellan called it an expression of "personal regard."[25]

McClellan also added to his staff, as aides-de-camp, members of French royalty. The duc de Chartres, known as Robert d'Orléans, and the comte de Paris, Louis-Philippe d'Orléans, both members of the exiled house of Orléans, had attached themselves to the Army of the Potomac even before McClellan became general in chief. The men were pretenders to the French throne and had as a constant escort their uncle, the prince de Joinville. McClellan was tempted to add the prince as an aide, for he frequently accompanied the general. Robert d'Orléans saw action on February 7, 1862, when he rode with five squadrons of cavalry to clear a road of Rebel pickets. In a sharp firefight, one of d'Orléans's companions was shot in the head. When the fight was over, the cavalry commander thanked d'Orléans for his "coolness, assistance, and advice."[26]

By the time McClellan was ready to depart for the Peninsula campaign in late March 1862, his personal staff had grown to twenty men. Fleshing

The duc de Chartres, comte de Paris, prince de Joinville, and others play dominoes in camp near Yorktown, Virginia, during the Peninsula campaign, 1862. The duc and the comte were both on McClellan's staff. This pose, presumably, does not reflect their official duties. (LIBRARY OF CONGRESS)

out the staff were Col. Edward H. Wright, aide-de-camp, a major in the Sixth U.S. Cavalry and former secretary to the American ministry in St. Petersburg, Russia; and Col. Thomas T. Gantt, aide-de-camp and judge advocate general. McClellan also assigned as aides-de-camp Lieutenant Col. Paul von Radowitz, Maj. Herbert von Hammerstein, Maj. W. W. Russell, of the Marines, and Maj. F. LeCompte, of the Swiss army. A host of captains also joined McClellan's headquarters as aides-de-camp: George A. Custer, Joseph Kirkland, Martin T. McMahon, William P. Mason Jr., William F. Biddle, E. A. Raymond, and Arthur McClellan, the general's brother. Of this last group, only Custer, class of 1861, was a West Pointer. Before the campaign ended, McClellan had lost LeCompte and gained as aides Capts. W. S. Abert and Charles R. Lowell. At the close of the campaign, Gantt, Astor, Russell, Robert and Louis-Philippe d'Orléans, and Raymond left the command.[27]

The Peninsula campaign was McClellan's second attempt that spring at a large assault on Richmond. The first, which had ended in failure in February even before it started, had prompted Lincoln to remove McClellan from the general in chief's job. McClellan called the first plan the "Urbanna plan": He would land an army at Urbanna, Virginia, near the mouth of the Rappahannock River, then march overland and capture Richmond. But McClellan first had to clear the Shenandoah Valley of Confederates. Any Union army going into the valley, however, needed a supply line, and McClellan proposed building a permanent bridge of pontoon boats across the Potomac River. Engineers floated the boats to the site on the Chesapeake and Ohio Canal, intending to pass them to the Potomac through locks. Only when the boats arrived did the engineers discover that the boats were six inches too wide to pass through the locks.

McClellan cancelled the campaign. Calling it a "damned fizzle," Secretary of War Edwin M. Stanton said it looked as if McClellan intended to do nothing. Now McClellan's chief, Marcy, found himself back on Lincoln's carpet, not at McClellan's behest but at the president's, who had long been exasperated with McClellan's lack of aggression. Lincoln did not let Marcy speak. "Why in the Nation . . . couldn't the general have known whether a boat would go through that lock before spending a million dollars getting them there?" thundered Lincoln. "I am almost despairing at these results." He dismissed Marcy before the soldier could offer an explanation.[28]

Hesitation had marked McClellan's tenure as commander of the Army of the Potomac; it also marked his personal staff usage. That began to change when McClellan embarked on the Peninsula campaign. The change was almost imperceptible, but it was present nonetheless.

The Peninsula campaign was an agonizingly slow push to the gates of Richmond; in the end, it was a failure. In late March McClellan assembled his 70,000-man army on boats, floated them down the Potomac River from Washington and into the Chesapeake Bay. In early April the army debarked at Fortress Monroe, on the tip of the Virginia Peninsula. Southern general Joseph E. Johnston had overall command of Rebel troops protecting Richmond, but when McClellan's men arrived he had only 17,000 troops, under Gen. John B. Magruder, on the Peninsula at Yorktown. McClellan's army drew up before Yorktown on April 5, but instead of attacking, the overcautious commander resorted to an unnecessary siege. Magruder stayed in his flimsy fortifications while McClellan wasted a month digging siege lines and positioning heavy guns. By the time Magruder slipped out of the lines on May 3, Johnston had brought 40,000 more Confederate troops to the Peninsula. Claiming a brilliant, bloodless victory, McClellan occupied Yorktown, then pushed ahead to Williamsburg. There, Federals caught up with Johnston's rear guard, the main Confederate army retreating to Richmond, and a daylong fight erupted May 5. Federals occupied Williamsburg on May 6, then pushed on toward Richmond. In the meantime, Gen. Irvin McDowell's corps of 35,000, left behind to protect Washington, headed south to join McClellan's right flank so that, by the end of May, when he reached Richmond, McClellan could count 100,000 troops at his command.

The Army of the Potomac was but five miles outside Richmond, split north and south by the Chickahominy River, when Johnston launched his counteroffensive. The battle of Fair Oaks, May 31 and June 1, was a fierce but confused fight on both sides. Men struggled through swamps and woods, and unit commanders lost control of the fight. When it was over, neither army had done much but lose men: Federals suffered 5,000 casualties, Rebels 6,000. McClellan, with overpowering strength, had been too timid to take Richmond. Johnston, on the other hand, had been unable to unseat McClellan. In the greatest consequence of the battle, Johnston suffered wounds that forced him to relinquish command. Within a day Confederate president Jefferson Davis gave command of the army to his top military adviser, Gen. Robert E. Lee.

The Army of the Potomac lingered near Richmond. Over the next several weeks, Lee took advantage of McClellan's idleness to refit the Southern army, which he dubbed the Army of Northern Virginia. On June 25 he initiated his own campaign to drive the Federals from Richmond. The counteroffensive became known as the battle of the Seven Days, with fighting at Oak Grove, June 25; Mechanicsville, June 26; Gaines's Mill, June 27; Savage's Station, June 29; Frayser's Farm, June 30; and Malvern Hill,

July 1. Casualties were staggering, with Confederates losing 3,286 killed, 15,909 wounded, and 946 missing. Federals lost 1,734 killed, 8,062 wounded, and 6,053 missing. Lee did not destroy the Army of the Potomac; in fact he lost at Malvern Hill, but he forced McClellan to retreat to the James River, thus ending the Federal threat to Richmond for the present. McClellan called his retreat simply a "change of base," but in truth the Peninsula campaign was over.[29]

Although the Peninsula campaign was another fizzle, McClellan did show a glimmer of enlightened staff usage on the Peninsula. But like the campaign itself, McClellan's staff assignments were tentative. At the outset, as McClellan was switching from the Urbanna to the Peninsula plan, he detailed John Jacob Astor Jr. to keep records of all information regarding transports. That way McClellan would "always know the exact conditions of the transports and their locality."[30]

No matter how it ended, the Peninsula campaign was a massive feat of organization and logistics. Naturally, the men of McClellan's special staff—the quartermaster general, commissary, and ordnance officers—coordinated transportation and supply. But the combat forces of the Army of the Potomac never could have marched without clear, concise orders from headquarters. McClellan's first assistant adjutant general, Seth Williams, handled that chore. Throughout the Army of the Potomac's time in Virginia, Williams wrote most of the general and special orders that kept the army running. Certainly, Williams's duties were traditional and standard; and, of course, Williams did not originate the orders, McClellan did. But Williams wrote understandable orders, made copies for the necessary field commanders, and saw that they safely reached their destination. The orders Williams drafted were mundane but crucial to the performance of the army. For instance, before the army had debarked in Virginia, Williams issued orders outlining leave and furlough policy for enlisted men. Those same orders gave division commanders responsibility for policing and disciplining soldiers.[31] In Europe, such provost duties belonged to a member of the commanding general's personal staff. As the campaign wore on, Williams issued new orders to division commanders to curtail rampant depredations against Southern civilians. Stealing had gotten out of hand after the army left Yorktown, Williams wrote. He added that anyone caught stealing would be "placed in irons, tried by a military commission, and punished to the extent of the law."[32]

Williams also regularly issued verbal orders, and he had a strict system for doing so. He required corps commanders, unattached divisions, and detachments to have messengers present at his office at 10:00 A.M. and

5:00 P.M. daily to receive orders. Each day at noon, Williams had a staff officer from corps and detached headquarters meet with him for orders. Williams also ordered that, after every march, corps and unattached unit commanders, or a representative staff officer, were to come to his head-quarters and report the locations of their headquarters. Finally, Williams wanted all the commanders of the various special staff departments to report to him after each march for orders. The system enabled the assistant adjutant general to stay in constant contact with field commanders.[33] Williams's system looked like a mixture of the duties that Berthier's general staff had performed for Napoleon. Williams probably was not attempting to copy a Napoleonic system, however; his regulations stemmed more from his own regimented mind and a need to bring administrative order to the large army.

Williams, and his assistant, Albert V. Colburn, also issued immediate orders of march to field commanders, and they used a topographical

McClellan staffer, Col. Albert V. Colburn, relaxes with Col. Delos B. Sacket and Gen. John Sedgewick at Harrison's Landing, Virginia, during McClellan's Peninsula campaign, 1862. (LIBRARY OF CONGRESS)

bureau to help them. For example, as the army moved from Williamsburg on May 6 and 7, Williams sent IV Corps commander, Maj. Gen. Erasmus D. Keys, orders to send a brigade to a specified point. Williams did not write out the brigade's destination, but he enclosed a map with the destination marked "A." Colburn sent similar orders to Col. George A. H. Blake, commanding a brigade of cavalry. He enclosed a map with "all the information in possession of the topographical bureau at these headquarters with regard to the region in question."[34]

The presence of a topographical bureau at McClellan's headquarters is interesting. None of McClellan's correspondence regarding staff composition, however, reveals who was in charge of the bureau or who worked in it. Napoleon had made topographical mapping a function of his cabinet, and members of Berthier's special staff had distributed maps to field units, so the notion of having a topographical bureau at headquarters was not new. Whether McClellan considered it special or personal staff duty is unclear, though.

Colburn proved as industrious as Williams. In a letter to his wife, McClellan said that Colburn rarely left his side. "He is one of the very best men I ever knew," wrote McClellan. He further commented that Colburn was "perfectly untiring. Day and night are about the same to him." Hard work, nevertheless, took its toll. In another, almost whimsical, letter to Nell, McClellan described a night at headquarters, which the general called a deserted "secesh" hut, before Yorktown. "Colburn is copying a long letter—Seth, standing by the fire, looking very sleepy. . . . I am sorry to say that your Father is snoring loudly in a corner."[35]

Other members of McClellan's staff were also busy with varied duties. The French "royals" carried orders to different parts of the field, and Robert d'Orléans once directed two companies of infantry to their destination. Louis-Philippe, Robert d'Orléans, and the prince de Joinville were with V Corps commander, Maj. Gen. Fitz-John Porter, throughout the battle of Gaines's Mill during the Seven Days fighting. D'Orléans delivered special instructions for troop placement from McClellan to the Fourth New Jersey Infantry, and Joinville helped reorganize part of Brig. Gen. Dan Butterfield's brigade after Confederates attacked it. Later, Joinville directed the fire of Battery A, New Jersey Light Artillery. Lt. Col. Paul von Radowitz and Maj. Herbert Hammerstein also helped Porter that day. Without citing their duties, Porter thanked McClellan's staffers for their "courage and energy [which was] conspicuous among many brave men on [the] field."[36]

Other McClellan staffers also did varied duty. Hammerstein and Nelson B. Sweitzer conducted reconnaissance for McClellan on May 6, the day following the Williamsburg fight, and Col. E. H. Wright helped position regiments in entrenchments following the Fair Oaks battle. On June 25, the first day of Lee's offensive, Hammerstein helped Brig. Gen. Daniel Sickles rally a portion of his Second Brigade, Second Division, who were fleeing their positions in panic. Col. Edward McKee Hudson and Capt. William P. Mason Jr. assisted Army of the Potomac chief engineer Brig. Gen. John G. Barnard, to lay out Union lines at Malvern Hill on July 1 before the final battle of the Seven Days, and Capt. Martin T. McMahon was with VI Corps commander, Brig. Gen. William B. Franklin, during at least part of the Seven Days. Franklin congratulated McMahon and others for "bravely carrying orders under the most trying circumstances."[37]

On the Peninsula, McClellan was expanding staff duty by sending his aides into the field to help unit commanders. Their help was no doubt valuable and won the appreciation of combat commanders. But to say McClellan was seeking a European model of staff work would be only partly correct. McClellan gives no hint that he was following a cogent plan for his staffers. He did not brief the men with his views or give them authority to issue orders in his absence. Frequently the men became just extra pairs of hands or couriers, passing along orders from McClellan or carrying orders for the commanders they were assisting. They never acted in an advisory capacity, which would have made them an extension of McClellan in the field. McClellan was only knocking at the door of expanded staff duty.

At the siege of Yorktown, however, McClellan did show a hint of progressive staff usage. On April 27, three weeks after the siege began, McClellan appointed Gen. Fitz-John Porter, then a division commander in the III Corps, as "director of the siege" and gave Porter two of his own staff aides, Capts. Joseph Kirkland and William P. Mason, as siege assistants. Porter said that he received the appointment "for reasons known only to the major general commanding." McClellan did have a reason, however. Siege work was not Chief of Staff Marcy's specialty, and "he cannot assist me in siege operations," said McClellan. McClellan wanted all generals in the trenches to report directly to Porter instead of Marcy, and Porter was to report in person to McClellan or Marcy at least twice daily to receive instructions. "I [will] give all my orders relating to the siege through . . . [Porter]—making him at the same time commandant of the siege operations and a chief of staff for that portion of the work." McClellan added that the new arrangement "will save me much trouble, relieve my mind greatly and save much time."[38]

Why McClellan gave Porter the job so late into the siege, only McClellan knew. And never mind that the siege was useless to begin with: McClellan's troops could have easily pushed Magruder from Yorktown. What is important is that McClellan was trying to use his staff to handle an extra burden and to free him to attend to operational matters. McClellan was not so much detaching staffers Kirkland and Mason to work with Porter, he was temporarily adding Porter to his own staff. McClellan said as much when he referred to Porter as "a chief of staff" for the siege.

As it worked out, though, Kirkland and Mason became permanent members of Porter's staff. In the Yorktown trenches, they toured the works with Porter and familiarized themselves with the siege. Porter fell ill in the last days of the siege and had to stay in his tent. He therefore relied on Kirkland, Mason, and his own staff officers for reports on Union progress and intelligence on enemy movements, which, said Porter, the men "obtained often by great exposure to the fire of the enemy." When the siege ended, Kirkland and Mason did not return to McClellan's staff. Whether McClellan officially detached them is uncertain, but Porter was soon referring to them as members of "my staff." They assisted Porter in a fight at Hanover Court House, May 27, and were with him throughout the Seven Days.[39]

McClellan used his father-in-law and chief of staff, Marcy, extensively as a link between headquarters and field commanders. Those men frequently received orders from Marcy, not McClellan, on everything from bivouac positions to artillery placements and reconnaissance missions. Marcy wanted to hear often from field commanders. "Do not lose sight of the absolute necessity of keeping me constantly and fully informed of everything which occurs in your front," he told Fitz-John Porter.[40] Although Marcy occasionally made spot decisions, he never had full rein to issue orders without first checking with his son-in-law. Marcy could, without hesitation, direct a division of troops to help construct a bridge and cross it to support other troops in battle, as he did at Savage's Station on June 28. But more often his comments left no doubt about who issued the orders. Marcy used phrases such as "I am directed by the commanding general to say . . ." or "the general commanding directs that you. . . ." Marcy frequently verified orders with McClellan,[41] but McClellan never authorized Marcy to speak with the full authority of the commanding general.

Throughout the Peninsula campaign and the Seven Days, just as he had after the battle of Rich Mountain, McClellan used Marcy to keep President Lincoln and Secretary of War Stanton apprised of his situation. Marcy put the best face on all of his reports. On May 10, from Yorktown, Marcy wrote to Stanton that McClellan was on the main road to Richmond—a heartening choice of words, considering the time McClellan had just wasted at Yorktown—and that gunboats were clearing the Pamunkey River of sunken Rebel vessels. On May 28 Marcy sent Stanton a brief report of the battle of Hanover Court House. He called the Union victory "decisive" and commented that Confederate "prisoners say [it] will have a demoralizing effect upon their army."[42]

On June 27, during the Seven Days, McClellan used Marcy to break bad news to Washington. Reporting that Federal troops had been fighting all day against superior numbers, which they had not, Marcy told Stanton, "We shall endeavor to hold our own, and if compelled to fall back, shall do it in good order, upon the James River." McClellan was planning just such a retreat, and Marcy softened the news by saying that the James would be a better supply conduit for the army.[43]

When the Seven Days ended at Malvern Hill, McClellan sent Marcy to Washington to personally request that Lincoln and Stanton send him 100,000 more troops to "accomplish the great task of capturing Richmond." Marcy met with Lincoln and Stanton on July 4, and he frightened Lincoln with the possibility that McClellan might have to surrender if Lee attacked him again. After their meeting, Lincoln gave Marcy a letter to deliver to McClellan saying that the most troops he could send would be about 25,000, and then not for a month or six weeks. Marcy forwarded the message to McClellan on July 4, adding that Lincoln and Stanton "speak very kindly of you and find no fault."[44]

McClellan would not try to capture Richmond again. President Lincoln, having lost faith in McClellan, split up the Army of the Potomac and gave most of it to Maj. Gen. John Pope. Pope had won a minor victory in the West, and Lincoln now called him to the Virginia theater to fight Lee. McClellan remained in command of a skeleton force around Washington, but when Lee trounced Pope at the second battle of Bull Run and invaded the North, Lincoln again turned to McClellan. He told the general to reorganize the Army of the Potomac and stop Lee.

In September 1862 Lee crossed his army into Maryland, hoping to move into Pennsylvania. A large Federal garrison at Harpers Ferry threatened his army's rear, however. Boldly, Lee split his small force. Part of it, under Stonewall Jackson, moved to capture the garrison, and the rest continued northward.

Groping blindly for Lee in the Maryland countryside, McClellan halted the Army of the Potomac near Frederick, Maryland, on September 13. On a campsite Lee's army had just abandoned, some of McClellan's soldiers found a copy of Lee's battle plan, detailing the exact destinations of his units. An excited McClellan wired Lincoln that he would soon catch Lee, and had he moved promptly he could have done so. Instead, McClellan moved as timidly as he had on the Peninsula, waiting sixteen hours before leaving Frederick. McClellan did bring one of the separated pieces of Lee's army to battle at South Mountain on September 14, and Union troops won the day. But, with a chance to destroy Lee's army in detail, McClellan again dawdled, wasting September 15 and 16 and allowing pieces of the Army of Northern Virginia time to reunite in a defensive position at Sharpsburg, Maryland, behind Antietam Creek.

At dawn on a foggy September 17, McClellan finally attacked. His plan, to hit three strategic points of Lee's line, was sound enough, but he executed it poorly. Instead of smashing the length of Lee's line simultaneously, McClellan committed piecemeal attacks never bringing the full weight of his superior numbers to bear on Lee's hard-pressed force. Instead, Lee, with the advantage of interior lines, moved troops from sector to sector to counter McClellan's separate blows. The battlefields became legendary: the Cornfield, the East Woods, Bloody Lane, Burnside's Bridge. By evening Lee's men had held fast, but the cost was terrific. Of about 40,000 men engaged, estimated Confederate casualties were 2,700 killed, 9,024 wounded, and 2,000 missing, totaling 13,724. Union casualties were estimated at 2,010 killed, 9,416 wounded, and 1,043 missing, or 12,469 out of about 75,000 men in battle.[45]

McClellan never increased staff duties to take advantage of the Confederate orders he had found, and, on the seventeenth, he did not use his staff officers to coordinate his triple attacks. In fact, when II Corps commander Maj. Gen. Edwin V. "Bull" Sumner arrived at McClellan's headquarters to complain that the attacks were proceeding "in driblets" and would do no good, McClellan's staffers refused to let him see McClellan. The commanding general had been up all night planning the battle and was asleep.[46]

McClellan's staff work throughout the campaign was unspectacular, and it varied little from what he had done on the Peninsula. Marcy, Colburn, and Seth Williams handled the bulk of headquarters correspondence.[47] On the day of battle, McClellan dispatched his staffers to accompany combat commanders. When Maj. Gen. Joseph Hooker's I Corps opened the battle on Lee's left at dawn, Chief of Staff Marcy and Maj. Herbert Hammerstein joined him. When Hooker fell with a wounded foot, Hammerstein notified McClellan's headquarters; Marcy soon had orders to put Maj. Gen. George G. Meade in command of Hooker's corps.[48]

On other parts of the field, Albert Colburn, assistant adjutant general, helped direct an artillery battery into position, and Capt. Martin T. McMahon was present with Maj. Gen. William B. Franklin's VI Corps. Franklin commended McMahon for his work but did not explain what duties he performed. On the southern end of the field, McClellan assigned Maj. Gen. Ambrose Burnside and his IX Corps to cross Antietam Creek and assail Lee's right. The creek was only knee-deep and easily fordable, but Burnside insisted on shoving his men across a narrow bridge. They became easy targets for Rebel snipers on high ground across the creek, and Burnside wasted precious hours trying to cross. Finally, McClellan sent Judge Key to urge Burnside along. Key arrived at about 1:00 P.M., just as Burnside's men got across the river. He rode back to headquarters and told McClellan that Burnside thought he could hold his position, but McClellan sent Key back with orders for Burnside to storm Sharpsburg itself. Key also carried orders removing Burnside from command if he did not obey.[49]

Antietam was McClellan's last battle. On September 18, Lee, his army badly cut up but undefeated, waited for McClellan to make a move. McClellan had a fresh reserve corps with which he could strike Lee, but he held back. Lincoln, exasperated, fired McClellan in November. Marcy remained with the army as an inspector general, and Seth Williams remained at its headquarters throughout the war, serving as adjutant to McClellan's successors Ambrose Burnside, Joseph Hooker, and George Meade.[50] McClellan retired to New York City to await orders, and he asked the War Department to allow ten of his personal staff officers to accompany him and help draft reports.[51]

For a soldier who had observed modern military staffs in action, McClellan did remarkably little with his own staff. Perhaps he did not trust his men. After the Peninsula campaign McClellan told his wife that he had little use for the civilians on his staff: "The most useless thing imaginable is one of these 'highly educated' civilians." He complained that they were slow to learn, that he would never take on another one. But McClellan did remarkably little with the trained men on his staff. Seth Williams ably ran the clerical end of McClellan's headquarters, and Randolph Marcy functioned efficiently, within the limits McClellan gave him, as a liaison with field officers and high command in Washington. The other staff officers, many of them West Point graduates, were used simply as couriers in shoulder straps. McClellan never asked them to help coordinate battles; he gave them no authority to issue orders in his absence; and, as general in chief, he did not dispatch them to assist in the operation of the various Union armies in the field. At times, such as during the siege of Yorktown, McClellan hinted at establishing a modern staff organization for his army. In the end, however, he hesitated to expand the role of his staff officers, just as he hesitated to deliver a crushing blow to the armies of the Confederacy.

CHAPTER THREE

Lee: Matters of Routine

1861–1865

ROBERT E. LEE, WHOM SOUTHERNERS REVERED AS PERHAPS THEIR greatest general, did nothing during the war to advance personal staff work at his headquarters. Lee had a personal staff, and they performed well the duties he gave them. But Lee never allowed himself a large staff and he never involved them in operational matters. Until early 1864, Col. Robert H. Chilton was Lee's chief of staff. Chilton was a chief in name only, performing duties little different from those of an assistant adjutant general. When attrition took members from his staff, Lee refused to replace them, choosing instead to heap excess work on the remaining staff officers. The small character of Lee's staff prompted Lee biographer Douglas Southall Freeman to comment that no other general "ever fought a campaign comparable to [Lee's of 1864] with only three men on his staff, and not one of them a professional soldier."[1]

Lee was no stranger to staff work. An 1829 graduate of West Point, he served as an engineer on Gen. Winfield Scott's special staff during the Mexican War. Lee became Scott's right-hand man, reconnoitering gun placements at Veracruz, picking a route over treacherous ground for artillery to approach Mexico City, and sighting guns on Chapultepec. Lee rose from captain to colonel during the war.[2]

Lee resigned from the United States Army and offered his services to the Confederacy soon after Virginia seceded from the Union in May 1861. He served briefly as an adviser to President Davis in Richmond, and he had a small staff to assist him with matters of army mobilization. In August 1861 Davis sent Lee with the rank of full general to coordinate the efforts of three independent Southern forces in northwest Virginia. Political rivals and inept military men commanded the forces, however, and Lee's hopes for a combined offensive in western Virginia vanished.[3]

As a general himself, Lee was cautious about putting together his own staff. In the summer of 1861 the Confederate Congress passed an act that allowed generals to request civilians for staff positions with the equivalent rank and pay of Regular Army positions. Generals frequently abused the act, however, requesting as many volunteer aides-de-camp as they could get. Many of those aides were relatives or politicians; few of them had the experience required for the job. Lee was not opposed to having relatives on staff, as long as they were competent and willing to work, but he decried large numbers of aides. While he was building one of his first headquarters staffs, Lee told his son, George Washington Custis Lee, that he had two experienced aides on his staff for the present, but he feared he would soon have to let them go. "I suppose it is in vain for me to expect to keep an instructed officer, there is such demand for their services with troops," Lee said. Realizing that the Confederate army had limited manpower, he feared that he might be keeping officers from duty on the line. As a result Lee failed to adequately staff his headquarters throughout the war.[4]

Lee took along a staff officer who would ultimately be with him until Appomattox: Capt. Walter Herron Taylor. Taylor, born in 1838 in Norfolk, Virginia, attended the Norfolk Military Institute, and he enrolled at age sixteen at the Virginia Military Institute. His military education ended abruptly in 1855, however, when his father's death forced him to withdraw.[5] Taylor was a member of a Virginia militia company when the Civil War began, and influential friends landed him a job helping Lee while the general was Davis's adviser. On the trip to western Virginia, Taylor and Lt. Col. John A. Washington, who had also been on Lee's Richmond staff, were Lee's only staff officers. Lee came to know the men well, as they shared a tent on the expedition. He commented in a letter to his wife, Mary, that Washington knelt in prayer morning and night. Tragedy befell the little headquarters, when, on September 13, Federal soldiers killed Washington when he rode out with Lee's nephew, Col. Fitzhugh Lee, to reconnoiter a position.[6]

With the western Virginia expedition over, Davis assigned Lee to command coastal defenses in South Carolina, Georgia, and east Florida in late 1861. Taylor followed Lee to Charleston, where the general put together a headquarters staff that reflected his attitudes about staff composition—small and efficient. Lee cast about for members of the Lee family to join his staff, and he asked his son, Custis, to recommend someone. Such

Walter Herron Taylor as a cadet at the Virginia Military Academy. Taylor would become Robert E. Lee's main adjutant and assist him throughout the war. (VMI ARCHIVES)

a selection would have to be mutually acceptable, he told Custis, "for I have so much to attend to, that I must have those with me who can be of service."[7]

Ultimately, Lee's small staff, seven men in all, included none of his relatives. Capt. Thornton A. Washington, adjutant general; Taylor, assistant adjutant general; and Capt. Joseph Manigault, volunteer aide-de-camp, made up Lee's personal staff. Capt. Joseph C. Ives, chief engineer, Lt. Col. William G. Gill, ordnance officer; a Captain Walker, chief of cavalry; and Maj. Armistead Lindsey Long, chief of artillery, composed the special staff.[8] Washington and Long were West Point graduates, Washington in 1849, Long in 1850.[9]

In Armistead Long, a friend of the extended Lee family, General Lee made another lasting association. Long would switch to Lee's personal staff and serve there until taking an artillery line command after the battle of Gettysburg in 1863. Long, previously an officer in the United States Army, had resigned his commission shortly before the first battle of Bull Run to join the Confederacy. He first met Lee at an interview in Richmond when Lee was Davis's adviser. Lee's "grace of . . . bearing and courteous but mild and decided manner" impressed Long. So did Lee's unpretentious attitude. The general wore only a gray suit, Long noted, and had "no handsomely dressed aides-de-camp or staff officers filling the anteroom." Only Taylor and some clerks attended Lee.[10]

Lee was also impressed with Long. He commissioned him a major and appointed him chief of artillery for Gen. W. W. Loring's Army of Northwest Virginia.[11] Loring, incidentally, was one of the generals who would complicate Lee's mission to western Virginia that August. Long's assignment to Loring was short-lived, however; in late November 1861 Long received orders to report to General Lee's headquarters in Charleston.[12]

For four months Lee and his staff strengthened the coastal defenses of their department, constructing batteries and earthworks and fortifying weak points. Although they saw no battle, Lee and his staff were present for a fire that destroyed half of Charleston the night of December 11. The men had noticed the fire as they crossed the Ashley River in a rowboat, but thought little of it. They went to their hotel, the Mills House, and were beginning their dinner when they heard more commotion outside. Going to the roof of the hotel, Lee and his staff saw that the fire was now out of control and threatening their building. They returned downstairs and found the lower levels in chaos as guests tried to escape. Lee and Long each carried a baby from the building, while Taylor, Joseph Ives, and the wives of Long and Thornton Washington followed them outside. Lee and his company spent the night at a private residence. The fire burned itself out, sparing the Mills House, but cutting a great swath between the Cooper and Ashley rivers.[13]

Such excitement cemented relationships on the staff, and Lee showed a fondness for Long when he took him to visit the grave of his father, Henry "Light-Horse Harry" Lee. The elder Lee had been returning from the West Indies in 1818 when he died near the estate of Revolutionary War general Nathanael Greene, on Cumberland Island, Georgia. Light-Horse Harry was buried in a corner of the Greene family cemetery. On their visit, Lee quietly regarded the dilapidated estate, then he and Long returned to their boat.[14]

In March 1862 Jefferson Davis called Lee back to Richmond, ostensibly to give him command of all Confederate armies. Davis did not make Lee general in chief, however, because he considered himself a hands-on military leader and did not want to lessen his own control of Southern forces. In reality, then, Lee returned to his old job as Davis's military adviser. Nevertheless, the Confederate Congress approved a staff for Lee, allowing him a military secretary, with the rank and pay of a cavalry colonel, and four aides-de-camp, with the rank and pay of cavalry majors.[15]

Walter Taylor followed his boss to Richmond. As all adjutants general were officially part of the Adjutant General's Department in Richmond and only assigned to field commanders, Lee offered Taylor the chance to remain with the adjutant general's office or to become one of the new aides-de-camp on his staff. Taylor replied that he would serve wherever Lee assigned him, but the general pressed him. Taylor decided that he would rather be an aide, reasoning that the job would spare him "much confinement about headquarters and the annoyance and trouble of attending to papers and routine work, and [I would] be more on the field."[16]

Armistead Long stayed in South Carolina for a time, but he received orders in May 1862 to join Lee in Richmond. He accepted Lee's offer of the military secretary's job and became a colonel on Lee's new staff.[17] Lee then rounded out his staff with Majs. Thomas Mann Randolph Talcott, Charles Marshall, and Charles Scott Venable. In Taylor, Marshall, and Venable, Lee had the nucleus of the staff that would remain with him for the rest of the war.

None of Lee's new staff officers were professional soldiers, but all were highly intelligent men of Virginia birth. Their intellect and standing no doubt influenced Lee to place them on his staff. T. M. R. Talcott was a family friend of Lee's before the war, and Talcott's father, Col. Andrew Talcott, was an engineer and one of Lee's old friends. Lee fondly referred to Talcott's mother, Harriet Randolph Hackley Talcott, as "the Beautiful Talcott." The younger Talcott enjoyed working mathematical problems and eventually became a colonel of engineers in the Confederate service.[18]

Venable was born in 1827 in Prince Edward County, Virginia, and attended Virginia's Hampden-Sydney College. He tutored mathematics there from 1843 to 1845, and in 1856 he became a professor of natural philosophy at the University of Georgia. In 1857 Venable moved to South Carolina College in Columbia, where he taught mathematics until 1860. After the Civil War, Venable would become a professor of mathematics at the University of Virginia. When the war began Venable volunteered his services to the Confederacy and saw action at Bull Run, acting as an aide to Capt. W. H. Stevens of the engineers. Venable's comrades on Lee's staff frequently referred to him as "Professor," and Confederate artillerist Edward Porter Alexander called him a man of "high type in intellect and character."[19]

Charles Marshall was born in 1830 at Warrenton, Virginia, into a family rich in Virginia heritage. His great-grandfather, Thomas Marshall, had been commander of the Third Virginia Regiment during the Revolution. Thomas' eldest son—Charles's great-uncle—was legendary U.S. Chief Justice John Marshall. Charles Marshall received a master's degree from the University of Virginia in 1849, taught for a while at the University of Indiana, then practiced law in Baltimore until the Civil War began.[20]

The staffers labored with Lee in Richmond until a threat to the Confederate capital changed their jobs for the rest of the war. Throughout the spring, Union major general George B. McClellan and his 100,000-man Army of the Potomac had been creeping up the Peninsula. Confederate general Joseph E. Johnston, who commanded the armies defending Richmond, had retreated before McClellan's advance, seemingly without a plan. Indeed, neither Jefferson Davis nor anyone at Lee's headquarters knew Johnston's plans, for the general in the field preferred secrecy. When Johnston finally struck back, in the battle of Fair Oaks, on May 31 and June 1, the battle incapacitated him for command.[21]

Near the end of the first day's fighting, a bullet struck Johnston in the right shoulder. An instant later a shell fragment hit him in the chest and knocked him from his horse and out of the battle. Command of the Confederate forces fell to Gen. Gustavus W. Smith, but he barely knew how to proceed, for Johnston had not informed Smith of his plans. Soon Davis and Lee, who had ridden from Richmond to check on the course of the battle, found Smith near nervous exhaustion under the strain of his unexpected command. Realizing that Smith could not handle the defense of Richmond, Davis transferred command to Lee.[22]

On June 1, at Lee's direction, Walter Taylor issued Special Orders No. 22, announcing Lee as general of the Confederate army before Richmond. Writing for Lee, Taylor reported that the new commander regretted the loss of Johnston and encouraged Rebel soldiers to continue the fight. Taylor also said that Lee was sure that every soldier would "maintain the ancient fame of the Army of Northern Virginia and . . . conquer or die in the approaching contest." With that, Lee christened the army, hitherto a collection of independent commands, with the name it would carry into legend.[23]

Suddenly Lee's staffers were catapulted from aiding a military adviser to assisting a field commander. Lee realized that he would need additional help at headquarters, and he quickly added two officers to his personal staff. By June 4 Lt. Col. Robert H. Chilton was at headquarters as Lee's chief of staff and principal assistant adjutant general, and by June 6 Capt. Arthur Pendleton "Penny" Mason was issuing orders as a second assistant adjutant general.[24]

Mason had served General Johnston as assistant adjutant general throughout the Peninsula campaign. After the first day of the battle of Seven Pines, Mason remained at headquarters even after the wounded Johnston and his other staffers quit the field. Upon assuming command, Lee made Mason his own assistant adjutant.[25]

Chilton had been an assistant adjutant and inspector general in the regular Confederate service before Lee chose him as his chief. Born in Virginia in 1817, Chilton entered West Point in 1833, graduating in 1837 with future generals Braxton Bragg, John Sedgwick, and Joseph Hooker. Chilton served in the First U.S. Dragoons until the Mexican War began in 1846, when he took a position on the staff of Gen. Zachary Taylor. Chilton carried orders for Taylor in the battle of Buena Vista, and when Col. Jefferson Davis of the Mississippi Rifles was wounded, Chilton helped him off the field. For his gallantry he earned a brevet promotion to major. Chilton remained in the army after the war, and in 1854 Davis, by then U.S. secretary of war, appointed him an army paymaster. When hostilities broke out Chilton followed Southern states out of the Union, resigning from the army on April 29, 1861.[26]

Chilton was immediately involved in the flurry of activity at Lee's headquarters as the general prepared the Army of Northern Virginia's defense against the Federals, yet his position on the staff seemed confused from the start. On June 4, the day Lee announced him as chief of staff, Chilton issued orders for Lee assigning generals to command. Throughout the next week Chilton drafted orders establishing provost guards in each division and corresponded with unit commanders. He did not sign his correspondence as "chief of staff," however, using instead his other title, "assistant adjutant general."[27] But Chilton's job as principal adjutant was short-lived.

Routine paperwork, which Lee hated, flooded his headquarters. The general spent much of each morning with a pile of documents on his desk and his staff officers arrayed in a semicircle before him, doling out papers to each staffer and instructing them on how to handle the work. The mundane work was soon too much for Lee, who needed to concentrate on operations instead, and he summoned Walter Taylor. "[He] said that he would have to put me back in the office," wrote Taylor. "I knew what he meant. . . . He had real work to do and wished to be rid of these matters of detail." By June 21 Taylor was signing himself "acting assistant adjutant general," and he said from that time on he, not Chilton, directed the staff adjutant general's department.[28]

Taylor always resented Chilton's presence on the staff. Once, when Chilton was away from camp, Taylor wrote to his sweetheart, Bettie Saunders, that he did not care if Chilton returned. "You see he has the rank and credit of A.A.G. and I have the unthankful and unremunerative part of the position, namely the labor and the responsibility."[29]

Chilton nevertheless remained busy drafting the general and special orders for Lee that largely affected army organization. Armistead Long communicated Lee's wishes to Rebel cavalry leader J.E.B. Stuart for the placement of cavalry pickets and to Maj. W. H. Stevens, Lee's chief of engineers, about laying out defensive lines. Mason and Taylor handled routine matters.[30]

Lee used cavalry commander J.E.B. Stuart's force to gather intelligence about McClellan's army. On June 12 Stuart's command left on a three-day dash around the Army of the Potomac, and they returned with the exact positions of McClellan's forces. Stuart told Lee that McClellan's right flank was vulnerable to attack.[31] With the information from Stuart, Lee prepared to push the stalled McClellan from the gates of Richmond. He outlined a plan to bring Gen. Thomas Jonathan "Stonewall" Jackson's army down from the Shenandoah Valley, where it had wreaked havoc on Federals during the spring, and have it fall on McClellan's exposed right flank, while Lee's main force struck McClellan from the front. Though the beginning of the campaign on June 25 was disjointed, Lee's army battered McClellan for a week in the battle of the Seven Days.

Little evidence of staff activity during the Seven Days exists, partly because Lee avoided detailed written orders, which staff officers would have drafted. The only elaborate order to come from Lee's headquarters was General Orders No. 75, which Chilton drafted for Lee and issued on June 24. The orders included precise instructions to all commanders participating in the fight. Any other orders Lee issued were verbal, and his brief comment that his staff officers "were continuously with me in the field" indicates the staffers were probably relaying those orders to their recipients. Walter Taylor did just that on June 27, when he delivered orders directly to Maj. Gen. Richard S. Ewell, and on June 30 Chilton rode out from headquarters to place Gen. John B. Magruder's division where Lee wanted it. Talcott met Brig. Gen. Lewis Armistead on the field July 1 to inform him of enemy positions.[32]

That Lee shunned elaborate written orders during the fighting re-veals something of his expectations of his staff. Taking a commander's operational ideas and crafting them into clearly understood orders, then getting them efficiently to line commanders, had always been a prime function of a personal staff officer. European staffers, especially chiefs of staff, often were involved in planning operations. In opting for verbal orders during combat, something he would do throughout the war, Lee was cutting his staff officers out of all but the courier phase. In part, Lee chose verbal orders to ensure the secrecy of his plans. The relatively small size of his army, which never approximated contemporary European armies or the Union forces he opposed, also enabled Lee to get away with using verbal orders.

But in a larger sense, Lee considered himself his own chief of staff and what historian Clifford Dowdey calls an "operations officer." The Seven Days campaign sprang fully from Lee's mind. He never consulted Chilton, his titular chief of staff. Lee's attitude toward the chief's job may, in fact, be the reason that Chilton never signed his correspondence as "chief of staff." Lee might occasionally use his staffers as a sounding board ("Now, Colonel Long, how can we get at those people?" Lee asked his military secretary when they reconnoitered Federal positions before the Seven Days) but he expected no informed military response. Walter Taylor said after the war that Lee typically asked such rhetorical questions of those around him, "not that he attached any importance to or expected any aid from what might be said in reply," but the questioning allowed him to think out loud. What he wanted from his staff was someone to shield him from what Taylor called "matters of routine."[33] He wanted his staffers to shield him from paperwork, headquarters housework, and griping soldiers. He also expected diligence and prompt service from his staff. When he had all that, things went well around headquarters.

Lee inherited his first headquarters, the home of widow Mary Dabbs outside of Richmond, from Joe Johnston, and he used it before and after the Seven Days, but on the march the job of selecting a headquarters location fell to Col. Armistead Long. Long was an experienced artillerist, and in future campaigns Lee would use his topographical skills to recon-noiter Federal positions and place Confederate artillery. But Lee also used those skills for everyday work; "He has a good eye for locality, let him find a place for camp," Lee reasoned. Long noted that Lee was easily satisfied with his selections, and only once did he refuse a site Long had picked. That was at Winchester, Virginia, when the whole of the Army of

Northern Virginia made camp before Lee, taking the best spots. Long found some bare ground on a farm, and its owners assured him that Lee and his staff were welcome to stay in their yard. Long ordered up the staff's modest baggage wagons, but when Lee arrived he ordered everything moved to a stony field nearby. "This is better than the yard," he commented. "We will not now disturb those good people."[34]

The Dabbs house was probably the most comfortable place Lee's staff would ever occupy. Lee conducted his business, with Long usually in attendance, in a back room of the house, while Taylor, Chilton, and Mason handled the duties of the adjutant general's office from a front room. The house also provided a comfortable place for staff officers to dine together.[35] In the field, though, headquarters accommodations were a good deal rougher. Lee's Mexican War experience had taught him that private soldiers on the line could become jealous of a staff officer's lot, and he tried to see that life at headquarters was little different from life at the front. His attitudes helped endear Lee to his army, but Walter Taylor and his comrades were just as likely to find themselves sleeping in a field of rocks when a combat division had a meadow for a bed. And Taylor once commented to his sweetheart in Richmond that Lee would "suffer any amount of discomfort and inconvenience sooner than to change a camp once established."[36]

Lee's headquarters were sparse, typically consisting of from five to eight pole tents. Staff officers usually slept two or three to a tent, while Lee stayed in a wall tent, usually no larger than the others in the assemblage. A few wagons hauled headquarters papers, equipment, and the staff officers' baggage, of which Lee allowed them only a small box each. Those wagons parked around camp in no particular order, and couriers and camp servants frequently slept beneath them at night. No banners or guards marked the headquarters as that of the army's commanding general.[37]

Meals were as Spartan as the headquarters. "While we never really wanted for food," said Taylor, "we only enjoyed what was allotted to the army generally. Ours was the regular army ration." Mess furniture was of tin, and Lee never used his rank to obtain "dainties for his table or any personal comfort for himself." Lee did not forbid liquor in camp, but none of the staff officers regularly imbibed.[38]

Of course, as military secretary, Armistead Long did more than just choose ground for headquarters camp. Long helped Lee with his correspondence, writing letters and some orders to line commanders. In one instance, however, Long's correspondence went to a higher authority. On September 2 Long drafted, from Lee's dictation, a letter to Pres. Jefferson Davis outlining Lee's reasons for taking the war into the North. The letter heralded Lee's first invasion of the Union.[39]

Most of the paperwork, however, landed squarely on Walter Taylor. Every day each corps or independent command of the army received reports and papers from its regiments, brigades, and divisions, and each day it sent its package of correspondence to Lee's headquarters. Taylor said that they included "matters great and small, important and unimportant," from furlough requests to "some intricate question of the relative rights of the officers of the line and of the staff." Couriers arrived with such documents around the clock. Lee hated trivial matters. As Taylor said, "matters of great import . . . caused him to lie awake for hours," and Lee trusted his chief adjutant to handle anything not requiring the general's direct action. So Taylor had to examine all correspondence arriving at headquarters and dispense with it properly. He became so adept at his job that a courier with a dispatch could wake him from sleep and he could "tell at a glance" whether the communication was important or just routine.[40]

Taylor became so involved in protecting his boss from unnecessary paperwork that it once caused his own temper to flare. He had saved a stack of documents for Lee to dispense with quickly. Noticing that Lee was in an "ill humor," Taylor noted, "I hastily concluded that my efforts to save him annoyance were not appreciated." The young adjutant threw down the papers, venting his own anger. Lee calmly looked up and said, "Colonel Taylor, when I lose my temper, don't let it make you angry."[41]

Taylor, however, was frequently exasperated with his boss. In letters to his sweetheart, Bettie, he complained about the small size of Lee's staff and how overworked he felt: "[Other generals] have ten, twenty, & thirty Ajt Generals, this army has only one and I assure you at times I can hardly stand up under the pressure of work." Despite his griping, Taylor was not disposed to seek relief from the work, for he had an intense desire to please Lee. In that Taylor was also frustrated. "I am not satisfied to have others say . . . my presence here is necessary. I want him to tell me, then I'll be satisfied," Taylor wrote.[42]

Robert Chilton, as titular chief of staff and assistant adjutant general, drafted most of Lee's general and special orders. Lee, of course, originated the orders, and Chilton penned them in order form, made the requisite copies, and distributed them to their recipients. Immediately after the Seven Days, general orders dealt with repositioning combat units in case of another Federal threat and with altering generals' assignments to better organize the Army of Northern Virginia. As summer wore on, orders covered a variety of topics, such as urging unit commanders to see that troops had uniform weapons, either smoothbore or rifled, so the ordnance department could distribute the right kind of ammunition. Another order directed units to locations that would be "conducive to the health of . . .

[the] command . . . where good water, ground, &c, would afford pure air and convenient camps."[43]

Perhaps the most literary job of the headquarters fell to bespectacled Charles Marshall, whom Lee assigned to write the general's official campaign reports. Every unit, from a company to a corps, submitted reports of their engagements, skirmishes, and battles. Marshall first waded through all of those accounts before he could write Lee's official reports. The task was not easy. "One of the most difficult things I had to do was to reconcile the many conflicting accounts of the same affair," said Marshall. When Marshall could not justify an important but confused point, he rode out to the army and interviewed the officers submitting the reports. Other times he summoned the correspondents to headquarters to settle a detail.[44]

Marshall did not have the last word on the reports, however; General Lee did. After completing a report, Marshall would submit it to Lee, who became headquarters editor, making any corrections, insertions, or deletions he thought would make the report clearer. Marshall often cringed while Lee struck from a manuscript some bit of detail he had spent hours verifying. Lee specifically asked Marshall if reports contained any conflicting material, and frequently he pored over the same sources his aide had queried to make his official reports, as Marshall said, "as truthful as possible."[45]

Marshall pulled no punches in his reports, and when he thought a commander had been lax or incompetent during a campaign, he said so. "Colonel, if you speak so strongly of this you will have nothing left to say of something better," Lee chided Marshall, and he usually deleted sentences condemning a subaltern's actions. Marshall countered that the reports should include such information, if only to shift blame for a failure from Lee. "The responsibility for this army is mine," Lee answered, preferring not to place blame in a public report. When Marshall penned Lee's official report of the July 1863 battle of Gettysburg, he pointedly blamed the Confederate defeat in part on cavalry general J.E.B. Stuart who, trying to re-create his ride around the Union army on the Peninsula, led his troopers on a similar jaunt in Pennsylvania. Stuart was nowhere to be found the first two days of the battle and left Lee without the intelligence he needed to conduct the battle. Characteristically, Lee removed the damning phrases from his report. In his postwar memoirs, however, Marshall wrote that "there are material facts . . . which in my opinion are necessary to a correct understanding of the [Gettysburg] campaign," and he proceeded to heap blame where he thought it should be—on Stuart.[46]

While the staffers stayed busy writing orders and reports, the work was sometimes so voluminous that Lee had to write a great deal of correspondence himself. That Lee wrote frequent letters to President Davis, the secretaries of war, and Inspector General Samuel Cooper is not unusual. But Lee spent much time passing on simple intelligence to unit commanders, and he once wrote detailed instructions to a colonel at Fredericksburg, Virginia, explaining how to break up a railroad and dispose of the ties.[47]

Besides handling paperwork, writing orders, and drafting official reports, Lee wanted his staffers to do one other thing—protect him from solicitous visitors at headquarters. Walter Taylor remembered that, between campaigns or in winter quarters, virtually every soldier in the Army of Northern Virginia went "to work with pen and ink to state his grievance or make known his wants and desires," which increased the paperwork at headquarters immensely. The odd complaint that slipped past Taylor and reached Lee usually returned to an aide with, as Charles Venable called it, "the old-fashioned phrase, ''Suage him, Colonel, 'suage him.'"[48]

Once, an aggrieved officer came to headquarters and would settle for nothing less than an interview with Lee. Staffers finally relented and allowed him into Lee's tent. After a time, the officer departed, and soon Lee, visibly angry, emerged from his tent. Entering his adjutants' tent he asked, "Why did you permit that man to come to my tent and make me show my temper?"[49]

As Lee's staff settled into their office routines, they became the general's family in the field. They learned his likes and dislikes and were in a unique position to take the true measure of the man, not the legend that the war would produce. They had every respect for their commander, but Lee's staff officers did not hold him in awe. Behind his back they called him "the Tycoon," a sarcastic reference to Lee's austere lifestyle.[50]

Walter Taylor noted that although some people found Lee generally unapproachable, the opposite was in fact true. He said that Lee was indeed dignified, but his manner with his staff "invited closer friendship." Taylor recalled, "In our small circle of the personal staff . . . there was . . . [with Lee] a degree of camaraderie that was perfectly delightful." Conversation at meals was relaxed, "unreserved as between equals," and Lee frequently jested with others at the table. Taylor wrote that, while staffers observed the protocols of rank and deference, Lee's headquarters had none of the "rigid formality and the irksome ceremonial regarded by some as essential . . . to the . . . commander-in-chief of an army."[51]

Lee had a certain dry wit, and he liked to use it on his staffers. His mealtime jesting was often good-naturedly at their expense. Charles Marshall once caught the brunt of the general's humor. Marshall was in his tent one night in late September 1862 when fellow aide T. M. R. Talcott and artillerist colonel E. Porter Alexander entered and started working out some complex mathematical problem. Marshall cared little for math and opted instead for whiskey. When the others declined to drink with him, he made as if to empty a bottle by himself. Just as he poured a drink, "a pretty stiff one," Alexander recalled, Lee poked his head through the tent flaps. The general's look petrified Marshall, and Talcott and Alexander teased him about what Lee would do to him the next day. At breakfast, when Marshall unwisely complained of a headache, Lee commented, "Too much application to mathematical problems at night, with the unknown quantities x and y represented by a demijohn and tumbler, was very apt to have for a result a headache in the morning."[52]

Lee had an irascible, petulant side as well, and staff officer Venable had plenty of opportunities to see it. Other staff members reasoned that Venable's age, thirty-six when the war started, and his dignified former position as a college professor, made him the logical choice to approach the Tycoon when he was in a foul humor. That dubious job left Venable with a slightly different portrait of Lee than Taylor had. "The views which prevail . . . as to the gentle temper of the great soldier . . . are not altogether correct," wrote Venable. "No man could see the flush come over that grand forehead and the temple veins swell on occasions of great trial of patience and doubt that Lee had the high, strong temper of a Washington, and habitually under the same strong control." Occasionally, though, Lee's control slipped and the mighty temper flared; Taylor had seen it, and Venable caught his share of it as well. In the fall of 1864, Lee told staffers and unit commanders to start a movement at 2:00 A.M. the next morning. Mistakenly thinking he had told them 1:00 A.M., Lee was in the saddle an hour early and hopping mad at everyone's absence. Venable scrambled to get everyone in line, and when all was in order Lee asked Venable to ride forward and act as a guide. Venable, talking to someone else, did not hear Lee. The general's anger flashed and he grabbed a courier named Evans. "Evans," he snapped, "I will have to ask you to act upon my staff today, for my officers are all disappointing me." Lee was cool toward Venable for two weeks. That episode notwithstanding, Lee was usually quick to make amends. Another time after he had snapped at Venable, the staffer left Lee's tent and went to sleep on the ground. Feeling sorry, Lee took off his own poncho and placed it over Venable before he too went to sleep.[53]

The routines and duties that Lee's staff established in the summer of 1862 varied little for the rest of the war. In the weeks before Lee's second Bull Run campaign in August, Chilton was one of the busiest men at headquarters, corresponding with line commanders and drafting orders. That work culminated with Special Orders No. 185, which launched the campaign.[54]

During the second Bull Run campaign, Lee sent units under Stonewall Jackson north from Richmond to counter a threat from Federal major general John Pope and his new Army of Virginia, created from independent commands and parts of McClellan's Army of the Potomac. When he became convinced that McClellan and his remaining army were going to stay idle on the Peninsula, Lee and the rest of the Army of Northern Virginia under Gen. James Longstreet turned north to help Jackson. On August 29, on the old Bull Run battlefield, Pope ordered a piecemeal attack, which Jackson halted. The next day Longstreet joined Jackson, and the force easily bent Pope's left flank back, sending his whole army in retreat. In his official report of the battle, Longstreet thanked Lee's staff officers for "great courtesy and kindness in assisting me on the different battle-fields," but he did not elaborate on what duties they performed.[55]

Lee's next campaign, the invasion of Maryland, ushered in changes in his staff. Victorious in the Seven Days and at second Bull Run, Lee wanted to continue his momentum, but also shift the theater of war from Virginia and allow his army to forage off Northern soil for a while. Also, many Confederates believed that their military presence in Maryland would ignite an anti-Union uprising there. In a letter to Jefferson Davis on September 3, Lee wrote that "the present seems to be the most propitious time since the commencement of the war" for such a campaign. He reasoned that Union forces were weak from their string of defeats, and since he could not successfully attack them in their Washington defenses, the campaign would draw them out and "harass" them. A victory on Northern soil might also win European diplomatic recognition for the South. Lee's 45,000-man army began a three-day crossing of the Potomac River into Maryland on September 4. But by September 7, when his army converged on Frederick, Maryland, Lee realized that no popular rising was coming: Confederate leaders had misjudged pro-Union sentiment in western Maryland.[56]

Lee could do some damage with his campaign, however, and he drafted orders to do just that. The plan was complex and risky. He would push his invasion into Pennsylvania, where he could cut the Pennsylvania Railroad, a major Federal artery. He could not succeed, however, unless he established secure supply lines in the Shenandoah Valley, and the Valley hosted a 10,000-man Union garrison at Harpers Ferry. That garrison would have to fall before Lee could go much farther. In camp at Frederick, Lee and Stonewall Jackson mapped out the operation. They planned to split the army into four pieces: divisions under Jackson, Gen. John Walker, and Gen. Lafayette McLaws would split off and attack Harpers Ferry from three directions while Lee and Longstreet waited at Boonsboro for their return. Splitting the army was decidedly risky, especially since J.E.B. Stuart's outriders had already informed Lee that George McClellan had refitted the Army of the Potomac and led it into Maryland. Trusting that McClellan would move as slowly in Maryland as he had on the Peninsula, Lee was certain that Jackson's expedition would have time to seize Harpers Ferry and reunite with Lee and Longstreet before the Federals posed any threat. Besides, Lee would keep South Mountain, a finger of the Blue Ridge Mountains, between his army and McClellan's, with Stuart's cavalry guarding the mountain passes.[57]

At Lee's headquarters, September 9, Robert Chilton went about his primary task, drafting Lee's operational plans into orders for the army. The resulting Special Orders No. 191 became perhaps the most controversial orders of the war. The orders themselves were an example of fine military writing, clearly laying out Lee's instructions for Jackson, McLaws, Walker, Longstreet, Stuart, and Daniel Harvey Hill, who would form the rear guard of the army at Boonsboro. The orders even directed Lee's primary aide, Walter Taylor, to return to Winchester, Virginia, and gather up all the sick and wounded Confederates from recent battles.[58]

The controversy of Special Orders No. 191 was not in its writing, but in its delivery. After drafting the orders, Chilton made the requisite copies and dispatched them to the generals with commands in the operation. Upon receiving his copy, Jackson made a copy for D. H. Hill, who had been in Jackson's command but was detached for service with Longstreet, in this instance to help guard South Mountain. Thus two copies of the orders were on their way to Hill, one without Chilton's knowledge.[59]

On September 10 Lee's army moved out of Frederick, putting the Harpers Ferry campaign in motion. Three days later, at Frederick, the Army of the Potomac happened to camp on the same site where Hill's division had camped. Two soldiers found an unusual package in some tall grass—three fine cigars wrapped in paper. The cigars were a great find, but as the men unwrapped them, they realized they had something more. The paper was labeled "Headquarters, Army of Northern Virginia, Special Orders No. 191," and was signed by someone named Chilton. The men quickly turned the paper over to their superiors, who ran it to XII Corps headquarters. There a colonel who had served with Chilton before the war verified the handwriting, and the orders went on to McClellan. At his headquarters, McClellan was entertaining a contingent of Frederick citizens when he received Lee's orders. He could not hide his elation, exclaiming, "Now I know what to do."[60]

When speculation arose that Harvey Hill was somehow to blame for losing Special Orders No. 191, he maintained that he had received only one copy, from Jackson. He carefully saved the copy to prove his story. He had always received his orders from Jackson, and he apparently thought it appropriate that the practice continue in Maryland, even though he was temporarily split from Jackson's corps. For his part, Chilton maintained that Lee's headquarters must have received a receipt from Hill for the orders, otherwise the staff would have attempted to verify that Hill had received it. Lee blamed no one, and he mounted no investigation of the incident. Hill continued trying to clear himself of fault in the matter, and after the war he wrote to Chilton hoping to learn anything that might absolve him.[61]

That the orders could fall into enemy hands represents a breakdown in staff work at Lee's headquarters. If Jackson was to have given orders to Hill, Chilton should have known that. If Chilton or other members of Lee's staff were to be the sole distributors of orders from headquarters, then line commanders should have known that as well. Given that the clear, precise, and prompt, not to mention secure, distribution of orders was a primary job for any headquarters staff, the loss of Special Orders No. 191 was a critical error.

Any opportunity the lost orders gave McClellan, however, he frittered away by delaying his march from Frederick. Moreover, one of the Frederick citizens who had been visiting McClellan when the lost orders arrived turned out to be a Southern sympathizer, and he quickly sent word to Lee that McClellan had the orders. When the Army of the Potomac tried to push across South Mountain on September 14, Harvey Hill's men met them with stiff resistance. McClellan won at South Mountain, but he did not destroy Lee's army, and the advance warning gave Lee time to prepare a retreat, putting Longstreet's units on the march to Sharpsburg. From Lee's headquarters, Chilton and Armistead Long fired messages to McLaws to abandon his operations at Harpers Ferry and rush back to the main army. Walter Taylor, back in Virginia, heard of the fight at South Mountain and raced back to be with his chief. On September 15 Lee received word that Harpers Ferry had fallen to Jackson, and Lee notified him to leave a contingent there to handle the surrender and hurry the rest of his force to Sharpsburg. There, near Antietam Creek, Lee and McClellan fought the bloody battle of Antietam on September 17.[62]

As he had during the Seven Days, Lee avoided elaborate written orders during the fight. A message from Chilton to Brig. Gen. William N. Pendelton, Lee's chief of artillery, asking him to be sure all reserve artillery and stragglers were on the field, was the only correspondence to come from Lee's headquarters during the battle.[63]

Nevertheless, Lee's staffers had plenty to do. In his official report of the Maryland campaign, Longstreet thanked Chilton, Long, Taylor, Marshall, Venable, Talcott, and Mason "for great courtesy and kindness in assisting me on the different battle-fields." Longstreet's acknowledgement was virtually the same as the one he penned after second Bull Run and offered no explanation of what Lee's staff officers did for him. Lee did not even mention their activities in his report of the campaign. Taylor, Long, and Chilton did ride orders out to brigade and division commanders during the campaign, and certainly Lee expanded the role of his military secretary, Armistead Long, at Antietam. Long rode about the battlefield, helping position artillery batteries for best effect. In so doing, Long was actually acting in the artillery department of Lee's special staff, but Lee was capitalizing on Long's prewar experience in artillery.[64]

With the exception of Long positioning cannon during battle and Taylor falling back to gather wounded Rebels at Winchester, Virginia, Lee asked nothing extra of his staff during the Maryland campaign. No staff officer helped Lee with operations; instead he used corps commander Jackson to help him plan the Harpers Ferry expedition. While staffers no doubt performed efficiently in drafting orders to draw the parts of the Army of Northern Virginia back together after the battle of South Mountain, they had also participated in the "lost orders" debacle that caused the emergency in the first place. Lee's staffers remained clerks at a battlefield headquarters, handling matters of routine on a campaign that was anything but routine.

After the Antietam Campaign, Lee returned to northern Virginia where he soon faced a new opponent. When Lincoln fired McClellan, he replaced him with Maj. Gen. Ambrose Burnside. Burnside did not want the job, but he did devise a plan that had merit. He would feint toward the vital Rebel supply line of the Orange and Alexandria Railroad, drawing Lee in that direction, then turn and mass at Falmouth, Virginia, across the Rappahannock River from Fredericksburg. From there Burnside could cross the river and use it as a supply line while he drove on to the undefended Richmond. Burnside moved with speed, but when he arrived at

Falmouth on November 19, the pontoon boats he needed to cross the river were not there. The boats did not arrive for two weeks. The delay allowed Lee, who had in fact lost Burnside, to assess his enemy's intentions and consolidate the Army of Northern Virginia at Fredericksburg to oppose Burnside's river crossing.[65]

Written staff work emanating from Lee's headquarters while he moved his army was sparse. Chilton, Taylor, and Penny Mason drafted general and special orders to facilitate the movement.[66] The lack of written orders, however, again shows Lee's fondness for verbal instruction.

Even though he had been watching Confederates take up defensive positions on hills behind Fredericksburg for weeks, Burnside decided that he would cross there anyway. On December 11, under heavy sniper fire from the town, engineers placed the belated pontoon boats. The next day Burnside massed his troops on the Rebel side of the river, and on December 13 he commenced one of the most ill-advised battles of the war. Federals had some success at Stonewall Jackson's position south of Fredericksburg, but they had to relent for lack of support. Immediately west of Fredericksburg, at a place called Marye's Heights, the Federals ran into a buzz saw. Secure in a sunken road behind a rock wall atop the Heights, James Longstreet's men had only to choose their targets as Burnside launched seven waves against them. The Union men never had a chance at Fredericksburg, and by nightfall their losses in killed, wounded, and missing were more than 12,600. Confederate casualties were about 5,300.[67]

Lee's headquarters issued no orders during the fight, but his staffers were busy anyway. Lee commented that "my personal staff were unremittingly engaged in conveying and bringing information from all parts of the field." In his official report of the battle, Lee commended Armistead Long, who again helped place artillery. Long, with the help of Charles Venable and T. M. R. Talcott, trained 200 guns on the hapless Federals. Talcott alone placed a four-gun battery four miles south of Fredericksburg, "in an excellent position," Lee said, to destroy Union gunboats trying to navigate the river. Taylor and Marshall were busy "communicating orders and intelligence," wrote Lee, and Venable and Talcott "examine[ed] the ground and the approaches of the enemy."[68]

The Army of Northern Virginia wintered behind—and improved—its old defenses at Fredericksburg. In April 1863 the Army of the Potomac, now under Maj. Gen. Joe Hooker, drew up across the Rappahannock from Fredericksburg. But Hooker did not intend to batter his army against Marye's Heights. He left about 40,000 men at Fredericksburg to feint an assault, and he quickly marched the bulk of his army west about ten miles to a crossroads tavern in Virginia's Wilderness known as Chancellorsville. Lee faced an enemy on both flanks but boldly attacked the situation. On May 1 he left 10,000 men under Gen. Jubal Early to protect Fredericksburg. Then, again splitting his army in the face of the Federals, he wheeled his remaining 46,000 men (Longstreet's were on detached duty south of Richmond) toward Chancellorsville. Suddenly Hooker relinquished the initiative, withdrawing to a five-mile perimeter around Chancellorsville, and Stuart's cavalry brought Lee word that Hooker's right flank was vulnerable. In a meeting in the woods of the Wilderness the night of May 1, Lee and Stonewall Jackson developed a bold plan. Lee would again divide his force. He would send Jackson and 28,000 men on a circuitous route landing them on Hooker's right. Lee would keep a scant 18,000 men in front of Hooker, with the hope that the Union commander did not realize he could swamp Lee and get between Jackson and Early.[69]

On May 2 Jackson moved out. Federal scouts detected the movement and reported it to Hooker, but as Lee had hoped, he thought the Confederates were retreating. That evening Lee began firing on Hooker's left as a distraction and, about 6:00 P.M., Jackson's men screamed out of the tangle of the Wilderness upon the unsuspecting Federals, knocking them back about two miles. Jackson was riding back to his lines that night when his own men, skittish after a day of hard campaigning, mistakenly shot him. The wound first cost Jackson his left arm, then his life. Command of Jackson's troops fell to J.E.B. Stuart, who on May 3 joined with Lee to drive Hooker from Chancellorsville. At Fredericksburg, however, Union general John Sedgwick began assaults that pushed Early's depleted numbers from Marye's Heights. Lee turned part of his force at Chancellorsville to help Early, and in fighting on May 3 and 4 the Rebels forced Sedgwick back across the Rappahannock.[70]

Lee's staff performed at Chancellorsville as they had throughout the war. Armistead Long again posted troops and artillery, while the other aides carried orders about the field. In the process of delivering an order on May 1, however, Chilton proved how risky verbal instructions could be. When Chilton arrived at Fredericksburg with orders for Early to march to Chancellorsville, leaving only a few troops and some of William Pendelton's artillery to counter the Federals across the Rappahannock, Early and Pendleton questioned the orders. Could Chilton have been mistaken? Why would Lee want to further deplete his right while planning an attack on his left? Chilton explained that Lee did not consider the threat at Fredericksburg great, and he convinced the men that the orders were correct. Chilton returned to headquarters and Early moved out, leaving

Pendleton at Fredericksburg. Soon, however, came written word from Lee that Chilton had misunderstood his wishes: Early was to leave Fredericksburg only if he considered the situation there safe. Chilton had failed to communicate the latitude Lee had given Early.[71]

Just as he received Lee's corrected orders, Early got word that Federals were advancing behind him, about to take Fredericksburg. If that was true, Lee's right was in danger of collapse, and so was his attack at Chancellorsville. Early had to decide whether to return to Fredericksburg and refortify defenses or march on to Lee, knowing that Federals might catch him from the rear. Eager subalterns convinced him to return to Fredericksburg, which he did, finding, happily, that reports of a Federal assault were incorrect. Lee's right remained intact.[72]

To be sure, Chilton had been mistaken in the orders he gave Early, and the calm manner in which he delivered and defended them before Early's questioning suggests he had no reason to believe he was in error. The insistence upon verbal orders, however, was Lee's. Having to remember several important details, execute a ride of several miles, and then repeat them was difficult enough. To do so in a tense battlefield situation was even worse. Certainly some of Lee's written orders had already fallen into enemy hands, in Maryland, but at Chancellorsville he had risked having his right immediately rolled up because of a forgotten phrase.

Lee used the momentum he gained at Chancellorsville to again invade the North. Hooker's Army of the Potomac shadowed the invaders, but in late June Abraham Lincoln replaced the timid Hooker with Pennsylvanian George G. Meade. On July 1 outriders of both armies collided at the crossroads town of Gettysburg, and as reinforcements rushed up, the battle developed seemingly out of the hands of Lee and Meade. Dismounted Union cavalry and Confederate infantry fought through the morning west of Gettysburg while two divisions of Federals rushed through the town to seize ground north of the town. Confederate pressure mounted, however, and units of Gen. Richard S. "Baldy" Ewell's corps pushed the Federals back through town. Union troops west of Gettysburg also retreated, and all the Federals made for a series of hills south of town known as Cemetery Hill and Cemetery Ridge. Lee arrived on the field late in the day and suggested that Ewell attack through Gettysburg and drive the Federals from the hills before the bulk of the Union army got up to reinforce them. Ewell did not strike, however, and through the night Union generals solidified their defenses south of Gettysburg. Lee massed his men about a mile west of Cemetery Ridge on a lower elevation known as Seminary Ridge.[73]

July 2 saw a series of disjointed Confederate attacks to knock the Army of the Potomac from its desirable high ground. Men of James Longstreet's corps, after marching and countermarching, attempted to flank and mount Little Round Top, a rocky and supposedly undefended hill on the far left of the Union line. Once there the Rebels could fire down into the Army of the Potomac, but Federals rushed to the hill and stubbornly repulsed assault after assault. Longstreet's men also attacked an exposed salient that Union general Dan Sickles had created when he ill-advisedly moved forward from the Union lines, hoping to protect his own flank. In engagements at the Peach Orchard, the Wheat Field, and Devil's Den, Longstreet drove Sickles back into the Union line, but accomplished little else. At the north end of the Federal defenses, Jubal Early's men of Ewell's corps gained some ground at Culp's Hill but failed to make an appreciable dent in Meade's line. At midday on July 3, Confederates opened an artillery barrage along the length of Cemetery Ridge, hoping to soften Union positions. Lee planned to send 15,000 men under Gen. George Pickett across the mile gap between the armies and have them assault the Union lines, much as Ambrose Burnside had done at Fredericksburg. Longstreet opposed the plan, but after two hours of bombardment, which hardly damaged the Federals, he ordered Pickett on his way. "Pickett's Charge" was a futile disaster; Union soldiers turned it back in vicious hand-to-hand fighting on Cemetery Ridge.[74]

The battle of Gettysburg marked the only time Lee used a staff officer in something resembling an operations role, but his help was mediocre at best. Armistead Long had won Lee's confidence by posting artillery in all the army's major battles since Antietam. Before marching into Pennsylvania in June 1863, Lee had called Long into his tent and traced his invasion plans on a map, asking the colonel his opinion. It was probably one of Lee's rhetorical questions, of the type that Walter Taylor said helped him think out loud, for when Long suggested engaging Hooker near Manassas Lee disagreed, saying that it would just let the Army of the Potomac fall back to Washington and regroup. Once at Gettysburg, however, Lee pressed Long into service posting and rechecking Confederate artillery and, with artillery chief William Pendleton, surveying the Union lines at Cemetery Ridge. Long brought Lee the news on July 2 that Federals were behind a stone wall and on a reverse slope, and he believed that an attack on that position probably would not succeed. Nevertheless, sitting in an apple orchard with Lee while the general planned Pickett's assault, Long assented that Confederate guns could silence the Union artillery. When Lee queried

Long about making the attack without Stuart's cavalry, Long answered that the attack should go in unsupported.[75]

Gettysburg was the nadir of the ongoing unspectacular staff work that came out of Lee's headquarters. Years later Walter Taylor unwittingly criticized Lee's use of his staff when he remarked that operations at Gettysburg were disjointed. "There was an utter absence of accord in the movements of the several commands and no decisive results attended the operations of the second day," he said. Lee's staff work also drew fire in the memoirs of another former member of his army. Artillerist E. Porter Alexander, commenting on the countermarching that preceded Longstreet's attack on the second day of Gettysburg, wrote that it showed "how time may be lost in handling troops, and . . . the need [for] an abundance of competent staff officers by the generals in command." Alexander noted that no Rebel general had the staff he needed to ensure proper execution of orders: "[A commander] should have a staff ample to supervise the execution of each step, and to promptly report any difficulty or misunderstanding."[76]

At least one prominent Civil War historian has also criticized Lee's staff work at Gettysburg. Lee typically gave his lieutenants great leeway in the execution of their orders, often including the phrase "if practicable" in his instructions. He had done just that when he urged Baldy Ewell to attack through Gettysburg and throw Federals off Cemetery Hill. He also had maintained his practice of issuing few orders during battle; on the second day at Gettysburg he sent only one message and received only one report. Kenneth Williams, in *Lincoln Finds a General,* comments that, while the vague and poor orders Lee often gave may have come from his "amiability and courtesy," they also dictated that "an adequate staff constantly [be] at hand, with sufficient rank and experience to raise searching questions about what was done" and challenge vague instructions. The possibility that Lee was sick at Gettysburg made the presence of an efficient staff doubly important. "There was no one who could do responsible planning other than himself," comments Williams. "Although he probably was compelled to depend upon Providence to 'raise up' another Jackson, he might have done something for himself in the matter of staff officers."[77]

The deficiencies in Lee's staff were of his own making. Lee chose to be his own chief of staff, essentially disenfranchising his titular chief, Chilton, who had shown no propensity for anything other than writing orders, from an integral part of staff work. Lee frequently sought information from his subordinate commanders, but when he did pose operational questions of his staff, as he did with Armistead Long, he heeded only suggestions that affirmed his own plans. And, by relying on verbal instructions, he denied himself the chance to use in battle the writing skills that his staff had developed handling the mountains of paperwork in camp. Regardless of how well a courier rehearsed his dispatches before leaving headquarters, by the time he rode through difficult battlefield situations the orders could never have been as clear at the recipient's end as if someone had first concisely written them.

Lee always had a small staff, and after Gettysburg it grew smaller. In September 1863 Armistead Long received a brigadier general's commission, and Lee gave him command of the II Corps's artillery. Lee aide T. M. R. Talcott was promoted to lieutenant colonel and took command of an engineer regiment. Penny Mason, whom Lee inherited from Gen. Joe Johnston after the battle of Seven Pines, returned to Johnston's staff when he recovered from his wounds enough to resume a command.[78]

Lee also lost his sometime chief of staff, Robert Chilton. Since the battle of Antietam, Chilton's staff career had been a curious one. While Lee never blamed Chilton for the lost orders during the Maryland campaign, just a few weeks after Antietam, Chilton, on paper at least, was off Lee's personal staff. Walter Taylor had bumped Chilton as primary adjutant soon after Chilton arrived at headquarters in June 1862. On October 28, 1862, Lee officially moved Chilton, who by then was a brigadier general, to his special staff as inspector general. Lee announced that all communications previously addressed to Chilton should be directed instead to assistant adjutant Penny Mason. On November 24, 1862, in orders that Chilton drafted, Lee officially moved Taylor from aide-de-camp to acting assistant adjutant general, and Taylor quickly took over Chilton's duties of writing general and special orders. Although Chilton had never truly acted as a chief of staff, Lee continued to address Chilton as both chief of staff and adjutant in future correspondence. Also, Chilton continued to sign himself as assistant adjutant general in correspondence. Chilton's status on the staff may indicate that Lee wanted some type of liaison between his personal and special staffs, or that Chilton was unsuited to staff work and Lee did not quite know what to do with him.[79]

A letter that Lee wrote to Chilton in April 1863 does indicate that Chilton was uncomfortable with staff work, or that someone else was questioning his fitness for a headquarters position. Indeed, when Jefferson Davis made Chilton a brigadier general, the Confederate Senate refused to confirm him. In response to a query from Chilton, Lee assured him that his staff duty had been "zealous and active . . . and I have never known you to be actuated by any other motive in the performance of them than the interests of the service." Lee said that he had always known Chilton to be "open and straightforward" and that he was entirely satisfied with Chilton's performance as chief of staff.[80]

Chilton remained at Lee's headquarters for another eleven months, acting as inspector general, titular chief of staff, and sometime adjutant. His inspector general's duties took him away from headquarters frequently, and he was thorough and conscientious in seeing that units he inspected were ready for service. He once irritated J.E.B. Stuart by pointing out that the guns and equipment of some cavalry artillery batteries needed routine care and cleaning. When Stuart complained to Lee, the general responded that Chilton's report was "a simple statement of facts," and that he trusted Stuart and his officers would "correct these evils." Chilton remained busy at headquarters, too. By early 1863 he was again helping Taylor draft special and general orders, and he frequently corresponded with unit commanders. Although Lee used him very little as a chief of staff, he apparently trusted Chilton. In February 1864, when Lee traveled to Richmond to see Davis, he left Lt. Gen. Baldy Ewell in command of the Army of Northern Virginia. Ewell, who had been ill, worried about taking the responsibility, but Lee assured him that Chilton would be at headquarters and that he should consult with Chilton "on all matters of importance connected with the army."[81]

Walter Taylor, who did not like Chilton, complained that the command arrangement between Chilton and Ewell was unsatisfactory. On February 23 Taylor wrote to Bettie Saunders that "Gen'l Ewell who is supposed to be in command doesn't relieve me at all, nor does my friend Chilton who terms himself 'Chief of Staff.' Neither has volunteered one single suggestion or in any way divided the responsibility." A week later, Taylor reported to Bettie that Union movements had alarmed him. Taylor thought the Confederate army should be rearranged to avoid danger, but Ewell was away at his own camp and unable to give advice. Taylor then consulted Chilton, but, said Taylor, "his reply to the first question I put to him was so very muddy and exhibited such ignorance of the situation that I was convinced I was to receive no help from this quarter." Taylor finally made the changes himself, and, no doubt to his own delight, earned Lee's praise when the general returned.[82]

Chilton departed from Lee's staff within two months, accepting a position in Gen. Samuel Cooper's adjutant general's department in Richmond. In a letter to Chilton on March 24, Lee wrote, "I shall miss your ever ready aid and regret your departure." He thanked Chilton for his service and wished him well, adding, "[I] trust that in your future sphere of action, your zeal, energy, and intelligence will be as conspicuous as in your former." Lee noted that he would try to find someone to fill Chilton's place, but he never did.[83] After all, Walter Taylor could write orders as well as Chilton, and indeed had been doing so since the start of the war.

With Chilton, Long, Talcott, and Mason gone, Lee's personal staff numbered three—Taylor, Marshall, and Venable—when he first engaged the Union's new general in chief, Lt. Gen. Ulysses S. Grant, in early May 1864. The fighting that began in the Wilderness was almost constant for eleven months, but Lee made no changes at headquarters except to heap extra work on the remaining three men. During the Wilderness fight, Lee's staffers maintained better contact with field commanders than they had in previous battles, corresponding with the likes of J.E.B. Stuart and Baldy Ewell almost hourly between May 5 and 7. Before the fight Lee also began riding out each morning with Marshall and Venable to examine Confederate lines. Taylor almost solely handled the writing of general and special orders.[84] Work at Lee's headquarters remained substantially unchanged for the rest of the war.

By now, Charles Venable had appointed himself as something of Lee's protector. During the Wilderness fight, when Lee threatened to personally lead a column of Texans into battle, Venable and Longstreet reined in the Tycoon from such rash behavior. When Lee tried to conduct operations from a sickbed on May 23, Venable suggested calling in P. G. T. Beauregard to take temporary command of the army. Lee would have none of it.[85]

In April 1865, as Lee's army prepared to evacuate its lines at Petersburg, Virginia, which Grant had invested for nine months, Walter Taylor approached his boss with an unusual request—he wanted to go to Richmond to get married. Lee was surprised, but Taylor explained that his sweetheart, Bettie Saunders, worked in a government bureau, her home was behind Union lines, and she wanted to "follow the fortunes of the Confederacy," if Lee established lines farther south. Lee agreed, and Taylor galloped off to a hurried wedding.[86]

Taylor returned on April 3 to only a week of war remaining for the Army of Northern Virginia. When Lee slipped west from Petersburg, Grant did likewise and caught the fleeing Confederates in a pincers grasp. On April 7 Grant opened correspondence with Lee, with a view to the latter's surrender. On April 9 Lee relented, and Charles Marshall, who had for three years recorded the history of the Army of Northern Virginia, recorded, at Lee's dictation, its final act, requesting a meeting with Grant to discuss the surrender of Lee's army. Marshall was the only member of Lee's staff to accompany him to the surrender at Appomattox Court House.[87]

Lee remained close to his staff after the war. He frequently corresponded with Chilton, who became president of the Columbus Manufacturing Company near Columbus, Georgia. In July 1865 Lee decided to write an account of the campaigns of the Army of Northern Virginia, and he requested that Walter Taylor send him accurate information about troop strengths, as Taylor had compiled such numbers to send to Richmond throughout the war. Lee's duties as president of Washington College in Virginia, however, kept him from writing the book, and Taylor used the figures in his own memoirs. Taylor led an impromptu reception for the old general in April 1870 when, after a lengthy tour of Florida and the southeastern seaboard that doctors had prescribed for his health, Lee and his daughter Agnes returned to Portsmouth, Virginia. Taylor and former Lee staff officer Charles Venable sat with the general's family at Lee's funeral in October 1870. In later years, not only Taylor but Venable, Charles Marshall, and Armistead Long would write memoirs of their experiences with Lee's army.[88]

Lee did little to expand the duties of his staff during the war. Even though Armistead Long made himself a minor reputation posting artillery and Walter Taylor might dash out to join a charge now and then, Lee's staffers were primarily clerks. Certainly they prepared marching orders that set the Army of Northern Virginia in motion and established communication lines, which Jomini had suggested were staff duties, and they made complex orders, such as Special Orders 191, easily understood. Still, staffers failed to always ensure proper delivery of orders and, again with Special Orders 191, were involved in a breakdown of communications that threatened the security of the entire army.

Lee's staff actually performed well within the limits he gave them, but the Tycoon hobbled his headquarters. Fearing he might keep qualified men from the line, he kept his staff small. When a staffer showed line qualifications, such as Armistead Long or T. M. R. Talcott, Lee sent him there, opting to deprive his headquarters of talent rather than the army in the field. Lee further hindered his headquarters, and subsequently the army, by relying on verbal orders. Though he thought he was securing his directives, he was in fact keeping his staff from doing what they had trained themselves to do best—write orders. Chilton's errant instructions to Early at Chancellorsville proved how dangerous the practice was.

Worst of all, Lee refused to adequately use his chief of staff. Chilton may have indeed been ill-suited for the job; such may never be known, as the memoir writers of the staff rarely mention Chilton, and Lee seems never to have regarded Chilton as anything but a friend. But Lee never replaced Chilton with an active chief of staff. He instead chose to remain his own chief, making all operational decisions and originating all the plans that his staffers subsequently drafted into orders. The embodiment of general and chief in one man was especially dangerous when Lee fell ill, and Charles Venable had recognized that fact when he suggested Beauregard temporarily replace Lee during the Wilderness fight.

Lee's personal staff bore the general's mark. Like Lee, his staffers did their best with what they had to use. If Lee wanted to use them primarily as clerks and couriers, so be it. They could do no more. And as the Army of Northern Virginia dwindled, so did their number at headquarters. Of course, Lee was not trying to emulate European staff systems during the Civil War—he was scrambling to keep his army alive. Nevertheless, the audacity he showed in some of his campaigns never spilled over into his conception of staff work.

CHAPTER FOUR

Grant: A Civilian Staff

1861–1862

ULYSSES S. GRANT WAS THE MOST VICTORIOUS GENERAL OF THE CIVIL War, winning signal campaigns in every major theater and ultimately forcing Robert E. Lee to surrender his Army of Northern Virginia. Grant also made more use of his personal staff than the other generals of this study. Grant's ideas of staff usage were not fully developed when he became a brigadier general in 1861, but they matured during the war until his headquarters was a professional unit functioning much like a small model of a Prussian staff. In 1861 Grant's staffers primarily were civilians just learning about war, but they were men Grant felt comfortable with. While some of the men ultimately proved useless as staff officers, in 1861 they were Grant's family away from home.

Two factors—an intense need for familial comradeship and a disastrous personal time between the Mexican and Civil Wars—directly influenced the way Grant built his first staff. Unlike Lee, who chose those he believed could adequately fulfill their duties, Grant gave staff jobs to men who had befriended him during a difficult time of his life. He created a staff that could support his emotional as well as military needs.

Stresses that influenced Grant's staff choices began in his childhood. Grant's parents were loving, but one was demanding, the other quiet and unemotional, which must have been hard on a little boy. Born April 27, 1822, in Point Pleasant, Ohio, Hiram Ulysses Grant (he did not become Ulysses Simpson Grant until a clerical mistake at West Point made him so) was the first of six children of driven businessman Jesse Root Grant and his taciturn wife Hannah Simpson Grant. Hannah spoke little about anything, even of her firstborn, and townsfolk in Point Pleasant and Georgetown, Ohio, where the family moved when Ulysses was eighteen months old, considered the woman somewhat neglectful of the child. Grant biographer Geoffrey Perret attributes the coolness to emotional restraint rather than uninterest.[1] Nevertheless, the atmosphere in which Grant grew up was quiet and undemonstrative.

Ulysses fared little better with his father. Jesse, who did not marry until he had established a successful leather-tanning business, was proud of his children—Samuel Simpson, Clara Rachel, Virginia Paine, Orvil Lynch,

Grant and staff, spring 1864. Recognizable are Rawlins, Badeau, Comstock, and J. G. Barnard (seated, flanking Grant), and Theodore Bowers, Peter T. Hudson, Ely Parker, and William McKee Dunn (standing to Grant's left). Others include Cols. Fred T. Dent, aide-de-camp, and William L. Duff, assistant inspector general, Maj. William Babcock, and Capt. Frederick Munther. (NATIONAL ARCHIVES AND RECORDS ADMINISTRATION)

and Mary Frances were Ulysses' siblings—and he attended their needs. He never neglected or abused them, but business, financial security, and social position ranked at least as high in his heart as his children. As the first child, Ulysses bore the brunt of Jesse's entrepreneurial hopes. Ulysses did not shine at athletics or academics, and he appeared to be a slow learner. Georgetownians twisted the boy's name to "Useless," which obviously upset Jesse. He sought to counter his son's deficiencies by giving him work at the tannery, but the boy considered the place odious. He hated the sights, smells, and sounds of it, especially when animals were being butchered for their hides. Jesse soon realized, to his chagrin, that Ulysses was no businessman. When an adult bested the eight-year-old Ulysses in a horse deal, the incident embarrassed both son and father. The deal, and his father's reaction, hurt the boy so much so that fifty years later the victorious general and former president recalled it in his memoirs with a hint of regret. Jesse finally recognized, however, that Ulysses was good with horses—the boy was as good with the animals as he was mediocre at school—and let him handle all the chores that required a horse or team. Still, even until Ulysses became a major general, Jesse, in veiled actions and phrases in letters, never let his son forget that he was not a businessman.[2]

Jesse, although he ultimately wanted his son to be a business success, allowed Ulysses a free boyhood. But when Ulysses turned seventeen, Jesse intervened and secured him an appointment to West Point. The education was free and guaranteed graduates careers as soldiers or engineers. To Jesse, it was the best of two worlds, but Ulysses did not want to go. His father was emphatic, however, surprising Ulysses by his firm stance, and the boy reluctantly went to the academy.[3]

Grant did sufficiently mediocre work at West Point to finish twenty-first of thirty-nine cadets in his class, but some of his classmates realized what the folks back in Georgetown—the ones who thought him slow—did not. Ulysses Grant had a keen, active mind, but without proper mental stimulation he quickly lost interest. Grant's roommate, Rufus B. Ingalls, also destined to be a Civil War general, recalled, "In his studies he was lazy and careless." Grant rarely studied a lesson thoroughly, reading it over only once or twice. Still, Ingalls said, "He was so quick in his perceptions that he usually made fair recitations even with so little preparation." Grant could blame his inattention on at least one distraction—homesickness. In 1871, as president, Grant revealed to a friend how he really felt about West Point. He said he looked forward to the day he would retire from public life. "That day is at hand . . . and I hail it as the happiest day of my life, except possibly the day I left West Point, a place I felt I had been at always and that my stay at had no end."[4]

After his graduation in 1843, the army assigned Grant to the Fourth U.S. Infantry at Jefferson Barracks in St. Louis. The city was the home of another of Grant's West Point friends, Frederick Tracy Dent, and he visited the Dent home often. There he met Fred's oldest sister, Julia, and found in her the companionship his family in Ohio had not offered. Grant determined to marry her, and they became engaged shortly before the Fourth U.S. Infantry received orders to join Gen. Zachary Taylor's army in Louisiana. That army was destined to move into Texas, where war between the United States and Mexico loomed.[5]

When he went to war in 1846, Lieutenant Grant was a staff officer himself, serving as quartermaster on the Fourth's special staff. The Fourth fought with Taylor in northern Mexico and with Gen. Winfield Scott in his campaign against Mexico City. Grant's duties kept him at the rear tending supplies, and while he occasionally stole to the front to be part of the action, he found his job as unrewarding as West Point had been.

After the war, in 1848, Grant and Julia were married. They traveled to Grant's assignments at Detroit, then Sackets Harbor, New York. Their first son, Frederick Dent Grant, was born in 1850, and, as the only child at the Sackets Harbor garrison, he became the darling of the post. Ulysses enjoyed his role as husband and father, taking to it as his own father never had. His family replaced the coolness he had felt with his parents, the disapproval he had known from his father, and the loneliness he had suffered at West Point. But the companionship Grant needed was short-lived, for in 1852 the army transferred the Fourth to the Pacific coast.[6]

The assignment devastated Grant. He did not let Julia, pregnant with their second child, accompany him to the West, a fortunate decision, for Grant's group crossed the Isthmus of Panama in July 1852 during a cholera epidemic that killed thirty-seven of them. Grant's decision perhaps saved his growing family's lives, but it indirectly cost him his career. First assigned to Columbia Barracks, Fort Vancouver, Washington Territory, Grant found peacetime quartermaster duties even more mundane than during wartime. Looking for diversion and a way to augment his army pay, and, perhaps, still trying to earn his father's favor, Grant tried several moneymaking schemes. None of them succeeded.[7]

Grant's business failures troubled him, and he missed his family, which now included infant son Ulysses Jr., but he had something of a surrogate family to support him. At Sackets Harbor, a career army couple, the Getzes, whom everyone knew simply as Maggy and Getz, were the Grants' servants. The couples were quite fond of each other, and Maggy and Getz went with Grant to Vancouver. Biographer McFeely writes that the Getzes "provided the domestic center without which Grant's world would not hold." Maggy cooked, Getz tended household chores, and they shared Grant's worry about his family. But in mid-1853 Maggy and Getz left the army to open a business, leaving Grant's home barren.[8]

The Fourth was soon reassigned to Fort Humboldt in northern California, and by the time he arrived there in February 1854, Grant was a man on the edge. Worse, he was under command of Lt. Col. Robert Buchanan, with whom he had clashed back at Jefferson Barracks in St. Louis when Buchanan fined Grant some bottles of wine for being late to mess. (The lieutenant had been at the Dent home seeing Julia.) Lonely, bored, stewing over his business failures, and unwilling to serve under Buchanan, Grant grew depressed and turned to drink. Alcohol was an escape, but he soon plotted another. Grant waited until he received a commission to the permanent rank of captain, then resigned from the army in April 1854.[9]

His life soon became a financial hell. Jesse Grant, fearful that his son had squandered the only job he could ever hold, petitioned Secretary of War Jefferson Davis to rescind the resignation. Davis declined, and Captain Grant's resignation stood. Jesse then offered Ulysses a job at his Galena, Illinois, tannery. Ulysses refused, having the same feeling toward the leather business as he did when he was eight. Between 1854 and 1858, Grant tried to sustain his family, which now included Nellie, born in 1855, and Jesse, in 1858, by farming. He worked farmland belonging to Julia's brother, Lewis Dent, near St. Louis, and erected a rough-hewn log farmhouse he called "Hardscrabble." His farming effort failed, however, and Julia secured Ulysses a job with one of her cousins, Harry Boggs, who ran a rent-collection business in St. Louis. But Grant hated bill collecting as much as he hated tanning, and he quickly wanted out of the firm. Some of his friends tried to get Ulysses the job of county engineer, for which his West Point schooling well qualified him, but the position went to another man. In 1860 Grant relented and accepted his father's offer of a job at the Galena leather goods store.[10]

When the Civil War erupted in April 1861, Grant helped muster and drill Galena men for armed service. With the help of political sponsor Republican congressman Elihu B. Washburne, himself a Galena man, Grant attained a colonelcy and command of the 21st Illinois Infantry Regiment. Sent to secure Federal presence in northeastern Missouri, which wavered between loyalty and rebellion, Grant learned in August 1861 that

Pres. Abraham Lincoln had submitted his name for promotion to brigadier general.[11]

With his general's commission, Grant had survived the bleakest time of his life. Those years, however, influenced the personal staff Grant put together to help him run his first general command. Grant selected men from Galena and others who had been kind to him during his trials. The many people who had been cruel to Grant in his younger years—bullies in Georgetown, Robert Buchanan, Jesse Root Grant, and even his mother in her silence—and the loneliness in which he had spent much of his life, from Ohio to West Point to Fort Humboldt, instilled in Grant certain needs. He knew he needed people around him whom he considered worthy of his trust. Most of all, Grant needed Julia and his children. But now, going to war, Grant knew that would be impossible, and as the Getzes had been his surrogate family at Columbia Barracks, he had to have a surrogate family with him on the battlefield. The men of his staff would, by their propinquity, be that surrogate family. They would eat with him, bunk with him, and come to know his innermost thoughts in a world that Julia could never be part of—the entirely male world of nineteenth-century warfare. Unfortunately, some of the men Grant selected to form his inner circle later proved unworthy of his trust, but their appointments helped Grant make the transition from devoted husband and father to fighting general.

Grant's commission as general sent men scrambling to get on his staff. Philip Drum, a Galena man whose cabinet shop was near Jesse Grant's leather goods shop, requested Grant appoint his son, 1st Lt. Thaddeus G. Drum, of the 19th Illinois Regiment, to his staff; E. A. Collins, a partner of Jesse Grant's some ten years earlier, tried to get a staff job for a friend. A Josh Sharp, probably a relative—Julia Grant's sister, Ellen, had married a Dr. Alexander Sharp (who did, in fact, become brigade surgeon on Grant's special staff)—offered to work for free on Grant's staff. Even Jesse Grant recommended a Mr. Foley for the staff. No less than Abraham Lincoln also endorsed an applicant, John Belser, a clerk at the Illinois adjutant general's office, for a spot on Grant's staff. Grant, knowing whom he wanted and needed, resisted all outside petitions.[12]

One of the first men Grant selected had supported him during his trying experience as a bill collector in St. Louis. Grant and his brother-in-law, Boggs, had rented office space from the law firm of Josiah G. McClellan, William S. Hillyer, and James C. Moody. The lawyers became friends of Grant's. On March 29, 1859, McClellan and Hillyer had witnessed Grant's manumission of a slave, William Jones, whom he had purchased from his father-in-law, Frederick Dent, during his farming days. All three men had also endorsed Grant in his bid for the St. Louis county engineer's job. Hillyer was closest to Grant, who later described Hillyer as "quite a young man, then in his twenties, and very brilliant." Grant chose Hillyer to join his staff, with the rank of captain, as an aide-de-camp.[13]

Grant also felt obliged that one of his aides come from the regiment he had commanded at the start of the war, the 21st Illinois; such a selection would honor the men who had given Grant his first successful job in seven years. He chose 1st Lt. Clark B. Lagow, who had joined the 21st on May 7, 1861. Lagow was perhaps "settling" for Grant, for he had unsuccessfully petitioned Illinois governor Richard Yates for a position on the staff of either Gen. John Charles Frémont or John Pope. Nevertheless, on August 11, 1861, Grant appointed Lagow to his staff as an aide-de-camp with the rank of captain.[14]

Perhaps the best appointment Grant ever made to his staff was that of assistant adjutant general John Aaron Rawlins, a Galena attorney. Rawlins became Grant's chief of staff and served Grant into his presidency, ultimately becoming secretary of war. Born February 13, 1831, Rawlins was the son of a charcoal burner who supplied charcoal to Galena's lead mines. Rawlins's father, James, was also an alcoholic. In him John saw early the effects of drink, and he pledged himself to a life of abstinence. When James

John Rawlins late in the war. Rawlins was Grant's first adjutant general and ultimately his chief of staff. A lawyer by trade, Rawlins had inspired Grant with a fiery pro-Union speech in Galena, Illinois, at the start of the war. His major general's stars indicate the photo was taken sometime after February 1865. (NATIONAL ARCHIVES AND RECORDS ADMINISTRATION)

followed the Gold Rush to California in 1849, John handled the charcoal burning, but he augmented his rudimentary education by reading and studying on his own, and he developed a keen interest in politics and debating. In 1853 he began to study law with Galena attorney Isaac P. Stevens, becoming Stevens's partner in 1854 and the next year taking over the practice. Rawlins shone at jury trials and public debates where he could use his dramatic oratorical skills. Once possessed of an opinion, Rawlins vehemently defended it with a booming voice and strident tones.[15]

While Rawlins was attorney for Jesse Grant's Galena leather shop, Ulysses did not take the measure of the man until he attended a patriotic meeting on April 16, 1861, held in response to the Confederacy's bombardment of Fort Sumter. Republican congressman Washburne spoke first, delivering a popular militant address. Then Rawlins, a Democrat, took the floor and proclaimed that the war cut through party lines. "It is simply Union or disunion, country, or no country," he declared. "Only one course is left for us. We will stand by the flag of our country and appeal to the God of Battles!" The address stirred Grant's military blood and he returned to the army. Two days later he was raising volunteers in Galena.[16]

On August 7, 1861, soon after receiving his brigadier general's commission, Grant offered Rawlins a staff job. "I . . . wanted to take one man from my new home, Galena," Grant explained, "and there was no man more ready to serve his country than he." Grant wanted Rawlins for assistant adjutant general, but a Montague S. Hasie held the job, so Grant offered Rawlins a position as aide-de-camp. Hasie was soon gone from the staff, however, and Grant amended his offer to Rawlins. On August 10 Grant wrote Julia, "I have invited Mr. Rollins [he evidently did not know Rawlins well enough to spell his name correctly] . . . a place on my Staff." He encouraged Julia to have his brother, Orvil, in Galena, hurry Rawlins to Grant's camp. Meanwhile, Rawlins had penned a flowery acceptance to Grant, calling the job a "compliment unexpected." He further stated that "whatever the duties and responsibilities devolved upon me . . . , I will with the help of God discharge them to the best of my ability."[17]

Still, a personal crisis kept Rawlins from hurrying to Grant's side. On August 30 his wife died of tuberculosis at her father's home in Goshen, New York, leaving Rawlins with three children under five years old. While Rawlins returned to New York to settle affairs, his supporters in Galena feared Grant would withdraw the staff offer, and several of them wrote to the general asking him not to change his mind. On August 31 Grant asked Julia to reassure Rawlins's friends that he had no intention of giving the job to anyone else. Three days later he told Washburne the same thing, noting,

"I never had an idea of withdrawing . . . [the offer] so long as he felt disposed to accept no matter how long his absence." Grant showed his loyalty to Rawlins and to his own decision, saying, "Mr. Rawlins was the first one I decided upon for a place with me and I very much regret that family affliction has kept him away so long."[18]

Rawlins was with Grant at Cairo, Illinois, by September 8, for that day he filed with the adjutant general's office in Washington General Orders No. 4 listing Grant's staff composition. Grant was thirty-nine years old, Lagow thirty-two, and Rawlins and Hillyer both thirty. Though none of the staffers had any real military experience, Grant called them "three of the cleverest men that can be found anywhere."[19]

Given command of the District of Southeast Missouri, Grant first went to Ironton, Missouri, in August, then to Cape Girardeau, and finally across the Mississippi River to the southern tip of Illinois at Cairo in early September. There he guarded the junction of the Ohio and Mississippi Rivers. At Cairo Grant finished building his staff. He brought aboard Maj. John Riggin Jr. as a volunteer aide-de-camp and Maj. Joseph Dana Webster as his chief of engineers. Although Webster was on Grant's special staff, he quickly bridged the gap between divisions of Grant's headquarters to become a trusted adviser to the general. By the end of December he was Grant's first chief of staff.[20]

Webster, whom Grant termed an "old soldier . . . of decided merit," brought the most military experience to Grant's staff. Gray-haired and steely-eyed with a bushy moustache and goatee, Webster was fifty years old when he joined Grant's staff. Born in Hampton, New Hampshire, he graduated from Dartmouth College in 1832. He studied law for a time, then engineering, and in 1835 he became a government civil engineer. In 1838 he joined the U.S. Army topographical engineers. He served in the Mexican War and left the army in 1854 as a captain. Moving to Chicago, the home of his wife, Webster helped lay out the city's early sewer system and elevate downtown Chicago above the level of Lake Michigan. When the Civil War opened, he rejoined the army, going to Cairo in late April as a paymaster with Illinois volunteers. On May 1 he was commissioned inspector of the First Brigade of Illinois Volunteers, but he continued to act as an engineer. On June 18 Illinois governor Richard Yates named Webster "engineer in chief" with the rank of colonel. Three days later he also took an appointment as an additional paymaster. On August 27 General Frémont, commanding the Department of the West, ordered Webster to erect defensive works around Cairo. When Grant arrived a few days later he brought Webster onto his staff.[21]

With Webster working on defenses and Rawlins drafting the orders that organized the command, Hillyer became something of an all-purpose man for Grant. While the general set up camp in Cairo, Hillyer brought him his uniform and horse from St. Louis. Hillyer also sent word to Capt. Reuben B. Hatch, assistant quartermaster at Cairo, that Grant needed office space and quarters for himself and the staff. Hillyer soon had to take emergency leave to be with his wife, whose father and brother had died suddenly, but when he returned Grant had additional duties for him. Grant had written to Capt. Chauncey McKeever, Frémont's assistant adjutant general in St. Louis, that many troops who had never been sworn in were serving around Cairo. Grant requested that Frémont's headquarters send or authorize someone in Grant's command to do the job. It fell to Hillyer, and on October 4 Rawlins issued orders making his fellow staffer mustering officer for the district. Finally, on October 30 Grant sent Hillyer, under flag of truce, to deliver a Southern prisoner into Rebel lines. The mission turned out to be a prisoner exchange of sorts, for Confederates told Hillyer that they had a man who wanted to go north. Hillyer took him aboard his steamer, but on the trip home the man jumped overboard and drowned.[22]

Grant enjoyed others' children as much as his own, and Hillyer's son, William S. Jr., was in Grant's camp in the fall of 1861, probably due to the family's losses in early September. Grant had quite a joke with the boy on November 1 when he issued a "general order" to "all whom it may concern." He appointed "Master Willie S. Hillyer Pony Aide de Camp with the rank of major. . . . All stable boys will take due notice and obey him accordingly."[23]

Grant could learn only so much about his staff officers and his army, and they about him, while sitting in camp. On November 7, 1861, at Belmont, Missouri, they all got their first taste of Civil War battle. Shortly before Maj. Gen. Henry W. Halleck replaced him as chief of the Department of the West, General Frémont had ordered Grant to demonstrate against Kentucky Confederates south of Cairo. Frémont feared that Rebels under Gen. Leonidas Polk might sweep out of their base at Columbus, Kentucky, on the Mississippi River, and into southern Missouri and join Confederates under Gen. Sterling Price. Frémont planned to bag Price himself—although Washington bagged Frémont for inactivity before he got the chance—and he wanted Grant to keep Rebel reinforcements from arriving. He cautioned Grant, however, not to bring on a fight. But Grant was a fighter. When he received intelligence (faulty, it turned out) that some of Price's men were massing at Belmont, immediately across the river from Columbus, to cut off a contingent Grant had sent into Missouri to capture a Rebel raiding party, he disregarded Frémont's order.

On November 6 Grant put 3,000 troops on navy gunboats at Cairo and headed down the Mississippi. At dawn the next day the troops unloaded three miles above Belmont, formed into line of battle, and quickly routed four regiments under Brig. Gen. Gideon Pillow that Polk had sent across the river to counter Grant. Elated at their quick victory, Grant's men began looting the tiny Confederate camp; the place had never been a staging area for a larger operation. While the Federals were taking spoils, reinforcements from Polk came ashore at Belmont and surrounded them. Grant was unperturbed when he had a horse shot from under him, however, and he remained cool in the face of the new development, dryly noting, "Well, we must cut our way out as we cut our way in." That they did, and during the sharp fight Grant stayed at the rear of his men, shepherding them back to their boats. He was the last one to board.[24]

As Civil War battles go, Belmont was merely a raid. The place had no strategic value, Confederates were not using it to base larger operations, and it was untenable, as Rebel guns at Columbus could rake it at will. But it was a classroom for Grant and his men. Although Grant had seen action in Mexico, he had never commanded men in battle. Likewise, Belmont was first blood for Grant's volunteers. All performed well and developed a measure of confidence in each other.[25]

All of Grant's staff officers were with him at Belmont, but Grant wrote little of their duties. In his report Grant expressed his gratitude to Rawlins, Lagow, and Hillyer, saying, "I am much indebted for the promptitude with which they discharged their several duties." He continued, "Major J. D. Webster . . . also accompanied me on the field and displayed soldierly qualities of a high order."[26]

Rawlins described the fight at Belmont in detail in a letter to his mother on November 15. While he revealed nothing about the duties he performed, he did stick close to his chief. "I was by the side of General Grant when his horse was shot under him," he wrote, explaining that when Grant's horse had balked for a moment, Rawlins took the lead as the men rode up to the ranks. When Rawlins turned back to Grant, "the General said his horse was shot so severely that it was necessary to leave him on the field." In a letter that surely would have been more unnerving than reassuring to a mother, Rawlins wrote, "I was in the midst of danger and within the reach of the rebel fire more than once during the day." Rawlins biographer James Harrison Wilson, who later served as an engineer on Grant's special staff, said that Belmont taught Rawlins the advantage of taking the initiative in battle and made him an "earnest advocate of striking the first blow."[27]

Belmont had proved that Rawlins was willing to stick close to Grant; by the end of the year he was sticking with Grant on an issue that would haunt the general throughout the war. After Grant's raid on Belmont, the public began to see him as a fighting general, but detractors surfaced as well. Some questioned Grant's competence, declaring the fight unnecessary. After all, Grant had gained nothing strategic, and casualties had amounted to 600 men on each side. Others opened an old wound, namely Grant's drinking in California and his resignation from the army. On December 17 a Benjamin Campbell of Galena wrote to Grant's political sponsor, Elihu Washburne, reporting that a "good authority" had told him that Grant was "drinking very hard." Campbell suggested Washburne write to Rawlins and get the real facts.

Washburne did write to Rawlins, who responded with fervor in defense of his commander. In a lengthy letter (Rawlins the wordsmith seldom wrote any other kind) dated December 30, Rawlins emphatically allayed Washburne's worries. He said that Grant was not "drinking very hard" and that such a statement "could have originated only in malice." Rawlins described Grant as a "strictly total abstinence man" and reported friends' observations that Grant had not taken a drink for five or six years, or since he left California. Rawlins did say that Grant had a few social drinks after the fight at Belmont, which was unusual to those around him because of his abstinence, but they were never enough to "unfit him for business." Rawlins also reported that in September Grant's doctor had prescribed two glasses of beer a day to cure dyspepsia; Grant had followed the prescription for two weeks but gave it up when it did no good.[28]

With his letter to Washburne, Rawlins assumed the job of Grant's protector, both from the bottle and from the public. Julia had done it at home, now Rawlins would do it in camp. Grant had not been on a bender since becoming a general, but he still had his problem with drink, and the astute Rawlins recognized it by late 1861. Over the next few years he willingly kept tabs on Grant's drinking, and early on, in this letter to Washburne, he revealed the source of his loyalty to Grant. "I regard his interest as my interest . . . ; I love him as a father; I respect him because I have studied him well, and the more I know him the more I respect and love him." Rawlins assured Washburne that Grant would never disgrace himself or his uniform with drink, and he pledged himself to that assurance.[29]

From the outset, Grant asked more of his personal staff than the terms adjutant general or aide-de-camp implied. Grant had already shown that when he made Hillyer a mustering officer. He used Hillyer again in December 1861 to investigate lumber contractors defrauding his army's quartermaster department. Hillyer cracked the case in St. Louis and recovered a great deal of money for the army. Grant also dispatched Maj. John Riggin that same month to investigate a river steamer reportedly running contraband goods into the Confederacy.[30]

Joseph D. Webster also did more than supervise engineering for Grant. On November 8, the day after the fight at Belmont, Grant sent Webster to confer with Leonidas Polk about tending the dead and wounded left on the field. Webster also returned sixty-four Confederate prisoners whom Grant had unconditionally released. In December Webster returned another seventeen prisoners to Polk, and in January he made another such trip, delivering a sick prisoner whom Polk had specially requested be released. By then Wesbster had joined Grant's inner circle as well. Rawlins described Webster as "a counsellor of the General . . . who was with him at and all through the Battle of Belmont, who has seen him daily and has every opportunity to know his habits." One can only surmise Rawlins's meaning of the word "counsellor," Grant shed no light on his relationship with Webster in his memoirs, and Webster left no collection of papers that might provide illumination. Throughout the war, however, Grant habitually listened to the opinions of his staffers and the generals he trusted, and he considered those opinions in making decisions. Webster was probably one of the earliest of those advisers. Regardless, Webster had gained Grant's trust enough that, by December 23, he was Grant's first chief of staff.[31]

To be sure, Grant's staff had its share of mundane duties to perform. Hillyer and Rawlins wrote most of the letters and orders at headquarters. James Harrison Wilson summed up Rawlins's clerical duties in late 1861 and early 1862 when he wrote, "Rawlins' duties . . . were confined to issuing orders, sending out instructions and making returns. These orders announced the staff, the creation of brigades and divisions, and the assignment of regiments thereto, but the greater number of them were dictated verbally by General Grant from his own personal experience and related to the discipline of the troops in camp and on the march, prohibiting them from leaving camp or going outside of the line of sentinels except upon duty, forbidding them to straggle, maraud, or fire away ammunition upon any pretext except in battle."[32]

During and after the war Grant detractors proclaimed that Rawlins was the mastermind of Grant's plans and that Grant would have had no operational success without Rawlins telling him what to do. But Wilson's comment about Rawlins writing orders that Grant had verbally dictated puts the lie to that story. Grant did indeed seek advice, but his decisions, and subsequently his orders, were his own. Rawlins simply wrote them for distribution to the army, a prime function of any staff officer. Wilson discusses the issue more directly, saying, "It cannot be contended that Rawlins was greater or wiser than Grant . . . nor can it be properly claimed that he . . . 'supplied Grant with brains,' as some have declared." Wilson concludes that, although he did not think for Grant, Rawlins gave the general "qualities and characteristics which . . . [he] did not possess." That is exactly the relationship that John Vermillion says is essential between a good chief of staff and his commander.[33]

In late 1861 and into the new year, Grant petitioned Halleck to let him take his army, grown now to near 20,000 men at Cairo, on an invasion of Tennessee. Confederate general Albert Sidney Johnston had stretched a poorly manned defensive line through northern Tennessee, and he knew that it would break if Federal troops pushed hard enough. He knew just where it would likely fail, too—at sister posts twelve miles apart, Forts Henry and Donelson. Henry guarded the Tennessee River, Donelson the Cumberland. Those rivers bisected Johnston's line, and, even though they flowed north, the Confederate commander knew that Federal gunboats could buck the current, get in his rear, and threaten the Confederacy's hold on Tennessee. Grant saw the weakness, too, and he tried to sell Halleck on a waterborne expedition into Tennessee. Halleck remembered Grant best for stories of his drunkenness, though, and besides, if any victories were to be won in the West, Halleck wanted to win them. So, when Grant traveled to St. Louis to persuade Halleck about an invasion, Halleck dismissed him. But when Grant returned to Cairo he received intelligence from Gen. C. F. Smith, an old Regular and one of Grant's West Point instructors and military idols, that troops could easily take Fort Henry. Grant went to work with U.S. Navy flag officer Andrew Hull Foote. Their joint plan to use gunboats on the Tennessee to soften up Fort Henry and float 17,000 of Grant's men upriver to capture the fort finally led Halleck, who trusted Foote, to relent.

Grant's expedition to the sister forts was a bona fide campaign, the first he and his staff had embarked upon, and during the next two weeks Webster proved himself worthy of his title as Grant's chief. On February 2 the expedition left Cairo, and the next day the transports stopped just below Fort Henry to disembark troops on either side of the river. Grant planned to have a column under C. F. Smith capture the heights across the fort while Brig. Gen. John A. McClernand's First Division moved behind the fort to cut off escape. In a move that foreshadows Grant's staff usage in

1864, he placed Webster with McClernand the day before the assault began. McClernand was a political general, and by the end of the year Grant recognized the man's incompetence as a field commander. Before Fort Henry, however, Grant did not yet suspect McClernand's abilities, so Webster was not along to hold McClernand's hand. More likely, Webster's job was to lend an old engineer's eye to the situation, for he participated in two scouting parties. On April 5 Webster rode out with Col. P. J. Oglesby and a detachment of the First Brigade, First Division, to reconnoiter the country near Fort Henry. Also that day Webster accompanied McClernand and engineers James B. McPherson and a Lieutenant Freeman on another reconnaissance, which confirmed to McClernand the strength of Fort Henry's guns.[34]

On February 6 Grant launched the assault, the ground columns moving on Fort Henry and a third sailing upriver with the navy. Foote's gunboats, however, started and finished the fight before Grant's infantrymen, bogged down in winter mud, could get into the fight. Fort Henry's commander, Brig. Gen. Lloyd Tilghman, realized his garrison could not withstand Grant's assault, and he sent 2,500 of his men to safety at Fort Donelson. He stayed behind with a contingent to put up a token fight, then surrendered to naval officers. Grant did not care who took the surrender; Fort Henry and, effectively, the Tennessee River had fallen. Fort Donelson and the Cumberland were next.

Although he had hoped to attack Fort Donelson on February 8, Grant had to delay his attack a few days. Foote needed time to get his gunboats back downriver to Cairo, pick up 10,000 reinforcements that Halleck had decided to send the expedition, and move up the Cumberland to Fort Donelson. The navy remained busy, however, and so did Joseph Dana Webster. On the seventh, three gunboats dashed up the Tennessee River, demonstrating their new control of the waterway. Webster, some other officers, perhaps including John Riggin, and two companies of sharpshooters went with Comdr. Henry Walke on the expedition, which destroyed the bridges of the Memphis and Bowling Green Railroad. On February 9 Webster accompanied Grant on a cross-country reconnaissance to within four miles of Fort Donelson. Hillyer also stayed busy, escorting prisoners captured at Fort Henry to Paducah, Kentucky, where Union officials would send them north.[35]

On February 12, leaving 2,500 men at Fort Henry, Grant started his men on their twelve-mile march to the rear of Fort Donelson. They started in beautiful, springlike weather, but by nightfall winter had returned, bringing sleet and snow and plunging temperatures. Grant took his men to within gunshot of Fort Donelson's defenses and, headquartering his staff in a farmhouse kitchen, deployed his army on the land side of Donelson. He posted Smith's division on the left and McClernand's on the right, although the line was not long enough to close an escape route along the Cumberland on Grant's far right. Halleck's replacements were late, so Grant ordered Brig. Gen. Lew Wallace to bring 2,000 of the reserves from Fort Henry to help close the gap. As it was, none of the reinforcements arrived until the fourteenth, and all went into line under Wallace's command.

When Foote arrived, Grant urged him to immediately attack the fort. He did and met with signal failure. Confederate gunners in Fort Donelson slammed solid shot into the iron-cased boats, sending them spinning out of control downriver and out of the fight. Foote himself suffered a wound in the battle. Before he retreated north with his battered armada, Grant conferred with him on the fifteenth.

While Grant was away, Confederates inside the fort, under the joint command of the generals Gideon Pillow, John B. Floyd, and Simon Bolivar Buckner, staged a counterattack to open an escape route through Grant's line. The attack smashed into McClernand's line, on Grant's right, sending it reeling. McClernand put up a desperate fight but could not hold on, and he sent a desperate plea for help to Wallace, whose Third Division was in line between McClernand and Smith. Before he left, Grant had emphatically ordered his men to hold their positions (McClernand had initiated a needless skirmish on the thirteenth and Grant wanted no more of that), and Wallace refused to lend McClernand a hand without orders. He sent a messenger to Grant's headquarters asking for permission to move, but at that critical hour of battle, Grant's staff officers failed him. None of the men, green in battle to be sure, would take the initiative and change the orders. Even though he could not get permission, Wallace finally sent two brigades to McClernand. Wallace's messenger to the farmhouse had bestirred Grant's staff, however, and John Rawlins quickly rode to Wallace's position. While the two men talked, a flood of retreating Federals overran them, one frantic man crying out, "We're cut to pieces!" Rawlins, the vehement patriot, unholstered his revolver and made as if to shoot the man; Wallace stopped him.[36]

Despite Wallace's assistance, the Confederates pried open their escape route. They hesitated, however, and Grant returned to find McClernand and Wallace dithering while the army disintegrated. Grant, angered, ordered the men to counterattack. Then, with Chief Webster riding by his side, Grant galloped up and down the line rallying the retreating men.

Grant recalled that he told Webster to "call out to the men . . . 'Fill your cartridge boxes, quick, and get into line; the enemy is trying to escape and he must not be permitted to do so.'" Webster's rally "acted like a charm. The men only wanted someone to give them a command."[37] Webster was by Grant's side much of the day, and a painting of the fight on the fifteenth depicts the chief of staff sitting on his horse amid snow and barren trees not fifteen feet from Grant, looking, with his gray beard and blue cloak blowing in the wind, like Father Winter himself.[38]

Grant found Smith and told the old general to attack the works guarding Fort Donelson. Smith did, gaining a secure hold in the entrenchments. Now the Confederates were reeling, and Webster raced back to the right, telling McClernand and Wallace that Smith had a foothold in the Rebel works and that they should press their attack.[39] They soon retook the ground on the right.

During the night, the Confederate generals decided to surrender Fort Donelson. Pillow and Floyd ingloriously escaped, however, leaving Buckner to surrender. On February 16 Grant sent Buckner his famous message calling for "unconditional and immediate surrender." Buckner had no choice but to accept Grant's demand; Donelson and the Cumberland were at last Grant's.[40]

In the days following the surrender Webster continued to act in an enlarged capacity. On February 19 he accompanied Foote on an "armed reconnaissance" up the Cumberland River some thirty miles to Clarksville, Tennessee. With the steamer *Conestoga* and the gunboat *Cairo* they neared Fort Defiance at Clarksville, where a white flag fluttered in the breeze. Foote's expedition troops landed and found the place deserted. Webster and a Lieutenant Commander Phelps, commander of the *Conestoga,* took possession of the fort and ran up the U.S. flag, while Webster gathered intelligence on the mission indicating that Grant's push in the northwest part of Tennessee had driven Sidney Johnston and his Confederates from Nashville, farther up the Cumberland. The Tennessee capital was apparently open for Federal occupation.[41]

In his official report of the surrender of Fort Donelson, Grant commended every member of his staff, saying that "all are deserving of personal mention for their gallantry and service,"[42] but he mentioned no particulars. To be sure, the Fort Donelson campaign had been testing grounds for inexperienced staff officers. The men had experienced an easy win at Fort Henry, perhaps so easy that it had imbued them with false confidence. Fort Donelson—with its winter weather, its delays, the spontaneous and dumbheaded behavior of McClernand, and a tenacious Rebel counterattack—was the opposite of Fort Henry. Grant no doubt felt obliged to commend all of his staff officers for their work, with which he may well have been satisfied. In fact, though, the staffers, and Grant, had much to learn about headquarters work. Grant failed to leave anyone in charge while he was with Foote on the fifteenth, nor did he give any of his aides authority to act in his stead in an emergency. While Webster performed yeoman service for Grant on the fifteenth, riding from field to field, often at Grant's side, Grant might have better used him at headquarters to direct operations and handle crises. Rawlins, too, had much to learn, for as adjutant his job was to coordinate troop movements and to monitor the fluid situation, not to threaten a frightened soldier with death.

Rawlins apparently realized he had much to learn. His friend, James Harrison Wilson, said that the Donelson campaign gave Rawlins "a clear insight into the difficulties and dangers of military life." He remarked that the campaign had taught Rawlins that he had to keep up with what was going on throughout Grant's command and at headquarters, and that he needed complete records of orders and communications. Wilson, always a Rawlins supporter, said that the adjutant was equal to the task. According to Wilson, Rawlins soon became "an acknowledged factor of great power and influence in the daily administration of the army, as well as in the personal and official fortunes of its chief."[43]

Rawlins did indeed quickly grasp the need for order around Grant's headquarters. On March 15, just a month after Fort Donelson, he issued General Orders No. 21, in which he perfectly stipulated the duties of each staff officer. That was something that no one, not Robert Chilton nor Walter Taylor, had done for Robert E. Lee's headquarters; the organized Seth Williams had not done it even for McClellan. Rawlins gave himself "special charge of the books of records, consolidating returns, and forwarding all documents to their proper destination." The job was not small, and Rawlins found someone to help him—Capt. William R. Rowley, a former lieutenant in the 45th Illinois Regiment. Rowley, a native of Gouveneur, New York, had been in Galena when the war started. He was a prominent Republican, clerk of the Jo Daviess County circuit court, and a man with Congressman Elihu Washburne's ear. Back in January Grant had agreed to try to get Rowley a spot on his staff, if the War Department would authorize him another man, and Rowley had petitioned Washburne for assignment to Grant. He had also supported Grant amid another spate of rumors about the general's drunkenness in late January. ("Any one who asserts that . . . [Grant] is becoming dissipated is either misinformed or else he lies," Rowley told Washburne.) Grant appointed Rowley to his staff on February 26, and Rawlins quickly made him his assistant. The two men hit it off immediately. By late March Rowley was urging Washburne to secure a major's commission for Rawlins. His commendation shows how immersed Rawlins had become in headquarters duty: "He works night and day and probably performs as much or more hard labor than any other Staff officer in the service of the United States."[44]

Also in General Orders No. 21, Rawlins assigned Hillyer to see that commanders of division level and below furnish returns to headquarters, and he put Lagow and Riggin in charge of applications for passes. He also directed Lagow and Riggin to "have a care to the amount of supplies on hand," both in commissary and quartermaster stores; apparently Rawlins did not trust the chief commissary or chief quartermaster of Grant's special staff to supply them with accurate information. Rawlins's delineation of Webster's duties reflected the trust Grant had in his chief of staff. Rawlins wrote that Webster "will be the advisor of the general commanding, and will give his attention to any portion of duties that may not receive proper attention." With General Orders No. 21, Rawlins was exercising what James Harrison Wilson called the "authority and responsibility" that Grant's headquarters needed.[45]

While Rawlins was lining out headquarters, Grant, now a major general by virtue of the Forts Henry and Donelson campaign, was seeking a promotion for his chief of staff. On March 14 Grant submitted Webster's name to Secretary of War Edwin M. Stanton for a brigadier generalship. For promotion Webster needed a field command, and Grant secured for him, nominally, command of the First Illinois Artillery. Aide-de-camp Hillyer also recommended Webster's promotion to Congressman William McKee Dunn of Indiana. Webster's promotion to general eventually came through, but not until November 29, 1862.[46]

The next test of Grant's staff would come at the battle of Shiloh, April 6–7, 1862, in southwest Tennessee. Confederate general Sidney Johnston and his army had retreated from Nashville across Tennessee to Corinth, Mississippi, a vital Rebel rail junction just across the state line. Grant intended to move his Army of the Tennessee up the Tennessee River to a place called Pittsburg Landing, on the west bank of the river and twenty miles northeast of Corinth. There Grant would await Maj. Gen. Don Carlos Buell's Army of the Ohio to join him from northeast Tennessee. The combined armies would go after Johnston's men at Corinth. Henry Halleck almost derailed Grant's plans, however, suggesting that Grant had been insubordinate when he left most of his army at Fort Donelson to check other areas under his command. Halleck also charged that Grant had refused to answer telegrams; but Grant had received them late, for a Rebel posing as a Union telegrapher impeded their delivery. Halleck ordered Grant back to Fort Henry and gave command of the expedition to General Smith. Grant obeyed and sent Smith on his way. Abraham Lincoln, pleased with Grant's victories, however, told Halleck to either press charges against Grant or drop the matter. Halleck relented and Grant hurried forward to join his army.[47]

By late March Grant had established his headquarters at Savannah, Tennessee, nine miles downstream from the bulk of his army at Pittsburg Landing. Grant and his staffers were all recuperating from illness (Grant had had diarrhea, chills, and fever for three weeks, he wrote Julia), and Hillyer had gone to Washington to have his position on Grant's staff formally recognized. Rawlins, who was also sick, continued to help Grant organize the army. Grant typically spent the night at Savannah and went upriver to Pittsburg Landing during the day. On March 26 Rawlins issued orders placing Smith in command at Pittsburg Landing whenever Grant was at Savannah and giving Brig. Gen. Benjamin M. Prentiss command of unattached troops at Pittsburg, thereafter called the Sixth Division. On April 2 Rawlins issued orders for Grant that further organized the command. General Orders No. 33 gave McClernand command of the First Division; Smith command of the Second Division (Brig. Gen. W. H. L. Wallace would take command of the division when Smith contracted a fatal disease); Maj. Gen. Lew Wallace the Third Division; Brig. Gen. Stephen A. Hurlbut the Fourth Division; Brig. Gen. William T. Sherman the Fifth Division; and Prentiss the Sixth.[48]

Meanwhile, Colonel Webster continued to conduct reconnaissance missions for Grant. On April 3, aboard the gunboat *Tyler,* he ran upriver from Pittsburg Landing to scout debarkation points for a crosscountry march to Corinth. He suggested that such a march, through ravines and over broken country, might be slow and dangerous, but once at Corinth Federals should have no trouble overcoming Rebel defenses.[49]

Grant soon had more immediate worries than the march to Corinth, for on the morning of April 6, 40,000 Confederates under Johnston and Gen. P. G. T. Beauregard slammed into his divisions on the plateau of land that extended west from Pittsburg Landing. Despite the claims of some Grant detractors, his men were not surprised: Pickets had clashed in the days before the sixth, and the Rebels had approached during the predawn hours with no degree of silence or secrecy. Nevertheless, Grant had expected no such attack, and neither he nor Sherman, who had assumed command at Pittsburg Landing from the ill Smith, had seen the need to entrench. The attack was fierce, especially where Sherman's Fifth Division camped, near a small chapel named Shiloh Church. In the fighting that bent back both the left and right ends of Grant's line, Sidney Johnston suffered a mortal wound; Benjamin Prentiss's Sixth Division became exposed in the center, and there his men fought savagely in what became known as the Hornet's Nest. Even though Prentiss had to eventually surrender 2,200 men, the action gave Sherman and the other division commanders time to fall back about two miles to a ridge near the Landing and regroup. Grant was at Savannah when the battle erupted. Hearing the firing, he hastened the first elements of Buell's army toward the Landing and ordered Lew Wallace and his division, which had been with Grant at Savannah, to hurry into the fight. Wallace, in an amazing display of incompetence, marched away from the battle and never got into the first day's fight. Grant and Buell soon arrived at the Landing, and, with Buell's 25,000 fresh troops and Wallace's division finally at the battlefield, Grant prepared a counterattack for the seventh. The Federal push retook the ground they had lost the day before and drove Beauregard's army from the field.[50]

Grant's staff officers performed far better at Shiloh than they had at Fort Donelson. They acted with an independence of thought and action that enabled them to make spot decisions without specific orders from Grant. The general commended them all, saying that they had been "engaged during the entire two days in conveying orders to every part of the field." In a flurry of dispatches early in the battle, Lagow, Hillyer, and Rawlins hurried off orders to lead elements of Buell's army, urging them to hurry to Pittsburg Landing.[51] Several of the staffers, however, did considerably more than send dispatches.

Grant and his staff were at his Savannah headquarters having breakfast when the battle started. Hillyer had returned about 3:00 A.M. from a trip to Cairo; his arrival had awakened Rawlins, who had since been up. While they were eating, at about 7:00 A.M., a private entered and reported heavy firing from Pittsburg Landing. Breakfast went unfinished. Grant's headquarters steamer, the *Tigress,* awaited him on the Tennessee River, and he ordered his horses and those of his staff taken aboard. Then general and staff boarded. Grant's horse had fallen on him several days earlier and injured his leg, and he leaned on Webster's shoulder as they went up the gangplank. Sailors on the *Tigress* kept steam up in the boilers in case of emergency, and the general was quickly on his way to the battle. Midway between Savannah and Pittsburg Landing was Crump's Landing, where

Lew Wallace had his division. Wallace was standing on his headquarters boat, and Grant ordered the *Tigress* close alongside Wallace's ship. Grant shouted for Wallace to get his division ready to march at a moment's notice; Wallace replied he had already done so. Grant and his staff sailed on.[52]

At Pittsburg Landing the men went to work. Hillyer said they met "hundreds of cowardly renegades" fleeing toward the rear. Grant and the staffers quickly quickly rode to the center of the line, trying to rally the men. "Soon I found myself in the midst of a shower of cannon and musket balls," he remembered, noting that Grant remained cool, issuing orders and sending "his aides flying over the field." Hillyer said that while he was issuing an order a cannonball passed within two feet of his horse's head.[53]

Once again, Grant expanded the duties of his chief of staff. Recognizing Webster's artillerist's eye and engineer's background, he placed the old soldier in charge of all the artillery on the field. Webster went to work. Down at the landing, amid stacks of supplies that Grant's quartermasters and commissaries were gathering for the Corinth campaign, was a five-gun battery, officially designated Battery B, Second Illinois Light Artillery. But the term "Light Artillery" was a misnomer; each of the guns were 24-pounder siege guns. Henry Halleck had said that teams of oxen would have to haul the guns to Corinth, but Webster reckoned they could be of service at Shiloh and he didn't have any oxen handy. Rounding up some soldiers, Webster had them manhandle the monsters onto the battlefield, where he positioned the guns a quarter mile from the river, facing south. There they covered the landing, and as the battered Federal divisions fell back, the guns became the left end of Grant's last defensive line of the day. As units fell back, Webster commandeered much of their artillery, some of them no less than 20-pounder Parrott guns, and added them to his end of the line. Before he was done Webster had fifty-two guns in place, and just in time.

By 5:30 P.M. Rebels had mounted an offensive against Grant's left, but their job was tough. To get to the Federals they first had to cross a watery, brush-choked ravine extending from the Tennessee, known as the Dill Branch. The Union gunboats *Tyler* and *Lexington,* floating in the river, had their 8-inch and 32-pounder guns aimed up the ravine to make the crossing hot, and any Confederate who forded the ravine found himself looking down the throats of Webster's killers. In his memoirs, in a typical understatement, Grant credited Webster's guns with "effectually check[ing . . . the] further progress" of the Rebels. Men in front of the guns, both Union and Confederate, had stronger words. When the guns opened up, some claimed that the noise knocked their hats off, other said that the concussion nearly broke their necks. Still others complained of bloody noses, bleeding ears, and deafness. Webster's overwhelming force had indeed checked the Rebels' further progress and allowed the lead element of Buell's army to slip into line relatively unassaulted.[54]

No less important, if perhaps less dramatic, were aide-de-camp William S. Hillyer's efforts to get troops on the battlefield. When General Buell arrived at Pittsburg Landing about 2:00 P.M., he told Grant that Brig. Gen. William Nelson's Fourth Division was soon to arrive and that Col. Thomas L. Crittenden's division was halted back at Savannah awaiting orders. Grant ordered Hillyer to escort enough boats back to Savannah to bring Crittenden on the field. Hillyer found Crittenden easily at about 3:30 P.M. and sent him on his way. He also discovered that divisions under brigadier generals Alexander McCook and Thomas J. Wood were also at Savannah awaiting orders. Hillyer wondered what to do: "I had no orders expect [sic] for Crittenden, but we needed all the reinforcements we could get." Grabbing pen and paper he wrote orders, under Grant's name, putting the divisions on the march. Then, remembering three idle regiments at Savannah, he ordered them, also, to march. Hillyer arranged for the troops' transportation, then made his way back to Grant. He arrived at the battlefield after dark, in a pouring rain, and found Grant, Rawlins, and some other staffers lying on the ground, with no shelter, trying to sleep. Hillyer reported to Grant what he had done, and "he said I had done exactly right." Hillyer's assumption of authority had brought badly needed troops onto the field for the second day's fight. "We needed them all!" Hillyer added.[55]

More frustrating duty fell to staff officers Rawlins and William R. Rowley. As Grant and the staffers had steamed up the Tennessee that morning, he had told Lew Wallace to prepare to march. After judging the situation on the field, Grant determined to get Wallace on the field right away. He sent Rawlins back to the Landing with orders to send assistant quartermaster Capt. A. S. Baxter downstream to put Wallace on the march, via the River Road that paralleled the Tennessee and would bring him immediately into Grant's rear. Baxter took the steamer *Tigress* to Crump's Landing, delivered the orders to Wallace, and reported back to Grant before noon. In the meantime, Grant sent a cavalry captain to make doubly sure that Wallace got the message. According to Rawlins, the rider returned and said that Wallace would not move without written orders. Rawlins's temper began to boil: "He should have been by this time on the field. His presence then would have turned the tide of battle . . . [and] saved the lives of many brave men."

Grant turned to Rowley and asked him if he had writing materials in his pouch. Rowley did, and Grant ordered him, the cavalry captain, and two orderlies to ride back to Wallace. "If he should require a written order of you, you will give him one," said Grant. As the men were leaving Grant called out, "See that you do not spare horse flesh." Rowley and company spurred off to Crump's Landing. Wallace had broken camp, but when Rawley followed the column he discovered Wallace on the wrong road. If left on his own course, Wallace would have ended up behind Confederate lines! Within earshot of the firing at the Shiloh church, Rowley was astounded to find many of Wallace's men resting and the general and his staff idling at the head of the column. When Rowley told Wallace about the report of his unwillingness to move without written orders, Wallace snapped that it was a "damned lie," and Rowley wouldn't have found him on the road if such was his intention. When Rowley questioned him about his choice of roads, Wallace replied that he was on the only road he knew of. (Rawlins later commented that Wallace had been in camp at Crump's Landing since mid-March and should have familiarized himself with the immediate area.) Rowley turned Wallace's column around and pointed them toward the River Road, but Wallace insisted he remain as a guide.

Meanwhile, Grant, having not heard from Rowley, sent Rawlins and Lt. Col. James B. McPherson to find him and Wallace's division. They found the division moving at a snail's pace, despite Rowley's urging. When it appeared that Confederates might be holding a bridge along their route, Wallace balked, asking the staff officers what he should do if the enemy was in the way. "Fight our way through until communication can be had with General Grant," was McPherson's reply. The men discovered the bridge was safe, but Wallace did not send forward a brigade to secure it until Rawlins suggested he do so. The staff officers kept Wallace headed toward the battle, but "he did not make a mile and a half an hour, although urged and appealed to push forward," said Rawlins. He got on the battlefield only after the day's fight was over.[56]

Grant did not publicly censure Wallace for his behavior at Shiloh, but staffers never forgave the errant general. In his memoirs, Grant's comments about Wallace were mild. He said that he could not understand why Wallace, with firing to his south, needed any other order than to come immediately to Pittsburg Landing. "His was one of three veteran divisions . . . ," said Grant, "and his absence was severely felt." But Grant's aides frequently—and vehemently—rehashed the affair in camp. Newspaperman

Sylvanus Cadwallader, who became close friends with Grant and the staffers and camped with them for much of the war, reported that the staff officers often spoke ill of Wallace, even in Grant's presence. "[Grant] always assented to their criticisms of Wallace's behavior," said Cadwallader, noting that he never again trusted Wallace with an important command.[57]

Grant's personal staff at Shiloh was, in effect, a different staff from the one that had served him at Fort Donelson. Back at Donelson, with Grant momentarily gone from the field, the men had dithered while the Confederates staged their counterattack. No one had attempted to rally the shocked and retreating Federals, and no one, even when a courier presented them with the opportunity, had taken the responsibility to put McClernand, Smith, or Wallace in charge of a renewed Federal offensive. At Shiloh, however, the men acted with speed, authority, and efficiency, from Webster's enthusiastic positioning of guns and Hillyer's troop roundup, to Rawlins's and Rowley's hounding of Lew Wallace. Their work helped secure Grant's last position on April 6 and prepare the army for its counterstrike on the seventh. Had Grant grasped the situation at Fort Donelson and told his staff officers what he expected of them at the next battle? Probably, for the men had become quite close in their few months together, but none of them ever mentioned it; staff work was not the foremost topic in the personal histories that appeared after the war. Certainly, though, Grant knew that he could only be in one place at a time. His two campaigns so far had been complex, involving close cooperation between navy and army units outside of his command. Grant needed the flexibility to freely converse with cooperating commanders and the assurance that, if he was temporarily off the field, things would go along without him. Grant's use of his staff at Shiloh was not necessarily by the book, but then he didn't fight by the book either, as Henry Halleck so fearfully acknowledged. The actions of Grant's staff, rather, reflected the personality of their commander; they were a necessity of war as Ulysses S. Grant chose to fight it.

CHAPTER FIVE

———◆———

Grant: An Accidental Staff

1862–1863

BETWEEN THE BATTLE OF SHILOH, IN APRIL 1862, AND THE SIEGE OF Vicksburg, May–July 1863, Grant began to realize that the friends he had placed around him in 1861 were not all efficient staff officers. While John Rawlins and other top aides groused about the ineptitude of their colleagues, Grant himself said little, choosing instead to cast about for effective duties for his staff. Indeed, Grant's command situation dictated that he experiment with broader staff usage. As Grant's star rose and he took command of larger military departments, his staff needs became more complex. No longer would he direct battles firsthand from the battlefield, as he had at Fort Donelson or Shiloh; he was certainly present on many battlefields, but he largely left the fighting to others, such as William Sherman or James B. McPherson. Instead, he crafted campaigns at headquarters and expected subalterns to carry them out. He no longer needed his staff officers solely to deliver messages or to look for errant division commanders; rather, he needed men to help him with overall campaigns, manage affairs in his vast Department of the Tennessee, and direct the operations of his increasingly larger armies. Grant realized this need gradually, and over the next fifteen months his staff usage often appeared disjointed. But slowly, as his command grew, Grant began expanding the role of his staff.

In the weeks following the battle of Shiloh, Grant beefed up his staff and recommended promotions for the staff officers who had served him well. On April 16 Grant requested promotions for Lagow and Hillyer to the rank of colonel for their "courage and good conduct" at Belmont, Fort

Donelson, and Shiloh. Only major generals of the Regular Army could forward the requests to the War Department, and as Grant was a volunteer, he hoped that Henry Halleck would make the recommendations. Their promotions came through on July 17, dating back to May 3. John Riggin Jr., who had served Grant as a volunteer aide with the honorary rank of captain, also received the official rank of colonel on May 3. In addition, Grant hoped to see Rawlins promoted. He wrote to Julia that "Hillyer and Lagow will be Colonels. Rawlins is a Major and ought to be a Brigadier General."[1]

Grant then brought aboard Theodore S. Bowers, born in 1832 in Pennsylvania and a newspaperman who edited and published the *Mount Carmel (Ill.) Register* from 1852 to 1861, as another aide-de-camp. At the start of the war, Bowers had joined the 48th Illinois Infantry as a private. He became a first lieutenant on March 24, 1862. The 48th saw action at Shiloh as part of McClernand's division. On April 26, 1862, Rawlins issued General Orders No. 45 announcing Bowers as Grant's aide-de-camp.[2]

The months after Shiloh were one of the lowest points of Grant's military career, during which he suffered both public and military criticism. Grant had won at Shiloh and sent Beauregard's troops fleeing back to Corinth. But the victory was marginal, and it ushered in another period of emotional trial for Grant. Rebels had surprised him, critics complained. He had been drunk at Savannah when the attack came, others added. With typical loyalty, staff officer William Hillyer tried to counter some of those criticisms in letters he sent Grant's father.

Bowers, the newcomer, once did more than write letters defending his boss's action at Shiloh. When in October Sylvanus Cadwallader, the reporter, was aboard a train full of soldiers headed for Cairo, Illinois, he overhead two men heatedly debating the merits of generals Grant and Rosecrans. One of them, a captain, began slandering Grant, saying that he had been in battle at Shiloh and knew all the rumors about Grant were true. Cadwallader noticed a "small, dark complexioned, quiet, unobtrusive" and "bilious" man take an interest in the argument and edge near it. Soon the man, with a "stony and cadaverous" expression and his eyes emitting "scorn, wrath and hate," confronted the belligerent captain. He stated that he could forgive misstatements, but he could not forgive someone slandering a friend by relating events that had never occurred. "You are a liar I know," said the little man. "You are a coward, I believe. I'll bet ten to one you were not in the battle of Shiloh." The crowd of soldiers, joining the side of the presumed underdog, cheered for the little man. Seeing that he could not win a fistfight if he started one, the captain backed down. At Cairo the men disappeared, but Cadwallader reported two days later that someone introduced him to the little man who had defended Grant— Theodore Bowers.[3]

Grant could handle public criticism, but rebuke from within his own army was another matter. General Halleck, in St. Louis, said nothing to support Grant. The scholarly Halleck had never had much confidence in Grant. Perhaps he had been drunk; perhaps he had been surprised. At any rate, he had let his victory go for naught by not pursuing Beauregard. The only thing for Halleck to do, he thought, was go to Pittsburg Landing and take command himself.

Halleck arrived at the Landing on April 11 and took field command of all the armies in his vast Department of the Mississippi—Don Carlos Buell's Army of the Ohio, John Pope's Army of the Mississippi, and Grant's Army of the Tennessee. Halleck then gave the Army of the Tennessee to Gen. George Henry Thomas and made Grant second in command of the department. Grant's new job was supposedly a promotion, but in reality it wrested from him all authority and put him right where Halleck could keep an eye on him. As Halleck prepared to move his combined army of more than 100,000 men to attack Corinth, he ignored Grant. He did not consult him on plans, and he kept Grant in the dark about preparations. Halleck began his campaign on April 30; it turned into a farce. Corinth was only twenty miles from Pittsburg Landing, but it took Halleck a month to reach it. Averaging less than a mile a day, Halleck stopped each night to build elaborate fortifications to avoid the same type of surprise he supposed had befallen Grant at Shiloh. By the time Halleck reached Corinth on May 30, the Rebels had slipped away. Even though Halleck claimed a great victory, his crawl toward Corinth disgusted Grant. In his memoirs Grant called Halleck's victory "barren," allowing, as it did, an entire Rebel army to escape unmolested. He added, "I am satisfied that Corinth could have been captured in a two days' campaign commenced promptly on the arrival of reinforcements after the battle of Shiloh."[4]

Grant endured his inactivity throughout the Corinth movement and the subsequent fortification of the town, but that was enough. Halleck had virtually suspended him after winning his last two battles; if that was how this army treated winning generals, he didn't know if he wanted to stay in it. As biographer William S. McFeely suspects, images of the critical Halleck must have mixed with memories of the berating Jesse Root Grant and the harsh colonel Buchanan at Fort Humboldt to bring the old Ulysses Grant—the failure—back to the surface. Hearing that his friend was thinking about resigning, William Sherman rode to Grant's headquarters. He found Rawlins, Lagow, and Hillyer outside, and they directed him into the tent, where Grant sat sorting papers. After a few minutes Sherman convinced Grant that matters might improve if Grant would just bide his time. Grant listened to his friend and soon discovered that he was right. In late June he received permission to move his headquarters and staff to Memphis, Tennessee, which Federals had recently liberated from Rebel control. He remained in an ineffective job, but at least he was away from Halleck. On July 11 Abraham Lincoln called Halleck to Washington to take command of all Union armies; Grant was rid of Halleck completely. Grant returned to make his headquarters at Corinth on July 15. In effect he became commander of all of Halleck's Department of the Mississippi, but orders making that official did not come until October 25.[5]

Although the summer of 1862 was an inactive period for Grant, his adjutant general, John Rawlins, became preeminent at headquarters. While Grant moved his headquarters from Corinth to Memphis and back again, Rawlins went along, setting up headquarters and tending to official correspondence. With occasional assistance from Bowers, who became Rawlins's right-hand man just as the former became Grant's, he drafted a spate of general and special orders which assigned commanders to units; banished from Memphis citizens who made unfounded accusations against occupying Federal troops; seized property in retaliation for guerrilla depredations; punished Federal troops who destroyed or stole Southern property; and outlawed Northern speculation in Rebel grain and cotton within Grant's district.[6] At the same time, Rawlins oversaw the activities of other staffers in the office. As his friend James Harrison Wilson later commented, "He made it his practice to see that every one else performed the services assigned him."[7]

In relieving Grant of mundane clerical worries, Rawlins was acting as a good adjutant should, and Grant appreciated it. In May, while Halleck was keeping him on ice, Grant wrote to Julia that Rawlins was making a good hand: "Rawlins has become thoroughly acquainted with the routine of the office and takes off my hands the examination of most all papers." The general revealed his growing fondness for Rawlins when he said, "I think he is one of the best men I ever knew." Rawlins had shown no penchant for operational planning, so Grant was laying it on thick when he commented that "if another war should break out, or this one be protracted, [Rawlins] . . . would make one of the best General officers . . . in the country."[8]

Grant had discovered in Rawlins a man who mirrored some of his own best qualities; "He unites talent with energy, and great honesty," Grant told Julia. But in other ways, Rawlins complemented Grant. Both men were industrious, but where Grant was often shy, reticent, and uncomfortable with public speaking, Rawlins, the lawyer, was fond of oratory and frequently expounded on a variety of topics. The unflappable Grant never cursed, but Rawlins could burn the air with profane outbursts, something incongruous with his straitlaced, Puritanical morality. Rawlins was not shy about voicing opinions on any topic to Grant, and Grant appreciated and respected Rawlins's candor. In his memoirs Grant wrote that Rawlins "could say 'no' so emphatically to a request which he thought it should not be granted that the person he was addressing would understand at once that there was no use pressing the matter." Grant concluded, "Rawlins was a very useful officer. . . . I became very much attached to him."[9]

Rawlins, dark and brooding, was not known around headquarters for jocosity, yet one day in late May 1862 he fell victim to Grant's well-cultivated sense of humor. Before he left Galena, friends there had presented Rawlins with a fine bay horse, and Rawlins became fond of showing off the animal's long tail. One morning, to his dismay and disgust, Rawlins suddenly found the horse's tail no more than two inches long. The adjutant fumed and sought his pistol to shoot whoever had committed the prank. Grant, standing nearby smoking a cigar, instantly realized what had happened—a wandering mule, not a delinquent soldier, had chomped off the horse's tail. Seeing Rawlins's rage and the absurdity of the situation, Grant burst into laughter. The swearing Rawlins wished the same fate on Grant's own horse. Nevertheless, Grant repeatedly had the last laugh; whenever the men rode anywhere together Grant needed only to glance at the horse's cropped tail to lapse again into laughter.[10]

While Rawlins established himself around headquarters, other positions on Grant's staff were in flux. During Grant's brief stay in Memphis he discovered that he needed administrative help. Of the places he had occupied so far, none had held a large Rebel population. Memphis did, however, and the townsfolk soon deluged Grant with complaints. "It took hours of my time every day to listen to complaints and requests," said Grant. To secure the help he needed, on June 24 he made his chief of staff, J. D. Webster, commander of the post of Memphis. The old soldier fell ill, however, and Grant soon made Col. T. Lyle Dickey commander. He later assigned Webster to supervise construction of fortifications on the south end of Memphis.[11]

Meanwhile, Grant's ablest aide at Shiloh, William S. Hillyer, had grown tired of war. "I have seen enough of war," he wrote to his wife after Shiloh. "God grant that it may be speedily terminated." He told her that he could not leave Grant until after "we have driven the enemy from

Corinth. When that is done I think I will leave it to others to finish up this rebellion."[12]

Grant and Hillyer were close, and the general saw that his friend from St. Louis was used up. He recalled in his memoirs that Hillyer had no "personal taste or special qualifications for the duties of the soldier," and he may have realized that as early at June 1862. Nevertheless he bore with the staffer who had served him so well at Shiloh and had treated him so kindly before the war. That month he gave Hillyer a job away from the battle-front, making him provost marshal in Memphis, where he wanted him to "devise ways of correcting some . . . abuses."[13]

Grant may also have realized that Clark B. Lagow was unsuited to duty at a combat headquarters; he made the same comment about Lagow that he made about Hillyer, and by July 1862 Grant was giving him assignments that took him away from headquarters. Grant's wife, Julia, and their children, were frequently in camp during slack times, and in early July Grant had Lagow escort them from camp back to Memphis. On July 10 Grant named Lagow acting inspector general for the army, a duty that shuttled him from camp to camp checking on their operational status. Five days later, however, Grant ordered Lagow to escort Confederate prisoners from Mississippi to a Federal prison in Alton, Illinois. No sooner had Lagow returned than Grant sent him to Hamburg, Tennessee, and East-port, Mississippi, to investigate alleged trade abuses between the army and private citizens.[14]

More changes at headquarters came in August 1862. With Lagow, Hillyer, and John Riggin away from headquarters, Grant sent William R. Rowley to deliver another group of prisoners to the prison at Alton. Then sickness dropped Rawlins. Grant commented in a letter to Julia on August 18 that his military family was "small. . . . Rawlins was obliged to have a serious surgical operation . . . to prevent his biles, or carbuncle, from turning into Fistula," he reported. He suspected Rawlins would be inca-pacitated for about ten days, but on August 22, with Rawlins's condition no better, Grant sent him home to Galena to recover. Theodore Bowers, who would soon be acting assistant adjutant, took over at headquarters for Rawlins. Rawlins fared better in Galena, where, on August 30, he delivered an hour-long speech in defense of Grant, who was still under public criti-cism for his conduct of the battle of Shiloh and his recent inactivity.[15]

Grant's headquarters family was indeed "small" just as he faced a dan-gerous military situation. After resuming command in mid-July, Grant found that Halleck had begun distributing units of the once-massive army to other commands. In August and early September, Grant received three orders to send troops to reinforce Don Carlos Buell for operations in eastern Tennessee, even though Grant was essentially on the defensive at an exposed forward point in Mississippi and facing the desultory raids of Rebel guerrillas and a more serious threat from Confederate generals Sterling Price and Earl Van Dorn. Union general Samuel Curtis had driven Price and Van Dorn from Arkansas at the battle of Pea Ridge in March, but now they were south of Grant, in independent commands, and could combine to bring 40,000 troops to bear on any spot they chose. Van Dorn, senior in rank to Price, wanted to drive Grant north, negating the Federal gains of the previous spring.[16]

Grant had other ideas, though, and in the resulting campaign he attempted to use his staff in a new way, one that foreshadows his later staff usage. By mid-September Grant had a plan to prevent Price and Van Dorn from consolidating their troops. Van Dorn was at Holly Springs, Mississippi, sixty miles west of Grant; Price was much closer, about twenty-two miles away at Iuka on the Memphis and Charleston rail line. Grant selected Price to fall first, and he moved his headquarters from Corinth to Burnsville, Mississippi, also on the Memphis and Charleston and within twelve miles of Iuka. His plan was complex: He would have Gen. Stephen A. Hurlbut move south out of Memphis on a demonstration designed to hold Van Dorn at Holly Springs, and, in case Van Dorn ventured eastward to help Price, Grant would leave a garrison at Corinth to handle him. He then planned to send Maj. Gen. E. O. C. Ord with two divisions north of Iuka and Maj. Gen. William S. Rosecrans, also with two divisions, south of Iuka. Between them they had 17,000 men (Price had 15,000), and Grant wanted them to catch Price in a pincers movement and destroy his force. Grant instructed Ord and Rosecrans to move from their staging areas— Ord at Burnsville, Rosecrans eight miles south at Jacinto—on September 18 and be in position to attack Price at Iuka at dawn September 19. Rosecrans was to move at least part of his troops by way of the Fulton Road from Iuka to block any escape Price might try that way.

Planning to have two separate armies converge simultaneously on a target was always complicated and risky, and the broken ground, poor roads, and swamps around Iuka made Grant's plan doubly so. Ord left on time, but Grant soon got word from Rosecrans that he was delayed and would not be in position to attack Price until noon on the nineteenth. Also, Rosecrans, for reasons of his own, decided to ignore the Fulton Road and travel solely by another route. Grant told Ord to go ahead and engage Price north of Iuka but warned him not to start a general fight until he heard Rosecrans's guns to the south.

Grant directed the overall Iuka campaign, but for the first time he let subalterns do the fighting, and he must have felt at a loss. While he had telegraph and courier contact with his field commanders, he could not be physically present with both. Grant spent some time with Ord, but he could not do likewise with Rosecrans. Telegrams and couriers were no replacement for the strength of Grant's personality, and he needed some way to transmit his presence and authority to the tardy Rosecrans. Grant knew that speed was essential, and he wanted Old Rosey to know it, too; for in truth Grant did not believe Rosecrans could be in place when he said he could. Grant needed personal representatives with Rosecrans, and he turned to two staff officers to fill the job.

Early on the 19th he sent Clark Lagow and Col. T. Lyle Dickey, chief of cavalry on Grant's special staff, to find Rosecrans, "explain to him the plan of operations," as Dickey later said, and prod the general into action. Shortly after noon the staffers found Rosecrans at Barnett's, a farmhouse seven miles south of Iuka, and they paused to have lunch with him. They then rode with the general to the head of his column, which was strung out over five miles. Rosecrans's lead troops soon encountered Price's skirmishers, and the fight quickly became general. "The shells burst around us—the bullets whistled through the air and it began to sound like some of the sharp passages at the battle of Shiloh," Dickey recalled. He and Lagow tarried about thirty minutes, then struck out to inform Grant that Rosecrans was engaged and Ord should begin his attack. Broken terrain and Rebel soldiers prevented Lagow and Dickey from going directly to Grant, and soon, with night falling and amid forests and grapevines, the men became lost. They attempted to travel by the North Star, but at one point Lagow's horse plunged into a ravine, landing on top of its rider. Neither man nor animal was seriously hurt, and they trudged on. By the time they reach Grant, however, dawn was breaking—they had been out all night. In fairness, a courier whom Rosecrans had sent to Grant independently of Lagow and Dickey arrived only shortly before they did.

In the meantime, Ord, who had been ready for a fight north of Iuka for more than a day, never got one. He had been waiting to hear Rosecrans's guns south of town, but a strong northerly wind had blown the sound away from him. By the time word arrived early September 20 that Rosecrans was engaged, Price had slipped the noose and escaped to the southwest.[17] Grant had preferred to destroy Price's army; nevertheless, his own troops had secured Iuka and prevented Price from entering Tennessee.

Price headed west and joined Van Dorn, who, in early October, launched an assault on Corinth. Grant had gone to St. Louis to discuss troop dispositions with Maj. Gen. Curtis, then to Jackson, Tennessee, so Rosecrans handled Van Dorn. On October 3 Van Dorn drove Rosecrans's men back into excellent fortifications around Corinth, which Grant had built after resuming command. From there, on the fourth, Rosecrans defeated Van Dorn in a savage fight.[18]

During the fight on October 4, Grant, at Jackson, took steps that showed he was settling into his role as an overall department commander. He hurried four regiments under Gen. James B. McPherson to Corinth to help Rosecrans, and, wanting to ensure Van Dorn's destruction, he ordered Hurlbut's division to get astride the Rebel line of retreat to Holly Springs, then he sent Ord to take command of that force. Once again he had Ord and Rosecrans on either prong of a pincers, but while Ord had a sharp fight with Van Dorn's lead elements, and got wounded in the melee, Rosecrans again moved slowly. The pincers didn't close and Van Dorn got away. Rosecrans's repeated tardiness dampened Grant's confidence in the man.[19]

Military historian J. F. C. Fuller commended Grant for his strategy during the Iuka-Corinth campaign. "He showed a strategic grasp that is quite amazing, seeing that hitherto he had no experience of a war of movement." Grant's weeks of inactivity under Halleck had given him time to study his maps and think. Fuller adds, the resulting campaign "marks him down as one of the most noteworthy generals of his age."[20]

Likewise, the campaign indicates Grant's first step, albeit small, toward an enlightened usage of his staff. Cavalry chief Dickey's comment that Grant wanted him and Lagow to "explain [to Rosecrans] . . . the plan of operations," shows that Grant wanted the staffers to do more than just hurry up the slow general. He wanted Rosecrans to know just when and how events were to take place and the consequences riding on them. Grant had a chance to defeat two armies in detail and see that they never took to the field again. Grant's concept of war centered on destruction of enemy armies, not merely putting them to flight, and he wanted that to be his field commanders' concept of war also. By sending staff officers to Rosecrans, Grant was trying to be in two places at once and see that his strategy went forward from both sides of Iuka. The complexity of his plan necessitated that he do no less. But Grant's dispatch of Dickey and Lagow has a spur-of-the-moment quality to it; he was thinking about getting Rosecrans into the fight, not forwarding nineteeth-century staff development. To have been truly effective, the staff officers should have been with Rosecrans from the start of the campaign; they should have insisted that he travel along Grant's prescribed route; and one of them at least should have stayed behind with Rosecrans to see that he prevented Price's escape until Ord could join the fray. Also, Lagow probably was not the staff officer to handle such assignments. Nevertheless, Grant had ventured forward, by necessity and somewhat unwittingly, into a new realm of staff usage.

Rosecrans left Grant's command October 24 to take over Don Carlos Buell's army in east Tennessee, but before he left he had some harsh words about Grant's staff. Old Rosey's departure was fine with both men, for the Iuka-Corinth campaign had soured them on each other. Grant could not abide Rosecrans's double failure to pounce on a defeated foe, nor could Rosecrans understand why Grant pulled him off the pursuit of Van Dorn he belatedly began after the fight at Corinth. Grant believed that a chase deeper into Mississippi would necessitate the Union force living off the land, and to him that spelled disaster. Back in Washington, Halleck and Lincoln also wondered at Grant's seeming ambivalence; indeed, the month following the battle of Corinth was another period of inactivity for Grant, of the type that had befallen him after Fort Donelson and Shiloh. A note from Rosecrans before he left for his own command could not have reassured the president and the general in chief, for he called Grant "sour and reticent." He also griped about "the spirit of mischief among the mousing politicians on Grant's staff." In short, he wanted to be away from Grant and his staff.[21]

Rosecrans did not elaborate about the "mousing politicians" comment. Certainly, Rawlins and Rowley were friends of Elihu B. Washburne, and Rowley had used his influence with the congressman to get on Grant's staff. But in late October came a controversy that Rosecrans's remark may have foretold. In October the Federal government arrested David Sheehan, a Galena attorney and former law partner of John Rawlins, and imprisoned him at Fort Lafayette in New York. Sheehan, like Rawlins, was a Democrat, and the government had charged him with treason. Rawlins took a brief leave from staff duties to investigate the charges and discovered that they were erroneous. Back at headquarters, Rawlins wrote to Secretary of War Stanton to ask for Sheehan's release. Getting no response, Rawlins got Grant, Rowley, and generals Hurlbut and John Logan to also write to Stanton. Grant's letter praised Rawlins and assured Stanton that he would ask no favors for Sheehan if he was guilty. Sheehan was released in December.[22] In the meantime, on October 25, Grant was given command of the entire Department of the Tennessee, and two days later he recommended Rawlins for promotion from major to lieutenant colonel, Rowley to major, and Bowers to captain.[23]

November 1862 was a watershed month at Grant's headquarters. It saw Grant stir from his month-long military lethargy and embark on the campaign that would virtually win the Civil War in the West. It also saw subtle changes within the staff, changes that set the staff on a road to professionalization.

Even when not campaigning, Ulysses S. Grant was not entirely idle. He had been studying his maps and had concluded, quite correctly, that the Mississippi River town of Vicksburg, Mississippi, was the key to victory in the West. Strongly fortified, Vicksburg not only guarded the river below its heights from Union boats, it also controlled rail lines that connected the western Confederacy to the east. A railroad ran east from Vicksburg to Jackson, Mississippi's capital, where it connected with other lines that ran into the heart of the Confederacy. Another line started on the Louisiana shore opposite Vicksburg and ran west. Capture of Vicksburg would cripple the rebellion, if not mortally then critically. Grant initially proposed to move south from his headquarters at Jackson, Tennessee, to Grand Junction, Tennessee, just short of the Mississippi line, and from there base an overland expedition to Vicksburg, more than 150 miles away.[24]

But Grant was hearing rumors around his camp, and he did not like them. In Washington, Abraham Lincoln had been studying his maps, too, and had also decided Vicksburg should be the Union's target in the West. Lincoln had supported Grant though rumors of the general's drunkenness, but Grant had been moving slowly the past month and Lincoln wanted to make sure Vicksburg fell. He dispatched Massachusetts politician-turned-general Nathaniel P. Banks to take command at New Orleans and mount an expedition up the Mississippi to grab Vicksburg. And, just to be sure, Lincoln would throw another column at the river town. In September Maj. Gen. John McClernand, who had caused Grant so much grief at Fort Donelson, had gone north on leave to visit an old Illinois friend—Abe Lincoln. The two had been lawyers together before the war, and Lincoln had supported McClernand's promotion to major general. Now McClernand figured Lincoln would support him in a scheme that would make him the hero of the war. McClernand wanted nothing less than permission to recruit troops from the West—largely Indiana, Iowa, and Illinois—and form an independent army with the sole purpose of floating down the Mississippi from Memphis and taking Vicksburg. Lincoln and Secretary of War Stanton believed the idea was sound, and they approved McClernand's plan. They did not consult Henry Halleck, though, and he and the rest of the army were in the dark about this plan to open the Mississippi.[25]

Such an expedition could not remain a secret for long, and Grant began to hear "newspaper rumors" about it. "I was very much disturbed by [them]," he said. Grant could not abide McClernand. He had proved himself incompetent on the battlefield, and now he showed himself as an intriguer. Grant refused to allow the politician to run an independent command within his department. He set out for Grand Junction, but not before he wired Halleck. He wanted to know if he was to sit still in Memphis while another force fitted out in that city and left on an expedition. He also asked whether Sherman, commanding the Memphis garrison, was subject to orders from the new command or from Grant. Halleck wired back that Grant had control of all troops in his department and could "fight the enemy where you please."[26]

Grant was on the move overland, but he wanted Sherman involved too. Grant knew that, although both Sherman and McClernand were major generals, the latter ranked the former in seniority. And even though Grant outranked McClernand, if McClernand arrived in Memphis, he could give orders to Sherman. Grant wanted Sherman with him on the push south, but first they had to make provisions for the safety of Memphis. They also had to do it quietly, lest McClernand hear that something was up and hurry to Memphis. So, Grant got his staffers in on the deception. William S. Hillyer had already been serving as something of a liaison between Sherman and Grant. On November 3 Sherman received Hillyer at his Memphis headquarters. "[He] can explain fully how satisfactory everything is here," Sherman wired Grant. He would say little more, other than that he had no trepidation about leaving a garrison force to guard Memphis. "The enemy would have to sacrifice more men than they can afford [to capture it]," he said. Within a week both Hillyer and Lagow were back at Sherman's camp. Again, Sherman declined to tell Grant in a letter what they had talked about. "[They] will tell you fully of all figures, numbers, and facts that I deem imprudent to trust by this route," Sherman told Grant. On November 15 the two generals finalized plans in a meeting at Columbus, Kentucky, where Grant ordered Sherman to bring two divisions to Grant's forward position and march them down the Mississippi Central Railroad. Sherman did as Grant asked, and by late November he was ten miles north of Oxford, Mississippi.[27]

Meanwhile, Grant moved from Grand Junction to La Grange, Tennessee. John Rawlins, traveling with him, began setting up headquarters there. "Move everything belonging to Hd Qrs including Printing . . . press to this place where Hd Qrs of the Dept. will for the present be established," Rawlins wired Bowers in Jackson. Rawlins told Bowers to hurry down on the first train, adding, "the Genl says for Mrs Grant to come with you."[28]

Rawlins might have been establishing headquarters at La Grange, but Grant was not sitting still. With McPherson on the left of his command, Gen. C. S. Hamilton in the center, and Sherman coming down with the right, Grant entered Mississippi, pushing an estimated 30,000 Confederates under Gen. John C. Pemberton before him. By November 13 Grant had frightened Pemberton across the Tallahatchie River and occupied Holly Springs, where he set up a forward supply depot for the expedition. By December 1 Grant was across the Tallahatchie, and by the eighth he had occupied Oxford, Mississippi, where he stopped briefly to repair his supply line, the Mississippi Central extending to his rear.[29]

Meanwhile, Grant was making changes in his personal staff back at La Grange. Grant's command encompassed three major railroads—the Mississippi Central, the Mobile and Ohio, and the Memphis and Charleston—and he recognized their importance in keeping his troops supplied. On November 1 he formally removed his chief of staff, Joseph Dana Webster, by then a brigadier general, from his staff and made him superintendent of all the military railroads in the department. He appointed Col. George G. Pride, who had been a volunteer aide with Grant since Shiloh, chief engineer of military railroads, responsible for keeping all the lines in the department in good repair. Grant had suggested the job for Pride to Halleck in early October.[30]

Grant made other changes in his staff, most notably giving John Rawlins the job as chief of staff as well as assistant adjutant general. In fact, most of the men on Grant's staff found themselves doing double duty as the general sought to get the most out of them. Hillyer remained as aide-de-camp and provost marshal, while Lagow was both an aide and acting inspector general. A Col. George P. Ihrie also served Grant as an aide and acting inspector general. William R. Rowley, for whom Grant had just requested promotion to major, was aide-de-camp and mustering officer; and John Riggin was aide and superintendent of Grant's military telegraph. Only Theodore Bowers, Rawlins's helper, appeared on the staff roll with only one job, that of aide-de-camp.[31]

Grant's appointment of Riggin as telegraph superintendent quickly caused a controversy. On November 14 Assistant Secretary of War P. H. Watson wired Grant's headquarters at La Grange that "some one signing himself John Riggin, superintendent of military telegraphs" was interfering with telegraphs in Grant's department. Watson claimed that the man did not have authority from Col. Anson Stager, general superintendent of military telegraphs, to use the wires. "[He] is an imposter," Watson said of Riggin. "Arrest him and send him north . . . before he does mischief by his interference."

Grant wired Watson, commenting dryly that "John Riggin . . . is my aide." Grant explained that he had authorized Riggin to send private dispatches over the wire before 10:00 A.M. so they would not interfere with military dispatches. Grant informed Watson that Riggin was departmental telegraph superintendent, "a position which interferes with no present arrangement, but is intended solely for my relief." Watson countered that Stager had deputies to help him with the operation of the telegraph, and that Riggin "must not interfere."

One of Stager's "deputies," J. C. Van Duzer, official telegraph superintendent in Grant's department, had in fact started the whole squabble. Van Duzer was absent in Cairo, Illinois, when Grant moved to La Grange, forcing the general to oversee construction of his own telegraph stations. When Van Duzer finally came on duty, he kept the wires so busy with commercial dispatches that Grant could not send military messages for a whole day. He suspended all private dispatches for a day, then had Riggin issue the order about sending private messages only before 10:00 A.M. In late November Grant again had difficulty with finding space for his dispatches on the wire, and his telegraph operator told him that Van Duzer was sending cotton dispatches. Van Duzer removed the tattling operator from Grant's headquarters, infuriating Grant. When Grant learned that Van Duzer had been promoted to oversee all the telegraphs in the department, Grant considered it an affront to himself and Riggin. He ordered Van Duzer arrested to prevent further interference. Secretary of War Stanton eventually directed Grant to release Van Duzer, but the general had defused the telegraph situation.[32]

Grant had made some changes in the structure and duties of his staff, but Rawlins, with full authority as chief of staff, wanted deeper changes. 1st Lt. James Harrison Wilson, a young engineer who had just served on George B. McClellan's special staff in the East, was assigned to duty in Grant's department, and arrived at his headquarters at La Grange on November 8. There he met John Rawlins, who was alone in the building. Rawlins, with a "dark and serious face," explained that Grant was away at Memphis but would probably assign Wilson to McPherson's special staff. Rawlins had done his homework on Wilson, learning about his family and background—Wilson was an Illinois man, as were many of Grant's staffers. Rawlins had apparently decided he could trust Wilson, for he launched into a lengthy discourse on conditions around Grant's headquarters. Wilson recalled that he spoke with "startling frankness, disguising nothing and extenuating nothing." Rawlins suspected that Wilson had heard rumors about Grant's drinking, and the chief quickly cut to the chase. He showed Wilson an abstinence pledge that Rawlins had made Grant sign. Rawlins perhaps intended to show Wilson that Grant recognized his problem, but, transparently, also let Wilson know that Rawlins had appointed himself Grant's conscience. Then, trying to play down the blemish of drink, Rawlins described the general as a "courageous officer . . . [who would] lead us to victory," cryptically adding, "if his friends could stay him from falling."

Preliminaries aside, Rawlins explained that Grant had some good officers on his staff, but some bad ones as well. He asked Wilson to "help clean them out." Rawlins "wanted to form an alliance . . . with me for the purpose of weeding out worthless officers, guarding the general against temptation and sustaining him in the performance of the great duties which he would be called on to perform."[33]

Wilson did not say whom Rawlins wanted rid of, but William R. Rowley made it fairly clear. On November 20 Rowley wrote to Elihu B. Washburne condemning some of his fellow staff officers. He complained that Col. John Riggin was an accidental staff officer. Someone higher up had mistaken a written compliment Grant gave Riggin as a request for the man's permanent service. Worse yet, Riggin was drinking buddies with colonels Hillyer and Lagow. "I doubt whether either of them have gone to bed sober for a week," Rowley said.[34]

Rowley's letter inspired a response from Washburne to Grant. That letter has been lost to history, but on December 16 Rowley wrote to Washburne again, saying that he hoped the congressman's letter would bring from Grant "an answer . . . of the right kind." He added, however, that he feared Grant would "hardly have the heart to cut loose from the . . . colonels." Rowley was away from headquarters when he wrote this second letter, and he commented that when he returned he hoped to find "fewer loafers about headquarters."[35]

Alcohol, then, had caused a rift at headquarters. Rawlins had seen drink destroy his own father, and he would not stand by and watch it destroy Grant. If men so close to Grant were drinking, they were a threat, and Rawlins wanted them gone. But the problem included idleness as well. None of the staffers had professional military training when the war started; Rawlins, Hillyer, and Lagow were even in that regard. But Rawlins had made it his purpose to study the duties of a staff officer and carry them out. For the others to do any less was an affront to Rawlins's Puritanical bent.

Certainly Hillyer had already expressed his war weariness, and Lagow had given a less than stellar performance at Iuka. But Grant was bearing with them, finding odd jobs for them, such as escorting his family and transporting prisoners. As chief, Rawlins had neither the power to hire nor fire; nevertheless, he would be glad if the slackers departed from headquarters.

Grant soon revealed that he, too, was dissatisfied with his staff, but he also had the tenderhearted loyalty that Rowley feared would saddle him with incompetent men. When Washburne wrote to Grant in response to Rowley's letter, he also talked to Henry Halleck in Washington. Halleck told the congressman that he would help with any staff recommendations Grant might make. Grant wrote to Halleck on December 16 that his "labors" with his army had been exceedingly hard, and he blamed his difficulties on "having an entire Staff of inexperienced men in Military matters." He noted that, of both his personal and special staffs, he regarded only two men as indispensable—Rawlins and Bowers, the latter of whom he had just recommended for promotion to major and the extra job of judge advocate. Grant's comment implied that everyone else on the staff was dispensable, but he talked ill about none of them. Hillyer was "very efficient" as provost marshal, relieving Grant of "much duty that I have heretofore had to attend to in person." Grant also said that he was "very much attached to [Lagow] personally" and described him as a "true honest man, willing to do all in his power for the service."[36] Grant recommended no one for dismissal, nor did he make any recommendations to better his staff.

Later, during the early stages of the Vicksburg campaign, Grant further revealed his dissatisfaction with his staff. Writing to Julia, Grant said, "Since I came down here I have felt the necessity of staff officers." Some had been away from camp, "and still others have been required," he said, adding cryptically, "that is of a class that can do something."[37] Grant's comment was loaded, implying that he had plenty of staffers who did nothing and that he could use no more of them. The context of his comment, the Vicksburg campaign, reveals again that the more complex his campaigns became, the more Grant realized he needed competent staff officers.

Grant's detractors, those who saw him as Rawlins's puppet, may suggest that Grant was following Rawlins's lead in trying to improve the staff. Such is doubtful. Grant respected Rawlins's views and encouraged him to speak his mind around headquarters, whether on matters of strategy or office business. Rawlins's outspoken nature makes it probable that Grant knew full well his chief's opinions of the other staffers. But Grant was the West

Point–trained general around headquarters, not Rawlins, and he knew how to run an army. He could spot an inefficient staff officer as well as Rawlins could. But Grant also had deep-seated loyalties, especially to men who had been nice to him, such as Hillyer in prewar St. Louis. That was perhaps a burden for a man of war. Nevertheless, Grant's personality won out over Rawlins's—and they both were men of strong, if opposite, personalities—in any effort to improve the staff. In the end it was Grant who decided who left the staff, and when and how they went. Rawlins could only contain the troublemakers and protect Grant from them as best he could.

Rawlins soon got his wish, at least temporarily, about Clark B. Lagow. Lagow fell ill in late November, and on the twenty-fifth Grant wired the staffer's brother, David, in Evansville, Illinois, to come to Grant's head-quarters and take the sick man home. On November 29 Rawlins issued special orders for Lagow to rejoin Grant's headquarters, "wherever the same may be," when he recovered. As late as March 27, 1863, however, Lagow was still sick. He was back in Memphis, though, within Grant's depart-ment and with staff colleague William S. Hillyer, but Grant was not opti-mistic about the man's health. "I am afraid it will be a long time before he gets strong again," he told Julia privately.[38]

In December 1862, however, Grant's main concern was his overland push toward Vicksburg, not his staff. Grant had created a supply depot at Holly Springs, Mississippi, to provision his thrust into Mississippi, left a garrison there, then moved twenty-five miles farther south to Oxford. There he gave new orders to Gen. William T. Sherman, who had arrived with troops from Memphis to form the right wing of Grant's invasion force. Grant now knew that John McClernand's foray down the Mississippi was definite, but he did not intend to sit back and let the political general pick the plum of his department. Grant sent Sherman back to Memphis with orders to take command of McClernand's recruits, integrate them with troops already present, and begin the expedition to Vicksburg. Grant "doubted McClernand's fitness" to command such an important cam-paign, and he wanted Sherman to hurry lest McClernand reach Memphis first, exercise his seniority in rank, and begin the invasion. Once Sherman had stolen McClernand's thunder and shoved off from Memphis, Grant had in mind another pincers movement, with Sherman assaulting Vicksburg from the river while Grant kept Pemberton occupied as far northeast of Vicksburg as he could.[39]

Soon Confederates under Earl Van Dorn stunned Grant with a raid that virtually ended Grant's overland campaign and nearly cost him one of his better staff officers. Raiders under Confederate cavalry leader Nathan

Bedford Forrest had bedeviled Grant's supply lines in Tennessee ever since he had moved into Mississippi. On December 20 Van Dorn compounded Grant's troubles when he led a column around Grant's left flank and dashed to the Holly Springs supply depot. Seeking to absolve himself of his loss at Corinth, Van Dorn easily overwhelmed the depot's small garrison. Grant's wife, Julia, and son Jesse, had just left Holly Springs on their way to meet the general at Oxford, so they escaped capture. Staff officer Theodore S. Bowers, Rawlins's assistant, was not so lucky.

Grant had sent Bowers to check on the strength and supply stores of every command in his department. Bowers finished checking the Holly Springs garrison late on December 19 and recorded his findings on a list. He then placed the document on the mantel of the fireplace in his quarters and went to bed. The next morning a noise outside awakened him. Wearing only his long underwear, Bowers stepped outside and saw two men threatening a Federal guard.

"What the devil are you interfering with that guard for?" Bowers asked. The Confederates cursed Bowers as a Yankee so-and-so and ordered him outside. Realizing Holly Springs had fallen to Rebels, Bowers stepped back inside and tossed on the fire the document containing unit strengths of Grant's command. The coals were nearly dead, though, and Bowers had to stall while the paper took fire. It finally flashed, and the Rebels, realizing that they had lost something important, futilely tried to save it. They had Bowers, though, and took him to Van Dorn. The general ordered his men to parole Bowers, but the staff officer, realizing that Van Dorn's small contingent could not stand against the Federal column that must surely be on its way, declined. When a Rebel officer threatened to drag him off behind a horse, Bowers replied, "Very well, we can stand that kind of treatment to prisoners if you can. It is your turn today, but it will be ours tomorrow."

Many others in the Federal garrison of 1,500 refused parole, and when the Union column that Bowers expected arrived, the Confederates abandoned them and fled. Before they left, however, the Rebels destroyed more than one million dollars in ordnance and commissary and medical supplies. Bowers's conduct delighted Grant, who presented him with an inscribed sword to show his appreciation.[40]

The raid left Grant little choice but to withdraw to Tennessee. With his main supply depot gone and Forrest menacing his northernmost supply lines, Grant realized that protecting such a line for a run at Vicksburg was impractical. He needed provisions to get home, though, and he ordered troops to fan out fifteen miles on either side of his route and take what they needed from Mississippi families. Federal troops easily garnered their needs, and the bounty of the countryside amazed Grant. It taught him a lesson about living off forage in Mississippi that he would not soon forget.[41]

The riverine phase of Grant's plan proceeded, though, for William Sherman had no way of knowing Grant had pulled back. Sherman and his army had sailed from Memphis on December 19 aboard Navy transports, part of a sixty-four-boat flotilla under Adm. David D. Porter operating jointly with Sherman. Sherman had left a full ten days before McClernand arrived and found himself without the special force Lincoln had promised. By Christmas Sherman was near Vicksburg and almost ready to start his land campaign. He planned to sail around Milliken's Bend, a sharp bend in the Mississippi about ten miles northwest of Vicksburg. Five miles beyond the bend he would have Porter swing the flotilla abruptly again, this time northeast and into the mouth of the Yazoo River. Five miles up that river he planned to unload his men and march them cross-country another five miles to the Walnut Hills, a high ridge that extended southwest to Vicksburg. If he could get a toehold on the ridge, Sherman would have a commanding position over the fortress city. The march from the Yazoo, however, was tortuous, with bayous and swamps impeding the army's movements. When Sherman finally launched his assault on the ridge, near Chickasaw Bayou, on December 29, Confederate sharpshooters were on the ridge waiting for him. The battle quickly went to the Rebels, who could fire straight down on hapless Federals trapped at the base of the ridge. Sherman had no choice but to withdraw, having suffered 1,776 casualties; on New Year's Day he abandoned a plan to assault the ridge again, at Haines Bluff farther up the Yazoo, when river fog stalled naval support. Sherman's attempt at Vicksburg was as dead as Grant's.[42]

Grant did not give up on Vicksburg, of course, and he spent the next four months slogging toward the city. On January 29, 1863, Grant arrived on the Mississippi to take command of his army. Gen. John McClernand had arrived at the mouth of the Yazoo on January 2, the day after Sherman had cancelled his Haines Bluff expedition, and, as Grant had feared, taken command of Sherman's force. McClernand ordered the force back up the Mississippi to Memphis, but on the way Sherman encouraged him to make a side trip up the Arkansas River to destroy a Confederate garrison known as Arkansas Post. Rebel prisoners had told Sherman that 5,000 men were garrisoned there, and he knew that such a force could threaten any further Union efforts down the Mississippi. On January 11 McClernand and Sherman forced the surrender of Arkansas Post, capturing all 5,000 men. Then McClernand paused at the town of Napoleon, at the mouth of the Arkansas. There, Sherman and Porter wired Grant, who had returned his headquarters to Memphis after withdrawing from Mississippi, and urged him to come down the river and take command himself. Grant visited Napoleon on January 17 and found subordinate commanders so wary of McClernand that their distrust gave the whole army an "element of weakness." Grant quickly decided to take command. He sent McClernand and Sherman back down to Young's Point, just beyond Milliken's Bend—the objective was toward the south, not north where McClernand had pointed the army—then he hastened to Memphis to arrange for his departure. He left Gen. Stephen Hurlbut in charge at Memphis, ordered all troops and guns not needed in Tennessee to move to Young's Point, then returned downriver himself.[43]

Arriving at Young's Point, Grant had much to conquer besides Vicksburg; one was the weather, the other was Northern public sentiment. Unionist newspapers had been grousing about the apparent lack of activity in the Mississippi theater after the defeats of Holly Springs and Chickasaw Bayou. Grant also knew that November elections had gone against Republicans, indicating war weariness among voters. Grant could not sit idle for long without jeopardizing his job, causing further disaffection among Northerners and demoralizing his troops. But unusually heavy winter rains were stopping him. Grant knew that he somehow had to get his army on dry land east of Vicksburg before he could subdue the city, but the swollen bayous networking the region would not permit any overland movement until March or perhaps April. To get east of Vicksburg immediately meant going back to Memphis to start another cross-country trek, but Grant believed that the movement would look too much like a retreat for Union sentiment to bear. He would have to bide his time until the waters receded, but he would have to look busy all the while.

Grant turned to what he called "a series of experiments to consume time, and to divert the attention of the enemy, of my troops and of the public generally." The experiments largely involved creating artificial shortcuts to Vicksburg, such as man-made canals, or cuts in the bayou system, northwest of the city. At Williams's Canal, Lake Providence, Yazoo Pass, Steele's Bayou, and New Carthage, Grant committed men to the work for the rest of the winter and into spring. Although he was prepared to exploit whatever success the efforts might produce, he "never felt great confidence that any of the experiments would prove successful." He was right, none did.[44] Meanwhile, he sought a truly viable plan for taking Vicksburg.

For the next six weeks, as experiment after experiment in the bayous failed, Grant studied his maps and plotted strategy in his room, the former ladies' cabin on the *Magnolia*. Ultimately he adopted another, bolder plan.

He would march his infantry down the Louisiana side of the Mississippi River to a designated point, gambling that the navy could run its gunboats and transports past Vicksburg's guns under cover of darkness without serious loss, steam to where the infantry waited, and ferry them to the east bank. The trip would place the army east of Vicksburg, which all of Grant's experiments in one form or another were designed to do. And more, Grant could accomplish it without making any northerly move that might resemble a withdrawal. "I had in contemplation the whole winter the movement by land to a point below Vicksburg from which to operate," he said. As he formulated the plan, Grant kept his thoughts to himself. The plan involved both daring and secrecy; it would not do to have Northern newspapers get wind of the plan and publish it, so Grant kept quiet until he was ready to proceed.[45]

In his *Life of Rawlins,* James Harrison Wilson, an engineer attached to Grant's special staff who was becoming something of a quasipersonal staff officer by virtue of his friendship with Rawlins, credits both himself and the chief of staff with the Vicksburg plan. Grant never mentions them regarding the plan in his memoirs, and the claim seems spurious.[46]

When a stranger at headquarters did threaten Grant's private plans, however, Rawlins and Wilson cooked up another scheme. On April 9 Charles M. Dana, a former newspaperman, arrived at Milliken's Bend as an official and confidential representative of Secretary of War Edwin Stanton. Stanton wanted Dana to check on the status of affairs in Grant's department, but Rawlins and Wilson quickly suspected Dana of spying. All of Grant's bayou experiments had failed, and he had halted active operations to prepare for his main Vicksburg campaign. Of course, the public knew nothing of Grant's real plan, and Northern newspapers were again attacking him as either incompetent or drunk. One ill word from Dana to Stanton would lead to Grant's ouster. Rawlins put on his mantle as Grant's protector, and he and Wilson decided their best defense was to make Dana a de facto staff officer. They told Dana about Grant's actual plan to take Vicksburg and informed him about affairs at headquarters. The staffers welcomed Dana into their offices and mess tent, and they always had Dana's tent pitched next to theirs. Wilson even wrote reports for Dana when the latter found his eyes overworked in the dim light of a lantern. According to Wilson, Grant fully approved of their plan to handle Dana, which succeeded beyond their expectations. "A genuine friendship, free from concealment or reservation, grew up between [Grant and Dana]," Wilson said. In fact, Dana became so close to Grant and his aides, particularly Rawlins and Wilson, that he "did all in his power to remove prejudice against Grant" from the minds of Lincoln and Stanton and replace it with "respect and confidence."[47] Dana became an astute observer of Grant's staff, and over the next two months noticed the same deficiencies that Rawlins had started complaining about months earlier.

Meanwhile, Grant had a campaign to finalize. He moved his route of march west several miles from the dry neck of land that Wilson had proposed. He would have troops march from Milliken's Bend, following Roundaway Bayou south to New Carthage on the Louisiana side of the river. By following the tops of levees and throwing bridges across otherwise impassable bayous, the men would have dry marching all the way. The navy, of course, had to be at New Carthage to transport them to the Mississippi shore, and to get there they had to run the Vicksburg batteries, just as Wilson said. Nevertheless, Admiral Porter was wholeheartedly behind the plan. By late March the winter rains had subsided, the ground was drying out, and Grant was ready to go. On March 29 Grant ordered General McClernand and his corps to move out first, preparing the route south for the other corps to follow.[48]

By April 16 Porter was ready to make the run. He had assembled on the Yazoo seven armored gunboats with coal barges lashed to their starboard sides, three army transports with supplies the army would need below Vicksburg, and a steam ram. Porter had banked the furnaces of his fleet's boilers to emit minimal smoke, doused lights, and covered windows to make the boats poor targets; and he had piled grain sacks on the decks and water-soaked cotton bails around boilers for protection from enemy fire. About 9:30 P.M., Porter began the run, sailing past Young's Point, where Grant, his wife, their two sons, his staff, and Charles Dana watched aboard the anchored *Magnolia,* and toward Vicksburg. Rebel gunners caught sight of them quickly and began firing. Porter's gunners returned fire, and after ninety minutes the river fell quiet again. Unable to await the outcome, Grant raced from the *Magnolia,* mounted his horse and galloped down the road to New Carthage. When he arrived, Grant found the fleet riding at anchor. Although all the boats were shot up, some badly, only one transport was lost. No men died and only thirteen suffered wounds. The run was a success.[49]

Still, the troops below Vicksburg needed more supplies than Porter's flotilla had been able to carry. More boats would have to run the batteries. The army would handle this run, though, not the navy, and Grant assembled six steamers and twelve barges to make it. Most of the steamers' civilian crews cowered from the trip, however, and Grant had to cast about in his own ranks for volunteers to man the boats. Fortunately, many of his soldiers had river experience: "I found that volunteers could be found in the ranks and among the commissioned officers to meet every call for aid." Lt. Col. William S. Oliver, of the Seventh Missouri Infantry, was master of transportation for the run, but Grant gave overall command of the army fleet to one of his staff officers, and an unlikely one at that—Col. Clark B. Lagow.[50]

Lagow, who had been on sick leave just a few months ago, was apparently well enough to take the assignment. Grant did not mention Lagow in his memoirs in connection with the second river run and offered no reason for giving Lagow the assignment. Julia Grant, however, remembered that Grant had been "much disturbed by the inefficiency of the officer who was ordered to make ready the boats." He relieved the man and assigned two of his staff officers to the duty. Julia did not say who the staff officers were; perhaps one was Lagow, and the command of the fleet was an extension of that duty. Regardless, Lagow took the job, and on April 21 Rawlins issued Special Order 111 putting him in charge of the fleet.[51]

Lagow's river run began about 11:30 P.M., April 22; it was his most harrowing duty of the war. Lagow sailed on Colonel Oliver's steamer, the flagship *Tigress,* which had been Grant's headquarters ship at Shiloh a year earlier. Five more steamers, lashed with barges, followed. The steamer *Empire City* soon passed the *Tigress* and was in the lead when the fleet reached Vicksburg at 12:20 A.M., April 23. Rebel gunners were ready for this second flotilla. Confederates had fired two buildings on the Louisiana shore opposite the city, and Oliver noted that "it was as light as day on the river." Rebel fire became terrific, and everything from minié balls to 200-pound shot and shell rained on the fleet. Gunfire tore away guylines and ropes on the *Tigress,* splintered its crew cabins, and destroyed an extra tiller wheel. The *Tigress* endured thirty-four hits, and Oliver thought the steamer should clear Vicksburg's last battery intact. But suddenly a large shot knocked a four-foot hole in her hull near the stern, "causing her to fill and settle fast."

Oliver ordered the *Tigress* grounded on the Louisiana side, which she reached just before going to the bottom. He hurriedly assembled his crew on the hurricane deck and hailed the steamer *J. W. Cheeseman,* which was coming alongside. Lagow ordered Oliver to move his crew to the second vessel. The fleet had more batteries to run at Warrenton, however, before they reached New Carthage, and Lagow put Oliver in command of the *Cheeseman* for the rest of the trip. Before they moved out, the *Empire City,* crippled with a cut steam pipe, floated near. Oliver took it in tow and the fleet pressed on.

At Warrenton, which the ships passed in daylight, Oliver discovered that the *Empire City* was dragging the *Cheeseman* out of control, and he ordered it cut loose to float. The *Cheeseman* took only three hits at Warrenton, none serious, and once out of range the crew waited for the free-floating *Empire City* to catch up.

Rebels at Vicksburg fired more than 500 shots at Lagow's fleet, damaging all of the boats and barges but sinking only the *Tigress.* Artillery and small arms fire from the shoreline injured many men, two of them mortally. Nevertheless, Grant was pleased: "I look upon this as a great success." At New Carthage, Lagow took reports from the various steamer commanders and submitted them to Grant. The general, however, never commended Lagow for his work or mentioned him in connection with the run in anything other than a brief report to General Halleck on April 25.[52]

Grant began the next phase of his Vicksburg campaign on April 30. He had shifted his infantry from New Carthage south to Hard Times, Louisiana, planning to cross the Mississippi and land at Grand Gulf, Mississippi. On April 29 Porter's gunboats had hammered Rebel batteries there, hoping to knock them out before the crossing, but to no avail. Grant moved his debarkation point farther south to Bruinsburg, and on the thirtieth McClernand's four divisions and one of McPherson's invaded Mississippi. On May 1 McClernand's men fought the battle of Port Gibson, dispatching a Rebel contingent and strengthening Grant's toehold in the state. Grant then ordered a move to the north and east, with McClernand's corps taking the left wing of Grant's army, Sherman's the center, and McPherson's the right. Vicksburg defender John C. Pemberton had his army between the city and the Mississippi capital of Jackson, forty miles east, where an army under Joseph E. Johnston was his only help if Grant attacked. Grant intended to get between Vicksburg and Jackson, cutting Pemberton off from Johnston, and hopefully destroying Pemberton's force before he could fall back to the Vicksburg defenses. On May 12 a Confederate brigade from Johnston's army hit Gen. John Logan's division of McPherson's corps near Raymond, fifteen miles from Jackson. Logan won, but the sharp fight prompted Grant to deal with Johnston outright before going on to Vicksburg. On May 14 Sherman's and McPherson's corps entered Jackson, putting Johnston to flight. With Jackson, a Confederate railhead, secure and Johnston dispersed, Grant feared no real Rebel counteroffensive at his rear. He turned his full attention to Vicksburg and pointed his army westward. Pemberton made an attempt to slip north and join Johnston, but Grant blocked him at Champion's Hill. A savage fight erupted May 16, with Federals suffering 2,441 casualties, Confederates

3,851. McClernand and McPherson handled the brunt of the fighting for Grant, but they were unable to destroy Pemberton's force. The Souhern general began withdrawing toward Vicksburg. Grant's army made another attempt to stop Pemberton at the Big Black River, just east of Vicksburg, on May 17, but the Confederates were able to duck inside the fortress city. On May 18 Grant's troops began entrenching around Vicksburg. On May 19 and again on May 22 Grant attempted to take the city by storm. Both assaults failed, however, and Grant began the serious work of besieging the city.[53]

The key to Grant's campaign had been rapidity, and, in another expansion of staff function, he adapted William S. Hillyer's staff duties to fit his needs. Grant, who made his headquarters with the forward elements of his army, left Hillyer behind at the Grand Gulf beachhead. Grant had essentially cut himself off from supply lines to the Northern states—his retreat from Holly Springs back in December had taught him Mississippi was rich in forage—but he still had something of a supply dump at Grand Gulf, full of ammunition, rations, and other provisions that had survived the battery runs in April. He needed someone there to get loaded wagons quickly from the Louisiana side to the front in good order.[54]

Grant's dispatches to Hillyer bristled with urgency. On May 5, from Hankinson's Ferry, Grant told Hillyer, "See that the [commissary] at Grand Gulf loads all wagons . . . with great promptness." And, in an order growing from the necessities of the campaign, Grant drastically increased his staff officer's authority when he told Hillyer, "Issue any order in my name that may be necessary to secure the greatest promptness in this respect." The order even placed Hillyer above the commissary officers, who in fact were part of Grant's special staff. Grant was especially worried about getting plenty of ammunition to the front, and he told Hillyer, "Every day's delay is worth two thousand men to the enemy. Give this your personal attention."[55] Hillyer performed well at Grand Gulf, and Grant ultimately commended his decisions there.[56]

Ironically, in Hillyer, Grant was getting yeoman service from a man who had resigned his staff position. On April 27 Hillyer, who more than a year earlier had reported his war weariness, had submitted his resignation to Adj. Gen. Lorenzo Thomas. He informed Thomas that he needed to attend to his law practice and real estate holdings in St. Louis as well as to the estates of three of his in-laws. Grant reluctantly approved Hillyer's request, saying that he had "served [me] faithfully and intelligently. . . . I am loathe to lose him." Thomas did not approve Hillyer's resignation until

May 15, however, so Grant had the staffer's services for much of the early Vicksburg campaign.[57]

If Grant was expanding staff officer duties by placing one in charge of supply transportation, then John Rawlins was expanding the role of chief of staff by taking the field with the spearhead of the invasion. Rawlins rode with his friend, James Harrison Wilson, near the front of Grant's invasion force. After the battle of Port Gibson, troops of John McClernand's XIII Corps occupied the town early May 2, then pushed on to the northeast. They stopped, however, at the South Fork of Bayou Pierre, where Rebels had fired a suspension bridge. Wilson sent dispatches to McClernand, urging him to repair the bridge, but when the troops took no action, Wilson and Rawlins rode out to the bridge. They personally supervised its repair, but five miles ahead, at the bayou's North Fork, they found another bridge in flames. Troops had difficulty finding timber to repair the bridge, but Rawlins took the matter in hand, detailing and accompanying detachments to find the necessary wood. Wilson credited Rawlins's prompt action, and he believed that Rawlins had a vested interest in keeping the campaign moving, having promoted it so vigorously to Grant. "[Rawlins] made it his personal business to see that not a minute should be lost, either in the repair of the bridges or in sending the troops across them in pursuit of the enemy," Wilson recalled. He commented that Rawlins was not content to simply issue orders for the work to be done—"This was not Rawlins' way of doing business."[58]

Grant generated a large volume of orders on the campaign to Vicksburg, and Rawlins, fulfilling one of the prime duties of a chief of staff, saw that copies of each reached its recipient in good order. But Rawlins's biographer, Wilson, implied that Rawlins also wrote the orders, a misconception that has lasted a century. "Not one [order] . . . was badly expressed, or was in any degree uncertain in tenor or obscure in meaning," Wilson says. Historians have always regarded Grant's orders as some of the clearest in the war, rarely leaving room for misunderstanding or misinterpretation, and the credit for that belongs to Grant, not Rawlins. Civil War writer Bruce Catton notes a special clarity in Grant's orders during the Vicksburg campaign, and readers need only consult the *Official Records* to confirm that. William T. Sherman recalled that Grant refused to let staffers write his orders. "He would sit down and scribble off an order easier than he could tell another what he wanted. If anyone came along and remarked to him, 'That was a clever order Rawlins put out for you today,' Grant would say right out, 'I wrote that myself.'" Sherman said that he had saved about

150 orders from Grant, all written in the general's hand. Furthermore, Rawlins was a fine orator but a slow writer and poor grammarian. Charles Dana commented that in executing his duties as adjutant Rawlins was "too slow, and can't write the English language correctly without a great deal of careful consideration." Rawlins's difficulties would hardly enable him to write quick, clear, and precise orders during a rapidly moving campaign. Grant had already shown a willingness to listen to Rawlins regarding strategy, and he may have listened to him again during the Vicksburg campaign—Wilson referred to Rawlins as Grant's "counsellor" on the movement. Perhaps, but the many orders that came out of headquarters originated with Grant.[59]

Grant made the most of his staff by spreading them over a wide area—he had Rawlins with him and Hillyer at the Grand Gulf beachhead, and he left Theodore S. Bowers back at the starting point, Milliken's Bend, to handle affairs there. Vicksburg's batteries were still trained on the Mississippi River, and supply steamers, easy marks on moonlit nights, had to cease operations. Instead, wagons hauled supplies forty-four miles south of Vicksburg, where soldiers transferred them to riverboats for safe passage to Grand Gulf. But commissary and quartermaster officers told Bowers that they did not have enough wagons and teams to keep the advancing army adequately supplied. On May 5 Bowers urged Major General Hurlbut, commanding the XVI Corps at Memphis, to send down any wagons and teams he could spare. Grant may have given Bowers the same authority to act on his own volition as he had given Hillyer, for Bowers commented, "General Grant is in the advance and cannot be consulted . . . , but the great importance of keeping the army supplied induces me to present these facts for your consideration."[60]

During the first week of the siege of Vicksburg, Grant sent another of his staff officers on a different kind of mission. Gen. Nathaniel P. Banks, commanding at New Orleans, planned a campaign to move up the Mississippi River and capture Port Hudson, another river fortress about 125 miles (?) south of Vicksburg. Grant had first considered sending McClernand's corps to help Banks, but on May 3 Grant received word from Banks that he would not be ready to start his campaign until May 10. Grant could not wait, and he pushed into Mississippi without telling Banks that he had changed his plans. In front of Vicksburg, however, on May 25, Grant began wondering if Banks might assist him. He sent staff officer John Riggin to find out. Grant did not give Riggin authority to do any arm-twisting, though, and he had little luck with Banks. Banks, who had started a siege of his own at Port Hudson on May 23, was miffed that Grant had not come to his aid. He refused to go to Grant, and instead sent Riggin back to Grant with the suggestion that Grant send 10,000 men to help invest Port Hudson. Grant would not go to Banks any more than Banks would go to Grant, so the two generals settled in to their respective sieges.[61]

Silent during the overland campaign was aide-de-camp colonel Clark B. Lagow. After Lagow commanded the second river run on April 22, Grant gave him no other special duty until May 24. That day Rawlins issued Special Orders No. 139 assigning Lagow to escort Confederate prisoners of war to Federal authorities up the Mississippi at Island No. 10. Troops guarding the prisoners were to go as far as Memphis, then hurry back down to Young's Point while Lagow took fresh guards for the remainder of his trip.[62]

Lagow performed poorly in his role as commander of the guard, however. On May 29 Memphis commander General Hurlbut wrote to Rawlins that Lagow had just arrived with 4,408 prisoners. Hurlbut switched the guards and ordered Lagow to start them back to Young's Point immediately. But Lagow apparently had not "paid any attention to this duty or . . . taken any care of the officers and men under his charge nor even . . . [knew] how many men constituted the Guard." Hulburt reported that the prisoners had not even had enough provisions. Lagow had insisted on loading all of the guard troops—1,000 men he estimated—on one boat for the return to Vicksburg. Hurlbut rebuked Lagow, though, for not splitting up the guard and sending them back on several steamers carrying supplies to Grant's army, all of which could have used guards.[63] Neither Grant nor Rawlins responded to Hurlbut's charges, but to be sure, the complaints went into Rawlins's own file against Lagow.

Excitement soon gave way to tedium as Grant's army settled in for the siege of Vicksburg; it took its toll on Grant, and Rawlins picked up anew his mantle as Grant's protector. Grant had not lived up to his reputation as a drinker over the past few months: Planning the Vicksburg campaign had taken all his time and energy, and he had on occasion refused to join others who were drinking socially, opting instead to stay with his topographical maps.[64] Once in Mississippi, though, Grant's resolve slipped. On the night of May 12, the day his troops had fought at Raymond and were poised to capture Jackson, Grant went to the tent of Col. William L. Duff, chief of artillery on Grant's special staff, and asked for a drink of whiskey. Grant was relieved that the crossing into Mississippi had gone so well,[65] and the drink, which turned into two, then three, was perhaps a way to reward himself while easing his fatigue. He knew that Duff and reporter Sylvanus Cadwallader had with them half a barrel of whiskey, left behind by Illinois governor Richard Yates after reviewing Illinois troops some weeks before. Duff had also supplied Grant's habit before, much to the chagrin of Rawlins, who suspected but could never prove the deed. Reporter Cadwallader, in Duff's tent when Grant entered, commented that the general was not shy about asking for a drink, despite his reputation. Cadwallader watched as Grant and Duff drank and toasted the campaign. Then Grant left, but he was not drunk; perhaps the knowledge that more hard campaigning lay before him kept him sober. Cadwallader had become a favorite around Grant's headquarters, and he wisely reported nothing about the incident.[66]

Through early June, with nothing before him other than more siege warfare, Grant continued drinking, ultimately provoking Rawlins's wrath. The chief of staff had done his best to outlaw whiskey anywhere near Grant. "Rawlins is death on liquor," was the word around camp, and officers found themselves sneaking drinks for fear that Rawlins would catch them. Figuring that a night or two of insobriety now, with the end of the siege not imminent, would do little harm, Grant did as he pleased. Rawlins scolded him harshly for it. At 1:00 A.M., June 6, Rawlins sat in his tent at headquarters some miles behind the lines and drafted a letter to Grant. It began, "The great solicitude I feel for the safety of this army leads me to mention, what I hoped never again to do, the subject of your drinking." Rawlins wrote that he hoped he was wrong, but he thought it better to err "on the side of the country's safety than in fear of offending a friend." Rawlins told Grant that he had the willpower to control his drinking, had proven it during the recent campaign. He also reminded the general of two pledges of abstinence he had made to the adjutant. But "I find you where the wine bottle has just been emptied," Rawlins scolded, "in company with those who drink and urge you to do likewise." Rawlins blamed drink for Grant's sudden indecisiveness, and he closed his letter by stating again that he hoped his suspicions were wrong. But, he said, if they were not, and Grant kept drinking, then "let my immediate relief from duty in this department be the result."[67]

Rawlins gave the letter to Grant and was apparently satisfied with its results. On a copy of the letter, which surfaced years after both men had died, Rawlins had scrawled the endorsement, "This is an exact copy of a letter given to . . . [Grant], about four miles from our headquarters in the rear of Vicksburg. Its admonitions were heeded and all went well.—John A. Rawlins."[68]

In truth, Grant slipped at least one more good bender past Rawlins. Charles M. Dana recalled Rawlins riding to where Grant, Dana, and some other men were talking some distance from headquarters and giving Grant, as Dana called it, "that admirable communication." Grant pocketed the letter and went about his business. Grant had planned a steamer trip up the Yazoo River to Satartia, Mississippi, where units of his army were poised to fight Confederate general Joe Johnston's men if they appeared to relieve Vicksburg. Dana accompanied the general, and, in an 1887 article in the *New York Sun,* which Dana then edited, he wrote that Grant got "as stupidly drunk as the immortal nature of man would allow." In his memoirs Dana referred to the incident more politely, recalling simply that Grant was "sick." Nevertheless, Dana said the next day that Grant "came out as fresh as a rose, without any trace or indication of the spree he had passed through." He added that Grant did the same thing on several more occasions.[69]

Reporter Cadwallader, in his own memoirs, embellished the story of the Satartia bender to include a drunken horseback ride across the Mississippi countryside. Cadwallader casts himself as the hero of the story, chasing down Grant and enticing him back to headquarters. There Cadwallader explained the drunken spree to Rawlins. Some historians doubt Cadwallader's veracity: He dates the bender vaguely, and writer Bruce Catton maintains it could not have happened before Rawlins wrote the letter to Grant, or the chief of staff would have referred to it directly. Likewise, it could not have happened after, or Rawlins would not have penned such a positive endorsement on his copy.[70]

Grant did go on some sort of a spree on his Satartia trip, perhaps not as spectacular as Cadwallader reported, and Rawlins did not catch him. Cadwallader undoubtedly took liberties with the story. While a newspaper dispatch suggests that Cadwallader may have been at Satartia about that time, Dana confirms that he did not travel there with Grant's party. Cadwallader probably picked up parts of the story around camp, for Grant's binge was apparently the subject of gossip for some time. Regardless, neither Cadwallader nor Dana, both of whom had found homes at Grant's headquarters, reported Grant's behavior to their respective bosses—the newspaper-reading public or Edwin M. Stanton—either of whom could have ended Grant's career.[71]

In reality, as much as John Rawlins would have hated to admit it, he had no true control of Ulysses S. Grant's behavior. Grant accepted Rawlins's frequently dramatic "protection" from drink not because he could not control himself—in fact, for someone so frequently labeled a drunkard, he went on relatively few benders in his life—but because he recognized he needed moral support in the matter from a trusted friend. "That Rawlins helped in this matter is apparent," says historian E. B. Long, "but that Grant was so defective a person that he had to have a constant caretaker is undoubtedly out of line."[72]

In a sidebar to the story, historian Catton questions Rawlins's motive for keeping a copy of the letter he wrote to Grant. When Julia Dent Grant heard of the letter in 1892, she neither confirmed nor denied the tale of her husband's drunkenness, but instead asked, "How could Rawlins have kept this letter? To me, it looks very like making a record for the future." Catton agrees. He says that Rawlins's training as a lawyer and as "head-quarters bureaucrat" gave him respect for the written record—a paper trail. Catton notes another time, in November 1863 at Chattanooga, Tennessee, when Rawlins wrote a letter rebuking Grant for drinking. His charge turned out to be false, though, for Grant was in a strategy meeting when Rawlins thought he was drinking. Nevertheless, Rawlins kept a copy of that letter, too. Catton sees Rawlins as "the keeper of Grant's conscience, and he did what he could to build up his own reputation. With a defender like Rawlins, Grant had no need of any enemies."[73]

Grant harbored no ill feelings toward Rawlins; he respected his adjutant's advice, even if he did not follow it. In fact, Grant frequently accepted public censure from Rawlins without letting it harm their friendship. "I have heard him curse Grant when, according to his judgment, the general was doing something he thought he had better not do," recalled Charles Dana. Grant, of course, also respected Rawlins as a friend and as a fine office administrator. Throughout the rest of the siege, Rawlins continued to run Grant's headquarters efficiently. Rawlins had little military bearing and "a rough style of conversation," said Dana. While he insisted that official army documents follow guidelines in the officer's handbook, he did not stand on formality. Wilson said that Rawlins made officers and enlisted men alike feel comfortable at headquarters. Even though Rawlins resorted to profanity if his booming voice was not enough to stress a point, he kept an air of cordiality around headquarters that Grant must have appreciated.[74]

On May 31 Grant sent Hillyer (who was serving as a favor to the general now, his resignation official since the fifteenth) to Memphis. Grant wanted Hillyer to tell General Hurlbut to "strip . . . [his district] to the very lowest possible standard" and send troops and supplies to reinforce Grant. Grant wanted to be sure the north end of his line near Haine's Bluff was secure in case Joe Johnston attacked. "The quartermaster in charge of transportation, and Col. Hillyer are specially instructed to see that this direction is fully enforced," Grant told Hurlbut.[75]

Hurlbut was a testy man, though, and something about Hillyer irritated him. Acknowledging receipt of Grant's orders, Hurlbut told Rawlins, "Col. Hillyer reported to me with orders . . . to assist in expediting movements of troops." Then he commented, "I am not aware of any assistance rendered by him, although his society was very agreeable . . . I am satisfied that his forte is not in Quarter Master's duty." Hurlbut also commented that colonels Duff, the artillerist, and Lagow had been in Memphis but had ignored protocol by not reporting to him.[76] Duff and Lagow both drank, and Hillyer probably did as well, from William R. Rowley's earlier comments. The thought of the three of them loose in Memphis is certainly grist for the imagination and probably set Rawlins's mind spinning.

In mid-June, however, Hillyer finally left Grant's staff and retired to St. Louis without saying good-bye to Grant. He blamed a terrible pain in his right arm, rheumatism he called it, for his discourtesy, and he said that medicine had eased the pain but left the arm virtually paralyzed. After ten days in St. Louis, Hillyer regained the use of his right hand, and he drafted a farewell letter to Grant: "I could not express to you . . . the day I left my heartfelt appreciation of your uniform kindness to me." But rumor had gone ahead of him that he left Grant's headquarters because of internal trouble there. Grant had always stood by Hillyer, notwithstanding his later comment that Hillyer was not cut out for staff work, and Hillyer had, in fact, rendered good service to Grant. Hillyer took "every occasion to make known the fact that there never had been an unkind word, thought, or expression between us." Hillyer also told Grant that "I have never had a truer, firmer, friend than you," and that if he ever rejoined the army, he would like to do so on Grant's staff.[77] In his comments Hillyer had struck a nail on the head—even if any man on his staff was a troublemaker, incompetent, or inefficient, Grant, who regarded friendships as for life, would rather let attrition take care of the problem than fire him outright.

Lagow was soon gone again, although temporarily, as well. He fell ill and Grant sent him home. On June 15 Grant wrote to Julia about conditions on his staff. He told her that Hillyer had resigned and that everyone else was well except Lagow. He "has gone home sick and I expect [him] never to recover," said Grant. "He may get up so as to return but will never be well."[78]

Grant may have lost some staffers during the Vicksburg siege, but he gained two as well, neither of which was well qualified for headquarters work. One was young lieutenant William McKee Dunn Jr., who became an aide on Grant's staff. Dunn, like so many others, had made it on Grant's staff not by his own qualifications, but through Grant's kindheartedness. Dunn, the son of Judge Adv. Gen. William McKee Dunn and sixteen years old when the war started, had run away from home, joined the army, and served several months until his father found him and secured his discharge. The boy ran away again. Finally, Grant learned that Dunn had joined his army. When Grant questioned him, the boy admitted his identity, but warned that he would run away again if Grant sent him home. Grant thought the least he could do for the boy's safety was transfer him from a combat command, and he made a place for him on his personal staff. Dunn primarily carried orders and messages.[79]

Dunn does not surface frequently in any examination of Grant's head-quarters; neither does Peter T. Hudson, whom Grant brought aboard early in the Vicksburg campaign. Hudson and his brother, Silas, were cousins of Julia Dent Grant. In January 1863 Silas queried Grant about a staff job for Peter. Grant, noting that it was his privilege to nominate whom he wanted for his staff, agreed for no other apparent reason than because of his famil-ial ties to the man. Grant urged Silas to send Peter on and advised him that everything he needed in the way of equipment he could find at Memphis.[80]

Grant's stranglehold on Vicksburg continued until July 4, 1863, when Rebel commander John C. Pemberton surrendered his 29,000-man garri-son. Lieutenant Dunn carried news of the surrender to the nearest telegraph office at Cairo, Illinois. Over Rawlins's objections, Grant paroled the Confederate prisoners rather than use part of his army to transport them north and oblige the Union to care for them.[81]

For all the wonderful clarity of his orders, Grant in July 1863 wrote few battle or campaign reports. After Shiloh, Grant had submitted only a brief letter to General Halleck informing him that a fight had occurred and the Federals had won. Grant claimed that when Halleck superseded him after the battle, he did not allow Grant access to his subalterns' reports. "For this reason I never made a full official report of this engagement," said Grant.[82]

But after Vicksburg fell there came from Grant's headquarters a lengthy, detailed report of the campaign and siege; and its composition reveals something about the way Grant's adjutants worked. Throughout the siege, Grant had been working on a draft of the report, covering events from the running of the Vicksburg batteries in mid-April to the investment of the city in May. Grant turned the draft over to Rawlins and Bowers for copyediting. They verified facts, added names and dates, and checked figures. In that manner the trio had completed by July 6 the official report of the Vicksburg campaign.[83]

In late July Grant assigned Rawlins to personally deliver the report and rolls of Confederate parolees to the adjutant general's office in Washington. He intended the trip to be something of a vacation for the chief of staff, who had worked so diligently for Grant the past two years. He also sent with Rawlins a letter introducing him to President Lincoln. Grant said he would be pleased if the president granted Rawlins an interview, noting that Rawlins could give Lincoln any information he wanted about affairs in the Department of the Tennessee. Grant ended by saying that he thought Lincoln would be relieved to know that Rawlins had no favor to ask. "Even in my position it is a great luxury to meet a gentleman who has no 'axe to grind' and I can appreciate that it is infinitely more so in yours," said Grant.[84] Lincoln must indeed have been relieved, recalling the visits of McClellan's chief of staff and father-in-law, Randolph Marcy, in 1862 when Marcy most certainly had an "axe to grind."

But Grant was shading the truth a bit, for in fact he wanted Rawlins to test the political waters on a decision he had made a month earlier. Throughout the Vicksburg campaign, Grant had wanted to fire his rival, Maj. Gen. John McClernand. Grant well understood the man's incompetence, but he wanted solid grounds for the man's removal. He got them in mid-June when McClernand, without Grant's approval, published in a Northern newspaper congratulatory orders to his XIII Corps. His corps had performed nobly, Grant pointed out, but McClernand's orders and his subsequent official report of operations exaggerated their role in the campaign and denigrated the efforts of other units. "The publication of his order . . . was in violation of War Department orders and of mine," said Grant, and on June 17 he canned McClernand, sending him home to Springfield, Illinois. Rawlins had earlier tried to heal the rift between Grant and McClernand, thinking it best for his boss, since McClernand and Lincoln were old friends from Springfield. But the political general's congratulatory orders angered Rawlins so much that he was wholeheartedly in favor of the man's dismissal. McClernand was still in the volunteer army, though, subject to recall, and still a close friend of Lincoln's. Grant wanted Rawlins to fully explain the facts of McClernand's performance to Lincoln and to ascertain if Grant could expect ramifications.[85]

What started as a vacation became a harrowing trip for Rawlins. Rawlins took a steamer up the Mississippi, then boarded an Illinois Central train for Chicago. But one hundred miles from the city, the train ran off the track. Rawlins wrote to Grant that he was on the most heavily damaged car and "came nearer being killed than ever before in my life." He commented that the wreck scared him nearly speechless, and he recognized how Grant must have appreciated that. Rawlins arrived at Washington after, as he called it, "one of the hardest trips one ever experienced, I reckon."[86]

Rawlins met with Maj. Gen. Henry Halleck and Col. John C. Kelton, assistant to Adj. Gen. Lorenzo Thomas, and he found them solicitous. He wrote to Grant that he should make a trip to Washington just to "see how delighted they are over your successes." He also found Halleck eager for Grant to submit names for promotions. Halleck explained that the nearby Army of the Potomac usually ate up all the vacancies on the promotion list, but three generalships in the Regular Army were now open. Seizing the opportunity and using the authority he knew Granted had vested in him, Rawlins recommended Sherman, McPherson, and Maj. Gen. George Thomas for the spots. He urged Grant to hurry along his recommendations and make it official.[87]

Rawlins's interview with Lincoln also went well. On July 31 Rawlins met with Lincoln and some of his cabinet members, giving details of the Vicksburg campaign and the people involved. Rawlins's "honest, unpretending, and unassuming manners" impressed Secretary of the Navy Gideon Welles. No doubt Rawlins spoke in the same straightforward style he used around camp, minus the cursing, but "the unpolished and unrefined deportment of this earnest and sincere man . . . pleased me more than that of almost any officer whom I have met," said Welles. That same earnest manner also convinced Lincoln and the cabinet that General McClernand was, as Welles put it, "an impracticable and unfit man." It was clear to Welles that Grant wanted the president on his side in the matter. "In this I think . . . [Rawlins] has succeeded," said Welles, "though the president feels kindly toward McClernand, Grant evidently hates him, and Rawlins is imbued with the feelings of his chief."[88]

Rawlins had impressed the Washington high command, but they soon received word that other members of Grant's staff were less competent. The Vicksburg campaign afforded Charles Dana plenty of opportunities to see Grant's staff in action. After Vicksburg surrendered, Dana penned his impressions of Grant's staff in a lengthy letter to Edwin M. Stanton. Dana started with general comments. "Grant's staff is a curious mixture of good, bad, and indifferent." Dana also said that Grant was "neither an organizer nor a disciplinarian himself," and that "his staff is naturally a mosaic of accidental elements and family friends. It contains four working men, two who are able to accomplish their duties without much work, and several who either don't think of working or who accomplish nothing no matter what they undertake."

Dana then got specific. In the same letter in which he criticized Rawlins's writing skills, Dana also praised the man. "Rawlins . . . is a very industrious, conscientious man, who never loses a moment and never gives himself any indulgence except swearing and scolding." Dana reported that Rawlins had "a great influence over [Grant]," watching over the general "day and night." Dana also praised Rawlins's assistant, Theodore Bowers, as "an excellent man . . . [who] always finds work to do."

Dana was not so generous with the rest of Grant's staff. Lt. Colonel William L. Duff, the artillerist on Grant's special staff who supplied the general with whiskey, was "unequal to [his] position," in part because he was ill, but largely because "he does not sufficiently understand the management of artillery." According to Dana, the siege of Vicksburg suffered for his incompetence, but he noted that Grant's personality had shaped his staff. "General Grant knows that he [Duff] is not the right person; but it is one of his weaknesses that he is unwilling to hurt the feelings of a friend, so he keeps him on."

Dana reserved his harshest words for Grant's aides-de-camp. The three captains serving as aides were virtually useless, but the colonels in that position, namely Lagow and Riggin, were worse: "[Lagow] is a worthless, whisky drinking, useless fellow. [Riggin] is decent and gentlemanly, but neither of them is worth his salt so far as service to the government goes. Indeed, in all my observation, I have never discovered the use of Grant's aides-de-camp at all. On the battlefield he sometimes sends orders by them, but everywhere else they are idle loafers."

Dana closed with this observation: "If . . . Grant had about him a staff of thoroughly competent men . . . the efficiency and fighting quality of his army would soon be much increased. As it is, things go too much by hazard and by spasms; or when the pinch comes, Grant forces through, by his own energy and main strength, what proper organization and proper staff officers would have done already."[89]

Dana had verbalized what Rawlins, Rowley, and even Grant—although he was quiet about it—already knew. Grant had tried using his aides as his operational proxy at the battle of Iuka, and he had given them a variety of jobs including provost marshal, transportation boss, and liaison with other department commanders. Still, his early policy of giving staff jobs to friends and men who had been kind to him left him with an untrained staff that his tenderhearted loyalty prevented remedying. As Dana noted, Grant had accidentally brought aboard good men, such as Rawlins and Bowers, but in general, the staff was inefficient. An abundance of drinkers on the staff, perhaps the norm at most headquarters but a particular problem where Grant and Rawlins were concerned, only created tension and impeded work. Dana's criticisms of Grant's staff were correct, but by the close of the siege of Vicksburg, changes at Grant's headquarters were already underway.

CHAPTER SIX

⎯⎯⎯⎯⎯≫●≪⎯⎯⎯⎯⎯

Sherman: An Economical Staff

1862–1865

THROUGHOUT THE VICKSBURG CAMPAIGN, GRANT WAS GROPING TOWARD a personal staff with expanded duties. Not so his friend, Maj. Gen. William T. Sherman. Certainly Sherman valued a good personal staff, but he kept its duties traditional. At the height of his Civil War career, during the Georgia campaign in 1864, Sherman did much of his own staff work and kept his staff small. He simply had no use for a large personal staff. He relegated staffers to the more routine duties of copying and delivering orders, while he met frequently with his army commanders to personally relay his ideas and strategies. He trusted those commanders enough to allow them to carry out his plans in the best possible way, with no staff representative from headquarters along to guide them.

Sherman made no specific comments about staffs until he wrote his memoirs in 1875. Those comments, even though the antithesis of broader staff thought occurring in other countries at that time, accurately reflected his Civil War attitudes toward staffs. While Sherman did not codify his thoughts on staffs and their performance, observers can break them into three parts: a personal staff should be small; it should perform limited duties, and the chief of staff should not be preeminent at headquarters.

Sherman insisted that his staff remain small. "A bulky staff implies . . . slowness of action and indecision," he wrote, but a small staff equaled "activity and concentration of purpose."[1] The size of Sherman's personal staff varied little during the war, whether he was commanding a division at Shiloh or three armies at Atlanta, and he equally thought that division, corps, and army commanders should have staffs of similar size. "The great

123

*The reverse image of the handwriting at the top of this print reads "Sherman's staff,"
but neither the men in the photo nor the year it was taken are identified. The
number of men—six—does, however, accurately depict the average size of Sherman's
personal staff.* (NATIONAL ARCHIVES AND RECORDS ADMINISTRATION)

retinues of staff officers with which some of our earlier generals began the war were simply ridiculous," he said. After he began the Atlanta campaign he proudly commented that his staff was "small, but select."[2] Sherman's brief duty as a combat commander at the first battle of Bull Run in July 1861 and as a lonely commander of troops in Kentucky later that year, shed little light on his attitudes about staff work. Not until he became a division commander in Grant's Army of the Tennessee, in early 1862, did he begin to establish any pattern of staff usage. It would always be economical.

Indeed, he kept his staff small, and he never allowed his chiefs of staff to gain the prominence around headquarters that John Rawlins had at Grant's. Sherman thought chiefs of staff were redundant to his own position as general. "I don't believe in a chief of staff at all," Sherman later wrote in his memoirs, "and any general . . . that has a staff officer who professes to know more than his [commander] is to be pitied." Sherman's comments are far

Sherman, leaning on the breech of a gun, and members of his staff at Atlanta, 1864. Again, the staffers are not identified, but the majority must be from Sherman's special staff for he took only three personal staffers with him on the Atlanta campaign.
(LIBRARY OF CONGRESS)

removed from those of Antoine-Henri Jomini, who said, "Woe to an Army whose commanding general and chief of staff did not work in concert."[3]

Still, the men who became Sherman's chiefs of staff were quite competent within the limited latitude Sherman gave them. The first of them was John Henry Hammond, who started with Sherman as an assistant adjutant general with the rank of captain. In Sherman's limited staff, working as assistant adjutant general was, in a sense, starting at the top, for Sherman expected his adjutant to do the work of a chief of staff: "[The] adjutant general . . . [should be able to] comprehend the scope of operations, and to make verbally and in writing all the orders . . . necessary to carry into effect the views of his general, as well as to keep the returns and records."[4]

Hammond proved an able aide for Sherman. Charles Dana, while observing Grant's army in 1863, had plenty of time to watch Sherman as well. He commented that Hammond was a "restless Kentuckian." That must have set well with Sherman, whom Dana said would allow "no idlers" on his staff.[5]

Hammond had firmly established himself at Sherman's headquarters by the battle of Shiloh in April 1862, when Sherman commanded a division in Grant's army. As Grant massed troops at Pittsburg Landing, Tennessee, in March, to march on Corinth, Mississippi, Hammond helped Sherman set up camp around the nearby Shiloh Church. He issued orders placing the brigades of Sherman's First Division (he did not take command of the Fifth Division, which he commanded during the battle, until April 2) in position. Hammond alerted soldiers that the division was the lead element of Grant's army, and he cautioned that "each brigade must encamp looking west, so that when the regiments are on their regimental parades the brigades will be in line of battle." Grant—and, by implication, his subalterns—often receive blame for letting Confederates surprise them at Shiloh. But Hammond's orders, which Sherman originated, indicate that the Union commanders were aware of the possibility of attack. Later, after Sherman had taken over the Fifth Division, Hammond drafted instructions for regimental and brigade commanders in case of attack. They should, Hammond wrote, form up and await orders "in case of alarm," but "if attacked, the immediate commanders . . . must give the necessary orders for defenses." Hammond also issued another warning. In the spring of 1862, army uniforms were not necessarily "uniform," and Hammond ordered commanders to not allow troops to leave camp in anything but Federal blue. "[A] regiment today went out in gray flannel shirts," scolded Hammond, "which at a distance of 100 yards resembles the secession uniform. Commanders of regiments must never leave their camps for action unless their men wear the blue coat, jacket, or blouse."[6]

Quite literate and efficient at writing orders, Hammond was not just a headquarters clerk; he was in the thick of the fight at Shiloh, for Sherman's Fifth Division held the far right of Grant's line during the battle. The Confederate attack on April 6 was savage up and down the line, and at one point Sherman's end was in danger of collapse. Hammond rode from Sherman's headquarters to those of Maj. Gen. John A. McClernand, whose First Division was in line next to Sherman's division. Hammond warned McClernand that Confederates were "hovering" on his left. McClernand borrowed Hammond for a time, ordering him to bring up a battery of artillery, which promptly opened fire and knocked the Rebels back. McClernand later thanked Hammond for his "prompt and valuable assistance." Later in the day, back with Sherman, Hammond ordered a battery into position on the right of the line, then sent the 53rd Ohio Infantry to support the guns. Then, riding in search of ammunition, Hammond ordered the 43rd Illinois Infantry "advanced . . . double-quick" to the front. The regiment tried, but, depleted in numbers and ammunition, it had to stop.[7] Shiloh was a bloody scrap requiring the urgent action of all men on the field. That Hammond was quick to order individual regiments and batteries to crisis points was an exercise in coolness and common sense, not indicative of an expansion of Sherman's staff expectations. Hammond was doing what an observant soldier should have done.

At another point in the fight, Sherman and Hammond had a near miss. As Sherman mounted his horse, the animal began prancing, tangling the reins around its neck. Hammond gathered the reins and handed them up to Sherman. When Sherman bent down to grab them, a cannonball shot between the two men, clipping the reins and carrying away part of Sherman's hat.[8]

The other men of Sherman's staff—aides-de-camp J. C. McCoy, Lewis M. Dayton, and William D. Sanger—also got into the action. After holding off the Rebel attack for five hours, Sherman ordered his line to retreat. All of the staffers, including Hammond, rode about giving orders to fall back. Sherman praised his staff officers after the fight: "I think they smelt as much gunpowder and heard as many cannon balls and bullets as must satisfy their ambition," he said. "McCoy and Dayton . . . were with me all the time, and act[ed] with coolness, spirit, and courage."[9]

The emergency of Shiloh required action from all soldiers present; after the battle, though, Hammond's role at Sherman's headquarters returned to routine. His work, however, reveals much about the nature of Sherman's headquarters and the commander's own temperament. On April 30, with the Army of the Tennessee still poised in south-central Tennessee, Sherman detected a laxity of discipline in the ranks, and he had Hammond pen an order to correct it. "The officers and men of this division must now bear in mind that we are in an enemy's country; that at any moment we may be assailed, or be called upon to assail our enemy, or repair to the assistance of our friends," Hammond wrote. He cautioned that officers and men must stay in their regimental camps. "The habit of wandering must be stopped, and all must bear in mind that we are not here to satisfy our individual pleasure, but to maintain the honor and character of a great nation." Hammond wrote that soldiers must routinely clean their weapons and have them stacked in line of battle; that regimental and brigade commanders must drill their units daily; that all must keep themselves well versed on the manual of arms. He also issued a stern warning to men causing unrest in the camp. "When soldiers or teamsters are noisy or mutinous or abusive, any officer on the spot must summarily prevent it, by tying them up, and using such other means as he may think proper."[10]

After Maj. Gen. Henry Halleck had temporarily superseded Grant in direct command of the Army of the Tennessee and begun his march toward Corinth, Sherman made Hammond his first official chief of staff. Even though Sherman sent Hammond on an expedition with a detached brigade,[11] Hammond's duties changed very little. Sherman did, however, wisely use Hammond as a conduit to keep his division abreast of developments in the army and encouraged about its goals. After a spring of vigorous advances under Grant, the army was now plodding indecisively under Halleck. Rain and boggy roads further slowed their progress, and spirits in Sherman's division were sagging. As a result, Sherman had Hammond write a circular on May 5 that had the double effect of making soldiers feel privy to the plan at headquarters and letting them know what Sherman expected of them. "Our situation from the rain and roads has become difficult, and it becomes the duty of every officer and man to anticipate our danger and labor," Hammond wrote. "Every ounce of food and forage must be regarded as precious as diamonds. Roads will be impassable and our bridges swept away. General Halleck and our superior officers will do all they can, but their power is limited by nature. We must do our part in full." Hammond gave instructions for rations and foraging, then noted that "particular attention must be given at once to our roads and defenses. Let every ax and spade be busy." Hammond continued, "We cannot be assailed by artillery, because the enemy cannot haul it up; but we may be assailed by hordes of infantry, night or day, and therefore vigilance must be kept at all times, and any neglect promptly punished."[12]

Throughout the summer of 1862, Hammond wrote detailed orders for Sherman, and he became quite prolific. Still, one can always imagine Sherman's freewheeling, rapid-fire mind working just behind Hammond's pen. Sherman had in Hammond a perfect conduit for getting his thoughts to the troops, and many of the orders continued to deal with camp order and discipline. On May 15 Hammond issued new orders detailing the posting of pickets, and in early June he again addressed the question of vigilance. "The general commanding thinks he observes . . . a partial relaxation of that activity and vigilance which characterized his command on the march to Corinth," Hammond wrote. "The enemy's army has fled away and there is no seeming danger present; but this may not be the real truth, and we must always act on the supposition that the enemy will do his worst." Hammond gave detailed instructions for setting out guards on the march and in camp, for laying out defensively sound camps, and for placing artillery. He concluded by stressing the necessity of alert guards. "The commanding general has frequently found sentinels negligent, sitting down, or even asleep, and has invariably been told by the sentinel 'he did not know any better'; 'had never been told by his officer,' &c. This will never do. Every sentinel must know that at least he should be well armed and wide awake."[13]

Much of Hammond's work for Sherman involved writing marching orders. Other orders dealt with repairing railroads, forbidding theft, and limiting family access to troops at a new post in Memphis.[14] Throughout, Hammond's duties were clerical. That is not surprising, given that Sherman himself was concerned only with the smooth operation of a division. He had not yet ascended to army command, and was not yet concerned—officially—with the larger elements of strategy and its execution. Hammond's duties reflected the smaller scope of Sherman's headquarters.

Hammond remained Sherman's chief in late 1862 as the general prepared for the Mississippi River phase of Grant's first attempt to take Vicksburg—the same campaign what would carry Sherman to defeat at Chickasaw Bayou on December 29. Even though the campaign marked his first large-scale independent command, Sherman made no substantive changes in the operation of his staff. Staffers McCoy and Dayton continued to back up Hammond as aides-de-camp. Sherman did not expand the duties of the staff officers, but continued to use them in an economical fashion.

As mentioned in a previous chapter, the campaign began in secrecy. Sherman had been commanding the Memphis district of Grant's army for some weeks, building fortifications and anticipating some action. He had Hammond issue orders organizing troops and alerting them to "prepare at once for field service" as early as November 12.[15] Still, Sherman did not know Grant's specific wishes until December 8, after he had already moved troops to join Grant's main body.

Countermarching to Memphis, Sherman and his staff quickly began rounding up the 40,000 troops there and integrating them into his XIII Corps—essentially the right wing of the Army of the Tennessee—for the expedition. On December 13 Hammond issued, at Sherman's instruction, General Orders No. 6, assigning division commands. Brig. Gen. A. J. Smith received the First Division, which would constitute the force's right wing; Brig. Gen. Morgan L. Smith got the Second Division, the army's center; and Brig. Gen. George W. Morgan took the Third Division, on the army's left. In the same orders, Hammond told troops to ready their gear, saying, "each soldier must carry his musket, 60 rounds of ammunition, knapsack, haversack, and canteen, and nothing else." Unit quartermasters would see that other necessary gear arrived at the front.[16]

Five days later, on December 18, Hammond penned for Sherman orders that briefed the infantry troops on proper conduct during an amphibious operation. Hammond explained the flag markings for boats carrying division and brigade commanders; briefed inexperienced privates on steamboat signals ("to hail a boat, five whistles; to land a boat, three whistles"); and cautioned the men to avoid the rowdiness that undoubtedly accompanied any body of soldiers cooped up on a small vessel for any amount of time. "All firing of guns, pistols, yelling or hallooing, or improper noises must be prevented. These are all false signals and mislead the commanders. A single gun from the flag-boat will be the signal for starting or closing up. . . . Three guns fired in rapid succession will be the signal for danger."[17]

By December 22 Sherman had his expedition aboard steamboats that Adm. David D. Porter had brought down from Cairo, Illinois. They left Memphis just a few beats ahead of McClernand, who had, indeed, realized he had been done in.[18]

Sherman established his headquarters on the steamer *Forest Queen*. There, on December 22 Hammond issued Special Orders No. 31, formalizing command of the expedition's divisions, which now numbered four, command of the last one going to Brig. Gen. Fred Steele. Hammond also made regimental boat assignments, with regiments occupying such boats as *War Eagle, Gladiator, Meteor,* and *Polar Star.*[19]

As the expedition entered the Yazoo River, from which troops would assail the Confederate high ground at Chickasaw Bluffs guarding Vicksburg, Hammond continued a flurry of writing that prepared troops for the coming land campaign. He wrote detailed marching orders, adding a cautionary note. "In case any men reach or are sent to the river at any point where they may encounter a gunboat, they must be carefully instructed to show the United States flag and two white handkerchiefs or cloths, on each side of the flag. This is the signal agreed on by myself and the admiral by which our troops can be distinguished from the rebels, who sometimes display our flag and wear our clothes."[20]

Despite its urgency and volume, Hammond's work on the way down the Mississippi was only traditional, routine staff work. Sherman did not use him to communicate any broad strategy or expectations to his division commanders. Of course, the expedition was small, and Sherman did not necessarily need a middleman. But Sherman was an able communicator, and on this trip he began a warlong tradition of communicating directly with his subcommanders before an engagement. He was retaining a prime function of a staff officer for himself.

On December 23 he sent each division commander a memo with a map of the projected campaign area that was, he said, "compiled from the best sources" and which was "the same used by Admiral Porter and myself." Sherman explained the current Confederate positions along the river—the Union holding it from the north to near Vicksburg; the Confederacy from Vicksburg to Baton Rouge. He commented that General Nathaniel Banks was working on the river from Louisiana. He also explained that their own expedition was part of a larger plan, which included Grant approaching Vicksburg overland from the northeast.

"Vicksburg is doubtless very strongly fortified both against the river and land approaches," Sherman wrote. He then laid out his broad expectations for the campaign.

> Before any actual collision with the enemy I propose, after assembling our whole land force at Gaines Landing, Ark., to proceed in order to Milliken's Bend and there dispatch a brigade without wagons or any encumbrances whatever to the Vicksburg and Shreveport Railroad to destroy that effectually and cut off that fruitful avenue of supply; then to proceed to the mouth of the Yazoo, and after possessing ourselves of the latest and most authentic information from the naval officers now there [the navy held the river about twenty-three miles ahead of the *Forest Queen*], to land our whole force on the Mississippi side and then reach the point where the Vicksburg and Jackson Railroad crosses the Big Black, after which to attack Vicksburg by land while the gunboats assail it by water.

Sherman relayed his wishes broadly. "The detailed manner of accomplishing these results will be communicated in due season," he said, "and these general points are only made known at this time that commanders may study the maps, and also that, in the event of non-receipt of orders, all may act in perfect concert by following the general movement."[21]

That memo is one of the best examples in the war of Sherman acting as his own chief of staff. In Europe, chiefs of staff might have been "partners" with their assigned commanders, imparting the thoughts, plans, and wishes of a general staff as a campaign progressed; but there was no need for such an intermediary in Sherman's army on the Mississippi—he could do the work himself. His official chief, Hammond, and his aides-de-camp had plenty of nuts-and-bolts work to do. Sherman, ever economical, saw no need to add staffers simply to liaison with field commanders. The pattern set, it was a job Sherman never relinquished, whether commanding a corps at Milliken's Bend or three armies in Georgia.

Sherman threw his troops at the bluffs on Chickasaw Bayou on December 29, and they met with resounding defeat. A smaller, yet well-positioned Confederate force inflicted about 1,700 casualties on Sherman's army, 208 of those killed. Sherman broke off the assault, and on December 30 and 31 he had Hammond issue orders keeping his troops vigilant and prepared for action. By January 3, however, Sherman knew he couldn't take the bluffs and was ready to depart.[22]

Sherman privately believed that he could have won at Chickasaw Bluffs had one of his division commanders, George Morgan, moved with more alacrity. Publicly, however, he shouldered the blame. He also sought a way to redeem his expedition and earn an independent victory for himself. Consulting with Porter, Sherman determined to sail up the Mississippi River about 125 miles, then turn into the Arkansas River and destroy a 5,000-man Confederate garrison called Arkansas Post. The men reasoned that, although it was small, the post could deter any future Union drive down the Mississippi.[23]

Sherman was delighted at the prospect of a redemptive campaign, but his enthusiasm dimmed even before he sailed out of the Yazoo when he learned that McClernand was on the river waiting to take over the expeditionary force. Sherman believed that his defeat at Chickasaw Bluffs was in part due to an influx of Confederates whom Grant had been driving back on his interior campaign. It had been McClernand who told him that Grant had been forced to pull back when Confederate raiders cut his supply lines at Holly Springs. McClernand had no doubt taken pleasure in relaying the news, for he knew that Grant and Sherman had schemed, albeit within legal channels, to take away his independent command.[24]

McClernand further irritated Sherman—not only did he take command of the force, but he also renamed it the Army of the Mississippi, broke it away from Grant's control, and made Sherman one of two corps commanders. On January 5, writing from the *Forest Queen*, Hammond issued a terse order listing Sherman as commander of the Second Corps, Army of the Mississippi.[25]

Sherman was not one to be insubordinate, and he endeavored to work with McClernand. He also sold the politician-general on the Arkansas Post plan. The river fleet reached a point three miles away from the post on January 9 and began disembarking from the boats. The next day Sherman, with Hammond riding at this side, led his corps overland in an attempt to stretch out his divisions and ring off the fort from above. Riding with Fred Steele's First Division, Sherman used black guides and gathered information from captured Confederates and some civilians. The men had already slogged through two miles of swamp, and their informants told them that they could not easily reach the fort—a distance of only two miles—without circuitously marching another seven. Sherman immediately saw the futility of the original plan, and he dispatched Hammond to tell McClernand the situation. Hammond crossed and recrossed the swamps, returning with McClernand to Sherman's and Steele's position. McClernand saw for himself that to push Steele any further would be to effectively take him out of the fight. He ordered Sherman to have Steele countermarch to the main body of the attack force, which was anchored on the Arkansas. Sherman rode ahead with McClernand and Brig. Gen. David Stuart's Second Division, which was within one-half mile of the fort. There they began preparing for the assault.[26]

Porter's gunboats opened the assault on the night of the tenth with what Sherman described as a "furious attack." Sherman stayed close to the garrison, listening to Confederates make last-minute defenses. "We became convinced [the enemy] was resolved on a determined resistance," said Sherman. During the next day's infantry assault, Sherman sent his staff to the rear, opting to go into the fray alone. Hammond, however, did not stay out of the fight. In his official report of the action, division commander Brig. Gen. A. J. Smith thanked Hammond, who "was near me during the latter part of the day and rendered important services." Smith, however, did not describe those services. The expedition captured the fort with little loss.[27]

McClernand's independent command on the Mississippi was short-lived. Grant soon arrived and took over, restoring Sherman's command in the Army of the Tennessee and giving McClernand a command as well. Then Grant settled into the "experiment" phase of his campaign to take Vicksburg.

Staff work at Sherman's headquarters, even during a combat expedition, had never ranged far from routine, and now, in winter and early spring 1863, things were little different. On February 6, writing from XV Corps headquarters "before Vicksburg," Hammond issued orders detailing part of Fred Steele's division to service on gunboats. Troops were occupied digging the canals that might alter the course of the Mississippi and deny Vicksburg its strategic strength. (Those were the experiments in which Grant had little faith, but which he rightly saw as a diversion until he could mount an effective spring campaign.) On February 8 Hammond issued specific orders for such work. "Each division of this corps will furnish a daily detail of 500 men to work on the canal, relief to be at the discretion of the division commander."[28]

As the canal projects proceeded, Sherman's camp was threatened with flooding, and Hammond, in early March, prepared the corps to move. "Our camps being threatened with overflow," he wrote, "preparations must be made to meet such an event. The water will enter the swamps to the rear of our camps, and will fill up the ditches and over the fields, until the . . . water inside is about eighteen inches below the level of the water outside." Hammond detailed the future positions of the divisions, then added that "these general instructions are now given, but the troops need not vacate their present camps till their respective division or brigade commanders think they are in danger, but all possible preparations will be made in advance."[29]

While the staff work at Sherman's corps headquarters was routine, it was plentiful enough to busy Hammond plus two other able staffers, assistant adjutants general Lewis M. Dayton and Roswell M. Sawyer. Dayton spent much of his time writing marching orders and announcing assignments to command. At one point he informed Gen. David Stuart that some of his men were going on what would be less-than-glorious duty. "Stuart . . . will detail from his command 1,000 men to report, with shovels and spades, . . . [to the] chief of engineers." They would board steamers and receive instructions, but obviously they were going to work on one of Grant's canal experiments. The detail would be continued daily until further orders.[30]

The canal digging lasted only until Grant began his real Vicksburg campaign on April 16, 1863. That night he began sending supply barges and steamboats past the Vicksburg river defenses, planning to send troops south down the opposite bank. When the infantry was ready to march, Grant instructed Sherman to make a demonstration toward Haines Bluff, near the old Chickasaw Bluffs battlefield, and detract attention from Grant's main invasion of Mississippi farther south.

Sherman was game, and he intended to make a great show of it. He decided to make the ten regiments of division commander, Gen. Frank Blair, seem as numerous as possible by marching them repeatedly across the same terrain—all conveniently within site of the enemy—in a tactic reminiscent of Confederate general John B. Magruder's on the Virginia Peninsula the previous spring. Sherman had Roswell Sawyer issue marching orders to the division commanders. Sawyer noted that "although there be no intention to make an attack on Haynes' [sic] Bluff, or, indeed to disembark the troops, all preparations should be made to take advantage of any opportunity afforded by events."[31] Sawyer's comment about not disembarking the troops shows the extent to which Sherman, not a staffer, relayed his final wishes to commanders.

Still, with action imminent, Sherman retained his earlier form of staff work. He kept his staff functioning at a minimal level, attending to the ever-present clerical duties at headquarters, while he personally communicated broad ideas of tactics and strategy to his division commanders. Indeed, communications bearing the signatures of Sherman's staffers fall to a low ebb at this point in the Vicksburg campaign. On April 28 Sherman penned a memo to Fred Steele in which he reveals the classic Sherman—thinking out loud, explaining intentions, asking for thoughts and recommendations.

> We must do all that is possible to make the enemy believe that the movement is a real attack, though it would be bad management to attempt a lodgment here and at Grand Gulf [Mississippi, where Grant intended to cross the river], as the enemy could fall on one or the other.
>
> If, by a diversion at Haynes' [sic] we enable General Grant to make a safe foothold at the mouth of the Big Black, he can then renew our old plan by moving on the Jackson road, and then we should make a real attack on Haynes', but until we know that Grant has secured a base at Grand Gulf, it would be bad war for us to make a foothold on the Yazoo. We should hold our forces in reserve to re-enforce Grant, or to operate after we know that Grant is able and intends to move inland from Grand Gulf.[32]

Sherman never had a problem letting his limited staff handle the clerical duties that cluttered warfare. But when the business of war turned to battle itself, Sherman wanted to communicate man-to-man with his subordinates. In so doing, Sherman revealed a double measure of trust—first in himself, then, in his division commanders. That trust is something he carried throughout the war, and it served to significantly limit the duties of his staffers.

Sherman's feint toward Haines Bluff was successful, so much so that some Confederate defenders considered Sherman's the main attack, and the movement they detected to the south at Grand Gulf merely a feint. Grant then ordered Sherman to break off the diversion, and soon Sherman and the XV Corps were at Grand Gulf themselves, then moving deep into Mississippi behind Grant. Roswell Sawyer continued to write detailed marching orders to facilitate the move, and Sherman stayed in close contact with his division commanders.[33]

Staff communiqués during the actual combat from Grand Gulf to Vicksburg are minimal. Indeed, staff activity is hard to trace until the XV Corps pulled into the siege lines around Vicksburg with the rest of Grant's army. On May 26 adjutant Lewis M. Dayton drafted orders for Sherman's corps, warning troops to be ever watchful. Several Confederate deserters had reported that "an attempt was to have been made . . . by the enemy to cut their way out; that the signals were given but the men failed to respond. . . . The general commanding directs that the utmost vigilance be exercised by the troops along our front to prevent the enemy succeeding, should they contemplate a like attempt to night."[34]

As the siege of Vicksburg dragged through June, staff work at Sherman's headquarters remained devoted to detailing troop positions encouraging the troops. In General Orders No. 44, June 9, 1863, adjutant Sawyer drafted a set of orders to "prevent communication between the enemy, now closely invested in Vicksburg, and their friends and adherents without." The orders have a detailed quality about them that other similar orders had not. "A continuous chain of sentinels must extend from the Mississippi River to the main Jackson road, along our front trenches," wrote Sawyer. "These sentinels will act as sharpshooters or pickets, and must be posted daily, and be instructed that no human being must pass into or out of Vicksburg, unless on strictly military duty, or as prisoners." Sawyers listed no fewer than ten points making dispositions that extended down to the regimental level. He concluded with the encouraging note, "The magnificent task assigned to this army should inspire every officer and soldier to sacrifice everything of comfort and ease, or pleasure to the one sole object, 'success,' now apparently within our grasp. A little more hard work, great vigilance, and a short struggle, and Vicksburg is ours."[35] The orders, of course, originated with Sherman, and they bear his same minute attention to detail. They also have much in common with the circular he had Hammond distribute to troops on the march to Corinth in

1862. Perhaps Sherman was allowing his staffers more room to communicate with subalterns in his stead. If so, it was an experiment that did not last.

On June 26 aide-de-camp Lewis M. Dayton penned equally detailed orders, adjusting elements of the line and encouraging officers and men to remain vigilant. The document manifests an underlying desire to see the siege end, and at the close of the orders Dayton added his own hint of encouragement embedded in a call for watchfulness. "The vast importance of events, now drawing to some conclusion, bids us guard against supposed combinations of the enemy rather than mere appearances. If [Confederate general Joseph E.] Johnston [who was hovering to the east between Vicksburg and Jackson—a possible threat to Grant's rear] attempts to relieve Vicksburg, which he is impelled to do by honor and the clamor of the Southern public, he will feign at many points, but attack with vehemence at some one. Let him appear at any point, he must be fought desperately."[36]

Montgomery Rochester, who had come aboard Sherman's staff as an assistant adjutant general, the same day issued a brief memo to Col. John Sanborn, brigade commander. It has in common with Dayton's writing the need for vigilance. "You will have your command in line under arms at 3:30 tomorrow morning, and remain so until 6 A.M., . . . In case of attack, the battle-cry will be 'Logan'."[37]

Sherman's worries of a Confederate breakout, or that Joe Johnston might stage a counterattack, were ultimately unfounded. No serious breakout came, and neither did Johnston. As Dayton had noted, the siege was drawing to a conclusion, and Grant and Sherman were making plans to execute after the fall of Vicksburg.

Even though Johnston was not making a move to relieve John C. Pemberton's trapped Rebels in Vicksburg, he was still a threat to Grant's army. As soon as the siege ended, Grant wanted Sherman to take a command on a rapid march east to Jackson and tackle Johnston. Sherman was to take his own XV Corps, Gen. E. O. C. Ord's XIII Corps, and the IX Corps under Gen. John G. Parke, collectively renamed the Expedition Army for the assignment. On July 4, the very day Pemberton surrendered Vicksburg, Roswell Sawyer wrote orders for the movement. "The moment Vicksburg surrenders and the investing army is relieved from the trenches . . . a movement will be made inland." He designated the routes of march for the various corps, and he made sure that commanders provided plenty of rations, ammunition, and water for the mission.[38]

The Expedition Army moved out from Vicksburg on July 6, pushing elements of Johnston's army before them. It was not a hard task, for

Johnston had no intention of fighting and Sherman knew it. Johnston instead had in mind a retreat to rebuilt fortifications at Jackson. As he neared Jackson, Sherman allowed his men to rush forward and pepper Johnston, but he stopped short of allowing a frontal assault. He had seen them fail both at Chickasaw Bluffs and at Vicksburg, so he opted for a bombardment and three-sided investiture of Jackson. The assault was successful, and on July 17 Johnston quit the place, recognizing the futile situation. The Expedition Army took Jackson.[39]

As the siege of Vicksburg had ended and the Jackson expedition approached, staff work at Sherman's headquarters picked up. Sawyer handled most of it. On July 6 he issued the marching orders that put the expedition on its way. He adjusted the columns as they marched, laid out positions as the army ringed Jackson, and, on July 17, issued orders that sent the army into the city.[40]

But again, the orders varied little from traditional staff work. The men were quite prolific order writers when the situation required, but Sherman held the privilege of personally communicating his ideas of broad strategy to his corps commanders. On July 8 Sawyer even drafted instructions ordering all corps commanders to meet with Sherman for a briefing. Sherman also kept in touch with his corps commanders through periodic memos.[41] If Sherman had allowed his staffers a larger measure of direct communication with subalterns during the Vicksburg siege, he reverted to his original scheme of staff work when he went on the march. Sherman's view of such work, of course, was not wrong—it was merely traditional and economical.

If Sawyer was doing most of the pen work around Sherman's headquarters in June and July 1863, it was because Sherman's chief, John Henry Hammond, was taking a more active combat role. On June 18, during the siege of Vicksburg, Hammond, then a major, engaged in a stirring cavalry fight at Birdsong (alternately known as Jones's) Ferry on the Big Black River. Hammond was still on Sherman's staff, and in his report of the affair he did not say why he was at the ferry and not at headquarters. Perhaps he was inspecting the lines of the army, for he introduced his report by saying, "I this morning started for [Birdsong] Ferry, distant 12 miles; good road, but hilly." Hammond was at the river crossing with a Maj. Cornelius Spearman and a company of Union cavalry, when about 120 Confederates, wielding carbines, rushed from a nearby swamp and attacked an advance party of about twenty-five cavalrymen. A fight erupted, and Spearman ordered a charge by the main body of cavalry, then concealed on the enemy's right. The sudden rush surprised the Rebels, who began to retreat. The cavalry—and Hammond—pursued, but a gully prevented many from hounding the enemy. Hammond's horse fell in the charge; Hammond hit the ground and was run over. The cavalrymen dismounted and chased the Confederates into a stand of timber. Discovering the enemy gone, they remounted and pursued them to within thirteen miles of Mechanicsburg, Mississippi, only to find the raiders scattered. Upon returning to the site of the skirmish, Hammond ordered the corn at two local farms burned, "as it was evidently used for hostile purposes."[42]

The end of Hammond's report sounds as if he was scouting enemy positions and topographical features. "Last Wednesday 200 Rebel cavalry . . . passed Big Black River at Birdsong Ford, yesterday 27. There is a regular picket stand at the ford. . . . There are three other fords above Big Black Bridge."[43]

Regardless of Hammond's original assignment at Birdsong Ferry, a few weeks later, on July 8, he was in a similar fight with a detachment of cavalry as Sherman's Expedition Army moved toward Jackson. Hammond, although officially still on Sherman's staff, was now a lieutenant colonel and had command of a company in the Fifth Illinois Cavalry. As a combined cavalry force neared Clinton, Mississippi, they discovered a strong force of Confederates from a General Whitefield's brigade in a wooded area and behind a fence. The Cavalry commander Col. Cyrus Bussey detached a company from the Third Iowa Cavalry and Hammond's company to flank the enemy, while a third column moved toward the Rebel center. Hammond reached a suitable spot, then ordered his men to open fire. The Confederates returned fire while Hammond's men dismantled a fence in their way. Soon, the combined force drove the Confederates from the fields. Hammond and others pursued, but they broke off the chase when darkness fell. At the conclusion of his report, which chronicled several days' activities, Bussey wrote, "Justice requires that I acknowledge the important service rendered me by Lieut. Col. J. H. Hammond, assistant adjutant general on the staff of General Sherman."[44]

Hammond's position with Sherman was obviously changing, and soon he would no longer serve the general. When Sherman took over command of the Army of the Tennessee at Grant's promotion to command the Division of the Mississippi, Hammond stayed at XV Corps headquarters to serve Maj. Gen. John Logan, first as assistant adjutant general, then as chief of staff.[45]

Sherman found an able replacement for Hammond in adjutant Roswell Sawyer. Throughout the siege of Vicksburg, Sawyer had proven himself a capable staff officer, writing special and general orders. His duties might have been mundane, but he performed them to Sherman's satisfaction. Ultimately, Sherman would make Sawyer his chief of staff.[46]

While Sawyer was doing capable work at headquarters, a new staffer, Joseph C. Audenried, was quickly becoming a Sherman favorite. Sherman would later say that Audenried, who was round of face and sported a neatly waxed moustache, was "one of the most polished gentlemen in the army, noted for his personal bearing and deportment." Sherman had met Audenried during the first Bull Run campaign of July 1861. Sherman, then a colonel, commanded a brigade in Brig. Gen. Daniel Tyler's division of the Army of Northeast Virginia. Lieutenant Audenried was on Tyler's personal staff. Audenried served briefly on Ulysses S. Grant's staff in 1863, and he served as something of a liaison between Grant and Sherman while the latter directed the expedition army toward Jackson. By October 1863 Audenried was an aide-de-camp on Sherman's staff. Over time, Sherman became close friends with Audenried and the staff officer's entire family. Long after the war, in fact, when Audenried was dead, Sherman had a flirtation—if not a full-fledged affair—with his widow.[47]

A rare photo of one of Sherman's favorite aides, Col. Joseph C. Audenried. Audenried joined Sherman's personal staff in 1863 and completed many special assignments for the general.
(National Archives and Records Administration)

After Grant's victory at Vicksburg, and against his wishes, the War Department ordered the Army of the Tennessee broken up and its pieces placed on garrison duty in Mississippi. The order miffed Grant and infuriated Sherman, but both men obeyed, albeit reluctantly. Grant proceeded to New Orleans to inspect troops, and there he suffered a leg injury in a horse accident. Meanwhile, although he did not officially assume temporary command, Sherman acted in Grant's stead with the Army of the Tennessee, basing his headquarters at the Big Black River near Vicksburg.

Earlier in the summer, Union major general William S. Rosecrans had maneuvered Confederate general Braxton Bragg's army out of central Tennessee and into northern Georgia. But Bragg staged a counterattack and defeated Rosecrans at the Battle of Chickamauga, September 19–20, 1863, and pursued Rosecrans's army back to Chattanooga, Tennessee, besieging it there. The crisis stirred the War Department, and General in Chief Halleck ordered Grant to move troops east from Memphis to threaten Bragg. Grant, in bed nursing his injuries, could not lead such an expedition, but Sherman could and Grant drafted orders for him to do so.

Sherman immediately prepared to move from Vicksburg to Memphis, then head east with his XV Corps. On the river trip, Sherman suffered a grave personal tragedy. In the lull after Vicksburg, he had brought his wife, Ellen, and their children to visit. But now his nine-year-old son, Willy, had contracted typhoid fever. At Memphis, Sherman ensconced the family in a hotel and brought doctors to care for Willy, but within a day he had died. Sherman, grief-stricken, could do no more than send his family home to Ohio, while he continued to build his expedition.[48]

Sherman threw himself even more deeply into his work to help ease the pain over his son's death. Roswell Sawyer, Sherman's chief of staff, was also central to the preparations, quickly drafting orders to facilitate the move. Back in Vicksburg, on September 22, Sawyer had begun writing orders of march to take most of the corps to Memphis. (Sherman had received orders from Grant's chief of staff, John Rawlins, to leave the remainder of the corps under command of Maj. Gen. James B. McPherson to cover the country between Vicksburg and the Yazoo River.) Between then and October 16, by which time Sherman's column had reached Corinth, Mississippi, Sawyer drafted eight sets of special and general orders, as well as compiled lists of Sherman's units and their placement. At all times, Sawyer's work remained clerical and never involved any direct communication of strategic ideas to division commanders. As usual, Sherman handled that himself.[49]

When Sherman and his staffers boarded a train east out of Memphis to begin the expedition, Joseph C. Audenried got his first taste of battle with the general, and he literally lost his shirt. Sherman, some staffers (although the record is unclear if all the staff officers went along, or if Sherman left some with the main body of infantry), and a guard of 600 men from the 13th U.S. Infantry, left for Corinth, which sat immediately south of the Tennessee line on the most direct railroad to Chattanooga. The train passed Colliersville, Tennessee, then stopped suddenly in the face of about 8,000 Confederate militiamen attempting to cut the line. The men of the 13th detrained to offer a fight, and Sherman ordered the train back to fortifications at Colliersville. Before Rebels could cut the telegraph line, Sherman got word back to the Fourth Division to hurry to the detachment's aid.

The Rebels initially drove in the pickets of a Colonel Anthony's 66th Indiana Infantry. Sherman was personally ordering the Regulars off the train when a Confederate rider with a flag of truce approached Anthony. Sherman staffer Lewis Dayton was with Anthony, and he hurriedly rode back to the train. The Confederates, commanded by a General Chalmers, had demanded the little detachment's surrender. "I instructed [Dayton] to demand an emphatic negation, and at once made preparations to resist the attack," wrote Sherman.

The men of the 13th got on high ground above the tracks and kept the Confederates from inflicting serious damage on the train, but they were unable to prevent individual Rebels from looting its rear baggage area and attempting to fire it. While trying to start a blaze, they used some of Audenried's clean shirts, and at one point they stole one of Sherman's uniforms and one of his horses. Help from the Fourth Division, four hours later, finally drove away the Confederates. After the engagement, Colonel Anthony wrote, "I am greatly indebted to Major General Sherman for his valuable advice during the engagement . . . [and to] Captains [H. S.] Fitch [provost marshal] and Dayton (of General Sherman's staff) for their action and aid."[50]

In Audenried, Sherman had brought to his staff a former Grant staff officer; now Sherman was also working closely with another of Grant's old aides, who also would soon be on Sherman's staff. Brig. Gen. Joseph Dana Webster, the "old soldier of decided merit" who had so ably helped Grant place artillery at Shiloh, was in Tennessee now directing the repair of rail lines and helping construct new ones for Federal movements.

After leaving Grant's personal staff, Webster had become superintendent of military railroads in Tennessee. At the same time Sherman prepared to leave with his expedition from Memphis and received orders from the ever-cautious Halleck to repair railroads in Union-occupied portions of the state. Thus Webster came under Sherman's ostensible command. Webster had, in fact, been in command of the left wing of Maj. Gen. Stephen A. Hurlbut's XVI Army Corps. Hurlbut made the assignment on September 1, but revoked it on September 3, giving the command instead to Brig. Gen. E. A. Carr. Hurlbut gave no reason for the revocation, but Webster remained supervisor of the railroads.[51]

On October 2 Hurlbut instructed Webster to prepare "material for reconstruction of the Memphis and Charleston Railroad to Decatur." The next day, when orders came from Hurlbut's corps headquarters that the division of Brig. Gen. John E. Smith was to move quickly by rail to the east, Hurlbut told Webster to "give every facility for this movement."[52]

With Confederate raiders always eager to cut Union lines of communication, any extension of the Union presence east of Memphis implied difficulty protecting the rails. Rightly fearing the safety of his workers, Webster asked Carr for a guard to protect them. Carr forwarded the request to Hurlbut, adding, "It will require a brigade to take and hold the crossing of the Big Bear . . . in order to repair the bridge." Sherman himself was on the Bear Creek, and he worried about it as well. A week later he wrote to Grant, "My own opinion is that we will have to rely on the Tennessee River or reopen the road from Corinth to Columbus. I have advised General Webster at once to look to that road, for it is certain this one from Memphis will be cut the moment I get east of Bear Creek."[53]

Soon, however, Webster was worrying about more than just repairing rail lines—he was concerned with moving troops and supplies over them as well. In truth, Webster was beginning to act as a de facto Sherman staff officer. Sherman warned Webster not to allow private citizens to travel the rails: They "betray us," he said. He also said that, at least for the time being, the railroad would be safe, and he ordered Webster to push as much forage and provisions ahead as possible. "And don't let any fancy freight come out till all forage and provisions are sent. Tomorrow I will organize working parties, so trains will be unloaded at night. Do the same there. Delay only consumes our stock on hand." Regardless of what he was doing, Sherman advocated quick movements. He did not like long waits during a campaign, believing them detrimental to any army.[54]

Webster was soon staging trains to run units to the developing front to the east. On October 15 Sherman notified Webster that two more regiments were to be in Colliersville the next day. "Have a train bring them to Corinth," ordered Sherman. "They will number, say, 500." Webster's reply shows that he did not have—or at least *believed* he did not have—full latitude in making decisions. "An extra is waiting at Colliersville in accordance with your telegram of yesterday. . . . There is an ambulance train at Colliersville asking for transportation to LaGrange [Tennessee] with twenty wounded men and thirty mules. Shall I ship them?" Webster did not fully understand whether shipping wounded men across the line would be legitimate use of the rails in Sherman's mind. Also, he had word that the two regiments to which Sherman had earlier referred would not be in, and the train could be used for the wounded. In a subsequent telegram, Sherman gave Webster the authority he needed to fully do his job. "Use the train for any purpose, and be ready to send the two regiments to Iuka the moment they reach the road."[55] The two may not have known it, but they were forming a working relationship that would carry them through Sherman's campaigns of 1864 and 1865.

On October 24, still pushing slowly east and trying to supervise railroad repairs as he went, Sherman received word that his friend Grant had been made commander of the new Division of the Mississippi—the combined armies of the Tennessee, the Ohio, and the Cumberland (which was now bottled up in Chattanooga). Sherman was to take over the Army of the Tennessee, now commanding not only his old XV Corps, but Hurlbut's XVI at Memphis and McPherson's XVII at Vicksburg.[56]

Sherman's staff grew to its largest at this point. His staff officers included the veterans Sawyer, McCoy, Dayton, Rochester, plus Audenried, John M. Corse, Willard Warner, Charles Ewing, William McKee Dunn (who later served on Grant's staff), and William D. Sanger. The men remained primarily clerks and couriers.[57]

That staff now jumped from running an army corps to a full army. Sherman faced essentially the same staff and command challenges that Grant had faced when his Army of the Tennessee had begun to grow in late 1862, and he found himself commanding scattered units. Ultimately Sherman did not make the same conclusions about staff work that Grant did. He continued to use them very little, choosing to use himself as his own top staff officer in communicating matters of strategy and tactics, trusting his subordinate commanders to carry out his orders without staff assistance from headquarters.

Sherman's first act as commander of the army was to make his lead assistant adjutant, Sawyer, his chief of staff, though Sawyer's duties changed little with his promotion. One of Sawyer's first acts was to pen General Orders No. 2 (No. 1 had been his own promotion to chief, which Sherman had written), which officially listed the subdivisions of Sherman's army and his expectations of commanders and troops. Hurlbut retained command of the XVI Corps; McPherson the XVII, and Maj. Gen. Frank

Blair took over the XV from Sherman. Blair's assignment was temporary, however; Maj. Gen. John Logan superseded him as corps commander on October 28, per orders from Grant. Writing for Sherman, of course, Sawyer ordered corps commanders to establish garrisons at fortified positions within their districts, then ready brigades and divisions for "offensive operations."

Sawyer reminded the corps commanders that, situated as they were in occupied areas of the Confederacy, they had more to think about than simply preparing for battle—they were, in effect, the top authority in a martial government. "All officers in command of corps and of fixed military posts will assume the very highest powers allowed by the laws of war and Congress," Sawyer wrote. "They must maintain the best possible discipline, and repress all disorders, alarms, and dangers in their reach." He called on the commanders to render assistance to any citizens cooperating with Union troops. But in areas "infested by guerrillas or held by the enemy, horses, mules, wagons, corn, forage, &c., are all means of war, and can be freely taken, but must be accounted for as public property. If the people do not want their [property] taken, they must organize and repress all guerrilla or hostile bands in their neighborhood." The same day he wrote those detailed instructions, Sawyer drafted orders bringing units of the various corps further east into Tennessee.[58]

Sawyer's work remained clerical; Sherman kept personal communications with commanders for himself. On October 25 he got up early to write Hurlbut in Memphis on what he called "some points." He explained that "it is now manifest that the 'powers that be' want the mass of available troops over toward Huntsville, and the only question is how to get them there, and feed them when there." Sherman noted that the Tennessee River was fine for navigation as far as Florence, Tennessee. "Thence we must haul." Tired of trying to repair railroads simultaneously with troop movements, he said, "the railroad must gradually take care of itself, for it is manifest that every soldier on our rolls will be needed till the draft comes." He concluded with an assessment of the army's new role: "The corps remain as hitherto . . . commanders the same, and we only point east now instead of south."[59]

Sherman's comment bore a trace of disgust with Halleck and the War Department for ordering the Army of the Tennessee scattered, rather than allowing it to campaign toward Mobile, Alabama, as Grant had suggested. Such a move would have threatened Bragg's rear and perhaps prevented the current siege at Chattanooga.[60] Nevertheless, the army would soon be in a full-fledged campaign to raise the siege. On October 27 Sherman received

word from Grant, who was in Chattanooga and had already opened a supply line to the besieged Federals. Grant was ready to force Bragg from natural defenses south and east of the town, which included such topographic
formations as Lookout Mountain and Missionary Ridge. Sherman and his
staffers immediately went to work. On October 30 Sawyer drafted Special
Orders No. 5, which ordered the XV Corps and Brig. Gen. Grenville M.
Dodge's division of the XVI Corps to march "with as much expedition as
possible," pursuant to Grant's orders.[61]

Dodge would become a close friend and confidant of Sherman during
and after the war. In his memoirs, Dodge verifies what the *Official Records*

*Gen. Grenville M. Dodge,
division commander in Sherman's
Georgia invasion force. While
Dodge was not on Sherman's staff,
his memoirs lend understanding to
Sherman's limited staff operations.*
(LIBRARY OF CONGRESS)

already reveal about Sherman's staff usage. Namely, Sherman preferred personal contact with his corps and division commanders, especially during a campaign, rather than trust it to staff officers. "As we marched along," wrote Dodge, "[Sherman] was in the habit of writing back personal letters to each of us who commanded a unit, and telling us where he thought we would find the best means of feeding our commands, because we were living off the country, only transporting sugar, coffee, bacon, and ammunition."[62]

No doubt Sherman preferred to be in personal contact with Grant as well, but such was becoming difficult with Sherman's new responsibilities. So, in early November, he had Audenried handle communications with Grant. Audenried wrote to Grant on November 7 from Decherd, Tennessee, indicating that Sherman and his staffers were not traveling together. (Records of the individual duties of the staffers at this point, however, remain sparse.) Audenried wrote to apprise Grant of the positions and progress of Sherman's units, but the picture he painted was a disappointing one in light of Grant's wish for a rapid march. "I left General Sherman at Richland Creek, 30 miles from Fayetteville, yesterday morning . . . with the Fourth Division. . . . The Elk Creek, containing four feet of water and 200 yards wide, was impassable. The direction of march was changed to Gilbertsborough, thence by way of Prospect toward Fayetteville. . . . Richland Creek was being bridged for General J. E. Smith, heavy rain having fallen. The roads area exceedingly hilly, rocky, and in some places very muddy; marching very difficult with wagons." Audenried closed by saying that Sherman suggested opening an existing railroad from Nashville to Decatur to speed movements, and he requested a reply on the idea from Grant.

The next day Audenried prompted Grant to reply. He wrote to John Rawlins, Grant's chief of staff, "Shall I await further orders before returning to General Sherman? If not, what does General Grant think about opening the railroad from Nashville to Decatur?" Grant replied personally to Audenried that he had already drafted orders to repair nearby rail lines and that he had sent both Sherman and Audenried copies of the orders for the upcoming campaign.[63] Audenried could return to Sherman. In conducting correspondence with Grant, Audenried had served as an information conduit for the two generals, much as he had done for them during the Vicksburg campaign when he was on Grant's staff. The activity fit largely into the category of courier work.

Meanwhile, Sherman moved ahead of his army. He and staff aide William D. Sanger rode to meet Grant at Chattanooga and learn the particulars of his plan to lift the siege. In brief, Sherman was to move against the extreme Confederate right, on the northeast end of Missionary Ridge, while Maj. Gen. Joe Hooker, the former commander of the Army of the Potomac who had brought two corps from Virginia, moved against the other Confederate flank atop Lookout Mountain. Maj. Gen. George Thomas, with whom Grant had replaced Rosecrans as commander of the Army of the Cumberland, would operate against the Rebel center on Missionary Ridge.

Chief of staff Roswell Sawyer stayed behind to help shepherd Sherman's troops to Chattanooga.[64] Sawyer brought up headquarters and stayed in communication with Sherman. On November 15 he telegraphed Sherman the exact locations of the various parts of the army, noting that the commanders were "all in good spirits, and will move forward rapidly."[65] To be sure, Sherman had not left Sawyer with a full measure of authority. He kept in touch, and told Sawyer exactly what he wanted to happen. On November 16 he wired Sawyer, "I will be down tomorrow. Order all the division commanders to be ready to march. . . . We will all move up to this vicinity [Chattanooga]."[66] If there was urgency in Sherman's note, it was because Grant had set the attack for November 22, only six days away. The next day Sherman wired Sawyer explicit orders. "I want John E. Smith's division to start tomorrow, to leave at Bridgeport the sick as camp guard, and all tents and baggage not absolutely necessary, and wagons to load with forage and provisions (roads are as bad as possible, and not a wagon should have more than 2,000 weight), to cross the Tennessee at Bridgeport and come up by Shellmound and Whiteside's. I will come down in a scow and expect to get there by 9 o'clock tonight. The other two divisions must follow the next day and all possible expedition used. Show this to all division and brigade commanders."[67] Sherman and his army were separated, albeit briefly. Had he been present, he would have passed the orders to his corps and division commanders personally. But recognizing the need for action, Sherman was forced, for one of the few times in the war, to pass such orders through his chief of staff.

In the midst of the rush to Chattanooga, Sherman also anticipated an addition to this staff. When Grant had ordered Sherman to come to Chattanooga with all haste, he had also told him to drop the railroad repairs upon which Halleck had insisted. That would have curtailed, if not done away with, Joseph Webster's job. On November 16, contemplating the end of the railroad work and pleased with Webster's performance, Sherman wrote to XVI Corps commander Hurlbut, "When General Webster is done with the railroad, I will put him on my staff."[68] With that decision

Sherman composed the staff that would assist him in the Georgia and Carolinas campaigns.

Meanwhile, Sherman's headquarters was at full speed. Audenried positioned himself on the gunboat *Hastings* on the river near Chattanooga, where he could watch troops and supplies arriving and report to Sherman. Men and matériel were arriving, he said, but "the great difficulty lies in the staging, and also from having to pull every wagon up the hill by mules."[69]

On November 21 Sawyer issued the orders that everyone knew were coming. "Every available man fit for duty in the Fifteenth Corps, now present, will at once be prepared for an important movement. Each man will carry a blanket or overcoat, three day's cooked rations, and as near 100 rounds of ammunition as possible." The twenty-third was the scheduled day of attack, and on the twenty-second Sawyer sent out a memo telling troops what they were to do. The communiqué was neither a general orders, nor was it a circular. It was conversational, a letter of the type Sherman had asked Hammond write to the troops before Shiloh. It was not the type of personal communication with commanders that Sherman reserved for himself, but an effort to make every man know exactly what he was to be part of.

Entitled "Operations for Monday, November 23," it read in part: "The Fifteenth Army Corps, re-enforced by one division of the Army of the Cumberland, is to cross the Tennessee at the mouth of East Chickamauga Creek, advance and take possession of the end of Missionary Ridge, viz., from the railroad tunnel to Chickamauga, hold, and fortify. The Army of the Cumberland and General Hooker's command are to assist by direct attacks to their front." Sawyer explained where each division would enter the attack, and he noted that Gen. William F. Smith would "give all the detailed arrangements for crossing over." Sawyer reaffirmed Sherman's habit of personally conferring with commanders when he said, "The commanding general will explain in person to the division commanders the ground and maps." Then Sawyer gave some cautionary notes. "The utmost silence, order, and patience must be displayed. The boats will take their loads from the heads of columns, and the men will resume their places the moment they reach the opposite bank of the Tennessee. Very great care must be taken by division commanders that the routes of march do not cross each other."[70] As far as Sherman's headquarters was concerned, everyone was ready.

But the weather did not cooperate. Heavy rains stopped Sherman from reaching his launching positions, and Grant postponed the attack for a day. Sawyer tersely related the news: "The operations of the Fifteenth

Corps planned for this morning are postponed for twenty-four hours. The instructions issued for this morning will, therefore, be carried out tomorrow morning."[71]

The assault did proceed the next day, but almost as no one had expected. Hooker had success against Bragg's left, on Lookout Mountain, but an unseen, rocky depression on the northeast end of Missionary Ridge slowed Sherman's approach. Finally, personal initiative by Thomas's troops in the center broke through the Confederate middle and forced Bragg off the high ground.

Evidence of staff work at Sherman's headquarters during the battle is almost nonexistent. The lack of documentation is not surprising, given that, in Sherman's style of staff work, once the battle is joined the staff work is done. The troop dispositions had been made, orders copied, routes of march handed out. It was clerical stuff, and it would resume when the battle ended. But during the fight, Sherman trusted and expected his division commanders to carry out his wishes, which he had already personally conveyed to them.

Bragg's army at Chattanooga had been shoved out of its siege lines, but not annihilated. Grant wanted to bag it if he could, and early November 26 he ordered Sherman, Hooker, and Maj. Gen. Phil Sheridan with elements of Thomas's army to go in pursuit. Audenried rode forward to Brown's Ferry that day and reported Confederate troop locations to Sherman. Grant, however, halted the pursuit the next day, and Sawyer relayed the orders to elements of Sherman's command. Sawyer informed generals Blair, Oliver O. Howard, and Jefferson C. Davis, in similar letters, that "the pursuit of the enemy has ceased, and . . . after the destruction of railroads and property liable to be put to hostile use, the army will return to its camp at or near Chattanooga."[72]

The pursuit had ended, but Grant had another expedition in mind for Sherman and his men. During the Confederate investment of Chattanooga, Confederate general James Longstreet, who had come to Tennessee from the Army of Northern Virginia to augment Bragg's force, had taken his corps northeast to threaten Union major general Ambrose Burnside's army at Knoxville, Tennessee. Longstreet placed the city under siege, and word soon reached a worried Abraham Lincoln, who believed Knoxville central to control of Unionist east Tennessee, which Burnside's army was starving and about to give way. Lincoln had barely congratulated Grant for relieving Chattanooga before he encouraged him to relieve Knoxville as well.

Grant was prepared to do so, and he sent a corps of men under Maj. Gen. Gordon Granger to the endangered Burnside. But Grant soon grew impatient with Granger's progress, and on November 30 he assigned Sherman to take his old XV Corps and march to Knoxville in Granger's stead. The same day, Sawyer drafted orders to Frank Blair, XV Corps commander, that he was going to Knoxville with Sherman, and that the corps was to "march with the utmost expedition, living upon the country." He also wrote to Granger, explaining that Grant wanted Sherman to "assume general command of all the forces moving to the relief of Knoxville." On December 1 Sawyer issued detailed marching orders for all units involved.[73]

The army, which had so recently marched across much of Tennessee to reach Chattanooga, now prepared to march another eighty-five miles hurriedly and on short rations. "[This force] had no idea of going beyond the Hiwassee at the time it marched from Graysville, and is therefore badly supplied with rations, but this country seems full of meat and corn, and we can easily reach Kingston without any help," Sawyer wrote. And march they did, arriving near Knoxville on December 3. Sawyer brought up the headquarters and prepared orders for an attack on December 4, but Sherman, entering the town with advance cavalry, found Burnside in not so serious straits as expected. Longstreet, fully aware that Sherman was coming to threaten his rear, quit the siege and prepared to leave. Sherman's goal had now vanished, and Sawyer passed the word to his subcommanders that the expedition was over.[74]

In December Sherman met in Nashville with Grant and other western commanders to discuss campaigns in spring 1864. Grant then gave Sherman a leave of absence to spend some time with his family in Ohio. Neither Sherman nor his wife, Ellen, had recovered from Willy's death, and Grant recognized that the loss, plus the constant campaigning, had taken a toll on Sherman. He needed a rest.[75]

Sherman left Maj. Gen. John Logan in temporary command of the Army of the Tennessee, but Roswell Sawyer continued to ramrod the work at headquarters. A lengthy letter Sawyer sent to Sherman on December 30 reveals much about Sawyer's duties.

> I left Bridgeport with headquarters on the road to Huntsville. Hearing that the roads were in a most terrible condition, I sent all the baggage belonging to headquarters, also all belonging to the Thirteenth Infantry and Third Cavalry, by rail as far as the road is finished, and took the road, with the troops and wagons lightly loaded with forage and rations. . . . The wagons and the infantry are still behind, but I push forward with the escort to Flint River, and borrow wagons of the troops there to move the baggage from the cars to

Huntsville. I do this as I am anxious to get the office open again as soon as possible. The work is very severe; accumulates rapidly. There is quite a package of inspection papers requiring action by the inspector general. Lieutenant Colonel Comstock, of General Grant's staff, is attempting to hurry them up. Will you please instruct me? Should not some officer be assigned to that duty?

Please instruct me as to what action I shall take on resignations and applications for leave. . . . I send this by . . . one of the orderlies, with instructions to stay with you if you should want an orderly, as you have none with you.[76]

The letter indicates several things. Regardless of whether he was physically present, the Army of the Tennessee was Sherman's; Sawyer turned to him, even on details of office minutiae, before he would turn to Logan. Surprisingly, for all the adeptness that emanates from Sawyer's writings, Sherman gave him little authority to act on his own, even in those same clerical matters. Where Grant trusted Rawlins to tend to all the mundane aspects of headquarters, where Robert E. Lee wanted his staffers to lift all routine matters from his shoulders, Sherman wanted Sawyer to consult him on virtually everything. Such items as inspection reports and leave applications were, in the overall scheme of Sherman's responsibilities, minor. Yet clearly Sherman wanted Sawyer to ask him about their dispensation.

Sherman began 1864 with a campaign that would foreshadow his work later in the year—a smashing advance on the Confederate railroad center of Meridian, Mississippi, about 150 miles east of Vicksburg. Even though Vicksburg had long since fallen and the Mississippi River was in Union hands, Meridian still posed a problem. With its railroads intact, it remained a conduit for Confederate provisions. Rebel troops near the crossroads also necessitated a strong Federal presence near the Mississippi. And Meridian was a supply base for guerrilla bands operating near the river. Sherman had long seen the value of crushing Meridian. If they attacked vigorously, cavalry attached to the expedition could drive and overwhelm Rebel troops under Nathan Bedford Forrest, who were then plaguing Union communications across Mississippi.[77] Sherman had wanted to attack Meridian following his expedition to Jackson after the fall of Vicksburg, but heat and the soldiers' weariness prevented it. Likewise, the rescue of Chattanooga had precluded it in the fall of 1863. Now Sherman had the time, a rested army, and cooler weather to conduct the campaign.[78]

At Vicksburg Sherman organized 25,000 men for the march—two corps, the XVI under Hurlbut and the XVII under McPherson. Sherman also attached to the expedition 7,000 cavalrymen under Maj. Gen. William Sooy Smith, Grant's chief of cavalry in the Division of the Mississippi. Sherman intended Smith to drive to Meridian independently of the infantry columns, engaging and destroying Forrest's men as he went.

Sherman kept his plans under wraps. He had long regarded newspaper reporters as, at best, nuisances with a great opportunity to wreck a well-laid plan. Confederate lieutenant general Leonidas Polk, commanding at Meridian, was unaware of the coming campaign, and Sherman wanted him to remain that way.

Sherman began his march on January 27. His men marched swiftly and steadily, pushing scattered Confederate resistance before them. Sherman also envisioned this campaign as one against the Southern populace who had sanctioned secession and war, and to that end Federals confiscated or burned Confederate property and matériel of war as they moved. The destruction, in a swath at times of more than fifty miles, was another foreshadowing of Sherman's campaigns to come.

Polk, whom Sherman kept befuddled, surmised that Sherman was heading to key points in Alabama, and he sent troops from Meridian to cover those areas. Thus, Meridian was open, and Sherman's troops marched in on February 14, facing only slight resistance.

Sherman was expecting to hear from Sooy Smith at any time; indeed, he had expected him on the tenth. In truth, Smith wasn't coming. Forrest's typically aggressive resistance had unnerved him, and instead of moving toward Meridian he headed back to Nashville to report to Grant. Sherman later expressed his utter dissatisfaction with Smith's campaigning.

But with his own men Sherman was satisfied. "My own movement was successful in an eminent degree," he reported to John Rawlins. Then he described the culmination of his plan. While Hurlbut's men destroyed railroads north and east of Meridian, McPherson's men did the same south and west. In Meridian proper, men under Sherman's supervision went to work. "I rested the army on the 15th, and on the 16th began a systematic and thorough destruction of the railroads centering on Meridian. The immense depots, warehouses, and length of sidetrack demonstrated the importance to the enemy of that place. . . . For five days 10,000 men worked hard and with a will in that work of destruction, with axes, crowbars, sledges, clawbars, and with fire, and I have no hesitation in pronouncing the work was well done. Meridian, with its depots, store-houses, arsenal, hospitals, offices, hotels, and cantonments no longer exists."[79]

In planning the Meridian campaign, Sherman split his staff—something he would do again. He left Sawyer at Huntsville to handle clerical matters, and he kept adjutant Lewis M. Dayton at his side to write the orders necessary to put the campaign in motion. Aides McCoy and Audenried also went on Sherman's expedition staff. Both in military objective and structure and function of his staff, Meridian was for Sherman a miniature type of the Atlanta campaign a few months away.

On January 27 Dayton drafted the first orders of march for the campaign, giving Hurlbut and McPherson their general assignments. On February 11, with the army nearing Meridian, Dayton issued orders that Sherman intended to speed up the march. "To each regiment will be allowed two wagons—one for cartridges and one for bread and cooking utensils—and two ambulances. To each general division and brigade headquarters one wagon. All other vehicles will constitute a general train under escort of one regiment to a division and one battery. . . . The army, thus relieved of baggage, will further be reduced by all men who are sick and unable to march. . . . [All others] must carry a full proportion of ammunition and provisions for five days."[80]

Once in Meridian, Dayton gave the word to begin the destruction. "The destruction of the railroad intersection at Meridian is of great importance, and should be done most effectually. Every tie and rail of iron for many miles in each direction should be absolutely destroyed . . . , and every bridge and culvert completely destroyed," he wrote. He detailed Hurlbut and McPherson their positions and prescribed the proper method of destruction. "Working parties should be composed of about one-half of the commands, and they should move by regiments, provided with their haversacks and arms, ready to repel attacks of cavalry."[81]

Finally, with the job done, on February 15 Dayton issued at Sherman's behest congratulatory orders. "The general commanding conveys his congratulations and thanks to the officers and men composing this command for their most successful accomplishment of one of the great problems of the war." Dayton reinforced that "secrecy in plan and rapidity of execution" brought the best results in war, and he commented that more such campaigning would inevitably bring "a peace that will never again be disturbed in our country by a discontented minority."[82]

Nowhere in the many special field orders Dayton drafted, however, did he offer elaborations or detailed expectations of the campaign to the corps commanders. As always, Sherman did that himself. On January 11 and 17, Sherman wrote to Hurlbut and McPherson, explaining to them his objectives and plans for leaving Vicksburg secure. He went so far as to delineate bridge crossings for the march. Sherman closed his note to McPherson with a line indicating his trust in the general, a quality that enabled Sherman to be his own chief of staff. "Knowing the objects of the movement, I will rely on your making all the preparations possible between this and the 25th instant."[83]

Following the Meridian campaign, Sherman praised his personal staff, although, like so many other generals, he gave no hint of what services they rendered. "In organizing and conducting the expedition, I have been admirably seconded by my personal staff, viz., Major McCoy and Captains Dayton and Audenried. I hardly know how to reward them substantially, further than to commend them to the favorable notice of our government."[84]

Sherman also took time to write Sawyer, in Huntsville, Alabama, a lengthy letter that offered his opinions on the war; in so doing, he wanted Sawyer to be a conduit of those opinions in Union-held territory. With Federal troops taking back land as far south as northern Alabama, Sawyer had inquired of Sherman what to do with Southerners who still offered resistance—either passive or active—to the United States. "In my former letters I have answered all your questions save one," Sherman replied in the introduction to a lengthy response, "and that relates to the treatment of inhabitants known or suspected to be hostile or 'secesh.' This is in truth the most difficult business of our army as it advances and occupies the Southern country. It is almost impossible to lay down rules, and I invariably leave this whole subject to local commanders, but am willing to give them the benefit of my acquired knowledge and experience."

Sherman told Sawyer that the Civil War was a war between societies and cultures—"races," he called them—and not just a war between armies. That conclusion, of course, had much bearing on the Meridian campaign and would have great impact on his upcoming Georgia and Carolinas campaigns. He allowed that, having resorted to war, all the adherents and supporters of the Confederacy must pay the consequences. "When men take arms to resist our rightful authority we are compelled to use force, because all reason and argument cease when arms are resorted to. When the provisions, forage, horses, mules, wagons, &c., are used by our enemy it is clearly our duty and right to take them, because otherwise they might be used against us. In like manner all houses left vacant by an inimical people are clearly our right, or such as are needed as store-houses, hospitals, and quarters." Private homes whose owners made no public display against the Federals should be passed by, Sherman said, but "if any one comes out into the public streets and creates disorder, he or she should be punished, restrained, or banished, either to the rear or front as the officer in command adjudges." Sherman continued, "These are well-established principles of war and the people of the South having appealed to war are barred from appealing to our Constitution, which they have practically and publicly defied. They have appealed to war, and must abide its rules and laws."[85]

The letter reveals more about Sherman's philosophies of war than it does about staff work at his headquarters. Nevertheless, it shows significant communication between Sherman and Sawyer, who, in fact, would be separated from Sherman for much of the rest of the war. Sawyer was inquiring of a subject beyond his experience, one more civil than military. Sherman knew that Sawyer needed instruction in the matter and a philosophical base to back up his actions. "I would advise the commanding officers at Huntsville, and such other towns as are occupied by our troops," said Sherman, "to assemble the inhabitants and explain to them these plain, self-evident propositions, and tell them that it is now for them to say whether they and their children shall inherit the beautiful land which by the accident of nature has fallen to their share."

He continued, "If you think it will do any good, call some of the better people together and explain these, my views. You may even read to them this letter and let them use it so as to prepare them for my coming."[86] Here Sherman was, in fact, giving Sawyer latitude to act within a larger body of Sherman's philosophy and wishes. That in itself marked an expansion of Sherman's staff expectations, had it continued. While distance and circumstance in the coming year forced him to do the same in other situations, such staff work was the exception and not the rule. Sherman preferred to remain his own most eminent staff officer.

Meanwhile, he was growing weary of tending railroads in western Tennessee when he could see future campaigns originating from east of that region. As such, he made plans to curtail rail work around Memphis. His decision would also affect his staff makeup. On January 27, 1864, Lewis M. Dayton penned Special Field Order No. 12 mandating that the Memphis and Charleston Railroad be dismantled, and all locomotives, cars, and equipment that the Nashville and Decatur Railroad needed be steamboated to Nashville. Also, Brig. Gen. Joseph D. Webster, who had been superintending the rail operations in western Tennessee, would "make any further directions necessary to carry out its objects . . . , and having completed the business will rejoin the general commanding wherever he may be."[87] Sherman was about to make good on his vow to place Webster on his staff.

In March Ulysses S. Grant became lieutenant general and commander of all United States armies, and Sherman ascended to command of the Division of the Mississippi. With his promotion, Sherman made some changes in his personal staff. Sawyer reverted to the job of assistant adjutant general—no demotion, to be sure, for Sherman's headquarters now oversaw three armies.[88]

Sawyer's move left Sherman's chief of staff position open, but he did not have to look far to fill it—he selected Webster for the job. When he made it official on March 24, in General Orders No. 3, which Sawyer wrote, Sherman simply listed Webster, with no title, on his special staff. With weeks, though, Webster was based in Nashville and using the title "chief of staff."[89]

Sherman's staff remained characteristically small, although he now had assumed command of the second largest military unit on the continent. In addition to Sawyer and Webster, Sherman retained the trusted Audenried, McCoy, and Dayton on his personal staff. Within a month, former Sherman staffer Montgomery Rochester, who had been briefly in service elsewhere, returned to Sherman's staff as assistant adjutant general, also based in Nashville with Webster and Sawyer.[90]

In mid-March, when the Union command shift was imminent, Sherman had gone to Nashville, then to Cincinnati, again to visit with Grant about the upcoming spring campaigns. Grant proffered his plan to attack the two remaining large Confederate armies—Lee's in Virginia and Joseph E. Johnston's in Georgia—at the same time. Grant, keeping his headquarters in the field with the Army of the Potomac, would handle Lee; Sherman would handle Johnston. The two men being essentially of the same mind about vigorous prosecution of the war, Sherman returned to Tennessee to plan his invasion of Georgia. Part of his plans included establishing a rearward base at Nashville under the supervision of half of his personal staff. As noted, Webster, Sawyer, and Rochester were there by late March.

In the early days of the command change, with Sherman meeting Grant in Cincinnati, Webster still en route to Nashville, and Sawyer presiding over a less-than-fully operational divisional headquarters there, word came from Brig. Gen. Grenville Dodge that Nathan Bedford Forrest was threatening Union supply lines. On March 22 Dodge wired Sawyer that one of his spies (who, by reputation, were quite accurate) had seen Forrest with a force of cavalry and infantry; equipped with a pontoon boat, they were preparing to cross the Tennessee River in northern Alabama, strike Union troops guarding the Tennessee and Alabama

Railroad—which Federals were using to supply their center—and attack Decatur, Alabama. Dodge reported that part of his command had already engaged Forrest near Moulton, Alabama.[91]

The crisis called for immediate action, for the spring campaigns necessitated unbroken rail lines from Nashville to the South. Sawyer initiated communication with army commanders to oppose the threat, although records indicate that he probably was playing catch-up to Dodge—who was already pulling together a defense—and not originating a plan on his own. Late that night, Sawyer wired Maj. Gen. George Thomas, commander of the Army of the Cumberland, news of Forrest and asked Thomas to have units of infantry and cavalry to move south and oppose Forrest simultaneously with Dodge. Sawyer signed the memo with both his own and Sherman's names.[92] Such may indicate that he had been in touch with Sherman (the records are unclear) or it may have been an extension of headquarters protocol in which staffers typically signed off "by order of the general commanding," then affixed their own names. Regardless, even though Sawyer had proved an essential link in putting together a Union defense, he had not acted on his own volition; in fact, it would have been uncharacteristic given his past headquarters experience.

Sherman arrived at Nashville the next day, apprised himself of the Forrest situation, then moved on to Chattanooga, from where he would launch his invasion of Georgia. He would trust local commanders to his rear to protect the supply lines. In the meantime, Webster arrived at Nashville to become top authority at Sherman's headquarters.

But Sherman did not expect Webster to single-handedly dispatch Forrest, who was still threatening the center. On March 31 Sherman advised Webster that he would be in Nashville the next day. Meanwhile, he wanted Webster to have Gen. M. Brayman, commander at Cairo, Illinois, to "give me by telegraph the most reliable news he can of Forrest. . . . Notify General Brayman to hold on to some veteran regiments and move against Forrest from Columbus if he supposes him to be near Mayfield or Union City. . . . Also notify Hurlbut where Veatch is and that he must not let Forrest escape us at this time."[93]

Webster's subsequent correspondence echoed Sherman. To Hurlbut, in Memphis, he wired, "General Veatch must be now at or near Purdy. Do not let Forrest escape us this time. Is [General Benjamin H.] Grierson after him?" To Brayman he wrote, "Sent to General Sherman by telegraph the most reliable news as to Forrest's movements. Hold on to some veteran regiments and move against Forrest from Columbus."[94] The correspondence shows that Sherman was clearly confident in his abilities to command the various portions of a separated army; Webster was, for the time being, simply a conduit for Sherman's orders.

Forrest's incursion led to one of the most notorious events of the war—the massacre of black troops at Fort Pillow, Tennessee. Hurlbut had garrisoned the place with both white and black troops. After Forrest's men assaulted it, they began murdering the blacks, many of whom were trying to surrender. Hurlbut was relieved from duty over the incident.[95]

Meanwhile, Sherman was planning his Georgia offensive, and his preparations well mark his economical view of staff work. On April 4 Grant sent Sherman official confirmation of his Southern strike, to move simultaneously with Grant's in Virginia. Sherman went to work. He realized that his campaign to Atlanta depended on speed and mobility, and that provisions coming from the rear must move forward without complication. In this, Sherman biographer Lloyd Lews says that Sherman acted as "his own chief quartermaster," sending aides (presumably from his special staff, as members of the personal staff performed no such duty) across Northern states procuring food and equipment for the three armies under Sherman's command—which totaled almost 100,000 men—and ensuring its delivery to Nashville.[96] That Sherman had no hesitancy acting as his own quartermaster is not surprising, given that he had always been willing to act as a staff officer.

Sherman intended Nashville to be a well-protected rearward supply depot. From there, supplies moved by rail and the Cumberland River to Chattanooga, Sherman's secondary base. Sherman took control of all railroads in the region, which departmental commanders had previously supervised. He also banned civil traffic on the rails, ensuring space for military cargo, whether troops or supplies. From Chattanooga, supplies moved on to Sherman's army by a single rail. Sherman wanted supplies moving out of Nashville daily, and he wanted twenty days' worth of supplies always on hand.[97]

The work to go on at Nashville was perhaps more suited to quartermasters and commissaries general, but Sherman intended it to be his clerical base as well. Following his economical view of staff work, Sherman left half of his personal staff—Webster, Sawyer, and Rochester—behind at Nashville to oversee both. On April 26 he informed Halleck of his intent to have a dual headquarters.[98]

That Sherman should leave his chief, Webster, in Nashville, underscores his comments in his memoirs about chiefs of staff, but it also reflects more. Sherman had no doubt about Webster's abilities; he trusted the man to do solid work. Plus, much of this campaign hinged on railroads. With

Webster's railroad and engineer experience, Sherman could count on him to keep provisions rolling to the front. Likewise, Webster could handle the clerical, housekeeping aspects of running a headquarters. In Webster, Sherman got two staff officers for the price of one—good economics.

The staff split also represented Sherman's desire for mobility. His field headquarters, habitually with the Army of the Cumberland, consisted of only three members of this personal staff—aides McCoy, Audenried, and Dayton—and three inspectors general, Brig. Gen. John M. Corse, Lt. Col. Willard Warner, and Lt. Col. Charles Ewing. The inspectors were, in fact, part of Sherman's special staff, but they frequently worked as personal staff, delivering messages for the general.[99] In that, Sherman also practiced good economics; he got double duty from the inspectors general performing on both sides of the staff.

Again recognizing the need for mobility, Sherman knew that knowledge of the Georgia topography was eminently important to his army. He appointed at division, corps, and army headquarters men to form and accompany reconnaissance parties, survey distances, and construct maps.[100] Thus organized, the topographical work did not affect Sherman's own personal staff, but it showed that he could be interested in enlarged staff duties when it suited military necessity.

Preparing for the invasion, Sherman now was overall commander of three armies—the Cumberland, under Thomas; the Tennessee, under James B. McPherson; and the Ohio, under Gen. John M. Schofield. On April 25, writing from Nashville, Sawyer issued General Orders No. 35, formalizing the command. "The armies now on the line of the Tennessee for the purpose of war will constitute one army, under the personal direction of the major-general commanding the division [Sherman], but for the purpose of administration will retain the separate department organizations. All department commanders will exercise as heretofore full control of all matters pertaining to troops properly belonging to them, and of the local districts which compose the field of their respective departments."[101] With each army retaining autonomy within the larger division, and, ostensibly, utilizing some staff system of its own commander's choice, Sherman could get by with a limited staff at his own headquarters.

Sawyer continued, "The effective Army of the Cumberland will be the center, that of the Ohio the left wing, and that of the Tennessee the right wing. . . . The commander-in-chief will be habitually with the center, but may shift from time to time to either flank, leaving a staff officer near the center to receive reports and make orders."[102] To be sure, that staff officer remaining in the center would be in close contact with Sherman, but he would not act in Sherman's stead.

Two other factors enabled Sherman to economize his personal staff. First, as he had done throughout the war, Sherman intended to personally correspond and meet with his army and corps commanders. That precluded the need for a permanent liaison officer. Second, Sherman trusted his army and corps commanders. Sherman liked and trusted McPherson implicitly. If he wasn't exactly warm with Thomas, he knew his abilities. He also got along well with Schofield, but did not have the battle experience with him that he had with Thomas and McPherson. He also had great respect for many of his corps commanders, especially Oliver O. Howard, commanding the IV Corps in the Army of the Cumberland, and John Logan, Grenville Dodge, and Frank Blair, commanding the XV, XVI, and XVII Corps, respectively, in the Army of the Tennessee.[103] That Sherman trusted the men to understand the intent behind his orders and achieve desired objectives negated any need for him to permanently assign staff officers to their headquarters, as per the new European style. There is no indication that such a thought ever crossed Sherman's mind.

Sherman early on resumed his practice of communicating personally with his army commanders. On April 24 he wrote a lengthy message to Schofield, explaining that he thought Grant's army in Virginia would be ready for its offensive earlier than his. "But let come what may we must attack Joe Johnston in position, or force him back of Coosa, at the moment the initiative is made in the East. I prefer that Johnston should not move at all, but receive us on his present ground. But I do not propose rushing on him rashly until I have in hand all the available strength of yours, Thomas', and McPherson's armies."[104]

By late April, with the Atlanta campaign approaching, Sherman's Nashville headquarters was in full operation with Webster and company handling a variety of tasks. Webster, of course, was to supervise transportation for the army. That frequently meant utilizing his railroad experience, but often as not Civil War transportation went on four legs. Webster soon found himself monitoring the status of mules for Sherman's army. On April 26 Brig. Gen. Robert Allen, quartermaster at Louisville, reported to Webster about some of the animals. He had already complained to Henry Halleck in Washington that "the sovereign difficulty that General Sherman has to contend with is in getting supplies forward to the advanced depots." He told Halleck that the necessary railroad cars to do the work were coming in from the East at a rate of only about fifteen cars per day; "from 1,500 to 2,000 are required to do the work." On April 25 he reported to Webster that 4,000 mules should be on their way from St. Louis by May 1. "Several hundred are being sent from Bowling Green and other points . . . ; 400 are on the river from Memphis . . . ; in all, between 5,000 and 6,000 [should arrive] at an early day. Allen, undoubtedly knowing that Sherman wanted to get as much efficiency out of his transportation lines as possible, noted, "I think General Sherman will be satisfied with this."[105]

Meanwhile, Sherman was on the move. He left Nashville headquarters in the hands of Webster, Sawyer, and Rochester, and went to Chattanooga, the starting point for his invasion of Georgia. When he arrived on April 29, he telegraphed Grant in Virginia that his armies were coming into place, then he telegraphed Webster. "I am here all right," he said. He also apprised Webster of the situation between the two cities. "Tell [Gen. Lovell H.] Rousseau [commanding the military district around Nashville] that the road appears thinly guarded about Wartrace; he had better send 100 men there for a short while till people get used to the diminution of the road guard."[106]

Then, showing that he was obviously uncomfortable using his chief of staff to transmit orders of a potentially critical nature, Sherman turned around and wired Rousseau himself. The communication reveals Sherman's capacity for detail and his ability to act as his own chief of staff. "Order General [Eleazer] Paine and the regiment now at Gallatin to Tullahoma, and give him charge of the defense of the road, embracing Duck and Elk River bridges. The road north of Nashville is not important to us, but that south is vital. Remember to place gun-racks and muskets in all the forts and strong buildings, so that citizens may, if necessary, assist in the defense of Nashville. But there is no danger there now and cannot be for a month to come."[107]

A flurry of correspondence between Sherman and his army commanders around the first of May confirms Sherman acting as his own chief. On April 29 he told Schofield in Knoxville and McPherson in Huntsville that Grant wanted him to begin his invasion by May 5. Sherman impressed upon them the need for quick positioning. Again, to McPherson, he conveyed his capacity for detail. "The Fifteenth Corps could march here by [May 5] but we would have to push up Dodge's command in cars, leaving the wagons . . . to overtake them at some point to be hereafter fixed; therefore, order Dodge's march by roads that will carry them near the railroad." Later that day, Sherman laid out McPherson's route of march. "Put everybody in motion at once for Chattanooga by roads north of the Tennessee, according to the figures we agreed on, viz., 10,000 of the Fifteenth corps and 10,000 of the Sixteenth Corps." Sherman reiterated that Grant wanted him moving by May 5. Then he uttered a classic understatement—"You know how I like to be on time."[108] The excitement of the coming campaign was beginning to show in Sherman's writing.

Sherman also made sure that his Nashville headquarters knew of his wishes. He telegraphed Sawyer the arrangements he had made with McPherson, and Sawyer took it from there. On April 30 Sawyer wired Col. Daniel C. McCallum, superintendent of Union military railroads, that Sherman wanted as many cars as possible carrying troops to the front. He specified that Dodge's corps was to go by rail from Huntsville to Chattanooga.[109]

When Dodge arrived at Chattanooga on May 5, well ahead of most of his army's provisions, he quickly saw Sherman's personal command style— that is, without staff officers. He found Sherman consulting with McPherson and realized that such face-to-face meetings were typical. Sherman quickly ordered Dodge's command to a point thirty miles distant, and when McPherson suggested finding a guide for the march, Sherman whipped out a map with route and objectives well marked.[110] Sherman was, in fact, a walking headquarters.

One need only look at the flurry of communications between Sherman and the army commanders around May 5 to see that he maintained his habit of personally corresponding with them. While some of the correspondence is with George Thomas, most of it is with McPherson and Schofield. Perhaps, because they were junior members of the command quartet, Sherman felt more need to be in constant touch with them. Much of Sherman's correspondence was so minutely detailed that the recipients could have no doubt about their instructions. By and large, correspondence coming the other way, from army commanders back up to Sherman, went directly to Sherman and not through a staff officer. Obviously, army commanders had no need to communicate with the Nashville office, but they also rarely had any need to communicate with Sherman's personal staff in the field. Sherman was a hands-on commander, regardless of the size of command under him. He had the confidence and ability to handle all but the most clerical of staff duties. Sherman wanted it that way, and his commanders knew it.[111]

On May 3 Sherman officially listed the members of his special and personal staffs accompanying him in the field. As advertised, the personal staff remained limited to Audenried, McCoy, and Dayton. The men would tend the traditional duties at Sherman's headquarters. Sherman also kept them busy running dispatches between the various army headquarters, at times bringing back to Sherman written verification of receipt.[112]Records do not show that at any time Sherman ever stationed a staff officer with a particular army or corps with authority to improvise orders in his stead. Such might have been the coming fashion in European armies, but not in Sherman's.

Sherman's initial campaign in Georgia became one of maneuver rather than one of set-piece battles. His opponent, Gen. Joseph E. Johnston, well knew that he did not have the manpower to face Sherman in a stand-up fight. Consequently, he opted to maneuver—feinting this way, sidestepping that way, all the while withdrawing south in an effort to preserve his army and stretch Sherman's supply lines. When Sherman was unable to get around Johnston at Dalton, Georgia, the Confederates left the town on May 12 and headed for Resaca. Early on May 17 Johnston crossed the Oostanaula River, and on May 20 the Etowah, with Sherman following close behind.[113]

Sherman continued to use his staff officers to ride information from headquarters to headquarters, more frequently now because distance demanded it. Nevertheless, they remained information conduits, not elements of command. Lewis M. Dayton continued to draft a variety of orders and carry out correspondence essential to the smooth operation of the army. But nothing in north Georgia indicated expanded staff usage.[114]

If staff duty in the field with Sherman was limited, Webster's duties at the Nashville headquarters were expanding. From the outset, Webster had more than just supplies to worry about. Sherman wanted no private citizens following his army, and the order went especially for newspaper correspondents. Sherman hated reporters. In a note to Schofield he likened them to spies, and to Webster he called them "mere traders in news like other men, who would make money out of the army." He told Webster to stop them at Nashville. If they journeyed any farther, they risked "being impressed for soldiers or other labor."[115]

Webster also had to contend with plantation lessees and freed blacks who wanted the Federal army to feed them. Sherman argued against it. "If we feed a mouth except soldiers on active duty we are lost," he told Webster. "Refugees and negroes of all sorts and kinds not in military use must move to the rear of Nashville, or provide food in some way independent of the railroad."[116]

Webster also became a news censor. Sherman knew, as much as he hated the press, that Northern newspapers would want information about his progress. Consequently, he let Webster dole out facts as they happened.

For instance, on May 20 Sherman told Webster, "You may let all the papers announce us in possession of the line of the Etowah." Later, when the armies captured roads leading to Marietta, Georgia, Sherman said, "You may give this publicity." He did not want Webster to elaborate too much, though. "Minor descriptions of the events will gradually become known to the public from letters of officers and soldiers to their families," said Sherman. "My official reports daily to General Halleck will in due time reach the public."[117]

Webster also dispatched troops to critical sites. He did not decide where they were needed, however; Sherman told him exactly where to send them. When Halleck told Sherman that he was sending 20,000 militia troops to the Division of the Mississippi, Sherman decided he wanted 5,000 sent to Nashville; 5,000 to Louisville, Kentucky; 5,000 to Columbus, Kentucky; and 5,000 to Memphis. Sherman told Webster to expect them soon and how to dispose of troops returning to the rear from the advancing army. Sherman said he was progressing well, and he ordered Webster to "back us up with troops in the rear, so I will not be forced to drop detachments as road guard, and I have an army that will make a deep hole in the Confederacy."[118]

While Webster was dealing with hungry Tennessee natives, newspaper reporters, and wandering Federal troops, he had yet another class of men to handle—Confederate raiders. Sherman's lengthy supply line, although it ran through Union-held territory, was a prize no Rebel cavalry commander could resist. In mid-May, Nathan Bedford Forrest and his raiders again made themselves a threat. In dealing with Forrest, and others like him, Webster had some autonomy. Sherman had already made it clear that he did not want to detach soldiers from his invasion force to protect his rear, so, while Sherman might help him with advice over the wires, Webster was fairly on his own. It would be the one time when distance and military necessity forced Sherman, usually conservative in staff assignments, to allow his chief some measure of independence.

On the morning of May 12, Webster wired Sherman that Forrest had a force of infantry, cavalry, and artillery massed at Florence. "It seems reliable that the force is large enough to cut the railroad, unless we take the offensive at once. . . . Is it not best to organize a force sufficient to drive or capture Forrest at once? There are so many trestles on that part of the road that we cannot hold there by acting solely on the defensive." Webster clearly was thinking on his own, and thinking ahead. The best defensive, he saw, would be a strong offensive. He informed Sherman that a brigade of cavalry was prepared to depart Columbia to join the Georgia invasion, and he asked if it wouldn't be best to "detain it a little while for this emergency?" He also had probably been planning with Nashville commander Rousseau. "Rousseau is arranging to send down some of our dismounted cavalry," he told Sherman.[119] In effect, while he was advocating offensive action to Sherman, Webster was already setting it in motion.

Sherman quickly wired back to Webster, telling him that Frank Blair's XVII Corps, which had not yet joined the invasion, was assembling near Florence. "[He] will be instructed to clear out the country about Florence before coming this way." Sherman also agreed with Webster. "The offensive should be assumed at once, and you may so instruct General Rousseau and General Blair in my name." He did say that the army in Georgia needed the cavalry force Webster had asked about, however, noting that Rousseau and Blair had "enough troops for any force that can possibly reach Tuscumbia."[120] An offensive wasn't necessary, as it turned out, for the threat ended when the raiders retreated.

Later, in June, when it appeared that Confederate cavalry might again stage a raid, Webster approved a plan of Rousseau's to take a force of 3,000 into Alabama near Selma and impede them. "Offensive operations from that point will give the enemy something else to do than plot and execute raids against our lines of communications," Rousseau wrote to Sherman, seeking the general's approval. "I have always thought the most effective way to guard the Tennessee River was by offensive operations on the other side." Not only did he intend to break up the plans of Rebel raiders, but he could "destroy fifty to one hundred millions' worth of property belonging to the rebel government, including a portion of the important road between Selma and Atlanta." Clearly, Rousseau had envisioned a miniature version of Sherman's Meridian expedition earlier in the year. He had laid the plans before Webster, who okayed them; after all, they were in line with Webster's own philosophy of offensive-defensive. Indeed, Webster may have helped Rousseau plan the raid, but that was as far as Webster's authority went. Rousseau asked Sherman twice for permission to carry it out. Ultimately, Sherman told Rousseau to plan the raid, but to not launch it until he gave specific orders. He wanted the situation on his own front to play out before authorizing a detached mission to his rear.[121] Sherman was willing to let his chief of staff have freer reign when it looked like attack on his rear was imminent. But to allow Webster to implement an offensive plan was speculative; Sherman would say when, where, or *if* it went.

Staff work otherwise remained routine. On May 12, the same day that Sherman and Webster were discussing Forrest, aide-de-camp Dayton, in the field with Sherman, was worrying about something less dramatic.

George Thomas's Army of the Cumberland was making too much noise, and Dayton had to tell him to quiet down. "The general commanding is desirous that as much silence shall be preserved in the army as possible, and in order that this end may be attained he wishes the use of the bass drum entirely discontinued, also the practice or use of any band music or field music save the usual bugle calls. All cheering of bodies of men, except in battle, should also be dispensed with." Dayton also continued drafting field orders and writing communiqués from general headquarters to those of the various armies.[122]

As Sherman's armies moved southeast, Union troops took Confederate prisoners. Sherman ordered them shipped north, to Nashville, where, for a time at least, they became Webster's responsibility. "My record of prisoners captured is not perfect," Sherman wired Webster. "Cause them on arrival . . . to be counted and make report of number, rank, &c, to General Halleck, Washington." Later in the summer, when the armies captured two Confederate factories at Roswell and Sweet Water, Sherman sent their operators to Webster with specific instructions. "When they reach Nashville," he said, "have them sent across the Ohio River and turned loose to earn a living where they won't do us any harm. If any of the principals seem to you dangerous, you may order them imprisoned for a time. The men were exempt from conscription by reason of their skill, but the women were simply laborers that must be removed from this district."[123] Sherman's orders not only added more to Webster's workload, but they underscored Sherman's intent for Georgia: He was there not only to beat Joe Johnston, but to destroy the Confederacy's ability to make war as well.

As Sherman's campaign progressed, Webster also learned that he had to deal with former Union prisoners of war. Dayton informed Webster that many Union men were escaping from Rebel captors and entering advancing Union lines. "I send [them] to you . . . and you will forward [them] to their regiments allowing, say, a week's leave at home."[124]

In late May, as Sherman's army took the Etowah River, he reinforced to Webster what the chief already knew—that supplies should continue to the front with all speed. He relayed that he wanted supply depots created now at Chattanooga and at Resaca, Georgia. He also wanted railroad cars pushing as far forward as the Etowah. Webster later acknowledged, "supplies are going forward well to Chattanooga, and will not be allowed to stop."[125]

Sherman's armies spent the summer slogging their way to Atlanta. Sherman continued to duel with Johnston, the latter sidestepping as he pulled back, the former seeking a way around his flanks. Weary of such a war of maneuver, Confederate president Jefferson Davis relieved Johnston of command on July 17, replacing him with John Bell Hood, a veteran of many Eastern fights, including Antietam and Gettysburg. Hood epitomized Southern aggression and agreed with the offensive-defensive Lee had been waging in Virginia. He was of the fiery demeanor that Southerners—and Davis—seemed to want in a commander, and he quickly carried the fight to Sherman. Hood attacked outside of Atlanta on July 20, then pulled back the next day. In fighting on the twenty-second, Sherman lost one of his favorite army commanders, when James McPherson was shot and killed. Sherman replaced him with Maj. Gen. Oliver O. Howard as commander of the Army of the Tennessee. There followed a month of maneuver and battle until, on September 1, Hood gave up Atlanta. Sherman's troops occupied the city.

As the campaign wore into August, Webster, back in Nashville, found that his job had changed little over the summer. Most of his duties still pertained to keeping the supply lines open and moving quickly. When Sherman learned that too many private citizens, even those acting with the Sanitary Commission, were reaching the front via the railroads, he warned Webster to shut them down. "Grant no passes beyond Chattanooga, and only the smallest number that far. Surgeons can fill the offices of the Sanitary Commission, and chaplains minister to the wants of the soldiers."[126]

Later, when Sherman learned that some newspaper vendors were slipping to the front on railroad cars, he penned a treatise to Webster that left no doubt about his wishes. He reiterated that precedence must be given to military supplies. Newspapers, which he regarded as freight, could come along, "but newsvenders [sic], like any other merchants, must not travel in the cars to sell their goods any more than grocers or hucksters. . . . Passes to citizens as far as Chattanooga, in very limited numbers, may be granted by . . . [any of the three army commanders], and they may send to the rear car-loads of prisoners, refugees and citizens, without limit, but I have ordered that on no pretense must citizens come this side of Chattanooga, for I find them useless mouths that we cannot afford to feed."[127]

Newspaper vendors and other people trying to reach the front were a nuisance, not a direct military threat. But as Sherman took Atlanta, Webster did face a direct threat closer to home, when Confederate cavalry under Gen. Joe Wheeler came to within ten miles of Nashville and threatened Sherman's rearmost supply base. Warning of Wheeler's approach had, in fact, come from Sherman himself on August 21. When Webster passed the word on to Gen. Stephen Gano Burbridge, the latter relayed his own intelligence—and fears—to Webster. "From all I can learn, I anticipate an invasion by the combined forces of Wheeler and [John Hunt] Morgan." Burbridge asked Webster if he could detach troops from Nashville to help with the defense. Webster, in turn, queried Sherman. The general replied, through Dayton, that Burbridge "must take care of Wheeler and Morgan with the force he has; troops, of course, cannot be sent from here. General Burbridge may telegraph General Halleck." The commands in central Tennessee were on their own. General Rousseau, commanding at Nashville, ultimately took the field to oppose Wheeler. Inside the city, Webster arranged for defense should Wheeler get through Rousseau. He ordered weapons handed out to everyone in the quartermaster's department, as well as to nurses and patients in the hospital. Webster ultimately thought no battle for the city would come, but, in a note to Rousseau, he wrote, "these [extra troops], with 500 men of the commissary department, will make us strong. We will make a good fight if the enemy leave your front and come against the town."[128]

Union skirmishing, plus Morgan's death on September 4, forced the Confederate raiders to retreat. Upon his immediate capture of Atlanta, Sherman had been several days out of contact with Webster. When they resumed communication, the chief of staff informed Sherman about the events and the defense that he and Rousseau had coordinated, lamenting that he had so little cavalry to pursue the raiders. He closed with a "hearty congratulations on the glorious success of your . . . campaign."[129]

Later in September, Forrest again threatened Webster, making to join Wheeler between Nashville and Sherman's rear. During the previous crisis, Webster had been on his own—as close as one of Sherman's staffers ever got to autonomy. Now, with Atlanta his, Sherman could once again concentrate on myriad items. "I will send some troops back to Chattanooga and Bridgeport," he told Webster, instructing him to have Burbridge move to Nashville and prepare to fight Forrest. On September 26 Sherman gave Webster direct orders and a policy to work within. "Recall Generals [James B.] Steedman and Schofield. The policy should be, small but well commanded bodies in the blockhouses, and a moveable force to act straight against Forrest, who must scatter for forage."[130] Forrest continued raiding in north Georgia and south-central Tennessee, but he did not go near Nashville. Webster apparently lost track of him, for he wired Schofield on October 1 that "there seems to be no definite knowledge of where Forrest is. Will advise you of everything important when known."[131]

Ultimately, Forrest's depredations forced Sherman to take sterner measures, and he sent George Thomas back to Nashville to handle the raids and defend the city. "General Thomas is now in full command of all the troops operating against Forrest," Sherman wrote to Webster, "and I want you to help him by making any orders he may ask." Thomas was in Nashville by October 3, and he and Webster began working together: "Major General Washburn . . . was directed by Webster before my arrival to land his infantry at Johnsonville to aide in the protection of the depot there, and to proceed up the river to Clifton with his cavalry, and to move toward Athens for the purpose of striking Forrest's flank."[132]

Two weeks after occupying Atlanta, Sherman, in his official report of the campaign, praised his personal staff, McCoy, Dayton, and Audenried, and inspectors general Corse, Warner, and Ewing. Sherman described the men as "ever zealous and most efficient" while delivering orders to distant units "with an intelligence and zeal that insured the proper working of machinery covering from ten to twenty-five miles of ground, when the least error in the delivery and explanation of an order would have produced confusion." Sherman, often stingy with praise, credited his staffers further, saying that "owing to the intelligence of these officers, orders have been made so clear that these vast armies have moved side-by-side, sometimes crossing each other's tracks, . . . [more than] 138 miles . . . without confusion or trouble."[133]

Implicit in Sherman's statement is that his personal staffers spent time with the separated armies of Sherman's division. But they were only delivering orders. Unlike Grant, Sherman never gave the staff officers authority to issue orders on the spot in response to an urgent situation. Sherman believed that job was his, and his alone.

In the meantime, he was planning what would become his famed "March to the Sea," a punitive expedition from Atlanta to Savannah that Sherman had designed to break the Southern populace's will to fight. Sherman needed Grant's approval before starting the march, and in September the two generals sent staffers back and forth between their headquarters to facilitate discussions. On September 20 Lt. Col. Horace Porter, of Grant's staff, arrived at Sherman's headquarters. Acknowledging his arrival, Sherman wrote to Grant, "I will have a long talk with Colonel Porter and tell him everything that may occur to me of interest to you. . . . If you can whip Lee and I can march to the Atlantic I think Uncle Abe will give us twenty days' leave of absence to see the young folks." Porter left for Virginia the next day, but Sherman apparently had more to add. On September 26 he dispatched Joseph C. Audenried, of his own staff, to Washington to confer with Halleck. Sherman wired Halleck, "I would like to know when Captain Audenried reaches Washington with my dispatches, that I may know that you and General Grant are in possession of my views."[134]

Of course, Sherman got the okay for the march. He began his expedition on November 16, cutting a swath across Georgia and occupying Savannah on December 21. Throughout, Sherman saw no reason to change his staff setup. He left Webster, Sawyer, and Rochester in Nashville to handle the rearward headquarters. This time, however, Webster need not worry about Rebel incursions, for Thomas was there to handle that. Although Webster and Sherman had kept in close touch during the Atlanta campaign, they did not correspond for the duration of the Savannah campaign. Webster knew his job—keep supplies moving south—and Sherman did not want northbound lines of communication slowing his progress. Sherman did add two aides to his personal staff in Georgia, Majs. Henry Hitchcock and G. Ward Nichols, while Dayton remained Sherman's adjutant general and Audenried a Sherman favorite.[135]

For the march, Sherman divided his army into two wings. The left, or northern wing, was under command of Maj. Gen. Henry Slocum; the right, the southern, wing was under Maj. Gen. Oliver O. Howard, who had taken over the Army of the Tennessee upon the death of Gen. James McPherson that summer. Sherman placed his cavalry under the command of Gen. Hugh Judson Kilpatrick, then renamed the force the Army of Georgia.[136]

The story of the great march is told well in a variety of places and needs no retelling here. Work at Sherman's headquarters proceeded much as it had throughout the war. Lewis M. Dayton kept busy, perhaps busier than he had ever been, writing general and special orders. As always, Sherman's quick mind and military capacities are evident in much of Dayton's writing, as in this dispatch to Maj. Gen. Jefferson C. Davis, commanding the XIV Corps. "The general-in-chief directs that you put your command in motion tomorrow morning by any road crossing Murder Creek and leading into the Monticello of Hillsborough and Milledgeville road, on which you will move to within about twelve miles of Milledgeville and camp tomorrow night. The brigade belonging to the Twentieth Corps he wishes you to send to report to General Slocum at Eatonton. You will also direct one regiment to feel for General Slocum . . . and bring back a report to himself." Sherman, as always, was directing things minutely, Dayton serving as an efficient conduit.[137]

For part of the march, Sherman assigned aide-de-camp Audenried to travel with Slocum's wing. Audenried was not with Slocum to relay orders from the commanding general, but rather to relay information on Slocum's progress back to Sherman. "We burned the bridge, about 120 feet long, over Brier Creek, four miles north of Waynesborough, during Saturday night," Audenried reported to Sherman on November 29. "Captured . . . a train of 8 box and 3 platform cares [sic] and a locomotive, all of which were burned, the cargo, hogs for Augusta, turned loose." Audenried reported that Rebel cavalry commander Joe Wheeler had assaulted the column, sparking a fight that cost 100 Federal casualties. He also kept Sherman abreast of what Georgia newspapers were reporting—that Sherman was, in fact, in "retreat." Audenried would continue to periodically ride ahead of Sherman and file reports on conditions from the field.[138]

By late December Sherman's army had reached Savannah and placed it under siege, although it was unable to block a Confederate escape route up the Savannah River. On December 20 Confederate general William J. Hardee led his small army out of Savannah, surrendering the city to the Federals, who then occupied it on the twenty-first. Sherman was away from the army, arranging for a naval blockade of the Rebel escape route, when the city fell. Sherman's adjutant, Dayton, sent him the message that Savannah was theirs.[139]

On December 24 Sherman wrote a report of his Savannah campaign to Webster. It was not an official report, although in length and detail it could have been, rather it was a message to bring Webster up to date on all that had happened since the two last communicated. Sherman drafted his official report to Grant and Halleck on January 1. In it he congratulated his personal staff, but, as usual, said nothing specific about their duties. "All have, as formerly, fulfilled their parts to my entire satisfaction."[140]

Sherman may have been entirely satisfied with the work of his personal staff, but a new member of that body saw things differently. Henry Hitchcock and G. Ward Nichols, added to the staff after the fall of Atlanta, published postwar memoirs of their experiences with Sherman. Nichols shed little light on the functioning of Sherman's staff,[141] but Hitchcock roundly criticized it. Hitchcock had been a St. Louis attorney before the Civil War. Thinking he could better serve the Union in his home state, Hitchcock stayed in Missouri as part of the Missouri Convention until September 1864. He then offered his services to the War Department. His uncle, Ethan Allen Hitchcock, an old soldier whom Sherman admired, asked Sherman if he had a place on his staff for Henry, and Sherman answered with an enthusiastic "yes." Hitchcock joined Sherman's staff on October 31, 1864, and Sherman immediately turned over to him much of his correspondence to answer. Other staff officers were impressed that Sherman should give such a confidential job to a newcomer.[142]

Such a sudden and close relationship with Sherman allowed Hitchcock to quickly take the measure of headquarters, and he did not like what he saw. Yes, Sherman's staffers worked efficiently, but the general's insistence upon limited staff work, in Hitchcock's estimation, robbed him of valuable services that the staff could perform. Hitchcock said that he could understand Sherman's desire to be his own chief of staff, for the general was "far-sighted, sagacious, clear, rapid as lightning,—personally indefatigable, but also something too impatient to see always to execution of orders in detail. He ought to have a first-rate AAG whom he fully sympathized with and trusted and liked personally, as well as officially, who would take it on himself sometimes to fill up this deficiency. Even then there would be occasion when he himself would have to act, and such an AAG would sometimes be in a delicate position. Dayton is not exactly he."[143]

Hitchcock described exactly what military historian John Vermillion outlines in his theory of corporate leadership, and what military theorist Antoine-Henri Jomini recommended in a relationship between a general and his chief of staff. Both agreed that a good chief, or, in his absence, the assistant adjutant general, should supply his general with qualities the latter did not have. Hitchcock also, unwittingly, described the type of relationship Ulysses S. Grant and John Rawlins had.

Sherman, however, was a tough soldier, and tough soldiers are often inflexible. Many times that is the key to victory—rigid adherence to a goal. But Sherman's attitude about staff work perhaps cost him efficiency on his march through the South.

In early January Sherman continued his habit of apprising his men of events in the war and their role in them. He had Dayton write, in the form of Special Field Orders No. 6, a synopsis for the last three months. "In order that all may understand the importance of events it is proper to revert to the situation of affairs in September last," wrote Dayton.

> We held Atlanta, a city of little value to us, but so important to the enemy that Mr. Davis, the head of the rebellious faction in the south, visited his army near Palmetto and commanded it to regain it, as well as to ruin and destroy us by a series of measures which he thought would be effectual. That army, by a rapid march, gained our railroad near Big Shanty, and afterward about Dalton. We pursued it, but it moved so rapidly that we could not overtake it, and General Hood led his army successfully far over toward Mississippi, in hopes to decoy us out of Georgia; but we were not then to be led away by him, and preferred to lead and control events ourselves. Generals

Thomas and Schofield, commanding the departments to our rear, returned to their posts and prepared to decoy General Hood into their meshes, whilst we came on to complete the original journey. We quietly and deliberately destroyed Atlanta . . . and then captured [the enemy's] commercial capital, which had been so strongly fortified from the sea as to defy approach from that quarter. Almost at the moment of our victorious entry into Savannah came the welcome and expected news that our comrades in Tennessee had also fulfilled nobly and well their part; had decoyed General Hood to Nashville and then turned on him, defeating his army thoroughly.[144]

The letter was much like the circulars Sherman had asked his staffers to issue in the past, and it served to keep the army assured of its own worth and valor.

In his strike north through the Carolinas, Sherman saw no need to change the function of his personal staff. The only thing he would change was its location. He would keep a small staff with him on the march and retain a rearward headquarters in Savannah under General Webster's control. On December 28, 1864, Dayton wrote to Webster that Sherman wanted him, Sawyer, and Rochester in Savannah. Webster was to properly dispose of all public property at headquarters, and he and the men were to leave their horses behind. They were to gather the official papers of headquarters, Sherman's trunk, the personal effects of staffers in the field with Sherman, and some staff officers assigned to lesser commands and go to New York. From there they would board a steamer for Savannah, where they would perform the same task of keeping Sherman's lengthy supply line secure. Webster had the base established by February 14, 1865.[145]

Again, Sherman's march through the Carolinas is well chronicled elsewhere; his staff usage did not change throughout the march. Webster continued to oversee activities rearward, while Dayton and the personal staffers handled the correspondence in the field. Audenried, always a favorite with Sherman, continued to get special duty. Before the army left Savannah, Audenried organized the removal of refugee families from Savannah to Charleston, South Carolina. Later, as the army neared Columbia, South Carolina, Audenried was involved in a more dramatic affair. On February 15 Audenried was assigned to ride ahead of Sherman's headquarters looking for information. He must have been in civilian clothes and therefore risked capture as a spy, for he stopped a Confederate lieutenant riding out of Columbia, passed himself off as a Rebel, and was able to obtain intelligence from the man. He returned to Sherman with the news that Columbia was not expecting the Federals, thinking instead they were headed for Augusta or Charleston.[146]

In the closing days of the war, Sherman leapfrogged his rear base, with Webster still in charge, to New Berne, North Carolina, then to Alexandria, Virginia, on April 28, 1865. When the war ended, Sherman detached Webster from headquarters and sent him to inspect all railroads in the beaten Confederacy.[147]

Sherman's campaigns succeeded, to be sure, and he was well pleased with his staff officers. His limited staff usage at a time when most European armies were using enlarged, well-educated staffs only shows the degree to which American personal staff work was unstructured in the early 1860s. That Sherman could manage three armies with an economical personal staff, of course, shows several things. Sherman understood that, as commander of the Division of the Mississippi, he need only craft broad strategies, then pass them on to his army and corps commanders for execution. He trusted them to do so, and he felt no need to place staff officers with each command to ensure the execution of his orders. Indeed, Sherman had such a military capacity that, apart from the routine, often grinding chore of writing and copying orders, he could—and did—frequently act as his own chief of staff. All of that played into Sherman's basic concept of a staff, which was that it should be small and its duties limited. Grant, of course, had arrived at something of a different conclusion about staff work, and, as Sherman pitched into Georgia in May 1864, was about to implement some changes with his personal staff in Virginia.

CHAPTER SEVEN

Grant: A Professional Staff

1863–1865

AFTER THE SIEGE OF VICKSBURG, ULYSSES S. GRANT'S PERSONAL STAFF underwent a subtle change, from civilian amateurism to military professionalism. Deadwood officers on his staff began to leave, albeit largely through attrition. Grant, however, did not make the same mistake in replacing them as he had when first organizing his staff. Instead of bringing in untrained friends to fill the vacancies, Grant chose military professionals, and their effect on the staff was far-reaching. By the time he began the Wilderness campaign in Virginia in May 1864, Grant's use of his staff officers resembled, crudely and unintentionally, Prussian staff usage.

Soon after Vicksburg fell, Grant sought a reward for chief of staff John Rawlins—a promotion to brigadier general. In his letter of recommendation to the War Department, Grant said, "I can safely say that he would make a good corps commander." Grant was overstating the case, for Rawlins had done nothing in his short military career to support that claim. Rawlins had spent all his time on the staff, not on the line, and had never commanded even so much as a company. In truth, Grant wanted the promotion for his friend as "a reward of merit." The army gave Rawlins a star, but the Senate did not confirm Rawlins's commission until mid-1864, and then only with Grant's repeated urging. Summing up his opinion of Rawlins, Grant told the Senate Committee on Military Affairs, "He comes nearest being indispensable to me of any officer in the service."[1]

Rawlins was also about to receive a promotion of a more personal sort. While his army occupied Vicksburg, Grant and his staff took as their headquarters the plantation home of a Mrs. Lum, widow of a wealthy planter. Confederate general John Pemberton had also used the place as his headquarters. Several young women of the family and one, a governess named Mary Emma Hurlbut, from Connecticut, naturally attracted Federal soldiers, so much so that Grant assigned Rawlins to protect the women from unwanted attentions. James Harrison Wilson remembered that Rawlins, a widower for two years now, was "singularly shy and restrained in the presence of ladies." His new headquarters job caught him unawares, however, for he and Emma Hurlbut became acquainted and fell in love. They planned their wedding for the following December in Danbury, Connecticut.[2]

Grant with some members of his staff and other officers, taken in June 1864. Rawlins, in a rare, clean-shaven pose, is seated at left; next to him is Cyrus B. Comstock. The names of the other men are certain, however their order is not. They are Capts. Peter T. Hudson and William McKee Dunn (believed seated), Grant, Col. Michael R. Morgan, who was Grant's commissary general, Maj. W. M. Babcock, and Capt. Henry Janes. (NATIONAL ARCHIVES AND RECORDS ADMINISTRATION)

Despite his newfound happiness, Rawlins could still take his boss to task. Trade restrictions in Grant's department forbade speculators to buy and ship Southern cotton to the North. When a relative of Grant's came to visit the general, and in the process bought cotton to send home, Rawlins, without Grant's knowledge, ordered the man expelled from the department. Grant asked Rawlins to repeal his order, and Rawlins flew into a rage. He cursed and suggested that Grant's relative should be hanged rather than expelled. The outburst embarrassed everyone within earshot, and Rawlins rushed from the tent, leaving Grant stunned.

Wilson followed Rawlins and told him to apologize to Grant immediately. Rawlins, mortified at his action, agreed, and he quickly begged Grant's pardon. He noted that, since meeting Emma he had been trying to curb his foul language. "I resolved to quit cursing and flattered myself that I had succeeded," he said. Grant had not let Rawlins's temper sour their friendship before, and he would not do so now. Unfazed, Grant explained that Rawlins was not cursing, just expressing his "intense vehemence on the subject matter." He let Rawlins's expulsion order stand.[3]

Grant showed just how much he trusted Rawlins when he left the chief of staff in virtual command of the whole army in September 1863. After Vicksburg fell, Grant was eager to move his army south and capture Mobile, Alabama. From there he could attack the interior of the Confederacy, force Gen. Braxton Bragg to disengage from operations in eastern Tennessee, and wreck supply lines that were feeding Robert E. Lee's army in Virginia. Henry Halleck disagreed and instead ordered Grant to disperse the elements of his army to various theaters and prepare to cooperate with Nathaniel Banks on the lower Mississippi River. When Grant traveled to New Orleans to confer with Banks, he left Rawlins in charge of the army remaining at Vicksburg. Either Sherman or McPherson should have taken command in Grant's absence, but both declined in favor of Rawlins. Sherman suggested for anyone but Rawlins to take charge would confuse headquarters records. Of course, Grant expected nothing major to occur in his absence, and none of his staffers issued an important order without first consulting Sherman.[4]

The Vicksburg area did indeed remain quiet, but affairs in eastern Tennessee were about to greatly affect Grant and his staff. Throughout the summer and early fall, Maj. Gen. William S. Rosecrans, who had departed Grant's army for an independent command after the battles of Iuka and Corinth in October 1862, had maneuvered Confederate general Braxton Bragg's army out of central Tennessee to near the Georgia border. On September 19, however, Bragg turned and engaged Rosecrans in the bloody two-day battle of Chickamauga. Bragg's army put Old Rosey's men to flight, but the Confederate victory was hollow; Rosecrans retreated to the important railroad junction of Chattanooga, which joined the Confederacy's two major east-west rail lines and linked Georgia war industries with the rest of the breakaway nation.[5]

Bragg could not leave Rosecrans in such a threatening position, and he moved to trap the Federals in the city. Chattanooga sat on the south bank of the twisting Tennessee River in a gap in the Cumberland Mountains. Just west of Chattanooga the river took a sudden turn south for about two miles before turning abruptly north again to swing wide around Raccoon Mountain west of the city. South of Chattanooga, where the Tennessee swung back north, mighty Lookout Mountain sat astride the Tennessee-Georgia border, and Missionary Ridge dominated the landscape east of the city. Bragg got his men atop Missionary Ridge and Lookout Mountain, then he let geography do the rest. With the Tennessee at his back and mountains beyond that, Rosecrans was effectively under siege. He had but one supply line, winding through the mountains to the north, and the weather or Rebel raiders could close it in a moment. By mid-October horses in the garrison were starving to death and the men were on quarter rations.[6]

Abraham Lincoln turned to Grant to relieve Chattanooga. In October the War Department consolidated Grant's Army of the Tennessee, Ambrose Burnside's Army of the Ohio, and Rosecrans's Army of the Cumberland into one command, the Military Division of the Mississippi. On October 16 Secretary of War Edwin M. Stanton personally gave Grant command of the new division, making him head of all Federal armies between the Alleghenies and the Mississippi. Stanton also gave William T. Sherman command of the Army of the Tennessee, and he fired Rosecrans from command of the Cumberland army, replacing him with Gen. George H. Thomas, who had saved the army from annihilation at Chickamauga.[7]

On October 20 Grant gathered up his staff and started for Chattanooga. They took a circuitous route, first to Nashville, then by train to northern Alabama, then on horseback over muddy, nearly impassable roads to Chattanooga. Grant had been on crutches since his trip to New Orleans, when his horse, frightened by a locomotive, collided with a carriage; and his companions had to carry him over several rough spots on the last leg to Chattanooga.[8]

Grant and his staff arrived at Chattanooga during a rainstorm after dark on October 23. Wet and tired, Chief of Staff John Rawlins's quick temper ignited over what he perceived as discourtesies at George Thomas's headquarters. Grant and his staff officers had headed straight to Thomas's tent to discuss the situation at Chattanooga, but neither Thomas nor any of his staff officers offered Grant's party warm drink or dry clothes. Rawlins fumed until James Harrison Wilson, who had been out inspecting units, arrived and broke the ice, asking if someone couldn't feed Grant and his men and offer them dry clothes. Thomas complied, but Rawlins never forgot the slight. He privately suspected that Thomas was angry that Grant had arrived to take over his command.[9]

Thomas had 45,000 men in Chattanooga, and the War Department was sending him reinforcements—17,000 men under Sherman from the Army of the Tennessee and 20,000 from the Army of the Potomac under Maj. Gen. Joseph Hooker. But Grant realized that reinforcements would do no good if they were starving, and he set about opening a new supply line into Chattanooga.[10]

Grant found that Thomas's chief engineer, William F. "Baldy" Smith, a former engineer in the Army of the Potomac, already had a plan to open a new supply line. The Tennessee River, when it turned south and then abruptly north again, formed a peninsula just west of Chattanooga, and a crossing on its far side, known as Brown's Ferry, was the key to Smith's plan. The crossing was out of range of Bragg's artillery, but Rebels held it. Smith would have three columns—one coming from the reinforcements approaching Chattanooga from the west, one marching across the neck of the peninsula from Chattanooga, and one floating silently down the Tennessee from Chattanooga—converge on Brown's Ferry under cover of darkness. Once they secured the ford, engineers would span it with pontoon bridges. Then the soldiers would brush Confederates away from Kelly's Gap at the south end of Raccoon Mountain, and the new line would be open. Smith's plan called for swift, daring action, and Grant liked it. Early October 27 Federal soldiers went into action. Smith's plan met resounding success and the "Cracker Line," as soldiers in Chattanooga called the new supply route, was open. Grant could now turn his attention to Bragg's army on the high ground south and east of Chattanooga.[11]

When Sherman's troops arrived in mid-November, Grant began planning an offensive to rid Chattanooga of Bragg. The Confederacy had sent Gen. James Longstreet and 15,000 men of the Army of Northern Virginia to help Bragg with the siege, but on November 4 Bragg sent Longstreet's force to drive Ambrose Burnside's Army of the Ohio out of Knoxville, Tennessee. Grant feared Longstreet would make short work of Burnside, and he wanted to dispatch Bragg before Longstreet could return. Nevertheless, having seen two frontal assaults fail at Vicksburg, Grant thought rushing Bragg's high positions would be a waste of Federal soldiers.

He devised a more complex plan. Sherman's army would get across the Tennessee northeast of Chattanooga and secure a foothold on the northeast end of Missionary Ridge. Meanwhile, Hooker and his men from the Army of the Potomac would move southwest of Chattanooga, either capture or bypass Lookout Mountain, and then step across a valley to the southwest end of Missionary Ridge. With Thomas's men attacking the center of the ridge, diverting Confederates from reinforcing either flank, Sherman and Hooker could sweep across the top of Missionary Ridge and destroy Bragg's army.[12]

Grant had hoped to begin the offensive November 21, but Sherman's men had not reached Chattanooga yet. Harsh weather and harsher terrain delayed them so they were not ready to cross the Tennessee above Chattanooga until the twenty-third. In the meantime, Rawlins, at Grant's headquarters, delivered information about the military situation at Chattanooga to Sherman. He told Sherman that Grant wanted him to leave his baggage trains behind and hurry on to the river ford.[13]

On November 24 everyone was in position, and Grant ordered the show to begin. In a spectacular engagement atop fog-shrouded Lookout Mountain, Hooker's men captured the summit then moved on to the valley separating the mountain from Missionary Ridge. There they bogged down, so it was early November 25 before they reached Missionary Ridge. At the other end, Sherman had a rougher time. Rocky ground slowed the Westerners, but not as much as a hard group of fighters under Confederate general Pat Cleburne. Sherman never secured the northeast end of the ridge.

Hooker was in position to sweep the ridge, though, and Grant ordered Thomas to begin a diversionary attack on the center. Blue lines swept forward, taking a line of Confederate trenches. Emboldened by their success and eager to avenge their loss at Chickamauga, the Federals rushed on without orders. The shock of the attack knocked Bragg's men rearward, then toppled them from the ridge.[14]

The Chattanooga campaign was Grant's first large unified command effort. Even though it ended in a great Federal victory, the battle of Chattanooga virtually proceeded out of Grant's hands. Yes, Grant had crafted a complex offensive to relieve the city, but his plans went awry almost as soon as they began. Sherman, whom Grant had intended to be the star of the show, was held up on the Federal left and never got into the act; Joe Hooker delivered a fine initial performance but stumbled trying to cross the gap between sky-high Lookout Mountain and Missionary Ridge. In the center, Thomas's men, whom Grant envisioned only as reserve players, stole the show. And they did it, much to Grant's chagrin, without orders. Grant wanted Thomas's Cumberland men to move up the ridge only when Sherman and Hooker were headed along its crest, keeping Bragg's men from swooping down on the attackers coming up the center. After noon, though, with Sherman and Hooker delayed, Grant could see through his field glasses Pat Cleburne's unit drifting back from the fight with Sherman to Bragg's main defenses. Suspecting Bragg was about to make a counterattack, Grant asked Thomas, who was staring through his own binoculars next to Grant, if he did not think it was time for his men to attack. Thomas ignored the remark, waiting instead for a direct order. Grant gave it a short while later, although he had to personally give the order to the attack's lead commander before it rolled forward. Even then, Grant ordered that the attackers stop and re-form after taking the first of three Rebel entrenchments. The Federals easily pushed the Rebels out of the way, though, and, flushed with battle, rushed up the hill, quickly taking the second and third entrenchments. Grant angrily quizzed his subordinate, "Thomas, who ordered those men up the ridge?" "I don't know," replied Thomas, "I did not." Grant knew full well that the battle had proceeded without him. "Damn the battle!" he reportedly said soon after it ended. "I had nothing to do with it." He still had something to learn about coordinating the efforts of three major armies.[15]

James Harrison Wilson attempted to credit Rawlins and himself, not Grant, with spurring Thomas's men into action on the afternoon of the twenty-fifth. Perhaps, but Wilson was a great self-promoter, and Grant mentions nothing of it in his memoirs. Rawlins was actually quiet during the Chattanooga campaign. Theodore Bowers and William R. Rowley handled more routine, day-to-day correspondence and order writing than did Rawlins.[16]

Rawlins had good reason for silence during the Chattanooga campaign, for in truth, he was sick. His friends at headquarters suspected that Rawlins, fatigued after the year's campaigning, had taken cold in the rainy Tennessee autumn. But his illness was more serious. His first wife had died of tuberculosis at the beginning of the war, and the onset of his cold, which did not abate with time, struck Rawlins with fear that he, too, had contracted the disease. Doctors with Grant's army, unsure about the communicability of the disease, assured Rawlins, however, that he was not consumptive and that his symptoms would fade. Rawlins ultimately took a leave of absence in December, not only to recuperate but also to marry his sweetheart, Emma.[17]

Before he left, Rawlins made sure he fulfilled the one task he had assigned himself, protecting Grant. On November 17 Rawlins wrote to Emma that drink was flowing around headquarters and that he feared for Grant's sobriety. Apparently suspecting that Grant's injury in New Orleans resulted more from alcohol than from a horse accident, Rawlins told

Emma that he had hoped that "experience would prevent him ever again indulging with this his worst enemy." Nevertheless, Rawlins considered himself indispensable in the matter: "I am the only one here ([Grant's] wife not being with him) who can stay it . . . and prevent evil consequences." That same day Rawlins drafted a lengthy letter to Grant, imploring him to "immediately desist from further tasting of liquors of any kind." Rawlins thought better of giving Grant the letter, and he talked to him instead. In an endorsement on the letter Rawlins said that his discussion with the general "had the desired effect."[18]

Rawlins's accusation of November 17 is the same one historian Bruce Catton says was unfounded, because Grant had been planning strategy, not drinking. But Rawlins had good cause for concern. A few days before Rawlins drafted his letters, a drinking party had erupted at headquarters. Though he could not abide the debauchery, it led to the resignation of a staff officer Rawlins could abide even less.

Col. Clark B. Lagow threw the drunken revel, and a relative of Grant's chronicled it in his diary. William Wrenshall Smith, a first cousin of Julia

Grant with Rawlins (left) and staff officer Theodore Bowers outside their City Point headquarters in early 1865. Bowers had been with Grant since he joined the staff in April 1862. (NATIONAL ARCHIVES AND RECORDS ADMINISTRATION)

Dent Grant's, was visiting the general and getting a firsthand look at the battle of Chattanooga. He also saw Lagow's shenanigans. On Saturday, November 14, Smith penned in his diary, "Quite a disgraceful party— friends of Col. Lagow, stay up nearly all night playing &c. Gen breaks up the party himself about 4 o'clock in the morning." The next day Smith wrote, "Lagow don't come to table today [he habitually dined with Grant]. He is greatly mortified at his conduct last night. Grant is much offended at him and I am fearful it will result in his removal."[19]

In truth, Grant had already decided to can Lagow; the party iced his decision. On November 1 Charles M. Dana had written to Secretary of War Stanton recommending Lagow's dismissal. Describing Lagow as a "worthless fellow" who earned "no part" of his pay, Dana reported that Grant wanted "rid of him." And after his drunken spree, Lagow saw that he had about worn out his welcome at headquarters. Both Rawlins and Grant treated him cooly, and on November 18 Lagow tendered his resignation to Adj. Gen. Lorenzo Thomas. Grant endorsed it and asked the War Department to disregard his request for Lagow's dismissal in lieu of the man's resignation. Grant tried to keep Lagow busy until his resignation became effective December 1. But on November 26 Lagow misdirected a scouting party, which Grant had accompanied, by erroneously reporting the existence of a bridge over Chickamauga Creek. The next day the aide caused a six-hour delay in the departure of a relief column bound for Knoxville, where Ambrose Burnside still faced James Longstreet, by failing to promptly deliver orders. Lagow fell into such disgrace that, as William Wrenshall Smith recalled, he slunk out of headquarters on November 30, one day before scheduled, in "sore, depressed spirits."[20]

Lagow's resignation no doubt delighted Rawlins, Rowley, and Bowers. His departure virtually ridded them of the staff undesirables they had complained about more than a year earlier. Hillyer had left during the Vicksburg campaign, and now Lagow was gone. The third man they despised, John Riggin Jr., had left a month before Lagow. On October 12, 1863, in a letter to Emma, Rawlins stated flatly, "Col. Riggin has tendered his resignation and gone; General Grant has approved it." In an understatement belying his pleasure, Rawlins said of Riggin's departure, "I have no regret . . . and shall express none."[21]

The resignations were part of major changes taking place on Grant's staff, changes that were coming just in time. Upon assuming command of the Division of the Mississippi, Grant faced more complex problems of combined operations than he had before, and he needed a more professional personal staff to help him. The victory at Chattanooga fixed Grant's fame with the public and with Abraham Lincoln, and the following

March, Congress revived the grade of lieutenant general specifically for Grant. On March 9, 1864, Lincoln commissioned Grant lieutenant general and gave him command of all United States armies, which further compounded his need for a professional staff. The resignations of Riggin, Lagow, and Hillyer cut some nonprofessionals from Grant's staff, but more important than the cuts were additions.

The first three additions were on the clerical side of Grant's personal staff. Back on May 2, the day after the battle of Port Gibson, James Harrison Wilson approached Grant with the idea of augmenting his staff with a military secretary. Grant agreed that he should have one, and Wilson suggested Adam Badeau, whom he had known on the Port Royal, South Carolina, campaign. Badeau, a New York native, was an established newspaper writer and publisher, as well as a clerk in the State Department before the war. He had joined the Port Royal expedition as a reporter for the *New York Express,* and while there he started a newspaper for soldiers called the *Port Royal New South.* He served unofficially as a volunteer aide-de-camp to Gen. Quincy Gilmore during the bombardment of Fort Pulaski, then joined the army as an aide to Gen. Thomas W. Sherman. Grant ordered Badeau to report to his headquarters, but before he could do so Badeau suf-

Col. Adam Badeau, Grant's military secretary, in civilian dress. Badeau was so stoop-shouldered that Grant found him a comical sight, exclaiming that Badeau looked like a "bent fo'pence." (NATIONAL ARCHIVES AND RECORDS ADMINISTRATION)

fered a foot wound at Port Hudson. He underwent a lengthy recuperation in New York City, and did not join Grant until February 1864.[22]

Badeau was a competent choice, but he was a comical sight. Short and heavy, with a red face, red hair, and glasses, he was so stoop-shouldered that Grant recalled he looked like a "bent fo'pence." He once tried to ride his horse between two trees, but he misjudged the space between them and found himself and his saddle on the ground. Grant laughed about the incident for days.[23]

In late September Grant and Rawlins also petitioned the adjutant general's office in Washington to promote Pvt. George K. Leet to captain and add him to Grant's staff as an assistant adjutant general to help Rawlins. Leet had served with the Chicago Mercantile Battery and had been present at the battles of Chickasaw Bayou, Arkansas Post, Port Gibson, Champion Hill, Black River Bridge; at the siege of Vicksburg; and at the investment of Jackson. In late July Rawlins detached the man for duty at Grant's headquarters. "By his industry and ability [he] has shown himself eminently fitted for the position," commented Rawlins. The adjutant general's office made Leet's promotion official on October 3.[24]

Grant also added Tonawanda Seneca Ely S. Parker to his staff. Born in 1828 in New York state, Parker was, by age eighteen, petitioning congressmen in Washington to repeal a treaty moving the Senecas off their land. Parker studied law and passed his board exam, but in 1849 he switched careers to engineering, finding it more interesting. He obtained an engineering degree from the Rensselaer Polytechnic Institute in Troy, New York, and worked on various engineering projects before becoming construction engineer for the Federal government at the Lighthouse District around Lakes Michigan, Huron, and Superior.[25]

Parker soon got an assignment that put him on an indirect course to service on Grant's staff. He met another Federal engineer, William F. Smith, who secured Parker an assignment to Galena, Illinois, to build a customshouse and marine hospital. There Parker became active in Galena's Masonic Lodge, and he made lasting friendships with two of the Lodge's top members—John Rawlins and William R. Rowley. Parker also met Grant in 1859, who was by then working in his father's leather goods store.[26]

When the Civil War began, Parker tried to enlist, but the Federal government denied his request because, as an Indian, he was not a citizen. Finally, in 1863, another of Parker's Masonic friends, John E. Smith, who had become a brigadier general in Grant's Army of the Tennessee, recommended Parker as his assistant adjutant general. The adjutant general's office delayed, and Grant, probably with Rawlins's and Rowley's support for their old friend, wrote an endorsement for Parker. He stated that Parker, "highly educated and very accomplished," was "eminently qualified for the position." Parker received a captain's commission and served Smith from July to September 1863.[27] Parker then received orders to join the staff of his friend William F. Smith, now a general. Parker fell ill, however, and when he recovered he found that Grant wanted him on his staff. By the end of October Parker was on board with Grant as an assistant adjutant general.[28]

Badeau, Leet, and Parker were all competent men, more so than some men Grant had selected earlier in the war. They were all well qualified for clerical duties, but they were not professionally trained soldiers. Others joining Grant's headquarters, however, were.

First among them was Cyrus B. Comstock, as professional a soldier as one could find in Grant's army. A colleague once noted of the Massachusetts native, "He had somewhat the air of a Yankee schoolmaster, buttoned

Adam Badeau and Cyrus B. Comstock (standing) converse behind the seated Grant and Rawlins at the left of this photo. Seated to the right of the tent pole, almost in shadow, are Horace Porter and Ely Parker. (National Archives and Records Administration)

in a military coat." Comstock graduated from West Point in 1855; he served in the Corps of Engineers, then as an assistant professor at West Point. When the Civil War began, Comstock helped construct defenses around Washington, then, as a first lieutenant, he served an assistant to Brig. Gen. J. G. Barnard, chief engineer of the Army of the Potomac.[29]

Comstock received a promotion to captain on March 3, 1863, and on June 8 he received orders to report to Grant's army. Reporting to Grant's chief engineer, Capt. F. E. Prime, Comstock immediately went to work on the siege lines at Vicksburg. His industry and intelligence won him a staunch supporter in Charles M. Dana, who, of course, had Secretary of War Stanton's ear. In late June 1863 Dana sent Stanton a series of brief messages about Comstock's work. "Captain Comstock takes general charge of the siege works on the lines of both [Generals] Lauman and Herron," he wrote on June 19. On June 25 he commented that siege works were "going forward well" under Comstock's eye. Finally, on June 28, Dana reported that Prime had gone north sick, and that Grant had made Comstock chief engineer. Later Dana told Stanton that Comstock was "an officer of great merit." He noted that Comstock had a quality that Prime had lacked—"a talent for organization. His accession to the army will be the source of much improvement."[30]

Grant also praised Comstock. After Vicksburg fell, while Comstock was destroying the siege approaches he had helped build, Grant commented that he had "ably filled" Prime's spot. What's more, Grant said that Comstock, along with Wilson and Prime, had passed on to his army experience such as "would enable any division . . . hereafter to conduct a siege with considerable skill in the absence of regular engineer officers."[31]

Comstock remained as Grant's chief engineer until October 19, 1863, when he took the same position at St. Louis. Grant wanted him back, though. A month later he notified Comstock that he wanted him for assistant inspector general, with the rank of lieutenant colonel, on his special staff. Comstock told Grant another general had made him a similar offer, but he chose to return to Grant. Although still on Grant's special staff, Comstock was working his way toward the personal staff; the next March, after becoming lieutenant general, Grant announced Comstock as his senior aide-de-camp.[32]

Comstock would become preeminent on Grant's newly professionalized staff. In January 1864, before Grant became lieutenant general, Comstock, along with Gen. William F. Smith, submitted to Grant a plan to land 60,000 men at Norfolk, Virginia, or at New Bern, North Carolina, and invade the North Carolina interior.[33] Grant ultimately used a similar plan, perhaps based on Comstock's. Regardless, that Comstock submitted such a plan reveals a strategic initiative never before present on Grant's personal staff.

In the midst of the Chattanooga campaign, Grant requested that another professional soldier, Capt. Horace Porter, join his staff. Porter, a Pennsylvania native, graduated from West Point in 1860 and went immediately into the ordnance department. He made it onto Gen. Thomas W. Sherman's staff and became friends with James Harrison Wilson. Like Wilson, he participated in the campaign against Fort Pulaski, Georgia, winning praise from Gen. Quincy Gillmore. Gillmore said that Porter had acted as chief of ordnance and artillery and that "he directed in person the transportation of nearly all the heavy ordnance and instructed the men in its use." On September 29, 1862, Porter became chief of ordnance for the Army of the Ohio, and on January 28, 1863, he took over the same posi-

Brig. Gen. Horace Porter, who joined Grant's staff as an aide-de-camp in April 1864. Porter's memoirs, Campaigning with Grant, *provide valuable insight into the workings of Grant's staff.* (NATIONAL ARCHIVES AND RECORDS ADMINISTRATION)

tion for the Army of the Cumberland. He was promoted to captain on March 3. When Grant entered Chattanooga as head of the Division of the Mississippi, he found that the officers around George Thomas's headquarters had everything good to say about Porter, but they were distressed that the War Department had called him to Washington to help with a reorganization of the ordnance department.[34]

Porter found the assignment "distasteful," but Grant tried to intervene on his behalf. He called Porter to his headquarters and told him that, while he had to obey his current call to Washington, he should take along a letter Grant had drafted to Henry Halleck. In it Grant told Halleck that Porter "is represented by all officers who know him as one of the most meritorious and valuable young officers in the service." He requested the War Department move Porter to his staff and make him a brigadier general in the process.[35]

Grant thought his strong comments on Porter's behalf would allow him to return to the field, but Halleck and Stanton surprised him. Upon arrival in Washington, Porter could not obtain an audience with Halleck. He settled for giving Grant's letter to Halleck's adjutant, but he never received acknowledgement of its receipt. Porter even met with Stanton to protest his retention in Washington, but the secretary insisted that he stay with the ordnance department. Porter did not see Grant again until the general arrived in Washington in March 1864 to receive his commission as lieutenant general. Grant continued to petition for Porter's assignment to his staff, and on April 27 the War Department relented, making Porter an aide-de-camp of Grant's.[36]

The next professional soldier whom Grant added to his personal staff was Orville E. Babcock. A Vermonter, Babcock graduated from West Point in 1861, going directly into the Corps of Engineers as a first lieutenant. He served in the Department of Pennsylvania the first summer of the war, then, along with Cyrus B. Comstock, served as an engineer in the Army of the Potomac. Babcock became a lieutenant colonel of volunteers January 1, 1863, and the next month, he joined Maj. Gen. Ambrose Burnside's IX Army Corps as chief engineer. He became a lieutenant colonel in the Regular Army on March 29, 1864. By April 6 Grant had picked Babcock to join his staff as an aide-de-camp. Grant biographer William McFeely calls Babcock "another of those totally unexceptional men whom Grant trusted"; nevertheless, he added more West Point experience to Grant's staff and soon grew close to the general.[37]

Finally, Grant selected his brother-in-law and old West Point roommate, Frederick Tracy Dent, to join his personal staff as an aide-de-camp.

Dent's appointment was not just a case of nepotism. He had made a life-long career of the army and was a major in the regular Fourth U.S. Infantry when Grant called him to his staff.[38]

Between 1861 and 1864, Grant had matured in his selection of staff officers. Though many of the new men on the staff were Grant's friends, they also had military educations and wartime experience. An exchange between Grant and Abraham Lincoln on March 29, 1864, shows just how adamant Grant was that his new staffers be well qualified. Lincoln had recommended a friend, a Captain Kinney, for a position on Grant's staff. Grant, mistakenly calling the man Kennedy, refused. "I would be glad to accommodate Capt. Kennedy but in the selection of my staff I do not want any one whom I do not personally know to be qualified for the position assigned them."[39]

By April 6, 1864, the composition of Grant's new staff was set. Brig. Gen. John A. Rawlins remained as chief of staff, with Lt. Col. Theodore S. Bowers, assistant adjutant general, retaining his role as Rawlins's principal assistant. Lt. Col. Cyrus B. Comstock was Grant's senior aide-de-camp,

John Rawlins at the rank of brigadier general. In petitioning for Rawlins's first general's commission, Grant said, "He comes nearest being indispensable to me of any officer in the service." (LIBRARY OF CONGRESS)

with Lt. Cols. Orville E. Babcock, Horace Porter, and Frederick Tracy Dent also serving as aides. Lt. Cols. William R. Rowley and Adam Badeau were Grant's military secretaries, and Capts. Ely S. Parker and George K. Leet were assistant adjutants general. Lt. Col. William L. Duff, the hard drinker who had been Grant's chief of artillery at Vicksburg, became an inspector general, and Grant retained Capt. Peter T. Hudson and 1st Lt. William McKee Dunn Jr. as aides-de-camp. Even though Hudson and Dunn were aides-de-camp, Grant never considered them equal to West-Pointers Comstock, Babcock, Porter, and Dent. Hudson and Dunn would be little more than couriers, and in fact Grant had confided to Comstock that he should probably get rid of Hudson, along with William L. Duff.[40]

The professionalism of this new staff was readily apparent. Newspaper reporter Sylvanus Cadwallader, who had ridden with Grant for more than two years, saw the change immediately. Grant's personal staff was "divided on the line of the regular and volunteer service," said Cadwallader. "Porter, Babcock, and . . . Comstock were sticklers for military authority. Duff, Rowley, Bowers, and others manifested their feelings by ominous shrugs of the shoulders rather than words. West Point training was quite apparent."[41]

Grant and his new staff had a massive job before them. When Grant pinned on his third star, he became commander of not just one army, as he had been at Vicksburg, or even three armies, as at Chattanooga, but of all the armies of the United States. Nineteen military departments and seventeen commanders were under his charge, and his new job was to move all of them in concert toward one goal—the destruction of the Confederacy. Two major Confederate armies stood in Grant's way, and he saw that the key to victory was Robert E. Lee's Army of Northern Virginia, guarding Richmond. The South's other major army, that under Gen. Joseph E. Johnston, in Georgia, Grant considered but an obstacle to the first, guarding as it did supply lines and industries that fed Lee's army. In designing his grand strategy for 1864, Grant decided to send Sherman, now commanding Grant's old, massive Division of the Mississippi, against Johnston in Georgia. At the same time, Maj. Gen. George G. Meade's Army of the Potomac would engage Lee in northern Virginia, and, moving from Fortress Monroe on the eastern tip of the Virginia Peninsula, political general Benjamin Butler and his Army of the James would demonstrate against Richmond and the important transportation junction of Petersburg, about fifteen miles south of the Rebel capital. The independent IX Army Corps, under Maj. Gen. Ambrose Burnside, would be held as a reserve at Annapolis, Maryland, ready to swing left or right to reinforce either Butler or Meade as Grant saw fit. Grant would leave skeleton commands on scattered fields to guard Union-held territory, such as the line of the Mississippi River, western Tennessee, and some beachfront toeholds in the Carolinas, and he would have Nathaniel Banks campaign up the Red River in Louisiana against trans-Mississippi Confederates, but he would rob as many soldiers as necessary from those commands to reinforce the three major thrusts.[42]

It was well that outside observers like Sylvanus Cadwallader could spot the new professionalism of Grant's personal staff, for the general would soon be using its members in a manner untried in an American army. Grant knew that coordinating the campaign he had designed would be a monumental task, and he knew he needed help. He no doubt realized, as Charles Dana had commented to Secretary of War Stanton, that things often were accomplished through force of his own will. He also realized that the various commanders now under him, whether in army or corps command, might not have the same view of the campaign as he had. He said as much to Horace Porter when he commented on the difficulty of finding generals with "sufficient breadth of view and administrative ability to confine their attention . . . giving a general supervision to their commands, instead of wasting their time upon details."[43] But he could no longer be present at every army headquarters to drive forward his plans. Grant did not have to worry about Sherman—his redheaded friend was fighter enough to accomplish any objective, and then some. He also did not have to worry about Meade, for he planned to make headquarters right next to Meade's, not to take command of the Army of the Potomac, but to nudge it the way he wanted it to go. He did have to worry about some other generals crucial to the campaign—Ambrose Burnside in particular, who had led the Army of the Potomac to disaster at Fredericksburg eighteen months earlier and whom Grant had been forced to bail out of a siege at Knoxville, Tennessee; and Ben Butler, whom neither Grant nor Rawlins trusted.[44] He needed someone at the headquarters of those generals to act with the knowledge, strategic understanding, and authority of Grant himself. He turned to the men of his personal staff to do the job.

Grant intended the grand campaign to begin in early May 1864. The Army of the Potomac sat on the north side of the Rapidan River in northern Virginia facing Lee's well-entrenched army on the south side. Grant wanted to cross the Rapidan on the night of May 3–4; Butler would start up the Virginia Peninsula as soon as the Army of the Potomac got across the Rapidan; Maj. Gen. Franz Sigel, with a small command, would attack down the Shenandoah Valley to keep Lee from pulling reinforcements from there; and down at Chattanooga, Tennessee, Sherman would head for Georgia on May 5.

On the night of May 3, Grant called all the members of his personal staff into the front room of a little house at Culpeper, Virginia, which he had taken for his headquarters. He was writing instructions when the men came in, and when he finished, he lighted a new cigar and turned to his staffers. He again explained to them the plan. He wanted to destroy Lee's army, or at least wound it mortally before it could crawl into Richmond's defenses. "I shall not give my attention so much to Richmond as to Lee's army, and I want all commanders to feel that hostile armies, and not cities, are to be their objective points," he told the men. Then, in a few sentences that elevated Grant's staff officers from office bureaucrats and couriers to members of a strategic body, Grant said, "I want you to discuss with me freely from time to time the details of the orders given for the conduct of a battle, and learn my views as fully as possible as to what course should be pursued in all the contingencies which may arise. I expect to send you to the critical points of the lines to keep me promptly advised of what is taking place, and in cases of great emergency, when new dispositions have to be made on the instant, or it becomes suddenly necessary to reinforce one command by sending to its aid troops from another, and there is not time to communicate with headquarters, I want you to explain my views to commanders, and urge immediate action, looking to cooperation, without waiting for specific orders from me."[45]

Grant had moved into the realm of modern staff usage. In a small way, he was asking his staff officers to perform much as Prussian general Helmuth von Moltke had been asking his staff to perform for years. In Prussia, of course, the Great General Staff trained staff officers in every facet of strategy and government objectives, then it attached them to field headquarters to direct commanders toward a common goal. In Culpeper, Virginia, the method was crude and simple, but the theory was the same. Grant, acting as his own "Great General Staff," imparted his views of the campaign to this staff officers, then sent them out to work alongside field commanders. Historian Richard J. Sommers calls these men "liaisons,"[46] but they were much more. They did not just facilitate communications between headquarters and field commands; they carried with them full authority to act in Grant's stead, to make critical spot decisions and issue orders in his absence. They were Grant's representatives, his proxies. They embodied all of the general's plans, ideas, and hopes for the campaign. They were to be, in effect, Grant himself.

Grant, of course, had hit on this enlightened bit of staff usage as a way to fill a need that his new command created, not by studying staff advances in other countries. He had been an indifferent student at West Point, and it is doubtful that his study habits had improved much over the past two decades. West Point French classes had presented him a great deal of trouble, and he never learned to speak or read it well, so it is equally doubtful that he ever read Paul Thiebault's *Manuel des Adjutants Généraux et des Adjoints Employés dans les Etats-Major Divisionairs des Armées*. Grant's senior aide, Comstock, was friends with former West Point instructor William P. Craighill, who wrote the staff officers' manual all the men carried in their saddle bags. While Craighill had concerned himself most with order writing in his book, he had highlighted French staff organizations.[47] If that influenced Grant, he never said. More likely, Grant's new contribution to staff work did not come from the books. Growing from necessity and experience, it was what Civil War historian Edward Hagerman calls a "mechanistic," or "practical if not theoretical,"[48] response to new combat conditions. Grant had tried something similar on the Iuka campaign in September 1862, but Clark B. Lagow had not been staff officer enough to help Grant much. Grant had also seen the large unified attack at Chattanooga, victorious though it was, stumble in its execution for lack of staff coordination. The armies under his command now were even larger—the Army of the Potomac had 115,000 troops, Butler's Army of the James had 30,000[49] And the scope of the cooperative operations Grant planned necessitated that he rely on staff officers to help coordinate them. The duties Grant handed his staff in May 1864 were also born of common sense and experience. But as most good military plans are born of just those elements, it is no wonder Grant's view of staff usage suddenly coincided with that of the Prussian Army's.

Grant's staffers may have seen the general's intentions coming, for he had been hinting at them by his actions. Grant had been corresponding with Sherman, in Chattanooga, in preparation for the spring campaign. On April 19 Grant sent Comstock personally to Sherman with details of his own plans. "Colonel Comstock . . . can spend a day with you, and fill up many a little gap of information not given in any of my letters," Grant wrote Sherman. Sherman had expected Grant to begin the campaign as early as April 27, but Comstock told Sherman it would probably be May 2, at least. Comstock also needed to judge the preparedness of Sherman's troops, information no one wanted to send across the telegraph wires, so Grant would know exactly when to begin. Comstock left Sherman's camp on April 24, and Sherman sent with him a letter to Grant saying that Comstock had the "facts and figures" about his armies. "As soon as you see them make your orders," said Sherman.[50]

Grant had also sent Orville Babcock to Franz Sigel's headquarters at Cumberland, Maryland, to help the German general iron out plans for his Valley campaign. Grant had recommended that Sigel start his campaign from Beverly, but Sigel soon reported that rains had made nearby roads impassable. He submitted another plan of attack, which Grant sent Babcock to check out. "Confer freely with Col. Babcock," Grant told Sigel, "and whilst he remains with you, let us settle, unalterably, the line to be pursued by your forces." Grant had not yet, however, fully given Babcock authority to issue orders in his name. Babcock soon reported back that Sigel's plan was satisfactory.[51]

On May 3 Grant issued orders for the great campaign to begin the next day, and soon after midnight, May 4, the Army of the Potomac began crossing the Rapidan at Germanna, Ely's, and Culpeper Mine Fords. Burnside's IX Corps began moving down from Annapolis, for Grant had ordered it to support Meade, not Butler, who that same day put his army on transports at Hampton Roads and began sailing up the James River toward Richmond. Immediately south of the Rapidan, and extending about seven miles farther south, was the dense area of trees and undergrowth known as the Wilderness. Travel through the Wilderness other than by the few roads that coursed through it was nearly impossible. Many soldiers of the Army of the Potomac had been there before, for exactly one year earlier Joe Hooker had engaged Lee near the crossroads landmark of Chancellorsville. At the same time Grant was slicing through Mississippi far to the west, Lee was whipping Hooker soundly. The soldiers, retracing their steps a year later and occasionally stumbling across the uncovered bones of comrades killed in Hooker's fiasco, feared Bobby Lee was about to do the same to them. But Grant had other plans. He knew the tangled woods undermined his numerical strength, and he wanted to get through the Wilderness quickly, moving around Lee's right to keep his supply lines as short as possible, and fight Lee in the open.[52]

Lee, encamped near Orange Court House and Gordonsville, also had other plans. The Army of the Potomac marched southeast via the Germanna Plank Road and Brock Road, and had to cross intersections with the Orange Turnpike, near Wilderness Tavern, and the Orange Plank Road about a mile farther south. Lee sent his II Corps, under Gen. Richard Ewell, pouring eastward on the Orange Turnpike and General A. P. Hill's corps along the Orange Plank Road to catch Grant. On May 5 the armies collided. Maj. Gen. Winfield Scott Hancock's II Corps was leading the

Army of the Potomac through the Wilderness; behind him was the V Corps of Maj. Gen. Gouvernor K. Warren; and behind him was the VI Corps of Maj. Gen. John Sedgwick. When the Confederates approached, the Army of the Potomac faced west, with Hancock fanning his forces out either side of the Orange Plank Road to meet Hill, and Warren deploying across the turnpike to meet Ewell. Sedgwick took his men off the Brock Road and into the Wilderness to come in on Warren's right to fight Ewell. The battle of the Wilderness was on, and the fighting quickly became fierce. The thick woods destroyed unit cohesion and hid the action from commanders. Soon Warren's corps veered into the tangled growth between the turnpike and the plank road. Rifle and artillery fire ignited the dry leaves that carpeted the Wilderness, trapping wounded soldiers and roasting them to death. Soldiers, fighting amid the screams of their burning friends, could barely see their enemies and had to fire at muzzle flashes.[53] By the end of May 5, the fighting had decided nothing.

On May 6 Grant ordered the fighting renewed, and he began dispatching his staff officers to help field commanders. Sedgwick and Warren drove back down the Orange Turnpike against Ewell, and Hancock down the Orange Plank Road against Hill. All the previous day, from Grant's headquarters near Wilderness Tavern, Cyrus B. Comstock and William R. Rowley had sent Burnside orders regarding his order of march and troop dispositions. Now he had come up, and at 6:20 A.M. Comstock sent orders for him to join the battle. Grant wanted Burnside to leave a division to guard the junction of the turnpike and Germanna Plank Road and use the rest of his IX Corps to fill a dangerous gap between Hancock's right flank and Warren's left. But Burnside, keeping in character with his past military accomplishments, got lost. South of the Germanna Plank Road, his men wandered about the Wilderness between and to rear of both Hancock's and Warren's flanks, never connecting with either. Hancock fumed at Burnside's absence, but at 9 A.M. he got news that Grant had sent Comstock to personally show Burnside where to place his army. Within an hour Comstock sent word to Grant that Burnside was nearing Hancock's position; they could hear the II Corps firing from less than a mile away. Grant was not content with Comstock holding Burnside's hand, and at 11:45 A.M. John Rawlins sent Burnside orders to "push in with all vigor so as to drive the enemy from General Hancock's front. . . . Hancock has been expecting you for the last three hours."[54]

Hancock, in fact, had gained some ground without Burnside. He had pushed Hill's men back to near a clearing where Lee himself had made camp. Lee tried to personally lead a counterattack, but his men demanded that he go to the rear. At that moment, Lee's best fighter, Gen. James Longstreet, whose corps had been ten miles away when the fighting started on the fifth, got his corps on the field and battered Hancock back to his starting place. Longstreet then took the initiative, driving on Hancock's exposed left flank. In an accident that resembled the shooting of Stonewall Jackson by his own men a year earlier, Longstreet's men mistakenly shot him. The wound incapacitated Longstreet for five months.

Meanwhile, Cyrus B. Comstock remained at Burnside's headquarters throughout the swirling fight. He kept Grant abreast of events there and in Warren's corps to the right.[55] At 3:30 P.M., Grant ordered Hancock to plan another assault for 6:00 P.M., and he sent word to Burnside to assist Hancock. Burnside's men got into position, and Grant sent word that Burnside's reserve division was on its way as reinforcements. Later, however, Grant cancelled the attack.[56]

On the right, near Grant's headquarters, the lieutenant general almost lost his army. Confederates under Gen. John B. Gordon found themselves on the extreme right flank of the Union line, and they swept down upon it. The attack captured two Federal generals and very nearly rolled up the entire Union line, but VI Corps commander Sedgwick rallied his men and averted a Confederate victory. The fight in the confused underbrush sputtered to a halt, with Hancock still astride the Orange Plank Road in earthworks, Burnside to his right, and Warren and Sedgwick's line still astride the Orange Turnpike but bent back almost ninety degrees so it touched the Germanna Plank Road

Lee may have whipped Grant in the Wilderness, but Grant was not prepared to retreat as his Eastern predecessors had done. Instead, he planned to keep moving south. On May 7, as the Army of the Potomac divisions pulled out of line, Grant, Meade, and their staffs clattered down the Brock Road trailing some cavalry troopers. Coming to a fork in the road, Grant and Meade chose the right path and started down it. Soon Comstock, "with the instinct of the engineer," Grant said, suspected that they were on the wrong road and spurred his horse ahead of the generals. Up ahead he spotted Lee's army on the move; had he not scouted the road, Grant and Meade would soon have been prisoners.[57]

Grant plotted a march to Spotsylvania Court House, a crossroads town in a clearing southeast of the Wilderness. There, between Lee and Richmond, he would force Lee into an open fight. Grant started his march by evening, May 7, but Lee, guessing Grant's intentions, got his men there first. Early May 8, Confederates scrambled behind rough earthworks and turned back a Federal assault. Grant regrouped, and on May 10 he threw his men at the Confederate works twice more. Both attempts failed. Grant sent his men against the works again on May 12, touching off one of the costliest battles of the war; no real territory changed hands, but Federal casualties were 6,800, while Confederates lost 5,000 men. The fight on May 12 was the last major battle at Spotsylvania, but Grant spent another week trying to maneuver Lee out of his trenches. When those tactics failed, Grant marched by Lee's flank to the North Anna River. Again Lee beat Grant to his objective. Rather than start another fight, Grant kept marching south. At Totopotomy Creek, Grant found Rebels again entrenched before him, so he slid around Lee's flank in one last attempt to get between the Grey Fox and Richmond. On June 1 Grant arrived at a crossroads about ten miles northeast of Richmond known as Cold Harbor. Lee's men were arriving, too, but they were not fully entrenched, and Grant ordered an assault on their unfinished works. The Army of the Potomac men were tired, though, and not all of them had arrived yet, so Grant had to postpone the attack. By the time the assault was ready, on June 3, the Rebels were secure behind new works. Grant's assault was as disastrous as the ones at Spotsylvania; he lost more than 7,000 in under an hour. Confederates lost only 1,500 men.[58]

Before the spring campaign started, Grant had told Army of the James commander Ben Butler that, if Lee evaded him and slipped back into Richmond's defenses, Grant would pull the Army of the Potomac into line next to Butler's army and together they would handle Lee. Grant was assuming, of course, that Butler would take his first objective—Petersburg. On May 5 Butler had sailed his troops up the James River to City Point, within ten miles of Petersburg. The next day his generals made a tentative attempt to take the town, but Confederate defenders drove the Federals back. To Grant's chagrin, Butler made no other serious attempt to take his objectives, but instead got himself so trapped by a few Rebel units and Virginia terrain that he was of no use to anyone.

Now, in mid-June, with the Army of the Potomac at Cold Harbor, Petersburg was still a prize for the taking. One more time around Lee's right flank, Grant saw, and Petersburg could be his; if Petersburg fell, Richmond would have to follow, and the Army of Northern Virginia would be stranded. On the night of June 12 Grant and Meade secretly slipped the 100,000 men of the Army of the Potomac out of their Cold Harbor defenses and across the James River. For three days, Lee did not know that they had gone. Southern general P. G. T. Beauregard, a hero of first Bull Run and Grant's old nemesis from Shiloh, was defending Petersburg with 2,500 men; the Federals now bearing down on him outnumbered his force greatly. Grant had borrowed Maj. Gen. William F. Smith's XVIII Corps from Butler's army to spearhead the attack, and Smith went in motion while Hancock's II Corps was coming up. On June 15 Smith's men carried some of Beauregard's outer defenses, and Petersburg lay virtually open to Federal occupation. But Smith inexplicably became convinced that Rebel defenders outnumbered him. At first he thought to wait for Hancock before mounting an attack, then, despite a moonlit night, he cancelled any attack at all. Grant was sorely vexed. When he got on the field, he and Meade ordered attacks on the Petersburg lines on June 16, 17, and 18. All failed. Lee, who had been holding his army north of the James to protect Richmond from an enemy that was no longer there, finally discovered his mistake and joined Beauregard in the Petersburg lines. If Grant wanted Petersburg now, he would have to resort to something he knew well—siege warfare. The siege of Petersburg began on June 18.[59]

The spring campaign had certainly not gone as Grant had hoped. Critics said that Lee had whipped him, and in fact the Confederate general had outmaneuvered Grant time and again. Others called Grant a butcher—the Army of the Potomac had lost 64,000 casualties since May 5. Still, Grant had refused to admit defeat, and he had placed two Federal armies before Richmond, where he intended to keep them—two things no Federal general had yet done in front of Lee. And, even though their usage had not ensured victory for Grant, he had, through the six weeks from the Wilderness to Petersburg, stuck to his plan of putting staff officers at "critical" spots of the battlefields.

Colonel Comstock had stayed with Burnside at IX Corps headquarters throughout the second day of the Wilderness fight, and, on the march to Spotsylvania, Grant had placed Orville Babcock with Burnside to hurry the slow-moving general along. To ensure that Burnside speed up his pace, John Rawlins, at Grant's headquarters, fired message after message to Burnside urging rapidity. Even so, Burnside did not arrive at Spotsylvania until after the fight on May 8.[60]

Remembering how Burnside had gotten lost trying to link up with Hancock in the Wilderness, Rawlins wanted to make sure it did not happen again at Spotsylvania. No fighting occurred May 9, but Rawlins urged Burnside to prepare for a fight the next day. He wired the muttonchop-whiskered general to carefully examine all roads near Spotsylvania and know positively where they led. Then, anticipating that one of Burnside's divisions would have to help Sedgwick's or Warren's men during the fight, Rawlins told Burnside to have staff officers of that division learn exactly what roads led to those other units. "When the division receives orders to move it must be conducted by one of those staff officers . . . that there may be no delay," admonished Rawlins.[61]

When Grant ordered the general attack at Spotsylvania on May 10, Orville Babcock was at the headquarters of Brig. Gen. Horatio G. Wright, who had assumed command of the VI Corps the day before, when a sharpshooter had killed Maj. Gen. John Sedgwick. Babcock kept Grant's headquarters informed of the situation at Wright's front. During the fight, one of Wright's divisions broke through Confederate lines, but a counterattack forced them back.[62]

On May 11, planning to attack at Spotsylvania again the next day, Grant sent Comstock to reconnoiter a spot between the VI and the IX Corps designated as the point of attack. Comstock took three officers from Hancock's II Corps and, riding for hours in a driving rain, the men tried to check the situation as close to enemy lines as they dared. Comstock, however, misled the quartet, and it was nearly nightfall before they had an accurate survey of the attack point.[63]

That same day Grant told Burnside that he and Hancock would attack "jointly and precisely at 4 A.M. May 12." He also informed Burnside that he would be getting more help from headquarters to help him execute the attack: "I send two of my staff officers, Colonels Comstock and Babcock, in whom I have great confidence, to remain with you and General Hancock." He added that they were acquainted with "the direction the attack is to be made from here, [and had] . . . instruction to rend[er] you every assistance in their power."[64]

Burnside did not like having the staff officers join his command. In his diary, Comstock noted that he and Babcock joined Burnside on May 11 "with orders to stay all night." Upon arrival, Comstock and Babcock discovered that Burnside, for no apparent reason, had moved his troops back some distance from their prescribed line. "He [returned] them at once without difficulty, but with some grumbling at the change," Comstock wrote.[65]

During the fight the next day, May 12, Comstock and Babcock stayed at Burnside's headquarters, keeping Grant abreast of the battle's progress. At one point during the fight, Grant telegraphed Burnside that he wanted his orders obeyed. Burnside, remembering how Grant's headquarters had prodded him the whole way to Spotsylvania, suspected that Comstock had been complaining to Grant about Burnside's slowness. When he challenged the staff officer, Comstock denied it, saying that he had only informed Grant about what was actually happening along Burnside's line. According to Comstock, at another instant, apparently chafing under the staff officer's watchful eye, Burnside snapped that he would "command his own divisions." Then, perhaps thinking better of it, he asked Comstock for advice. In his diary's entry for May 12, Comstock summed up his attitude toward Burnside: "Rather weak and not fit for a corps command."[66]

If Burnside had problems working with Comstock, he was not alone. Back at Grant's headquarters, Chief of Staff Rawlins disliked the man as well. Rawlins, the Galena lawyer, had done his best to learn military matters in the three years he had been with Grant, and he may have felt uneasy among the army professionals who had arrived on Grant's staff in the last six months. Although they did not interfere with his running of the office, Rawlins suspected that Comstock was exerting more and more influence over Grant. In fact, he blamed Comstock for the way Grant was conducting the spring campaign. Rawlins recalled the finesse and fluidity with which Grant had dropped below Vicksburg, then up to its rear. Now Grant was using a sledgehammer, it seemed, exhausting men's lives with the same kind of attacks that had failed at Vicksburg. James Harrison Wilson was no longer part of Grant's special staff, but as a cavalry commander he had plenty of opportunity to visit his friend Rawlins. He noticed Rawlins's agitation over the "slipshod" way Grant was conducting operations. According to Wilson, Rawlins pointedly blamed Comstock for Grant's insistence on frontal attacks. Comstock's "advice and constant refrain was 'Smash 'em up! Smash 'em up!'" The words haunted Rawlins so much that he repeated them himself, turning pale and shaking with anger as he did so.[67] If Rawlins was as vociferous about Comstock as he was about Grant's drinking, the general certainly knew his chief's opinion of the staff officer.

Nevertheless, Grant continued using Comstock, and other staff officers, in the field, and he gave Comstock a great deal of latitude. On June 16, near Petersburg, Comstock wrote orders to V Corps commander, Maj. Gen. Gouvernor K. Warren. "General Grant directed that you should get up to the enemy on the Jerusalem road," Comstock wrote, but then he explained that such a move would put a large swamp between Warren's corps and the rest of the army. Then Comstock gave his own idea. "I think General Grant, if he knew the circumstance (he is now at Bermuda Hundred), would desire you to get up on Norfolk and Petersburg road instead. I would so advise." In those orders Comstock had done just as Grant had wanted; he had acted on his own in the absence of Grant, without wasting time getting the general's approval.[68]

As Grant slipped from the North Anna down to Cold Harbor and Petersburg, he sent his staff aides from command to command. Grant began dispatching them to help the Army of the James, and Comstock,

Babcock, and Horace Porter worked with Benjamin Butler and his XVIII Corps leader, William F. Smith. The work largely involved reconnoitering lines and transmitting orders, but Grant especially wanted Comstock to check the safety of Butler's lines. Grant was about to send the Army of the Potomac across the James River, and he knew that if Lee discovered the movement, the Confederates could pounce on Butler while Grant's troops were astride the river. Before ordering the move, he first wanted Comstock to see if Butler needed reinforcements. Grant also sent aide Frederick Tracy Dent to round up river transportation for Smith's assault on Petersburg.[69]

By the start of the Petersburg siege, Grant's subaltern army and corps commanders were accustomed to the general's staff officers frequenting their headquarters. And, perhaps grudgingly or because they feared to make a move without Grant's approval, they even began requesting staff assistance. Meade was the first. Back on May 20, when the army was pulling away from Spotsylvania, General Wright's VI Corps was to hold the right flank while the rest of the army moved out. Meade was worried about his position, though, and wrote to Grant, "I think it would be well if you should send either Comstock or Babcock to consult and advise with him." Grant agreed and sent Babcock, who helped Wright establish his defensive line.[70] On June 21, in the growing siege lines around Petersburg, Meade called for help again. Consulting a map that Comstock and engineer General J. G. Barnard had drawn, Grant ordered Meade to position artillery on his left to hold Confederates in place while he moved to a better location. Meade sent to Grant, "I do not fully understand your views. Can you not send Barnard and Comstock here to explain them?"[71]

Even crusty Ben Butler called for help. On June 20 Butler's chief engineer, Maj. Gen. Godfrey Weitzel, had been reconnoitering a bridge. Butler told Grant that Weitzel considered the problem "of the most difficult solution," which he did not think himself capable of making. "He does not feel justified to decide what to recommend, and suggests that Colonel Comstock be sent over and look at the position with him," said Butler. Grant wanted to oblige, but Comstock was busy elsewhere. "I think General Weitzel had better give the problem the best solution he can," advised Grant.[72]

The West Point professionals on Grant's staff had plenty of work during the spring 1864 campaign, but Grant kept his staff clerics busy as well. He had left George K. Leet behind in Washington to run a liaison headquarters office there. Theodore S. Bowers and Ely Parker traveled with the field headquarters, both devoting much of their time to writing special orders. Parker drafted orders easing supply and transportation problems and assigning J. G. Barnard as chief engineer for all armies in the field. Bowers handled assignments to command, and on May 24 he issued Special Orders No. 25 attaching Burnside's independent IX Corps to the Army of the Potomac.[73] When military secretary William R. Rowley went on sick leave in late June, Ely Parker took his place. He wrote Rowley frequent letters keeping him abreast of events at headquarters.[74]

Chief of Staff John Rawlins, still suffering the initial symptoms of tuberculosis, continued to manage Grant's headquarters. During battles, he spurred generals on with urgent missives. At other times he facilitated communications between Grant and unit commanders. He also issued orders designed to ease and protect the many marches that characterized Grant's thrust toward Richmond.[75]

Rawlins also remained alert for signs of Grant's drinking. On June 30 Maj. Gen. William F. Smith, of Butler's army, informed Rawlins that Grant had taken a drink at his headquarters and gone away drunk. Rawlins thanked Smith for the information and said, "Thus timely advised of the slippery ground he is on, I shall not fail to use my utmost endeavors to stay him from falling." Though he reported the incident to his wife, Rawlins apparently did not challenge Grant as he had in times past. Indeed, Smith's charge against Grant may have been slanderous. Grant had lost faith in Smith when the latter failed to follow up his advantage in the initial assault on Petersburg. Smith had also publicly criticized Grant and Meade for their handling of the campaign. Grant had determined to fire Smith, and on July 19 he relieved him from duty.[76]

Whether relations between Grant and Rawlins had cooled after Comstock joined the staff, Rawlins remained dedicated to the general. He traveled with Grant between their headquarters at City Point and Meade's headquarters near the Petersburg front. He served as a communication link between Theodore S. Bowers and Ely Parker, who stayed at City Point handling special orders and other mundane office work, and he helped iron out problems of supply and transportation between army units.[77]

Rawlins's health was deteriorating, however. The "cold" he had contracted at Chattanooga in November 1863 lingered, and his friends at Grant's headquarters feared for his well-being. Grant wrote to Julia from City Point in July 1864, that Rawlins was "as well as he ever will be." Even though a leave of absence from the army in late September and early October temporarily rejuvenated Rawlins, Grant's prognosis would ultimately prove correct.[78]

Perhaps to get his friend away from the stresses of the front line, much as he had done after Vicksburg fell, in late July 1864, Grant sent Rawlins to

Washington. The trip had an official purpose as well. Grant sent Rawlins to discuss with President Lincoln a plan the general had for reorganizing forces in the East. He had in mind creating a military division of four armies, much like his old Division of the Mississippi, and giving its command to George Meade. Winfield Scott Hancock, Meade's II Corps commander, would take charge of the Army of the Potomac. In a note to Lincoln, Grant said he had "many reasons," none of which he wanted to "commit to paper," for suggesting the change. "Rawlins . . . will be able to give more information of the situation here than I could give you in a letter." Rawlins met with Lincoln on July 26, but the president wanted to meet with Grant later. Ultimately, nothing came of the reorganization plan.[79]

Even though the presence of Grant's personal staff officers had not ensured success in the campaign from the Wilderness to Petersburg, he continued the practice throughout the summer. When Grant's chief of engineers, Maj. Gen. J. G. Barnard, temporarily left the army in July, Cyrus B. Comstock took his place in addition to remaining as Grant's senior aide-de-camp. Comstock continued to shuttle between Grant's and Meade's headquarters, explaining to Meade just how Grant wanted siege approaches constructed, and he examined intelligence gleaned from Confederate deserters. Grant also sent Comstock to Washington on July 14 to give Maj. Gen. Henry Halleck an overview of the military situation at the front.[80]

When soldiers in Ambrose Burnside's IX Corps dug a 500-foot-long mine shaft under the Confederate lines southeast of Petersburg, intending to pack it with explosives and blow an exploitable breech in the Rebel works, Grant had high hopes for the plan. He left the planning to Burnside and his men, however; none of Grant's staff officers lent expertise or advice to the plan. By the end of July, soldiers had the end of the shaft—just twelve feet below a Rebel fort—loaded with 8,000 pounds of explosives. Burnside set the blast for 3:30 A.M., Saturday, July 30, and Grant and all his staffers were present near Burnside's headquarters to watch the show. The appointed time came, but the blast did not, and courageous miners venturing into the shaft found that the match-lit fuse had gone out. They relighted it, then sprinted for safety. The resulting explosion sent a mushroom cloud of fire and dirt billowing into the air, stunning both Confederates and Federals alike. Burnside had trained a black division to lead the attack through the gap, but Grant, fearing that abolitionists would charge him with butchering blacks if the attack failed, had ordered Burnside to change his plans. Now the lead division was disoriented, not only by the blast, but by unfamiliar terrain, and they lurched ahead, Burnside also had failed to clear their path of enemy abatis, and the men had only a ten-foot wide opening in the works through which to reach the smoking crater in the ground. Grant had planned for the other corps of the Army of the Potomac to help Burnside exploit the gap, but Burnside's men, instead of going around the edges of the crater where they could fight, went into it. When the Rebels, recovering their senses, returned to the hole, they began shooting Federals like fish in a barrel. Cyrus B. Comstock watched from V Corps headquarters, and Grant and Horace Porter watched from horseback, riding close to the crater when they realized the attack was fizzling. About 9:30 A.M., having seen enough, Grant had Burnside withdraw his attackers.[81]

Grant's staffers may not have been involved in planning and executing the attack, but they all roundly criticized Burnside, whom they blamed for the debacle. Theodore Bowers stated, "The chances of success were so great—the failure so utter." Ely Parker said, "I have had the biggest kind of disgust on and dare not express myself on the Potomac Army." George K. Leet reported that the staffers were generally "gloomy." He suspected that, in Burnside's army, at least, if not within the whole Army of the Potomac, "There were screws loose somewhere and the machine would not work." The battle of the Crater, in which Federals lost 4,000 men, made Grant physically sick, and he took to his bed. "His illness is real," said Bowers, recalling times when friends had labeled Grant sick when he was really drunk, "and I think resulted from his grief at the disaster of Saturday."[82]

Since the battle of the Wilderness, Grant had practiced an enlightened, more modern approach to staff work by placing his staff officers with different commands. Prior to the mine explosion, Grant could have stepped up staff work again, but he did not. He had planned for two extra corps to help exploit the gap in the Confederate line that the crater would create, and he lined up 144 pieces of artillery to support the attack. The whole thing, from digging the mine to assaulting the crater, required a degree of coordination every bit as complex as Grant's overland run to Vicksburg or the march south from the Wilderness. Yet Grant assigned none of his own people to it. Though Grant understood that he could, and should, get more work from his staff officers than just writing and carrying orders, he still had much to learn about truly efficient staff work.

As the summer of 1864 wore on, Grant used his personal staff members less to help him manage the siege of Petersburg and more to act as his representatives with expeditions farther afield. After Sherman's armies captured Atlanta on September 2, Grant had some ideas of his own for new campaigns, and he wanted to know what Sherman planned after occupying Atlanta. He trusted neither the army mails nor the telegraph for such a lengthy discourse, so he sent staff officer Horace Porter to Atlanta. Porter found Sherman relaxed after his victory but fully possessed of the nervous energy with which friends frequently described Sherman. Grant's intention in sending Porter to Sherman was not to suggest operations, however, but learn Sherman's plans so Grant could incorporate them with his own and draft the appropriate orders. In a lengthy letter that Sherman gave Porter to deliver to Grant, Sherman outlined his tentative plans for a march across Georgia. He said he would discuss all the ramifications of such a campaign with Porter before he left. Porter left for Grant's headquarters on September 21.[83]

Next, in October, Grant sent his most trusted aide, Chief of Staff John Rawlins, on a far-flung mission of his own. Grant had determined that Confederate resistance in far-Western theaters had deteriorated so much that Federal troops there could move to support armies still actively engaged in the East. He instructed Rawlins to go to St. Louis, Missouri, meet with Maj. Gen. William S. Rosecrans, who had taken command of the Department of the Missouri, and draw from that department as many troops as possible. Their destination was at Rawlins's discretion, depending on the most urgent need when Rawlins issued his orders. Grant wanted to have them in the siege lines before Petersburg, but, in southern Tennessee, Maj. Gen. George Thomas's Army of the Cumberland faced invasion by Gen. John Bell Hood's Confederates. Sherman had just tossed Hood out of Atlanta, and the Rebel general reckoned that an invasion of Tennessee would force Sherman to withdraw from Georgia. To expedite his mission, Grant gave Rawlins full "authority to issue orders in the name of the . . . 'Lieut General.'" Grant's old friend and former aide, William S. Hillyer, wrote the general a letter about the time of Rawlins's trip, commenting that he had read in a newspaper that the chief was in St. Louis. "I thought that Rosecrans had a tough customer to deal with in John," said Hillyer. But Rawlins met with Rosecrans's full cooperation. In fact, Henry Halleck, from his office in Washington, had sent a telegram ahead of Rawlins stating that the situation in Tennessee had worsened and that Rosecrans should direct troops there. Old Rosey already had them headed for Tennessee when Rawlins arrived. Rawlins made sure that all the details of their departure were arranged, then he returned to City Point in mid-November.[84]

Meanwhile, Grant had decided to send an expedition to capture Fort Fisher, at the mouth of the Cape Fear River in North Carolina, then sail up that river and capture Wilmington. Wilmington was one of the last harbors where Rebel blockade runners could deliver foreign supplies to the Confederacy, and Grant wanted it shut down. His plan, to send 6,000 to 10,000 men against Fort Fisher,[85] sounded much like the one staff aide Cyrus B. Comstock had submitted to Grant earlier in the year. Whether it was Comstock's plan, Grant never said. Regardless, he chose Comstock to accompany the expedition.

Grant gave command of the Fort Fisher expedition to Gen. Ben Butler, who was to cooperate with Adm. David D. Porter. Butler fitted out 6,500 troops for the trip, which left Fortress Monroe on December 18. Comstock went along to help Butler in any way possible, both as a member of Grant's staff and as an engineer. Bad weather slowed the flotilla's progress, but the transports arrived off Cape Fear on December 23. Butler planned to devastate Fort Fisher by loading an old boat with explosives, floating it near the fort, and exploding it. He exploded the boat, but the blast had no impact on the fort. Porter's boats then laid down a barrage on the fort, which also had little effect. On Christmas Day, Federal troops landed on the peninsula north of Fort Fisher and made great headway, some troops even getting close enough to the fort to capture a flag. Butler had suffered few casualties and taken many prisoners, but those prisoners told him that 1,600 Rebels were about to hit him from the north. Butler paled and decided to withdraw his men from the peninsula. Porter urged him to change his mind, saying his gunners could step up their covering fire, but Butler would not relent. By December 28 his expedition was back at Fortress Monroe.[86]

Butler's cowardice enraged Grant. He had told Butler that, if he should effect a landing, he must hold the ground at all costs and begin a siege of Fort Fisher. On January 8 Grant relieved Butler of command of the Army of the James, sending Horace Porter and Orville Babcock to break the news.[87] Grant put Maj. Gen. E. O. C. Ord in command of the Army of the James, then he began forming another Fort Fisher expedition.

The new expedition, consisting mostly of veterans of Butler's debacle, gathered at Bermuda Hundred under Brig. Gen. Alfred H. Terry. Admiral Porter again supplied transportation, marines, and sea firepower for the mission. Grant again assigned Comstock to assist. The expedition left Virginia on January 6, 1865, and reached the North Carolina shore a few days later, but rough seas again held up the operation. On January 13 Porter began one of the heaviest bombardments of the war, laying 20,000 projectiles on Fort Fisher over the course of two days. Terry landed his men and guns north of Fort Fisher, and marines went ashore on the seacoast side of the fort. On January 14, under cover of Porter's barrage, Terry and Comstock led a reconnaissance expedition to within 600 yards of the fort. The reconnaissance, along with the temperamental seas off the cape that made landing supplies risky, convinced Terry that a siege of Fort Fisher was impractical. He ordered the combined army and navy forces to assault the works the next day. On January 15 at 3:00 P.M., the attack began. By evening Terry's army had taken the fort. Terry had nothing but praise for Comstock. "For the final success of our part of the operations the country is more indebted to him than to me," said Terry. The second Fort Fisher expedition confirmed Terry as a major general of volunteers and brigadier general in the Regular Army, and it earned Comstock a brevet to brigadier general.[88]

In February 1865 Grant sent Comstock to another theater that needed a staff officer's attention; the assignment, however, would keep Comstock out of the final act of the Civil War in the East. In Alabama, Maj. Gen. E. R. S. Canby, who had helped drive Confederates out of New Mexico three years earlier, had been planning to capture Mobile for weeks. But Grant had grown impatient. After all, Adm. David G. Farragut had captured Mobile Bay back in August 1864, negating the city's importance as a gulf port. Canby had an expedition against Mobile planned, though, and Grant consented as long as Canby got moving. Grant wanted his troops cut loose so they could move against the industrial city of Selma, Alabama, to create a diversion from Sherman's push through the Carolinas. But Canby stalled, and Grant sent Comstock west to spur him on.

Comstock was in Washington testifying before the Congressional Committee on the Conduct of the War when he received Grant's orders on March 1. He caught a train to Cairo, Illinois, then dropped down to New Orleans. He then traveled east, arriving at Canby's headquarters on March 15. In the meantime, Grant had written to Canby, instructing him to keep Comstock until he had captured Mobile or had determined a lengthy siege was the only way to reduce it.[89] Canby finally moved on March 17. He should have easily taken the city, considering he had 32,000 troops facing only 2,800 Confederate defenders. Nevertheless, he was overcautious. He finally laid siege to the city on March 25, did not occupy it until April 12, and then only after the defenders had evacuated Mobile the night before. Canby finally relieved Comstock to return to Grant on April 15, almost a week after Lee had surrendered at Appomattox.[90]

Back in Virginia, Grant's final campaign had begun on March 25. Since going into the trenches at Petersburg, Grant had continuously had soldiers lengthening the Federal lines to the west, trying to flank Lee's right. On the morning of the twenty-fifth, Lee staged an attack on Grant's right, hoping to make the Federal leader pull support troops from his left, opening an escape route for Lee to the west and south. The Confederate attack captured a fort in the Union line and seized a mile of trenches, but a vigorous Union counterattack knocked the Rebels back. Sensing Lee's desperation, Grant quickly sent 12,000 cavalry troopers and two infantry corps west to again try to get around Lee's right flank.[91]

Grant gave command of the flanking movement to Army of the Potomac cavalry leader, Maj. Gen. Phil Sheridan. When Sheridan arrived at Grant's headquarters on March 26, he found Rawlins, true to form, giving the lieutenant general a piece of his mind. Part of Sheridan's orders intimated that he might turn his cavalry south and meet Sherman's troops coming through North Carolina. Rawlins, who had been opposed to "Sherman's March," was equally opposed to Sheridan going to Sherman's aid, and he said so in "vigorous language . . . [that] left no room to doubt" his meaning, according to Sheridan. Sheridan was concerned, too, but Grant soon told both men that he intended to modify that part of the orders. Rawlins quieted on the point, but something else bothered him. Rains had settled in, and Grant had wondered aloud about postponing the move to the left. Rawlins again disagreed. Grant, who had heard enough, quietly said, "Well, Rawlins, I think you had better take command." Grant, of course, decided to go despite the rains, and Sheridan headed west.[92]

A few days later, Grant, continuing his policy of placing staff officers at critical points, sent Horace Porter to Sheridan. After months in the trenches, Grant finally saw the opportunity to fight Lee on open ground, and he trusted Sheridan, who had lain waste to the Shenandoah Valley last year in support of Grant's 1864 campaign, to get the job done. Still, he wanted Sheridan to have headquarters assistance if he needed it. "You know my views," Grant told Porter, "and I want you to give them to Sheridan fully." Grant told the staffer to "send me a bulletin every half-hour or so," updating the general on Sheridan's progress.[93]

Porter caught up with Sheridan April 1 at a crossroads called Five Forks. Sheridan had been pressing the Rebels all day and wanted to deliver a final blow before nightfall, but delays in getting the infantry of the V Corps placed irritated him. Finally the battle was on, and it quickly became a rout. Sheridan smashed into the 10,000 Confederates before him, inflicting 50 percent casualties. Porter, elated, raced back to Grant's headquarters with the news. Night was falling, and Porter found Grant and most of his staff sitting outside headquarters by a fire. Porter began shouting the news before he dismounted, causing, he said, "boisterous demonstrations of joy" among the officers. Porter was so excited that, when he dismounted, he ran to Grant and started clapping him on the back. Grant listened to Porter's full report, then he ordered a general assault on the Petersburg lines for the next morning.[94]

That assault, on April 2, pushed Confederates into retreat. Lee's army escaped to the west, leaving Petersburg and Richmond open to the Federals. The Confederate government quickly abandoned the Southern capital, and Union troops occupied it April 3. Federals raced west trying to get ahead of Lee, delivering another costly blow to the Confederates at Sayler's Creek on April 6. By April 8 Sheridan's left wing of the Union army had flanked Lee, stopping the Grey Fox near Appomattox Court House about 100 miles west of Petersburg.[95]

John Rawlins used his lawyer's intellect to help Grant in a presurrender dialogue with Lee. On April 7 Grant wrote to Lee that he thought further resistance was futile. Lee sent a note asking what terms Grant offered, and the Northern general replied that, as his goal was "peace," he wanted Lee's men disqualified from service until properly exchanged. Lee seized upon Grant's use of the word "peace" in an effort to trap Grant into treating for peace for the entire South. Rawlins recognized the Rebel's snare and alerted Grant. "He wants to entrap us into making a treaty of peace . . . ," said Rawlins, "something to embrace the whole Confederacy if possible. No sir,—no, sir!" Rawlins reminded Grant that President Lincoln had the only legal authority to treat for a general peace; Grant could only take the surrender of Lee's army. After discussing the situation with Rawlins, Grant, early on April 9, penned another note to Lee, saying that he had "no authority to treat on the subject of peace." He reminded Lee that the South could have peace by "laying down their arms." Grant's letter returned the focus of the dialogue to Lee surrendering his army.[96]

Throughout the correspondence, a terrible headache plagued Grant. Staff aide Horace Porter blamed it on "fatigue, anxiety, scant fare, and loss of sleep." His staffers, recognizing his agony, tried to get Grant some relief with hot foot baths, mustard plasters on the wrists and neck, and sleep. But Grant could not sleep. When Rawlins went to deliver Lee's "peace" message to Grant early April 9, he feared waking the general if he had fallen asleep. He opened the door to Grant's room in the double house they had taken for headquarters and listened quietly. "Come in, I am awake," said Grant. "I am suffering too much to get any sleep." Grant's pain did not abate until later that day, when he received another note from Lee, this one asking to discuss the surrender of the Army of Northern Virginia.[97]

Grant was riding along his lines when the letter came, and he sent aide Orville Babcock to find Lee and tell him where they could meet. Babcock found Lee and escorted him and his aide, Col. Charles Marshall, to Appomattox Court House. There they occupied a room in the home of Wilmer McLean until Grant, other members of his staff, and Generals Sheridan and Ord arrived.

Grant and Lee discussed terms of surrender, and Grant wrote a rough copy for Lee to read. When they had agreed on conditions, Grant called Theodore S. Bowers to write a copy for signing. Bowers was nervous, however, and turned the job to Ely Parker "whose handwriting," said Porter, "presented a better appearance than that of anyone else on the staff." Lee, in the meantime, had Marshall draft a short letter acknowledging his acceptance of Grant's terms. While the letters were being copied, Grant introduced the generals and staff officers with him to Lee. Lee said nothing, but Porter noticed his expression change when he met Parker, the Seneca. "What was passing through his mind no one knew," said Porter, "but the natural surmise was that he at first mistook Parker for a negro, and was . . . [astonished] to find that . . . [Grant] had one of that race on his personal staff."[98]

While Lee had done little with his personal staff during the war, Grant had attempted much. Now, as the generals faced each other in the McLean house, their staff officers had the final act of the war in Virginia. Horace Porter remembered, "Colonel Parker folded up the terms, and gave them to Colonel Marshall. Marshall handed Lee's acceptance to Parker."[99]

CHAPTER EIGHT

Conclusion

THE IMPROVEMENTS THAT ULYSSES S. GRANT MADE TO HIS PERSONAL staff lasted only the duration of the Civil War. Rapid downsizing of the army after the war, plus a "raiding" style of fighting during the Indian Wars, negated the need for efficient, modern personal staffs. Had Grant wanted to improve staffing throughout the army—which is doubtful, for his improvements were an attempt to meet the immediate needs of combat, not overall reform—he had little time to do so. In the immediate postwar years, he wrestled with the problems of the Federal army during Reconstruction, then, in 1868, he was elected president. Gen. William T. Sherman, who believed that staffs should be small and their work limited, took over Grant's job as general in chief in 1869. Staff advances languished under Sherman. Likewise, Sherman's successors—Phil Sheridan, John Schofield, and Nelson Miles—presided over a small army fighting a Western war of post and contended with special staff bureau chiefs in Washington who had assumed much of the army's power. Not until after the Spanish-American War, when the United States designed for itself an enlarged military presence on the world stage, did the three factors necessary for staff improvements again emerge: a large army, the need for assistance with combined operations, and commanders willing to use efficient personal staffs. Only then did army reformers and Congress pass legislation that officially created personal staffs of the type Grant had experimented with in the Civil War.

In 1866 the United States Army transferred thirty-three-year-old captain William J. Fetterman, a Civil War veteran, to Fort Phil Kearny,

213

Wyoming Territory, where troops endeavored to protect the Bozeman Trail from Sioux Indians. Fetterman immediately began pressing post commander Col. Henry Carrington to attack the Sioux. "A single company of regulars could whip a thousand Indians," Fetterman said. "A full regiment could whip the entire array of hostile tribes," he continued; finally boasting, "With eighty men I could ride through the Sioux nation." Ironically, Fetterman did take an eighty-man command into battle against a combined force of Sioux, Cheyenne, and Arapaho on December 21, 1866; the Indians wiped out Fetterman's entire command.[1]

Fetterman's bold comments before the fight revealed more than just the impetuosity of a young army captain; they revealed a general philosophy of the post–Civil War American army. Soon after armed Southern resistance ended, the Union army dismissed its volunteers. The army that had grown to more than one million men in 1865 suddenly shrank to slightly more than 57,000. Civilian politicians would have made it even smaller—about 25,000 men—had army brass not explained that garrisoning Southern states required additional men.[2] Nevertheless, neither army high command nor officers in the field, like Fetterman, believed that they needed large armies to subdue Western Indians, which was the postwar army's principal mission. Over the next few years, the army's size continued to dwindle: In 1871 the entire force was down to 29,115 troops; in 1876, the year Lt. Col. George Armstrong Custer and most of the Seventh U.S. Cavalry died at the Little Bighorn, the number was at 28,565; by 1880 it had dropped to 26,594, where it would hover until the Spanish-American War in 1898 sent total enlistments to more than 209,000 men.[3]

Just as the size of the army shrank, the nature of campaigning changed. Campaigns against Indians were usually raids from fixed fortifications, unlike the complex combined strategic operations that characterized the final Civil War campaigns of Ulysses S. Grant and William T. Sherman. In part, the size of the army meant Indian-fighting commanders could do little other than conduct raids. The small forces at their disposal were easy marks outside of their fortifications, so they would periodically sally forth from their forts, attack a target, then retreat to the safety of their defenses. Custer exhibited this tactic in November 1868 when he led his Seventh Cavalry south from Fort Supply, Indian Territory, to attack Cheyenne on the Washita River. Marching through snow, Custer's men found and massacred Black Kettle's Cheyenne, then returned to Fort Supply. The entire campaign took less than a week.

Size was not the only factor in the new style of campaigning, for in fact, large armies would have been a detriment to operations in the West. Indian forces were typically small. Only rarely, as the Fetterman fight or at the Little Bighorn, did combined forces number more than 2,000. They were extremely mobile, whether on horseback or afoot. They knew well the ground they covered and easily took advantage of natural hiding places— the Palo Duro Canyon in the Texas panhandle proved an ideal hiding place for Comanches until Col. Ranald Mackenzie, another Civil War veteran, found and routed a band of them there in 1874. Quite simply, large American armies could never hope to match the speed and maneuverability of the Indians. Only twice, during the Sioux campaign of 1876 and the Nez Perce campaign of 1877, did combined United States forces total 3,000 to 4,000 men. Even then, in the case of the former, commanders had to separate the expedition to achieve mobility and speed, and Custer's defeat well demonstrated the danger of doing so in enemy territory.[4] In general, if soldiers hoped to achieve victories, they had to do it with small raids.

Using small, quick armies of regimental size or less negated a commander's need for a large personal staff, or any staff for that matter. He could communicate directly with his entire command with the wave of a hand or by dispatching a courier with a scrawled note. Buglers often doubled as couriers, making them cut-rate staff officers.[5] Aides-de-camp, several adjutants, chiefs of staff, military secretaries, all were just excess baggage. Obviously, in such a hostile environment to staff development, personal staff functioning could do nothing but wither.

In the 1870s, however, one officer took an interest in reforming the staff system, along with almost everything else about the United States Army. Emory Upton, an 1861 graduate of West Point, went straight into Civil War combat, first with a Regular artillery unit, then as colonel of a volunteer infantry regiment. He won a commission to brigadier general on May 12, 1864, during the battle of Spotsylvania. There, as commander of the Second Brigade, First Division, VI Corps, Army of the Potomac, Upton briefly gained Confederate works at the "Bloody Angle" but had to withdraw for lack of support.[6]

Even though Upton had a knack for handling troops, he could not credit most of his colleagues with the same skill. Upton fired the first gun at the battle of Bull Run, July 21, 1861, and after the battle, a Union defeat, he commented, "Our troops fought well, but were badly mismanaged." Three years later, after the battle of Cold Harbor, Upton further derided fellow generals. He recalled, "I have seen but little generalship during the campaign. Some of our corps commanders are not fit to be corporals."[7] Some of Upton's disgust no doubt stemmed from the inability of other generals to exploit his push into the angle at Spotsylvania. After the war, Upton devoted himself to studying ways to improve the army.

In 1874 General Sherman took Upton as his protégé, and the next year he sent Upton on a tour to inspect the world's major armies. In 1877 Upton published his findings in *The Armies of Asia and Europe*. The work offered Upton's assessments of the armies of Japan, China, India, Persia, Italy, Russia, Austria, Germany, France, and England. The German—née Prussian—Army fascinated Upton most, and he advocated that the U.S. Army imitate many of its systems, including the Great General Staff.[8] "In every military system which has triumphed in modern war," Upton wrote, "the [staff] officers have been recognized as the brain of the army, and to prepare them for this trust, governments have spared no pains to give them special education or training."[9] Upton was talking primarily about general staffs, but he recognized that the U.S. Army's staff system needed major reforms.

Upton went on to serve as commandant of cadets at West Point and as commander of the Presidio in San Francisco. He began writing a history of American military policy from the Revolution to the Civil War, but he suffered a chronic illness, perhaps a brain tumor that caused horrible headaches, which stopped his work. He also became despondent over the lack of progress he saw in army reforms. On March 15, 1881, Upton shot and killed himself in his quarters.[10]

Only after Upton's death did his work begin to bear fruit, and then only minimally. In 1881 Upton's sponsor, General Sherman, followed one of his protégé's recommendations and began a postgraduate school for army officers. That school, the School of Application for Infantry and Cavalry, ultimately became the United States Army Command and General Staff College. Sherman's motives for establishing the school were spurious, however. The general in chief had never had much use for staff officers in the Civil War, and it seems that sixteen years did little to change his sentiments. He once told a friend that "I confess I made the order [establishing the school] as a concession to the everlasting demands of friends and families to have their boys detailed to signal duty, or to the school [of application for artillery] at Fort Monroe to escape company duty in the Indian Country. The school at Leavenworth may do some good, and be a safety valve for those who are resolved to escape from the drudgery of garrison life at small posts."[11] Each regiment of infantry and cavalry sent one lieutenant to the first class of the Leavenworth school for a two-year course of instruction, but the men attending may not have been the best choices. Many could barely read, write, or do simple math. Their education was probably little better, for 100 percent of the first class passed. That number dropped to 75 percent under a stricter commandant for the second class.[12]

As Sherman's school got off to a rocky start, Upton's writings were getting shoved aside in military archives, not coming to light again until after the Spanish-American War in 1898. That summer the United States armies and navies defeated Spanish forces in the Philippines and Cuba. But the army of more than 200,000 men operated inefficiently. Both the War Department and field commanders mismanaged mobilization, quartermasters botched supply duties, and commanders in Cuba suffered from poor intelligence of the enemy.[13] American military insiders realized that victory in the war was never certain.

Elihu Root, a lawyer who became secretary of war during Pres. William McKinley's administration in 1899, realized, too, that the army needed reforms, but he considered himself too deficient in military knowledge to implement them. So he began to study military history and European armies, and he discovered Emory Upton's *The Armies of Asia and Europe* and British writer Spenser Wilkinson's *The Brain of the Army,* which also praised the German (Prussian) General Staff. Like Upton, Root realized that the United States needed a general staff functioning along the German model.[14]

Root saw that without a general staff to coordinate supply and logistics problems, plan for war, and help generals execute plans, the army would continue to operate inefficiently. Such could not be the case, Root reasoned, if the United States was to become a world power, as its interest in Cuba and the Philippines indicated. But Root's insistence on modeling a staff after the German General Staff smacked too much of "Germanization" for most Americans, so he proceeded slowly.[15]

Not until 1901 did Root have the military and congressional support to push through Congress an act creating the War College Board. Root gave the board duties that made it a forerunner of an American general staff.[16] Two years later Root convinced Congress to accept a limited general staff with the General Staff Act of 1903. The act provided for a general staff corps consisting of a chief of staff (replacing the general in chief as the army's top officer), two other general officers, and forty-two junior officers. Section Two of the act summarized the staff's responsibilities: "The duties of the general staff corps shall be to prepare plans for the national defense and for the mobilization of the military forces in time of war; to investigate and report upon all questions affecting the efficiency of the army and its state of preparation for military operations; to render professional aid and assistance to the secretary of war and to general officers and other superior commanders and to act as their agents in informing and coordinating the action of all the different officers who are subject under the terms of this act to the supervision of the chief of staff; and to perform such other military duties not otherwise assigned by law as may from time to time be prescribed by the President."[17]

Root's reforms and the General Staff Act targeted first the several special staff bureaus that handled army supply and transportation. Headquartered in Washington, they were mired in politics and power struggles that impeded their efficiency. As general in chief, Sheridan had wrestled against them to no effect, and the situation changed little under Schofield and Miles. But the Root reforms and the General Staff Act also affected field commanders' personal staffs. Military historian John Dickinson notes, "The general staff fell roughly into two parts, the War Department general staff, consisting of staff officers on duty in Washington, and the general staff serving with troops, i.e., staff officers assigned to duty with the commanders of various geographical divisions and departments."[18] With the act of 1903, educated, trained, and professional staff officers would take their places alongside generals at field headquarters. Their jobs were to transmit national military policy, as set by the General Staff in Washington, on to combat commanders. With that knowledge, they would also help craft field operations. Thus, the War Department officially recognized what Ulysses S. Grant had known forty years earlier—that field commanders needed help getting large commands to operate efficiently and that staff officers were the logical men to supply it.

Meanwhile, the School of Application that Sherman had established at Fort Leavenworth had evolved to include a School of the Line and a Staff College. In 1907 the Staff College began a course to explore the duties of general staff officers. Students, who knew little about staff work going into the class, learned the basics—reconnaissance, making reports, relaying orders to subalterns. As Timothy K. Nenninger, historian of the Leavenworth schools, explains, students on the staff college learned to gather information, assist the commander prepare plans based on that information, and translate the plans into orders. "In each of these tasks, they relieved the commander of much detail," writes Nenninger. "They were the men in the middle, not commanding directly but sometimes issuing orders in the name of the commander."[19]

The four generals of this study—Grant, McClellan, Sherman, and Lee—are examples of both the problems staff reformers had to overcome and the vision they had to embody to enact personal staff advances. Two of the men, Sherman and Lee, had little use for personal staffs. McClellan periodically showed insightfulness about his staff but did little with it. Only Grant improved his personal staff, changing it from a group of amateur volunteers to trained professionals with expanded duties.

Grant's staff achievements do not fit into an organized plan to modernize staff work throughout the U.S. Army during the Civil War. His efforts were just a practical response to complicated command situations. When the war ended, so did Grant's vision of personal staff work. But such only reinforces historian Mark Neely's assertion that the Civil War was something less than "total" or completely modern.[20]

It is impossible to know if Grant's staff system hurried the end of the Civil War, but that is not the thrust of this study. Of more importance is that the Civil War was not a static period of American staff work. It proved that, if the War Department would not take the lead in expanding personal staff duties, individuals would have to. Only Grant did so, proving himself as much an innovator within his headquarters as he was on the battlefield. In Grant, all of the factors compatible with staff advancement came together: large armies, cooperative operations, and a willingness to experiment with staff improvements. Grant was not a staff reformer; he was a competent, intelligent general looking for more efficient ways to fight a complicated war. As such, he spent no time talking or writing about staff work. He did not promote his innovations as a model for the whole United States Army. He simply found a creative way to use an organizational element available to all Civil War generals—the personal staff—and made it his right hand of command.

NOTES

PREFACE

1. Herman Hattaway and Archer Jones, *How the North Won: A Military History of the Civil War* (Urbana: Chicago University of Illinois Press, 1983), 42; Archer Jones, *Civil War Command and Strategy: The Process of Victory and Defeat* (New York: Free Press, 1992), 41; Shelby Foote, *The Civil War: A Narrative* (New York: Random House, 1958–74; reprint, New York: Vintage Books, 1986), 1:73–75; Bruce Catton, *The Coming Fury* (New York: Washington Square Press, 1961; reprint, New York: Pocket Books, 1967), 449.

2. John M. Vermillion, "The Pillars of Generalship," *Parameters* 17 (summer 1987): 4–5.

3. Hattaway and Jones, *How the North Won*, 42, 102–3.

4. Ibid., 102–4; James D. Hittle, *The Military Staff: Its History and Development* (Harrisburg, Pa.: Military Service, 1944; reprint, Harrisburg, Pa.: Stackpole, 1961), 190; Oliver L. Spaulding, *The United States Army in War and Peace* (New York: G. P. Putnam's Sons, 1937), 266.

5. Hittle, *Military Staff*, 187, 190; Hattaway and Jones, *How the North Won*, 106; Spaulding, *United States Army in War and Peace*, 266.

6. Hattaway and Jones, *How the North Won*, 102.

7. Alfred D. Chandler Jr., *The Visible Hand: The Managerial Revolution in American Business* (Cambridge: Harvard University Press, Belknap Press, 1977), 120.

8. Russell F. Weigley, *Towards an American Army: Military Thought from Washington to Marshall* (New York: Columbia University Press, 1962); Russell F. Weigley, *History of the United States Army* (New York: Macmillan, 1967); Allan R. Millett and Peter Maslowski, *For the Common Defense: A Military History of the United States of America* (New York: Free Press, 1984); Walter Millis, *American Military Thought* (Indianapolis: Bobbs-Merrill, 1966); Edward Hagerman, *The American Civil War and the Origin of Modern Warfare: Ideas, Organization, and Field Command* (Bloomington: Indiana University Press, 1988); T. Harry Williams, *Lincoln and His Generals* (New York: Alfred A. Knopf, 1952); Fred Shannon, *The Organization and Administration*

of the Union Army, 1861–1862, 2 vols. (Cleveland: Arthur H. Clark, 1928); Allan Nevins, *Ordeal of the Union* (New York: Scribner's), vol. 5, *The Improvised War, 1861–1862* (1959), vol.6, *War Becomes Revolution, 1862–1863* (1960), vol. 7, *The Organized War, 1863–1864* (1971), and vol. 8, *The Organized War to Victory, 1864–1865* (1971).

9. Hittle, *Military Staff;* Hattaway and Jones, *How the North Won;* Jones, *Civil War Command and Strategy.*

10. Bruce Catton, *Bruce Catton's Civil War: Three Volumes in One* including *Mr. Lincoln's Army, Glory Road,* and *A Stillness at Appomattox* (New York: Fairfax Press, 1984); Bruce Catton, *Grant Moves South* (Boston: Little, Brown, 1960).

11. Geoffrey Perret, *Ulysses S. Grant: Soldier and President* (New York: Random House, 1997); William S. McFeely, *Grant: A Biography* (New York: W. W. Norton, 1981); Brooks D. Simpson, *Let Us Have Peace: Ulysses S. Grant and the Politics of War and Reconstruction, 1861–1868* (Chapel Hill: University of North Carolina Press, 1991); J. F. C. Fuller, *The Generalship of Ulysses S. Grant* (New York: Dodd, Mead, 1929); Albert D. Richardson, *Personal History of Ulysses S. Grant* (Hartford, Conn.: American Publishing, 1868). Other books about Grant and his campaigns, which reveal little insight about his staff usage, include Don Lowry, *Dark and Cruel War: The Decisive Months of the Civil War, September–December 1864* (New York: Hippocrene Books, 1993); Noah Andre Trudeau, *The Last Citadel: Petersburg, Virginia, June 1864–April 1865* (Baton Rouge: Louisiana State University Press, 1991); Noah Andre Trudeau, *Bloody Roads South: The Wilderness to Cold Harbor, May–June 1864* (Boston: Little, Brown, 1989); Earl Schenck Miers, *Web of Victory: Grant at Vicksburg* (New York: Knopf, 1955); Edward Steere, *The Wilderness Campaign* (Harrisburg, Pa.: Stackpole, 1960); Nathaniel Cheairs Hughes Jr., *The Battle of Belmont: Grant Strikes South* (Chapel Hill: University of North Carolina Press, 1991); William D. Matter, *If It Takes All Summer: The Battle of Spotsylvania* (Chapel Hill: University of North Carolina Press, 1988); Wiley Sword, *Shiloh: Bloody April* (New York: William Morrow, 1974); and Richard J. Sommers, *Richmond Redeemed: The Siege at Petersburg* (Garden City, N. Y.: Doubleday, 1981). Some, like Sommers, Trudeau, and Matter, faintly touch on an aspect of Grant's personal staff, but fail to grasp its context and import. Trudeau seems typical in that he uses Grant's staff officers merely as diarists to forward battle narratives; he never attempts to examine the true function of Grant's staff.

12. Such books about McClellan include Stephen W. Sears, *George B. McClellan: The Young Napoleon* (Boston: Ticknor and Fields, 1988); Clarence Edward Macartney, *Little Mac: The Life of General George B. McClellan* (Philadelphia: Dorrance, 1940); Warren W. Hassler Jr., *General George B. McClellan: Shield of the Union* (Baton Rouge: Louisiana State University Press, 1957); and Richard Wheeler, *Sword over Richmond: An Eyewitness History of McClellan's Peninsula Campaign* (New York: Harper and Row, 1986).

13. Edward Hagerman, "The Professionalization of George B. McClellan and Early Civil War Field Command: An Institutional Perspective," *Civil War History* 21, no. 2 (1975): 116–18.

14. B. H. Liddell Hart, *Sherman: Soldier, Realist, American* (New York: Praeger, 1958); Lloyd Lewis, *Sherman: Fighting Prophet* (New York: Harcourt, Brace, 1932); John F. Marszalek, *Sherman: A Soldier's Passion for Order* (New York: Free Press, 1993); Albert Castel, *Decision in the West: The Atlanta Campaign of 1864* (Lawrence: University Press of Kansas, 1992), 260. Other books, which offer little information on Sherman's staff, include William Key, *The Battle of Atlanta and the Georgia Cam-*

paign (New York: Twayne, 1958); Theodore P. Savas and David A. Woodbury, eds., *The Campaign for Atlanta and Sherman's March to the Sea: Essays on the 1864 Georgia Campaigns* (Campbell, Calif.: Savas Woodbury Publishers, 1992); Charles Edmund Vetter, *Sherman: Merchant of Terror, Advocate of Peace* (Gretna, La.: Pelican Publishing, 1992); and Charles Royster, *The Destructive War: William Tecumseh Sherman, Stonewall Jackson, and the Americans* (New York: Knopf, 1991).

15. Douglas Southall Freeman, *Lee's Lieutenants: A Study in Command,* 3 vols. (New York: Scribner's, 1942–44); Clifford Dowdey, *Lee's Last Campaign: The Story of Lee and His Men against Grant—1864* (Boston: Little, Brown, 1960).

16. Clifford Dowdey, *Lee* (Boston: Little, Brown, 1965), 217–18, 252–53.

17. Emory M. Thomas, *Robert E. Lee: A Biography* (New York: W. W. Norton, 1995).

18. J. Boone Bartholomees Jr., *Buff Facings and Gilt Buttons: Staff and Headquarters Operations in the Army of Northern Virginia, 1861–1865* (Columbia: University of South Carolina Press, 1998), 6, 172.

19. Ibid., xiv.

CHAPTER 1: HERITAGE

1. Hittle, *Military Staff,* 52–54, 89, 93–95.

2. Ibid., 94–95.

3. Ibid., 104–6.

4. Ibid., 106–8.

5. Ibid., 95–96, 101.

6. Antoine-Henri Jomini, *The Art of War,* trans. G.H. Mendell and W. P. Craighill (1862; reprint, Westport, Conn.: Greenwood Press for West Point Military Library, n.d.), 232–34.

7. Hittle, *Military Staff,* 98, 100–101.

8. Gordon A. Craig, *The Politics of the Prussian Army, 1640–1945* (Oxford: Clarendon Press, 1955), 6, 31–32; Hittle, *Military Staff,* 56–57; Walter Goerlitz, *History of the German General Staff* (New York: Frederick A. Praeger, 1953), 21–22.

9. Goerlitz, *German General Staff,* 21–22, 25.

10. Hittle, *Military Staff,* 66–68; Goerlitz, *German General Staff,* 34.

11. Hittle, *Military Staff,* 70, 76.

12. Ibid., 59, 90–92.

13. Ibid., 114, 117.

14. William P. Craighill, *The Army Officer's Pocket Companion: Principally Designed for Staff Officers in the Field* (New York: Nostrand, 1862), 6–12.

15. Craig, *Politics of the Prussian Army,* 45; Goerlitz, *German General Staff,* 36; Hittle, *Military Staff,* 58–60.

16. Jomini, *The Art of War,* 231–36; Hittle, *Military Staff,* 95.

17. Hittle, *Military Staff,* 110–11.

18. Ibid., 113; Vermillion, "Pillars of Generalship," 4–5.

19. Hittle, *Military Staff,* 109–10; Vermillion, "Pillars of Generalship," 4–5.

20. Vermillion, "Pillars of Generalship," 4–5.

21. Goerlitz, *German General Staff,* 15–17, 25–27.

22. Ibid., 20, 41; Hittle, *Military Staff,* 66–67, 102.

23. Hattaway and Jones, *How the North Won,* 104; Hittle, *Military Staff,* 140–151.

24. Hittle, *Military Staff,* 167–72; James Thomas Flexner, *Washington: The Indispensable Man* (New York: Little, Brown, 1969; reprint, New York: Plume Books, 1974), 111–15.

25. Hittle, *Military Staff,* 173–81; Hattaway and Jones, *How the North Won,* 104.

26. T. Harry Williams, "Military Leadership, North and South," in *Why the North Won the Civil War,* ed. David Donald (Baton Rouge: Louisiana State University Press, 1960), 23; Hittle, *Military Staff,* 186–87; Hattaway and Jones, *How the North Won,* 28.

27. Jones, *Civil War Command and Strategy,* 79, 112–13, 225; Frank J. Welcher, *The Union Army, 1861–1865: Organization and Operations,* vol. 1, *The Eastern Theater* (Bloomington: Indiana University Press, 1989), 1–2.

28. Sears, *McClellan,* 6, 9–10; Sidney Forman, *West Point: A History of the United States Military Academy* (New York: Columbia University Press, 1950), 58.

29. Halleck, Henry Wager, *Elements of Military Art and Science; or, Course of Instruction in Strategy, Fortification, Tactics of Battles, &c;* (New York: D. Appleton, 1846), 235–55; Hittle, *Military Staff,* 98, 185.

30. Craighill, *Officer's Pocket Companion,* 3, 15–17, 18–34, 38–42, 50–51, 52–62.

CHAPTER 2: McCLELLAN, 1861–1862

1. Hittle, *Military Staff,* 187, 189; Hagerman, "Professionalization of George B. McClellan," 116.

2. Sears, *McClellan,* 3–13, 31.

3. Ibid., 17–18, 44; Hittle, *Military Staff,* 188.

4. Sears, *McClellan,* 44–46.

5. Ibid., 47–48.

6. Ibid., 48; Hittle, *Military Staff,* 188; Hagerman, "Professionalization of George B. McClellan," 116.

7. Chandler, *The Visible Hand,* 81, 95, 120.

8. Sears, *McClellan,* 69–72.

9. McClellan to Winfield Scott, 9 May 1861, Stephen Sears, ed., *The Civil War Papers of George B. McClellan: Selected Correspondence, 1860–1865,* (New York: Ticknor and Fields, 1989), 18 (hereafter cited as *Papers of McClellan*).

10. George W. Cullum, *Biographical Register of the Officers and Graduates of the U.S. Military Academy at West Point, New York* (Boston: Houghton, Mifflin, 1891), 2:130–32.

11. Sears, *McClellan,* 72; Theodore Lyman, *Meade's Headquarters, 1863–1865: Letters of Colonel Theodore Lyman from the Wilderness to Appomattox* (Boston: Atlantic Monthly Press, 1922), 28.

12. "Red River Diary," George B. McClellan Papers, National Archives; Sears, *McClellan,* 63.

13. Will Huett, "A Man Called 'Mary Anne,'" *True West* (November 1991): 42; Randolph B. Marcy, *The Prairie Traveler* (Washington, D.C.: U.S. War Department, 1859; reprint New York: Perigree Books, 1994), passim.

14. Hagerman, "Professionalization of George B. McClellan," 118; Hittle, *Military Staff,* 190.

15. General Orders No. 1, *War of the Rebellion: A Compilation of the Official Records of the Union and Confederate Armies* (hereinafter cited as *O.R.*), 1st ser., vol. 5, 575; *Papers of McClellan,* 39–40, 50.

16. McClellan to Nell McClellan, 7 July 1861, *Papers of McClellan,* 50.

17. E. B. Long, *The Civil War Day by Day* (Garden City, N.Y.: Doubleday, 1971), 92–94; *O.R.,* 1st ser., vol. 2, 259.

18. Sears, *McClellan,* 89–93; *O.R.,* 1st ser., vol. 2, 210–11.

19. General Orders No. 1, *O.R.,* 1st ser., vol. 5, 575.

20. Cullum, *Biographical Register*, 2:387, 543, 621

21. Ibid., 1:656; ibid, 2:347.

22. *O.R.*, 1st ser., vol. 1, 246, 248; vol. 2, 160, 184.

23. McClellan's general report, *O.R.*, 1st ser., vol. 5, 23.

24. Sears, *McClellan*, 122–23.

25. McClellan to Nell McClellan, 18 November 1861, *Papers of McClellan*, 136, 535; *O.R.*, 1st ser., vol. 1, 414–15.

26. *Papers of McClellan*, 136; report of Capt. L. D. H Currie, 7 February 1862, *O.R.*, 1st ser., vol. 5, 505–6.

27. McClellan's general report, *O.R.*, 1st ser., vol. 5, 23; Edward H. Wright Papers, New Jersey Historical Society, Newark; Cullum, *Biographical Register*, 2: 837.

28. Sears, *McClellan*, 156–57.

29. James M. McPherson, *Ordeal by Fire: The Civil War and Reconstruction* (New York: Knopf, 1982), 238–48; E. B. Long, *Civil War Day by Day*, 193–206, 218–20, 230–35.

30. McClellan to Assistant Secretary of War John Tucker, 13 March 1862, *O.R.*, 1st ser., vol. 5, 752, 757.

31. General Orders No. 102, items I–III, 24 March 1862, *O.R.*, 1st ser., vol. 11, pt. 3, 33.

32. Special Orders No. 144, 10 May 1862, ibid., 163.

33. General Orders No. 102, item IX, 24 March 1862, ibid., 34; for other duties of Seth Williams see ibid., 39–40, 152–53, 161, 167–68, 172, 181, 188–89, 198–99, 227.

34. Williams to E. D. Keyes, 6 May 1862; Colburn to George A. H. Blake, 7 May 1862, ibid., 148.

35. McClellan to Nell McClellan, 27, 6 April 1862, *Papers of McClellan*, 250, 230.

36. Report of Maj. Gen. Winfield Scott Hancock, *O.R.*, 1st ser., vol. 11, pt. 1, 534; reports of Col. James H. Simpson, 4th New Jersey Infantry; Brig. Gen. Dan Butterfield, 3rd Brigade, 1st Div., V Corps; Capt. William Hexamer, Battery A, New Jersey Light Artillery; Maj. Gen. Fitz-John Porter, V Corps, ibid., pt. 2, 444–45, 317, 436–37, 227.

37. Reports of Brig. Gen. John G. Barnard, chief of engineers; Brig. Gen. Daniel Sickles, commander, 2nd Brigade, 2nd Division, III Corps; McClellan, commander, Army of the Potomac; Lt. Col. Joseph Trawin, 8th New Jersey Infantry; Brig. Gen. William B. Franklin, commander, VI Corps, *O.R.*, 1st ser., vol. 11, pt. 2, 120, 135, 22, 837, 432.

38. Porter's siege report, *O.R.*, 1st ser., vol. 11, pt. 1, 313–15; Special Orders No. 126, 27 April 1862, ibid., pt. 3, 125; McClellan to Nell McClellan, 27 April 1862, *Papers of McClellan*, 249.

39. Porter's siege report; reports of Col. James McQuade, 14th New York Infantry, and Col. Jesse A. Grove, 22nd Massachusetts Infantry, of action at Hanover Court House, *O.R.*, 1st ser., vol. 11, pt. 1, 315, 713, 717; Porter's report of Seven Days' battles, ibid., pt. 2, 226.

40. For examples of Marcy's correspondence see reports of Col. John Farnsworth, 8th Illinois Cavalry; Brig. Gen. Dan Sickles; Lt. Col. John Kimball, 15th Massachusetts Infantry; Brig. Gen. George W. Morrell, 1st Division, V Corps; Capt. J. Howard Carlisle, Battery E, 2nd U.S. Artillery, *O.R.*, 1st ser., vol. 11, pt. 2, 234, 135, 89, 274, 269; Marcy to Phillip St. George Cooke, 25 May 1862; Marcy to Porter, 23 June 1862; Erasmus D. Keyes to Marcy, 5 April 1862, ibid., pt. 3, 191, 247, 70–71.

41. Report of Brig. Gen. George W. Morrell, ibid., pt. 2, 274; Marcy to McClellan, 19 March and 5 May 1862, ibid., pt. 3, 20, 141, 254–55.

42. Marcy to Stanton, 10, 29 May 1862, ibid., pt. 3, 163, 200.

43. Marcy to Stanton, 27 June 1862, ibid., pt. 3, 265.
44. McClellan to Stanton, 3 July 1862; Marcy to McClellan, 4 July 1862, ibid., pt. 3, 291, 294; Lincoln to McClellan, 4 July 1862, ibid., pt. 1, 72–73; Sears, *McClellan*, 223, 226.
45. E. B. Long, *Civil War Day by Day,* 267–68.
46. Sears, *McClellan*, 305.
47. For duties of Marcy, Colburn, and Williams see *O.R.,* 1st ser., vol. 19, pt. 2, 176–79, 183–86, 188, 190–95, 202, 226–27, 290, 295, 297.
48. Hooker's report of Antietam, ibid., pt. 1, 216; Colburn to Marcy, 17 Sept 1862, ibid., pt. 2, 315; Sears, *McClellan*, 308.
49. Reports of 1st Lt. George A. Woodruff, Company L, 1st Artillery; Maj. Gen. William B. Franklin, VI Corps; McClellan, *O.R.,* 1st ser., vol. 19, pt. 1, 310, 378, 63–64; Sears, *McClellan*, 313.
50. Cullum, *Biographical Register,* 1:521–22; ibid., 2:130–32.
51. McClellan to Adj. Gen. Lorenzo Thomas, 9 December 1862, *Papers of McClellan,* 528.

CHAPTER 3: LEE, 1861–1865

1. Douglas Southall Freeman, *R. E. Lee: A Biography* (New York: Scribner's. 1934–35), 3:230. Readers should note that one source, Joseph H. Crute Jr., *Confederate Staff Officers, 1861–1865* (Powhatan, Va.: Derwent Books, 1982), 115–17, lists as many as forty-five officers passing through Lee's personal staff during the war. For some reason, Lee appointed many of the men on November 2, 1863. Nevertheless, their impact on Lee's staff was minimal at best, for they hold no preeminence in primary source material.
2. Gene Smith, *Lee and Grant: A Dual Biography* (New York: McGraw-Hill, 1984), 26, 44–48.
3. Thomas, *Robert E. Lee,* 195–96; Clifford Dowdey and Louis H. Manarin, eds.,*The Wartime Papers of R. E. Lee* (New York: Bramhall House for the Virginia Civil War Commission, 1961), 60 (hereafter cited as *Wartime Papers*); Smith, *Lee and Grant,* 103–4.
4. Freeman, *Lee's Lieutenants,* 2:433–34; Lee to George Washington Custis Lee, 29 December 1861, *Wartime Papers,* 98.
5. R. Lockwood Tower and John S. Belmont, eds., *Lee's Adjutant: The Wartime Letters of Colonel Walter Herron Taylor, 1862–1865* (Columbia: University of South Carolina Press, 1995), 2–3.
6. Armistead L. Long, *Memoirs of Robert E. Lee* (New York: J. M. Stoddart, 1886), 112; Thomas, *Robert E. Lee,* 195, 201–2; Lee to Mary Custis Lee, 9 August and 17 September 1861, and Lee to Virginia governor John Letcher, 17 September 1861, *Wartime Papers,* 63, 73–75.
7. Lee to Custis Lee, 29 December 1861, *Wartime Papers,* 98.
8. A. Long, *Memoirs of Lee,* 141; *O.R.,* 1st ser., vol. 6, 312.
9. Cullum, *Biographical Register,* 4:77–78.
10. A. Long, *Memoirs of Lee,* 111–112.
11. Ibid., 112, 117.
12. Ibid., 130.
13. Ibid., 134–36; Walter H. Taylor, *General Lee: His Campaigns in Virginia, 1861–1865, with Personal Reminiscences* (Norfolk, Va.: Nusbaum, 1906), 40–41.
14. Lee to Mary Custis Lee, 18 January 1862, *Wartime Papers,* 103; Smith, *Lee and Grant,* 106.

15. Frederick Maurice, ed., *An Aide-de-Camp of Lee: Being the Papers of Colonel Charles Marshall, Sometime Aide-de-Camp, Military Secretary, and Assistant Adjutant General on the Staff of Robert E. Lee, 1862-1865* (Boston: Little, Brown, 1927), 4–6, 8–9.

16. Taylor, *General Lee*, 42; Walter H. Taylor, *Four Years with General Lee: Being a Summary of the More Important Events touching the Career of General Robert E. Lee in the War between the States* (New York: D. Appleton, 1877), 11.

17. Taylor, *General Lee*, 42; Long, *Memoirs of Lee*, 143.

18. Gary W. Gallagher, ed., *Fighting for the Confederacy: The Personal Recollections of General Edward Porter Alexander* (Chapel Hill: University of North Carolina Press, 1989), 156, 565 n. 6.

19. "Biographical Note," Charles Scott Venable Papers, University of North Carolina, Chapel Hill; *O.R.,* 1st ser., vol. 2, 520, 527; Gallagher, *Fighting for the Confederacy,* 482.

20. Maurice, *Aide-de-Camp of Lee*, xiii.

21. Foote, *The Civil War,* 1:445–50; Long, *Civil War Day by Day,* 218–20.

22. Foote, *The Civil War,* 1:449–50.

23. Special Orders No. 22, 1 June 1862, *O.R.,* 1st ser., vol. 11, pt. 3, 569.

24. Taylor, *General Lee*, 55; General Orders No. 61, 4 June 1862; Mason to A. P. Hill, 6 June 1862, *O.R.,* 1st ser., vol. 11, pt. 3, 574, 577–78.

25. Taylor, *General Lee*, 55; see *O.R.,* 1st ser., vol. 11, pt. 1, 568, and pt. 3, 555, 558, 564, for Mason's duties with Johnston.

26. Freeman, *Lee's Lieutenants,* 1:85 n; "Biographical Sketch," Robert H. Chilton Papers, Eleanor S. Brockenbrough Library, Museum of the Confederacy, Richmond (hereafter cited as Chilton papers); Jefferson Davis to Chilton, 10 August 1854, Chilton Papers; U.S. adjutant general Lorenzo Thomas to Chilton, 1 May 1861, Chilton Papers; *O.R.,* 1st ser., vol. 8, 726.

27. Special Orders No. 123, 4 June 1862; General Orders No. 63, 5 June 1862; Chilton to Col. Thomas R. R. Cobb, 8 June 1862; Maj. Gen. John B. Magruder to Chilton, 10, 11 June 1862, *O.R.,* 1st ser., vol. 11, pt. 3, 574, 577, 582, 586, 593.

28. Taylor, *General Lee*, 56; Taylor to Brig. Gen. Joseph Finnegan, 21 June 1862, *O.R.,* 1st ser., vol. 11, pt. 3, 611.

29. Taylor to Bettie Saunders, 13 December 1863, in Tower, *Lee's Adjutant,* 97–98.

30. General Orders No. 68, 14 June 1862; General Orders No. 70, 21 June 1862; General Orders No. 71, 22 June 1862; Long to Maj. Gen. J.E.B. Stuart, 17 June 1862; Long to Maj. W. H. Stevens, 17 June 1862; Special Orders No. 137, 18 June 1862, *O.R.,* 1st ser., vol. 11, pt. 3, 599, 611, 612–13, 606, 609.

31. McPherson, *Ordeal by Fire,* 243–44.

32. General Orders No. 75, 24 June 1862, and Lee's report of the Seven Days, *Wartime Papers,* 198–200, 222; Magruder's, Ewell's, and Armistead's reports of the Seven Days, *O.R.,* 1st ser., vol. 11, pt. 2, 666–67, 605, 818.

33. Maurice, *Aide-de-Camp of Lee,* xxvi; Freeman, *R. E. Lee,* 3:228–30; Dowdey, *Lee,* 252–53, 272–73; Taylor, *General Lee*, 56; Long, *Memoirs of Lee,* 168; Taylor, *Four Years with Lee,* 151–52.

34. Smith, *Lee and Grant,* 127; Lee to Mary Custis Lee, 9 July 1862, *Wartime Papers,* 229; Long, *Memoirs of Lee,* 227.

35. Maurice, *Aide-de-Camp of Lee,* xix.

36. Ibid., xxi–xxii; Freeman, *R. E. Lee,* 218 n.

37. Maurice, *Aide-de-Camp of Lee,* xx–xxi; Taylor, *General Lee*, 154; *Wartime Papers,* 119; Charles S. Venable, "General Lee in the Wilderness Campaign," in Robert U. Johnson and Clarence C. Buel, eds., *Battles and Leaders of the Civil War,* (New York:

Century, 1881–88; reprint, New York: Thomas Yoseloff, 1956), 4:240 (page citations are to the reprint edition).

38. Taylor, *General Lee*, 157–58.

39. A. Long, *Memoirs of Lee*, 204; for some of Long's correspondence duties see *O.R.*, 1st ser., vol. 11, pt. 3, 567, 606, 643, 672.

40. Taylor, *General Lee*, 155.

41. Taylor, *Four Years with Lee*, 77–78.

42. Taylor to Bettie Saunders, 8 August 1863, in Tower, *Lee's Adjutant*, 68–69.

43. For some duties of Chilton see Special Field Orders No.–, 3 July 1862; Special Orders No.–, 7 July 1862; Special Orders No.–, 8 July 1862; General Orders No. 78, 12 July 1862; Chilton to Gen. Lafayette McLaws, 27 July 1862, *O.R.*, 1st ser., vol. 11, pt. 3, 630, 636–37, 640–41, 656.

44. Maurice, *Aide-de-Camp of Lee*, xv.

45. Ibid., 178–80.

46. Ibid., xvii–xviii, 178–81, 214–24; Freeman, *Lee's Lieutenants*, 3:206–8.

47. For some of Lee's correspondence in late 1862 see *O.R.*, 1st ser., vol. 21, 1013–14, 1027–37, 1038–39, 1048.

48. Taylor, *General Lee*, 154; Venable, "Lee in the Wilderness," *Battles and Leaders*, 240.

49. Venable, "Lee in the Wilderness," in *Battles and Leaders*, 4:240.

50. Freeman, *R. E. Lee*, 3:228, 229.

51. Maurice, *Aide-de-Camp of Lee*, xix; Taylor, *General Lee*, 157.

52. Gallagher, *Fighting for the Confederacy*, 156–57.

53. Venable, "Lee in the Wilderness," *Battles and Leaders*, 4:240; Gallagher, *Fighting for the Confederacy*, 481–82; J. F. C. Fuller, *Grant and Lee: A Study in Personality and Generalship* (London: Eyre and Spottiswode, 1933), 99.

54. For some of Chilton's correspondence in July and August 1862 see *O.R.*, 1st ser., vol. 12, pt. 3, 920–21, 928, 934–35; Special Orders No. 185, 19 August 1862, *Wartime Papers*, 259–60.

55. McPherson, *Ordeal by Fire*, 254–59; Longstreet's report of second Manassas, *O.R.*, 1st ser., vol. 12, pt. 2, 568.

56. Lee to Davis, 3 September 1862, *Wartime Papers*, 292–93; Stephen W. Sears, *Landscape Turned Red: The Battle of Antietam* (New York: Warner Books, 1983), 79–80; McPherson, *Ordeal by Fire*, 280.

57. Sears, *Landscape Turned Red*, 98–100; McPherson, *Ordeal by Fire*, 280–81.

58. Special Orders No. 191, *Wartime Papers*, 301–3; Taylor, *General Lee*, 120–21.

59. Sears, *Landscape Turned Red*, 100–101.

60. Ibid., 122–25.

61. Ibid., 126–27; letter from D. H. Hill, 11 December 1867, Chilton Papers.

62. Chilton to McLaws, 14 September 1862; Long to McLaws, 15 September 1862, *Wartime Papers*, 307–9; Taylor, *General Lee*, 121; McPherson, *Ordeal by Fire*, 281.

63. Chilton to William N. Pendleton, 17 September 1862, *O.R.*, 1st ser., vol. 19, pt. 2, 610.

64. Reports of Gens. Pendleton, Longstreet, McLaws, David R. Jones, Walker, Robert Rodes, and Capt. John G. Barnwell, Maryland Campaign, *O.R.*, 1st ser., vol. 19, pt. 1, 831, 842, 858, 887, 914, 1036, 838; Freeman, *R. E. Lee*, 3:229.

65. McPherson, *Ordeal by Fire*, 303.

66. See Special Orders No. 246, 18 November 1862; Special Orders No. 253, 26 November 1862; General Orders No. 130, 4 December 1862; and Chilton to chief commissary, Lt. Col. Cole, 4 December 1862, *O.R.*, 1st ser., vol. 21, 1020, 1033–34, 1046.

67. McPherson, *Ordeal by Fire,* 304; Long, *Civil War Day by Day,* 296.

68. Lee's report of battle of Fredericksburg, *O.R.,* 1st ser., 21, 552, 556; Long, *Memoirs of Lee,* 236.

69. McPherson, *Ordeal by Fire,* 320; Long, *Civil War Day by Day,* 344–45.

70. McPherson, *Ordeal by Fire,* 321–23; Long, *Civil War Day by Day,* 346–48.

71. Lee's and Pendleton's reports of battle of Chancellorsville, *O.R.,* 1st ser., vol. 25, 805, 811–12; Freeman, *Lee's Lieutenants,* vol. 2, 607–10.

72. Freeman, *Lee's Lieutenants,* 2:610–13; Edward J. Stackpole, *Chancellorsville: Lee's Greatest Battle,* 2nd ed. (Harrisburg, Pa.: Stackpole, 1988), 284.

73. Long, *Civil War Day by Day,* 374–75.

74. Ibid., 375–77.

75. A. Long, *Memoirs of Lee,* 268, 277–78, 280; Pendleton's report of battle of Gettysburg, *O.R.,* 1st ser., vol. 27, pt. 2, 349–50; Freeman, *R. E. Lee,* 3:75, 92–93; Freeman, *Lee's Lieutenant's,* 3:145.

76. A. Long, *Memoirs of Lee,* 286; Gallagher, *Fighting for the Confederacy,* 236.

77. Gallagher, *Fighting for the Confederacy,* 233; Maurice, *Aide-de-Camp of Lee,* xxvii; Kenneth Williams, *Lincoln Finds a General: A Military Study of the Civil War,* (New York: Macmillan, 1959), 2:617–18, 664.

78. *O.R.,* 1st ser., vol. 29, ibid., pt. 1, 403; pt. 2, 745, 864; Taylor, *General Lee,* 57.

79. General Orders No. 124, 28 October 1862, *O.R.,* 1st ser., vol. 19, pt. 2, 688; Special Orders No. 251, 24 November 1862; ibid., vol. 21, 1028; General Orders No. 130, and Special Orders Nos. 253, 277, 281, ibid., 1033–34, 1046, 1077, 1080–81; Lee's report of battle of Fredericksburg, ibid., 556; Lee's report of battle of Chancellorsville, ibid., vol. 25, pt. 1, 805.

80. Taylor to Bettie Saunders, 13 December 1863, Tower, *Lee's Adjutant,* 97; Lee to Chilton, 23 April 1863, *O.R.,* 1st ser., vol. 25, pt. 2, 745–46.

81. For some of Chilton's duties in early 1863 see General Orders 20, 21, 43, 52, 58, *O.R.,* 1st ser., vol. 25, pt. 2, 625–26, 629, 681–82, 708, 739–40; Lee to Stuart, 2 November 1863, *O.R.,* 1st ser., vol. 29, pt. 2, 816; Venable to Ewell, 22 February 1864, *O.R.,* 1st ser., vol. 33, 1193; Freeman, *R. E. Lee,* vol. 3, 224.

82. Taylor to Bettie Saunders, 23 February and 4 March 1864, Tower, *Lee's Adjutant,* 128, 130, 132.

83. Lee to Chilton, 24 March 1864, Chilton Papers.

84. Freeman, *R. E. Lee,* 3:218; for examples of orders and correspondence of Lee's staff in May 1864 see *O.R.,* 1st ser., vol. 36, pt. 3, 948, 952–53, 961, 967–68, 801, 813–14, 826, 832, 834, 836–39, 844, 846.

85. Freeman, *Lee's Lieutenants,* 3:357–58; Venable, "Lee in the Wilderness," in *Battles and Leaders,* 4:244.

86. Taylor, *General Lee,* 276–77.

87. Maurice, *Aide-de-Camp of Lee,* 263–74; Gallagher, *Fighting for the Confederacy,* 535, 539.

88. "The Sudden and Sad Death of Gen. R. H. Chilton," obituary, Chilton Papers; Taylor, *Four Years with Lee,* 156; Long, *Memoirs of Lee,* 477; Charles Bracelen Flood, *Lee: The Last Years* (Boston: Houghton Mifflin, 1981), 245–46.

CHAPTER 4: GRANT, 1861–1862

1. McFeely, *Grant,* 8–9; Perret, *Grant: Soldier and President,* 28.

2. McFeely, *Grant,* 6–8, 10–11; Smith, *Lee and Grant,* 12–13.

3. Perret, *Grant: Soldier and President,* 19.

4. McFeely, *Grant*, 12; Smith, *Lee and Grant*, 18–19; Thomas J. Fleming, *West Point: The Men and Times of the U.S. Military Academy* (New York: William Morrow, 1969), 103; Joseph Ellis and Robert Moore, *School for Soldiers: West Point and the Profession of Arms* (New York: Oxford University Press, 1974), 12.

5. Perret, *Grant: Soldier and President*, 32–44.

6. McFeely, *Grant*, 43–45.

7. Ibid., 42; Smith, *Lee and Grant*, 58–59.

8. McFeely, *Grant*, 51–52.

9. Perret, *Grant: Soldier and President*, 102; McFeely, *Grant*, 41–56.

10. McFeely, *Grant*, 58–65.

11. Ibid., 75, 80–83.

12. John Y. Simon, ed., *The Papers of Ulysses S. Grant* (Carbondale: Southern Illinois University Press, 1967–1995), 2:116–17, 141, 145–46, 160–61 (hereafter cited *Papers of Grant*).

13. *Papers of Grant*, 1:347–49; Ulysses S. Grant, *Personal Memoirs of U. S. Grant* (New York: C. L. Webster, 1885–86), 1:254–55.

14. Grant, *Memoirs*, 1:254–55; *Papers of Grant*, 2:98–99; Grant's report of skirmish at Potosi, Missouri, *O.R.*, 1st ser., vol. 3, 131.

15. James H. Wilson, *The Life of John A. Rawlins: Lawyer, Assistant Adjutant-General, Chief of Staff, Major General of Volunteers, and Secretary of War* (New York: Neale Publishing, 1916), 24; E. B. Long, "John A. Rawlins: Staff Officer Par Excellence," *Civil War Times Illustrated*, 12, no. 9 (1974): 6.

16. Ibid., 7; *Papers of Grant*, 2:7.

17. Grant, *Memoirs*, 1:255; *Papers of Grant*, 2:96–97, 126, 117.

18. E. B. Long, "Rawlins: Staff Officer," 8; *Papers of Grant*, 2:160–61, 182.

19. *Papers of Grant*, 2:206–207, 145–46, 141.

20. General Orders No. 22, Cairo, 23 December 1861, *O.R.*, 1st ser., vol. 7, 515.

21. Ezra J. Warner, *Generals in Blue* (Baton Rouge: Louisiana State University Press, 1964), 546–47; Webster to Capt. William McMichael, *Papers of Grant*, 3:217–18.

22. For duties of Webster and Rawlins see Frémont to Grant, 5 September 1861; Charles F. Smith to Frémont, 9 September 1861; Webster to Grant, 27 September 1861, *Papers of Grant*, 2:191, 204–6, 353; and Grant to Webster, 2 November 1861; and General Orders No. 11, 14 October 1861, ibid., 3:107, 38–39. For Hillyer's duties see Hillyer to Hatch, 3 September 1861; Grant to Julia Dent Grant, 20 September 1861; Grant to McKeever, 29 September 1861; special orders, 4 October 1861; and Grant to McKeever, 30 October 1861; ibid., 2:168, 182, 290, 323, and 3:85–86.

23. Grant to All Whom it May Concern, 1 November 1861, *Papers of Grant*, 3:102.

24. McFeely, *Grant*, 92–93; Foote, *The Civil War*, 1:149–51.

25. McFeely, *Grant*, 93–94.

26. Grant's report of Belmont engagement, 17 November 1861, *O.R.*, 1st ser., vol. 3, 271; Grant to Seth Williams, 10 November 1861, *Papers of Grant*, 3:143.

27. Wilson, *Life of Rawlins*, 65–67.

28. Ibid., 68–71.

29. Ibid., 71.

30. *Papers of Grant*, 3:289–90, 324–27, 351–52, 292.

31. Ibid., 131, 323; ibid., 4:87; General Orders No. 22, 23 December 1861, *O.R.*, 1st ser., vol. 7, 513.

32. For examples of Hillyer's and Rawlins's writing see *Papers of Grant*, 2:154, 190, 194, 195, 200, 203, 204, 205, 215, 222, 251, 256, 254–55, 256, 261, 284; *O.R.*, 1st ser., vol. 8, 430, 433; Wilson, *Life of Rawlins*, 72.

33. Wilson, *Life of Rawlins,* 72, 62.

34. McClernand to Grant, 10 February 1862, *O.R.,* 1st ser., vol. 7, 128; McClernand to Grant, 5 February 1862, *Papers of Grant,* 4:148.

35. *Papers of Grant,* 4:169, 180, 167.

36. David Nevin et al., eds., *The Civil War: The Road to Shiloh* (Alexandria, Va.: Time-Life Books, 1983), 86–87; Wallace's report of battle of Fort Donelson, *O.R.,* 1st ser., vol. 7, 237.

37. Grant, *Memoirs,* 1:308.

38. Nevin, *The Road to Shiloh,* 88–89.

39. McClernand's report of battle of Fort Donelson, *O.R.,* 1st ser., vol. 7, 178.

40. For accounts of the Forts Henry and Donelson campaigns see E. B. *Long, Civil War Day by Day,* 170–72; Nevin, *The Road to Shiloh,* 61–67, 78–95; Foote, *The Civil War,* 1:173–76, 181–91, 195–215; McFeely, *Grant,* 96–101.

41. Foote's report of occupation of Clarksville, 20 February 1862, *O.R.,* 1st ser., vol. 7, 422; Grant to Brig. Gen. George W. Cullum, St. Louis, 21 February 1862, *Papers of Grant,* 4:258.

42. Grant's report of surrender of Fort Donelson, *O.R.,* 1st ser., vol. 7, 160.

43. Wilson, *Life of Rawlins,* 80–81.

44. General Orders No. 21, 15 March 1862, *O.R.,* 1st ser., vol. 10, pt. 2, 41; *Papers of Grant,* 4:277–78, 445.

45. *O.R.,* vol. 10, pt. 2, 41; Wilson, *Life of Rawlins,* 81.

46. Grant to Stanton, 14 March 1862, *O.R.,* 1st ser., vol. 10, pt. 2, 35; *Papers of Grant,* 4:357.

47. Grant, *Memoirs,* 1:318–29.

48. Ibid., 329; Grant to Julia Dent Grant, 29 March 1862, *Papers of Grant,* 4:443; Special Orders No. 36, 26 March 1862, and General Orders No. 33, 2 April 1862, *O.R.,* 1st ser., vol. 10, pt. 2, 67, 87–88.

49. Webster to Grant, 3 April 1862, *O.R.,* 1st ser., vol. 10, pt. 1, 84–86.

50. Grant, *Memoirs,* 1:330–51; McPherson, *Ordeal by Fire,* 226–28.

51. *O.R.,* 1st ser., vol. 10, pt. 1, 110, 95–96.

52. William S. Hillyer, "Pittsburg, April 11, 1862: On the Battlefield," *Ulysses S. Grant Association Newsletter,* 1, no. 2 (January 1964): 10; Rawlins to Grant, report of Battle of Shiloh, *O.R.,* 1st ser., vol. 10, 184–85.

53. Hillyer, "On the Battlefield," 10.

54. Sword, *Shiloh: Bloody April,* 352–53, 361; James Lee McDonough, *Shiloh: In Hell before Night* (Knoxville: University of Tennessee Press, 1977), 171, 175, 180; Grant, *Memoirs,* 1:345–47.

55. Hillyer, "On the Battlefield," 11–12.

56. Rawlins's, Rowley's, and McPherson's reports to Grant, *O.R.,* 1st ser., vol. 10, pt. 1, 178–88.

57. Grant, *Memoirs,* 1:337; Sylvanus Cadwallader, *Three Years with Grant* (New York: Knopf, 1956), 229.

CHAPTER 5: GRANT, 1862–1863

1. *Papers of Grant,* 3:292; ibid., 5:52–53, 73.

2. Ibid., 5:103–104.

3. Cadwallader, *Three Years with Grant,* 7–9.

4. McFeely, *Grant,* 116–17; Grant, *Memoirs,* 1:381.

5. McFeely, *Grant,* 118–20; Grant, *Memoirs,* 1:385, 392–93.

6. General Orders No. 56, 20 June 1862; Special Orders No. 123, 29 June 1862; General Orders No. 60, 3 July 1862; General Orders No. 61, 4 July 1862; Special Orders No. 133, 9 July 1862; Special Orders No. 136, 16 July 1862, General Orders No. 64, 25 July 1862; *O.R.*, 1st ser., vol. 17, pt. 2, 20, 51, 69, 70, 87–88, 102, 123.

7. E. B. Long, "Rawlins: Staff Officer," 8.

8. Grant to Julia Dent Grant, 24 May and 9 June 1862, *Papers of Grant,* 5:130, 140.

9. Ibid.; E. B. Long, "Rawlins: Staff Officer," 9–11; Grant, *Memoirs,* 1:256.

10. Richardson, *Personal History,* 258–59.

11. Grant, *Memoirs,* 1:390; Special Orders No. 118, 24 June 1862, *O.R.,* 1st ser., vol. 17, pt. 2, 30–31; *Papers of Grant,* 5:199.

12. Hillyer, "On the Battlefield," 13.

13. Special Orders No. 118, *O.R.,* 1st ser., vol. 17, pt. 2, 30–31; *Papers of Grant,* 7:397; ibid., 5:149; Grant, *Memoirs,* 1:255.

14. Grant, *Memoirs,* 1:255; *Papers of Grant,* 5:207, 219, 268.

15. Grant to Julia Dent Grant, 18, 22 August 1862, *Papers of Grant,* 5:308, 309, 328; Special Orders 187, 190, *O.R.,* 1st ser., vol. 17, pt. 2, 207, 211.

16. Grant, *Memoirs,* 1:396–401; Foote, *The Civil War,* 1:716–17.

17. *O.R.,* 1st ser., vol. 17, pt. 1, 67, 69; Grant, *Memoirs,* 1:411–12; *Papers of Grant,* 6:177–78; Foote, *The Civil War,* 1:718–19; Catton, *Grant Moves South,* 309–11; C. S. Hamilton, "The Battle of Iuka," in *Battles and Leaders of the Civil War,* 2:734.

18. Foote, *The Civil War,* 1:722–25; E. B. Long, *Civil War Day by Day,* 274–75.

19. Catton, *Grant Moves South,* 316–17.

20. Fuller, *Generalship of Grant,* 121–22.

21. Foote, *The Civil War,* 1:744, 762.

22. Wilson, *Life of Rawlins,* 102; Grant to Stanton, 27 October 1862, *Papers of Grant,* 6:220–21.

23. Grant, *Memoirs,* 1:421; *Papers of Grant,* 6:203.

24. Grant, *Memoirs,* 1:422–24.

25. Foote, *The Civil War,* 1:763.

26. Ibid., 764; Grant, *Memoirs,* 1:426–27.

27. Sherman to Grant, 3, 8 November 1862, *Papers of Grant,* 6:256, 264; Grant, *Memoirs,* 1:427.

28. Rawlins to Bowers, 5 November 1862, *Papers of Grant,* 6:256.

29. Grant, *Memoirs,* 1:423–24, 427–28.

30. Special Order No. 5, 1 November 1862, *O.R.,* 1st ser., vol. 17, pt. 2, 300; *Papers of Grant,* 6:120–22.

31. Grant to Washburne, 7 November 1862, and General Order No. 6, 11 November 1862, *Papers of Grant,* 6:275, 294–95.

32. *O.R.,* 1st ser., vol. 17, pt. 2, 346–47, 378–79.

33. Wilson, *Life of Rawlins,* 99–100.

34. Rowley to Washburne, 20 November 1862, *Papers of Grant,* 7:32.

35. Ibid.

36. Grant to Halleck, 16 December 1962, *Papers of Grant,* 7:28–29.

37. Grant to Julia Dent Grant, 9 February 1863, *Papers of Grant,* 7:309.

38. *Papers of Grant,* 6:295; ibid., 7:480; ibid., 8:163.

39. Grant, *Memoirs,* 1:428–31.

40. John Y. Simon, ed., *The Personal Memoirs of Julia Dent Grant* (New York: G. P. Putnam's Sons, 1975), 107 (hereafter cited as *Julia Grant*); Richardson, *Personal History,* 282–84; Foote, *The Civil War,* 2:70–71.

41. Grant, *Memoirs,* 1:435.

42. Foote, *The Civil War*, 2:73–77.
43. Grant, *Memoirs*, 1:438–41.
44. Ibid., 442–55; Richardson, *Personal History*, 287–92; Foote, *The Civil War*, 2:190–94.
45. Grant, *Memoirs*, 1:460; Foote, *The Civil War*, 2:323–26.
46. Wilson, *Life of Rawlins*, 113–14.
47. Ibid., 120–22; Cadwallader, *Three Years with Grant*, 62.
48. Foote, *The Civil War*, 2:323–24; Grant, *Memoirs*, 1:465–66.
49. Grant, *Memoirs*, 1:463; Foote, *The Civil War*, 2:326–29.
50. Grant, *Memoirs*, 1:471–72; Foote, *The Civil War*, 2:330; *O.R.*, 1st ser., vol. 24, pt. 1, 565.
51. *Julia Grant*, 112; *O.R.*, 1st ser., vol. 24, pt. 3, 216–17.
52. Report of U.S. Army adjutant general Lorenzo Thomas, 23 April 1863; report of Col. William S. Oliver, 24 April 1863; Grant to Halleck, 25 April 1863, *O.R.*, 1st ser., vol. 24, pt. 1, 564–67, 31.
53. E. B. Long, *Civil War Day by Day*, 343–54; Foote, *The Civil War*, 2:347–80.
54. Special Orders No. 120, 30 April 1863, *Papers of Grant*, 8:137.
55. Ibid., 162; Fuller, *Generalship of Grant*, 143.
56. *Papers of Grant*, 8:175, 186.
57. Ibid., 219.
58. Report of Capt. Andrew Hickenlooper, chief engineer, 17th Corps, *O.R.*, 1st ser., vol. 24, pt. 2, 198; report of James Harrison Wilson, 4 May 1863, pt. 1, 130; Wilson, *Life of Rawlins*, 125–26.
59. Wilson, *Life of Rawlins*, 127; E. B. Long, "Rawlins: Staff Officer," 45; Catton, *Grant Moves South*, 392; Charles A. Dana, *Recollections of the Civil War* (New York: D. Appleton, 1898), 72; see also *O.R.*, 1 ser., vol. 24, pt. 3, 259–321 for the many orders coming from Grant's headquarters on the campaign.
60. Bowers to Hurlbut, 5 May 1863, *O.R.*, 1st ser., vol. 24, pt. 3, 275–76.
61. Grant, *Memoirs*, 1:491–92; Grant to Banks, 25 May 1863, *Papers of Grant*, 8:268–71; Dana to Stanton, 8 June 1863, *O.R.*, 1st ser., vol. 24, pt. 1, 94–95.
62. Special Orders No. 139, 24 May 1863, *Papers of Grant*, 8:243.
63. Hurlbut to Rawlins, 29 May 1863; *Papers of Grant*, 8:243.
64. Foote, *The Civil War*, 2:219–20.
65. Grant, *Memoirs*, 1:480.
66. Cadwallader, *Three Years with Grant*, 71.
67. Wilson, *Life of Rawlins*, 128–29.
68. Catton, *Grant Moves South*, 464.
69. *Papers of Grant*, 8:324–25.
70. Cadwallader, *Three Years with Grant*, 103–12; *Papers of Grant*, 8:324; Catton, *Grant Moves South*, 463–64.
71. *Papers of Grant*, 8:324–25.
72. E. B. Long, "Rawlins: Staff Officer," 44.
73. *Julia Grant*, 5.
74. Wilson, *Life of Rawlins*, 148; Dana, *Recollections*, 62.
75. Grant to Hurlbut, 31 May 1863, *Papers of Grant*, 8:297–98.
76. Hurlbut to Rawlins, 10 June 1863, *Papers of Grant*, 8:306.
77. Hillyer to Grant, 30 June 1863, *Papers of Grant*, 8:219.
78. Grant to Julia Dent Grant, 15 June 1863, *Papers of Grant*, 8:377.
79. Grant, *Memoirs*, 1:567; Jesse R. Grant, *In the Days of My Father, General Grant* (New York: Harper and Brothers, 1925), 27–28; *O.R.*, 1st ser., vol. 30, pt. 2, 805, 807.
80. *Papers of Grant*, 7:224–25.

81. E. B. Long, *Civil War Day by Day,* 137–79; Catton, *Grant Moves South,* 473–74; Wilson, *Life of Rawlins,* 152.

82. Grant, *Memoirs,* 1:370.

83. Report of Vicksburg campaign, 6 July 1863, *Papers of Grant,* 8:485–523; Wilson, *Life of Rawlins,* 147, 157–58.

84. Grant to Lorenzo Thomas, 19 July 1863, and Grant to Abraham Lincoln, 20 July 1863, *Papers of Grant,* 9:78–91.

85. Ibid., 78–79; Grant, *Memoirs,* 1:546–47; Wilson, *Life of Rawlins,* 125, 130–34.

86. Grant to Lorenzo Thomas, 19 July 1863, and Grant to Abraham Lincoln, 20 July 1863, *Papers of Grant,* 9:78–81.

87. Ibid.

88. Welles's diary entry, 31 July 1863, in Wilson, *Life of Rawlins,* 158–59; also *Papers of Grant,* 9:82–83.

89. Dana, *Recollections,* 74–75.

CHAPTER 6: SHERMAN, 1862–1865

1. William T. Sherman, *Memoirs of General William T. Sherman* (New York: Charles Webster, 1891), 2:402.

2. Sherman's report of Atlanta campaign, *O.R.,* 1st ser., vol. 38, pt. 1, 84.

3. Sherman, *Memoirs,* 2:402.

4. Ibid.

5. Dana, *Recollections,* 75–76.

6. Special Orders Number 15, 19 March 1862, and Orders Number 19, 4 April 1862, *O.R.,* 1st ser., vol. 10, pt. 2, 50, 92.

7. Reports of John A. McClernand; Lt. Col. Robert D. Fulton, 53rd Ohio Infantry; and Lt. Col. Adolph Engleman, 43rd Illinois Infantry, of the battle of Shiloh, *O.R.,* 1st ser., vol. 10, pt. 1, 120, 122, 144, 265.

8. Lewis, *Fighting Prophet,* 228.

9. Col. John A. McDowell's and Sherman's reports of battle of Shiloh, *O.R.,* 1st ser., vol. 10, pt. 1, 254–55.

10. Orders Number 23, 30 April 1862, ibid., pt. 2, 145–46.

11. Hammond's and Sherman's reports of Corinth campaign, *O.R.,* vol. 10, pt. 1, 744, 857–59.

12. Circular, Headquarters, Fifth Division, 5 May 1862, ibid., pt. 2, 164–65.

13. General Orders No. 33, 7 June 1862, ibid., 269–70.

14. For examples of Hammond's writing at this time see *O.R.,* 1st ser., vol. 17, pt. 2, 4, 8, 10, 13, 15–16, 33, 50, 81, 102–3, 112–13, 118–19, 158–60, 204.

15. General Orders No. 93, 12 November 1862, ibid., 344–45.

16. General Orders No. 6, 13 December 1862, ibid., 617–18.

17. General Orders No. 7, 18 December 1862, ibid., 618–19.

18. Lewis, *Fighting Prophet,* 256–57.

19. Special Orders No. 31, 22 December 1862, *O.R.,* 1st ser., vol. 17, pt. 2, 614–15.

20. Special Orders No. 34 and 36, 25, 26 December 1862, ibid., 620–22.

21. Sherman to division commanders, 23 December 1862, ibid., 616–17.

22. Special Orders 38, 39, and 1, 30, 31 December 1862, and 3 January 1863, ibid., 623–24; Lewis, *Fighting Prophet,* 259.

23. Lewis, *Fighting Prophet,* 259.

24. Ibid., 260.

25. Ibid., 260–61; General Orders No. 1, 5 January 1863, *O.R.,* 1st ser., vol. 17, pt. 2, 538–39.

26. Reports of Sherman and McClernand on the capture of Arkansas Post, 13, 20 January 1863, ibid., 754–55, 702–3.

27. Reports of Sherman and A. J. Smith, *O.R.*, 755, 727; Lewis, *Fighting Prophet*, 261.

28. Special Orders No. 34 and 36, 6, 8 February 1863, *O.R.*, 1st ser., vol. 24, pt. 3, 37, 40.

29. General Orders No. 10, 7 March 1863, ibid., 89–90.

30. For examples of Dayton's writing see ibid., 118, 165, 171.

31. Special Orders No. 96, 28 April 1863, ibid., 245–46.

32. Sherman to Steele, 28 April 1863, ibid., 245.

33. Sherman to Frank Blair, 2 May 1863; General Orders Nos. 29 and 30, 2 May 1863, ibid., 263–64.

34. Circular, 26 May 1863, ibid., 352.

35. General Orders No. 44, 9 June 1863, ibid., 394–95.

36. Special Orders No. 135, 26 June 1863, ibid., 442–43.

37. Rochester to Sanborn, 26 June 1863, ibid., 443.

38. General Orders No. 52, 4 July 1863, ibid., 475–76.

39. Lewis, *Fighting Prophet*, 294–95; Foote, *The Civil War*, 2:618–19.

40. For examples of Sawyer's writing at the time see: General Orders No. 53, 6 July 1863; Circular, 8 July 1863; General Orders Nos. 55 and 56, 9, 10 July 1863; General Orders Nos. 57, 58, 59, 11, 12, 17 July 1863, *O.R.*, 1st ser., vol. 24, pt. 3, 481–82, 490–91, 496, 502–3, 507, 524–25.

41. See Sherman to Cyruss Bussey and E. O. C. Ord, 15 July 1863 and to John G. Parke, 16 July 1863, ibid., 514–16, 520.

42. Hammond's report of fight at Birdsong Ferry, ibid., 508–9.

43. Ibid.

44. Report of Col. Cyrus Bussey, 22 July 1863, ibid., 551–54.

45. *O.R.*, 1st ser., vol. 31, pt. 3, 543; ibid., vol. 32, pt. 2, 7, 23.

46. General Orders No. 69, 30 August 1863; General Orders No. 71, 22 September 1863; General Orders Nos. 75, 76, Special Orders No. 185, 26 September 1863, *O.R.*, 1st ser., vol. 30, pt. 3, 225–26, 772–73, 868–69; Special Orders No. 188, 6 October 1863, ibid., pt. 4, 117; General Orders No. 1, 24 October 1863, ibid., vol. 31, pt. 1, 712.

47. Sherman, *Memoirs*, 2:445; Brig. Gen. Daniel Tyler's report of Bull Run campaign, *O.R.*, 1st ser., vol. 2, 351; Sherman to Grant, 14 July 1863, ibid., vol. 24, pt. 2, 524, 527; Special Orders No. 188, 6 October 1863, ibid., vol. 30, pt. 4, 117; Michael Fellman, *Citizen Sherman: A Life of William Tecumseh Sherman* (New York: Random House, 1995), 358–70; Marszalek, *Sherman: A Soldier's Passion for Order*, 418–20.

48. Lewis, *Fighting Prophet*, 308–9.

49. For examples of Sawyer's writing at this time, see General Orders No. 71, 22 September 1863; General Orders Nos. 75 and 76, 26 September 1863; Special Orders No. 185, 26 September 1883; *O.R.*, 1st ser., vol. 30, pt. 3, 772–73, 868–69; Special Orders No. 186, 3 October 1863; General Orders No. 77, 6 October 1863; Special Orders No. 192, 10 October 1863; General Orders No. 80 and Special Orders No. 196, 16 October 1863, ibid., pt. 4, 51, 116, 237, 410.

50. Lewis, *Fighting Prophet*, 310–11; Sherman to Rawlins, 14 October 1863, and report of Colonel Anthony, *O.R.*, 1st ser., vol. 30, pt. 2, 731, 754.

51. General Orders Nos. 120 and 121, 1, 3 September 1863, *O.R.*, 1st ser., vol. 30, pt. 3, 278, 320; Hart, *Soldier, Realist, American*, 212.

52. Hurlbut to Webster, 2 October 1863; Special Orders No. 239, 3 October 1863, *O.R.*, 1st ser., vol. 30, pt. 4, 30, 51.

53. Carr to Hurlbut, 3 October 1863; Sherman to Grant, 10 October 1863; ibid., 55, 236.

54. Sherman to Webster, 12 October 1863, ibid., 305.

55. Sherman to Webster, 15 October 1863; Webster to Sherman, Sherman to Webster, 16 October 1863, ibid., 382, 409–10.

56. Hart, *Soldier, Realist, American,* 314.

57. For duties of Rochester see *O.R.,* 1st ser., vol. 32, pt. 3, 178; McCoy, ibid., vol. 24, pt.2, 575, vol. 30, pt. 2, 865, and vol. 31, pt. 2, 578; Sanger, ibid., vol. 31, pt. 3, 168; Corse, ibid., vol. 30, pt. 2, 8, 98, 278, 885; Warner, ibid., vol. 31, pt. 2, 602, 605–6, 608–9, 613, 617; Dayton, ibid., vol. 17, pt. 2, 10, vol. 30, pt. 2, 731, and vol. 31, pt. 3, 329; Dunn, ibid., vol. 30, pt. 4, 380, vol. 31, pt. 1, 713, 720.

58. General Orders No. 1, 24 October 1863; Special Orders No. 4, Division of the Mississippi, 28 October 1863; General Orders No. 2 and Special Orders No. 1, 25 October 1863; *O.R.,* 1st ser., vol. 31, pt. 1, 712, 768, 730–32.

59. Sherman to Hurlbut, 25 October 1863, ibid., 732–33.

60. Hart, *Soldier, Realist, American,* 212.

61. Special Orders No. 5, 30 October 1863, *O.R.,* 1st ser., vol. 31, pt. 1, 792.

62. Grenville M. Dodge, *Personal Recollections of Lincoln, Grant, and Sherman* (Council Bluffs, Iowa: Monarch Printing, 1914; reprint, New York: Sage Books, 1965), 137.

63. Correspondence between Audenried and Grant, 7, 8 November 1863, *O.R.,* 1st ser., vol. 31, pt. 3, 79–80, 91–92.

64. Sherman to Grant, 14 November 1863, *O.R.,* 1st ser., vol. 31, pt. 3, 152.

65. Sawyer to Sherman, 15 November 1863, ibid., 159.

66. Correspondence between Sherman and Sawyer, 15, 16 November 1863, ibid., 159, 168.

67. Sherman to Sawyer, 16, 17 November 1863, ibid., 168, 178–79.

68. Sherman to Hurlbut, 16 November 1863, ibid., 169.

69. Audenried to Sherman, 20 November 1863, ibid., 200.

70. "Operations for Monday, November 23," ibid., pt. 2, 589–90.

71. Special Orders No. 15, 23 November 1863, ibid., 590.

72. Audenried to Sherman, 26 November 1863; Sawyer to Blair, Davis, and Howard, 27 November 1863, ibid., 592–95.

73. Sawyer to Blair and Granger, 30 November 1863, Special Orders No. 16, 1 December 1863; ibid., pt. 3, 278–79, 299, 300.

74. Lewis, *Fighting Prophet,* 327–28; Field Orders, 4 December 1863; Sawyer to Granger, Davis, and Howard, 5 December 1863; ibid., 329, 340–41.

75. Lewis, *Fighting Prophet,* 328–32.

76. Sawyer to Sherman, 30 December 1863, *O.R.,* 1st ser., vol. 31, pt. 3, 534–35.

77. Lewis, *Fighting Prophet,* 332; Royster, *Destructive War,* 324.

78. Sherman's report of Meridian campaign, 7 March 1864, *O.R.,* 1st ser., vol. 32, pt. 1, 173–74.

79. Ibid., 175–76; Lewis, *Fighting Prophet,* 333; Royster, *Destructive War,* 324–25.

80. Special Field Orders Nos. 11 and 16, *O.R.,* 1st ser., vol. 32, pt. 1, 182, 185–86.

81. Special Field Orders No. 17, ibid., 186.

82. Special Field Orders No. 18, ibid., 187.

83. Sherman to Hurlbut and McPherson, 17 January 1864, ibid., 179–82.

84. Sherman's report of Meridian campaign, ibid., 179.

85. Sherman to Sawyer, 31 January 1864, ibid., pt. 2, 278–81.

86. Ibid.

87. Special Field Orders No. 12, 12 January 1864, ibid., 243.

88. General Orders No. 1, Item II, 18 March 1864, *O.R.,* 1st ser., vol. 32, pt. 3, 87.
89. General Orders No. 3, 24 March 1864, and Brig. Gen. Mason Brayman to Webster, 1 April 1864, ibid., 147, 216.
90. General Orders No. 3, 24 March 1864; Rochester to Sherman, 29 April 1864, ibid., 147, 532.
91. Dodge to Sawyer, and Sawyer to McPherson, 22 March 1864, ibid., 114.
92. Sawyer to Thomas, ibid., 110.
93. Sherman to Webster, 31 March 1864, ibid., 202–3.
94. Webster to Hurlbut and Brayman, 31 March 1864, ibid., 203.
95. Lewis, *Fighting Prophet,* 353.
96. Ibid., 351; Hart, *Soldier, Realist, American,* 231–32.
97. Hart, *Soldier, Realist, American,* 234–35; Sherman, *Memoirs,* 2:389; Sherman to Sawyer, 3 April 1864, *O.R.,* 1st ser., vol. 32, pt. 3, 542.
98. Sherman to Halleck, 26 April 1864, *O.R.,* 1st ser., vol. 32, pt. 3, 498.
99. Hart, *Soldier, Realist, American,* 237.
100. Ibid., 258.
101. General Orders No. 35, 25 April 1864, *O.R.,* 1st ser., vol. 32, pt. 3, 496–97.
102. Ibid.
103. Lewis, *Fighting Prophet,* 348–50.
104. Sherman to Schofield, 24 April 1864, *O.R.,* 1st ser., vol. 32, pt. 3, 474–75.
105. Allen to Halleck, 12 April 1864, and to Webster, 25 April 1864, ibid., 330, 494.
106. Sherman to Webster, 29 April 1864, ibid., 532.
107. Sherman to Rousseau, ibid.
108. Sherman to McPherson and Schofield, ibid., 533–34.
109. Sawyer to McCallum, 30 April 1864, ibid., 543–44.
110. Dodge, *Recollections,* 146.
111. For correspondence among Sherman and his commanders around 5 May 1864 see *O.R.,* 1st ser., vol. 38, pt. 4, 28–39.
112. Dayton to Thomas, O. O. Howard to Schofield, Sherman to Schofield, 6 May 1864, ibid., 43–46.
113. McPherson, *Ordeal by Fire,* 430–32; Long, *Civil War Day by Day,* 502–6.
114. Sherman to George Stoneman, 17 May 1864; Schofield to Sherman, 22 May 1864; Special Field Orders Nos. 6 and 7, 15 May 1864; Dayton to Schofield and Special Field Orders No. 8, 16 May 1864, *O.R.,* 1st ser., vol. 38, pt. 4, 224, 285, 199, 200, 209, 216–17.
115. Sherman to Webster, 1 May 1863, *O.R.,* 1st ser., vol. 38, pt. 4, 3.
116. Ibid., 26.
117. Sherman to Webster, 20 May and 6 June 1864, ibid., 262, 418.
118. Sherman to Webster, 19 May 1864, ibid., 249.
119. Webster to Sherman, 12 May 1864, ibid., 146.
120. Correspondence between Webster and Sherman, ibid.
121. Correspondence between Rousseau and Sherman, 19 June 1864, ibid., 530–31, 625, 630.
122. Dayton to Thomas, 12 May 1864, and other samples of Dayton's writing, ibid., 533, 338–39, 341–42.
123. Sherman to Webster, ibid., 294; ibid., pt. 5, 93.
124. Dayton to Webster, 31 July 1864, ibid., 308.
125. Correspondence between Sherman and Webster, ibid., pt. 4, 294, 351.
126. Sherman to Webster, 2 August 1864, ibid., pt. 5, 329.
127. Sherman to Webster, 4 August 1864, ibid., 351.

128. Correspondence between Webster and Rousseau, ibid., 757–58; among Webster, Burbridge, and Sherman, ibid., 1st ser., vol. 39, pt. 2, 285, 291–92, 300.

129. Webster to Sherman, 8 September 1864, *O.R.,* 1st ser., vol. 38, pt. 5, 831.

130. Sherman to Webster, 23 September 1864, ibid., vol. 39, pt. 2, 442, 480.

131. Webster to Schofield, 1 October 1864, ibid., pt. 3, 11.

132. Sherman to Webster, 1 October 1864; Thomas to Sherman, 3 October 1864, ibid., 3, 55.

133. Sherman's report of Atlanta campaign, *O.R.,* 1st ser., vol. 38, pt. 1, 84.

134. Sherman to Grant, 20, 21 September 1864, Sherman to Halleck, 26 September 1864, ibid., vol. 39, pt. 2, 411–13, 432, 479.

135. Sherman to Webster, 23 December 1864; Sherman to Grant, ibid., vol. 44, 787, 14.

136. Burke Davis, *Sherman's March* (New York: Random House, 1980), 26.

137. Dayton to Davis, 20 November 1864, *O.R.,* 1st ser., vol. 44, 501–2; for more examples of Dayton's writing on the march see ibid., 460, 465, 519, 527–28, 556, 582, 606, 609, 611, 771, 772, 776–77.

138. Audenried to Sherman, 29 November 1864, ibid., 570–71, 667.

139. Davis, *Sherman's March,* 116.

140. Sherman to Webster, 24 December 1864; Sherman's official report of Savannah campaign, 1 January 1865, *O.R.,* 1st ser., vol. 44, 787–93, 14.

141. George Ward Nichols, *The Story of the Great March* (New York: Harper and Brothers, 1865; reprint, Williamstown, Mass.: Corner House, 1972), passim.

142. M. A. DeWolfe Howe, ed., *Marching with Sherman: Passages from the Letters and Campaign Diaries of Henry Hitchcock, Major and Assistant Adjutant General of Volunteers, November 1864–May 1865* (New Haven, Conn.: Yale University Press, 1927), 3, 7, 19, 24.

143. Ibid., 131.

144. Special Field Orders No. 6, 8 January 1865, *O.R.,* 1st ser., vol. 44, 17.

145. Special Field Orders No. 144, 27 December 1864; Dayton to Webster, 28 December 1864, ibid., 826; Sawyer to Maj. Gen. Quincy Gillmore, 14 February 1865, ibid., vol. 47, pt. 2, 424.

146. Sherman to Easton, 9 January 1865; Sherman to O. O. Howard, 15 February 1865, ibid., 29, 429.

147. Special Field Orders No. 68, 28 April 1865; orders from adjutant general's office, 23 June 1865, ibid., pt. 3, 338, 661.

CHAPTER 7: GRANT, 1863–1865

1. Wilson, *Life of Rawlins,* 139–40.

2. Cadwallader, *Three Years with Grant,* 123; Wilson, *Life of Rawlins,* 150–51.

3. Wilson, *Life of Rawlins,* 155–56.

4. Grant, *Memoirs,* 1:580–82; Wilson, *Life of Rawlins,* 154.

5. E. B. Long, *Civil War Day by Day,* 411–12; McPherson, *Ordeal by Fire,* 334–37.

6. McPherson, *Ordeal by Fire,* 338–40.

7. Foote, *The Civil War,* 2:784–85.

8. Grant, *Memoirs,* 2:26–29; Foote, *The Civil War,* 2:774.

9. Wilson, *Life of Rawlins,* 165–66.

10. Foote, *The Civil War,* 2:805; McPherson, *Ordeal by Fire,* 338.

11. Foote, *The Civil War,* 2:806–7; McPherson, *Ordeal by Fire,* 339; Grant, *Memoirs,* 2:29, 35–37.

12. McPherson, *Ordeal by Fire*, 339; Foote, *The Civil War*, 2:836–37.

13. Foote, *The Civil War*, 2:837; Rawlins to Sherman, 21, 23 November 1863, *O.R.*, 1st ser., vol. 31, pt. 2, 39, 41–42.

14. McPherson, *Ordeal by Fire*, 341.

15. Foote, *The Civil War*, 2:853–59; Grant, *Memoirs*, 2:78–81.

16. Wilson, *Life of Rawlins*, 172; for correspondence and orders of Bowers and Rowley see *O.R.*, 1st ser., vol. 31, pt. 3, 48–49, 64, 38, 74–75, 84, 93, 94, 107–8, 123, 115.

17. Wilson, *Life of Rawlins*, 151, 175.

18. Rawlins to Emma Hurlbut, and Rawlins to Grant, 17 November 1863, *Papers of Grant*, 9:475–76.

19. William Wrenshall Smith, "Holocaust Holiday," *Civil War Times Illustrated* 18 (October 1979): 31.

20. Ibid., 40; Dana to Stanton, 1, 18 November 1863, *O.R.*, 1st ser., vol. 31, pt. 2, 54, 60; Lagow to Lorenzo Thomas, 18 November 1863, *Papers of Grant*, 476.

21. Rawlins to Mary Emma Hurlbut, 12 October 1863, John A. Rawlins Papers, Chicago Historical Society.

22. Adam Badeau, "Adam Badeau, on Appomattox," *The Ulysses S. Grant Association Newsletter* 3 (October 1965): 28–29.

23. Ibid.

24. *Papers of Grant*, 10:161.

25. David William Smith, "Ely Samuel Parker, 1828–1895: Military Secretary, Indian Commissioner, and Commissioner of Indian Affairs" (master's thesis, Southern Illinois University, Carbondale, 1973), 10–18.

26. Ibid., 19–22.

27. Ibid., 24–28; *Papers of Grant*, 8:414.

28. Smith, "Ely Parker," 29; *O.R.*, 1st ser., vol. 30, pt. 4, 27.

29. Lyman, *Meade's Headquarters*, 81; *Papers of Grant*, 8:446; *O.R.*, 1st ser., vol. 5, 24.

30. Dana to Stanton, 17, 19, 25, 28 June 1863, *O.R.*, 1st ser., vol. 24, 101, 103, 108, 111; *Papers of Grant*, 9:126; Dana, *Recollections*, 75.

31. *Papers of Grant*, 8:464–65; ibid., 9:126; Grant to Halleck, 6 July 1863, *O.R.*, 1st ser., vol. 24, pt. 1, 56–57.

32. *O.R.*, 1st ser., vol. 30, pt. 4, 471; *Papers of Grant*, 10:160–61, 220.

33. Cyrus B. Comstock Diary, 18 January 1864, Library of Congress; *Papers of Grant*, 10:41.

34. *O.R.*, 1st ser., 6:142, 146, 156, 160; *Papers of Grant*, vol. 9, 358–59.

35. Grant to Halleck, 5 November 1863, *O.R.*, 1st ser., vol. 31, pt. 3, 49; Horace Porter, *Campaigning with Grant* (1897; reprint, Secaucus, N. J.: Blue and Grey Press, 1984), 11–13.

36. Porter, *Campaigning with Grant*, 17, 22–24.

37. *Papers of Grant*, 10:221, 261–62; report of Maj. Gen. Richard Patterson, *O.R.*, 1st ser., vol. 2, 170; *O.R.*, 1st ser., vol. 5, 24, 677, 692; McFeely, *Grant*, 88, 338.

38. McFeely, *Grant*, 20; *Papers of Grant*, 10:220.

39. Grant to Lincoln, *Papers of Grant*, 10:221.

40. Grant to Halleck, 6 April 1864, *Papers of Grant*, 10:221–22; Comstock Diary, 11 March 1864.

41. Cadwallader, *Three Years with Grant*, 208.

42. Grant, *Memoirs*, 2:124–32.

43. Porter, *Campaigning with Grant*, 25.

44. Cadwallader, *Three Years with Grant*, 202.

45. Porter, *Campaigning with Grant,* 37–38.

46. Richard J. Sommers, *Richmond Redeemed,* 53.

47. Fleming, *West Point: Men and Times,* 103; Ellis and Moore, *School for Soldiers,* 12; Lyman, *Meade's Headquarters,* 178; Comstock Diary, 8 March 1864.

48. Hagerman,*American Civil War and Origin of Modern Warfare,* xvi.

49. McPherson, *Ordeal by Fire,* 411.

50. Grant to Sherman, 19 April 1864; Sherman to George Thomas, 23 April 1864; Sherman to McPherson, 24 April 1864; Sherman to Grant, 25 April 1864, *O.R.,* 1st ser., vol. 32, pt. 3, 409, 455, 479, 489.

51. Grant to Sigel, 15 April 1864; Babcock to Rawlins, 18 April 1864, *Papers of Grant,* 10:286, 310–11.

52. E. B. Long, *Civil War Day by Day,* 492; McPherson, *Ordeal by Fire,* 414–15; Foote, *The Civil War,* 3:146–47.

53. E. B. Long, *Civil War Day by Day,* 493; McPherson, *Ordeal by Fire,* 415.

54. Comstock and Rowley to Burnside, 5 May 1864; Comstock to Burnside, 6 May 1864, 6:20 A.M.; A. A. Humphreys to Hancock, 6 May, 1864, 9:00 A.M.; Comstock to Grant, 6 May 1864, 10:00 A.M.; Rawlins to Burnside, 6 May 1864, 11:45 A.M., *O.R.,* 1st ser., vol. 36, pt. 2, 424–25, 460, 442, 461; Hancock's report of Wilderness fight, ibid., pt. 1, 322.

55. Comstock to Grant, 6 May 1864, 2:45 P.M., ibid., pt. 2, 461.

56. Grant to Burnside, 6 May 1864, 3:30 P.M.; Comstock to Grant, 6 May 1864, 3:45 P.M.; Grant to Comstock, 6 May 1864, 4:00 P.M.; Grant to Burnside, 6 May 1864, ibid., 462.

57. Grant, *Memoirs,* 2:211.

58. McPherson, *Ordeal by Fire,* 416–22; Long, *Civil War Day by Day,* 496–514.

59. McPherson, *Ordeal by Fire,* 422–26; Long, *Civil War Day by Day,* 515–524.

60. Rawlins to Burnside, 8 May 1864, 1:00 P.M., 3:00 P.M., 7:30 P.M.; Babcock to Rawlins, 8 May 1864, 4:20 P.M., *O.R.,* 1st ser., vol. 36, pt. 2, 546–47.

61. Rawlins to Burnside, 9 May 1864, 8:45 A.M. and 10:00 A.M., ibid., 480–81.

62. Babcock to Rawlins, 10 May 1864, 9:00 A.M., ibid., 609.

63. Report of Maj. W. G. Mitchell, A.D.C., II Corps, ibid., pt. 1, 357–58.

64. Grant to Burnside, 11 May 1864, 4:00 P.M., ibid., pt. 2, 643; Burnside's report, ibid., pt. 1, 908–9.

65. Comstock Diary, 11 May 1864.

66. Comstock Diary, 12 May 1864.

67. Wilson, *Life of Rawlins,* 198–99.

68. Comstock to Warren, 16 June 1864, *O.R.,* 1st ser., vol. 40, pt. 2, 95.

69. Charles M. Dana to Stanton, 10, 12 June 1864; report of Maj. Gen. William F. Smith; Grant to Butler, 11 June 1864, ibid., vol. 36, pt. 1, 94–95, 1004, 754–55, 662.

70. Meade to Grant, 20 May 1864, 10:30 A.M.; A. A. Humphreys to Wright, 20 May 1864, 5:20 P.M., ibid., pt. 3, 5, 17.

71. Grant to Meade, 21 June 1864, 10:00 A.M.; Meade to Grant, 21 June 1864, 11:00 A.M., ibid., vol. 40, pt. 2, 268–69.

72. Butler to Grant, 20 June 1864, 2:45 P.M.; Grant to Butler, 20 June 1864, 3:25 P.M., ibid., 257.

73. Special Orders No. 27, 4 June 1864; Special Orders No. 28, 5 June 1864; Special Orders No. 25, 24 May 1864, ibid., vol. 36, pt. 3, 569–70, 600, 169.

74. Smith, "Ely Parker," 37.

75. For Rawlins's duties during this campaign see *O.R.,* 1st ser., vol. 36, pt. 3, 26, 64–65, 96, 100, 135–36, 167; ibid., vol. 40, pt. 2, 12, 321.

76. *Papers of Grant,* 11:207–9.

77. Bowers to Butler, 17 June 1864; Bowers to Rawlins, 24 June 1864; Grant to Bowers, 24 June 1864; Rawlins to Butler, 22 June 1864; correspondence among Rawlins, Bowers, and William F. Smith, *O.R.,* 1st ser., vol. 40, pt. 2, 143, 374, 321; for duties of Bowers and Parker see ibid., pt. 1, 40–41, 284; ibid., pt. 2, 143, 88, 236, 305, 464, 499, 584; ibid., pt. 3, 6, 389–90.

78. Grant to Julia, 1 July 1864, *Papers of Grant,* 11:151; Grant to Julia, 23 September, 4, 26 October 1864, *Papers of Grant,* 12:200, 277, 351.

79. Grant to Lincoln, 25 July 1864; Stanton to Grant, 26 July 1864, *O.R.,* 1st ser., vol. 40, pt. 3, 436, 456.

80. Special Orders No. 49, 5 July 1864; Grant to Meade, 8 July 1864; Meade to Grant, 9 July 1864; Meade to A. A. Humphreys, 13 July 1864; Grant to Halleck, 14 July 1864; Comstock to Grant, 15 July 1864, ibid., 6, 72, 94, 208, 223, 253.

81. Foote, *The Civil War,* 3:531–38; Porter, *Campaigning with Grant,* 261–67; Comstock to Grant, 30 July 1864, 7:00 A.M. and 8:00 A.M., *O.R.,* 1st ser., vol. 40, pt. 1, 142–43.

82. Bowers to James Harrison Wilson, 1, 2 August 1864; Lee to William R. Rowley, 9 August 1864, *Papers of Grant,* 11:363.

83. Grant to Sherman, 12 September 1864; Sherman to Grant, 19 September 1864, *Papers of Grant,* 12:154–57.

84. Grant to Rawlins, 29 October 1864; Special Orders No. 114, 29 October 1864; Halleck to Rawlins, 3, 4 November 1864; Rawlins to Grant, 4 November 1864; Rosecrans to Bowers, 4 November 1864, *Papers of Grant,* 12:363–67.

85. Grant to Sherman, 12 September 1864; Sherman to Grant, 19 September 1864, *Papers of Grant,* 12:154–57; Grant, *Memoirs,* 2:387.

86. E. B. Long, *Civil War Day by Day,* 612–15; Grant, *Memoirs,* 2:390–92.

87. Grant, *Memoirs,* 2:392; Porter, *Campaigning with Grant,* 373.

88. E. B. Long, *Civil War Day by Day,* 620–25; Grant, *Memoirs,* 2:395–99; Alfred H. Terry's report of Fort Fisher expedition, *O.R.,* 1st ser., vol. 46, pt. 1, 397, 400; Grant to Stanton, *O.R.,* vol. 46, pt. 3, 1257.

89. Grant to Canby, 27 February 1865, *Papers of Grant,* 14:61; Comstock Diary, 1–15 March 1865.

90. E. B. Long, *Civil War Day by Day,* 653, 657, 673.

91. McPherson, *Ordeal by Fire,* 479

92. Philip Henry Sheridan, *Personal Memoirs of Philip Henry Sheridan, General, United States Army,* 2 vols. (New York: Charles L. Webster, 1888; reprint, 2 vols., New York: Appleton, 1902), 2:126, 128–29, 144–45.

93. Porter, *Campaigning with Grant,* 434.

94. Ibid., 434–35, 441–43.

95. McPherson, *Ordeal by Fire,* 481.

96. Wilson, *Life of Rawlins,* 318–23.

97. Porter, *Campaigning with Grant,* 462–65.

98. Ibid., 467–81.

99. Ibid., 484.

CHAPTER 8: CONCLUSION

1. Bill O'Neal, *Fighting Men of the Indian Wars: A Biographical Encyclopedia of the Mountain Men, Soldiers, Cowboys, and Pioneers Who Took Up Arms during America's Westward Expansion* (Stillwater, Okla.: Barbed Wire Press, 1991), 113–14.

2. Weigley, *History of the United States Army,* 266.

3. Ibid., 567–68.

4. Ibid., 268.

5. R. Joshua Sherman, "The Bugler—Unsung Hero," *True West* vol. 40, no. 11 (November 1993): 17

6. Stephen E. Ambrose, *Upton and the Army* (Baton Rouge: Louisiana State University Press, 1964), 16–27; Warner, *Generals in Blue,* 519–20.

7. Ambrose, *Upton,* 17–18; Roger J. Spiller, "The U S Army Command and General Staff College: The Beginnings of the Kindergarten (pt. 1)," *Military Review,* 61, no. 5 (1981): 7–8.

8. Spiller, "Kindergarten," 8; Wallace E. Walker, "Emory Upton and the Army Officer's Creed," *Military Review* 61, no. 4 (1981): 66; Weigley, *Towards an American Army,* 120.

9. Weigley, *Towards an American Army,* 121.

10. Warner, *Generals in Blue,* 520.

11. Spiller, "Kindergarten," 4–5.

12. Ibid., 2–9.

13. Millett, *For the Common Defense,* 274–80.

14. Weigley, *History of the United States Army,* 314–15.

15. Millett, *For the Common Defense,* 310.

16. Weigley, *History of the United States Army,* 317.

17. John Dickinson, *The Building of an Army: A Detailed Account of Legislation, Administration, and Opinion in the United States, 1915–1920* (New York: Century, 1922), 257.

18. Paul Hutton, *Phil Sheridan and His Army* (Lincoln: University of Nebraska Press, 1985), 346–51; Dickinson, *Building an Army,* 259; Millett, *For the Common Defense,* 311.

19. Timothy K. Nenninger, *The Leavenworth Schools and the Old Army: Education, Professionalism, and the Officer Corps of the United States Army, 1881–1918* (Westport, Conn.: Greenwod Press, 1978), 99–100.

20. Mark E. Neely Jr., "Was the Civil War a Total War?" *Civil War History* 37 (March 1991): passim.

BIBLIOGRAPHY

PRIMARY SOURCES

Manuscripts

Chilton, Robert H. Papers. Eleanor S. Brockenbrough Library, Museum of the Confederacy, Richmond.

Comstock, Cyrus B. Diary. Library of Congress.

———. Papers. National Archives.

McClellan, George B. Papers. National Archives.

Rawlins, John A. Papers. Chicago Historical Society.

Sherman, William T. Papers. Library of Congress.

Venable, Charles Scott. Papers. University of North Carolina, Chapel Hill.

Wright, Edward H. Papers. New Jersey Historical Association, Newark.

Government Documents

Atlas to Accompany the Official Records of the Union and Confederate Armies. Washington, D.C.: Government Printing Office, 1891–95.

Craighill, William P. *The Army Officer's Pocket Companion: Principally Designed for Staff Officers in the Field.* New York: Nostrand, 1862.

Halleck, Henry Wager. *Elements of Military Art and Science; or, Course of Instruction in Strategy, Fortification, Tactics of Battles, &c;* New York: D. Appleton, 1846.

War of the Rebellion: A Compilation of the Official Records of the Union and Confederate Armies. 70 vols., 120 books. Washington D.C.: Government Printing Office, 1880–1901.

Other Published Documents

Badeau, Adam. "Adam Badeau, on Appomattox." *The Ulysses S. Grant Association Newsletter* 3 (October 1965).

———. *The Military History of U. S. Grant.* New York: D. Appleton, 1885.

Cadwallader, Sylvanus. *Three Years with Grant.* New York: Knopf, 1956.

Clausewitz, Carl von. *On War.* Edited and translated by Michael Howard and Peter Paret. Princeton, N.J.: Princeton University Press, 1976.

Dana, Charles A. *Recollections of the Civil War.* New York: D. Appleton, 1898.

Dodge, Grenville M. *Personal Recollections of Lincoln, Grant, and Sherman.* Council Bluffs, Iowa: Monarch Printing, 1914. Reprint, New York: Sage Books, 1965.

Dowdey, Clifford, and Louis H. Manarin, eds. *The Wartime Papers of R. E. Lee.* New York: Bramhall House for the Virginia Civil War Commission, 1961.

Gallagher, Gary W., ed. *Fighting for the Confederacy: The Personal Recollections of General Edward Porter Alexander.* Chapel Hill: University of North Carolina Press, 1989.

Grant, Jesse R. *In the Days of My Father General Grant.* New York: Harper and Brothers, 1925.

Grant, Ulysses S. *Personal Memoirs of U. S. Grant.* 2 vols. New York: C. L. Webster, 1885–86.

Hillyer, William S. "Pittsburg, April 11, 1862: On the Battlefield." *Ulysses S. Grant Association Newsletter* 1, no. 2 (January 1964): 10.

Howe, M. A. deWolfe, ed. *Marching with Sherman: Passages from the Letters and Campaign Diaries of Henry Hitchcock, Major and Assistant Adjutant General of Volunteers, November 1864–May 1865.* New Haven, Conn.: Yale University Press, 1927.

Johnson, Robert U., and Clarence Buel, eds. *Battles and Leaders of the Civil War.* 4 vols. New York: Century, 1887–88. Reprint (4 vols.), New York: Thomas Yoseloff, 1956.

Jomini, Antoine-Henri. *The Art of War.* Translated by G. H. Mendell and W. P. Craighill. 1862. Reprint, Westport, Conn.: Greenwood Press, n.d.

Long, Armistead L. *Memoirs of Robert E. Lee.* New York: J. M. Stoddart, 1886.

Lyman, Theodore. *Meade's Headquarters, 1863–1865: Letters of Colonel Theodore Lyman from the Wilderness to Appomattox.* Boston: Atlantic Monthly Press, 1922.

Marcy, Randolph B. *The Prairie Traveler.* Washington, D.C.: U.S. War Department, 1859. Reprint, New York: Perigree Books, 1994.

Maurice, Frederick, ed. *An Aide-de-Camp of Lee: Being the Papers of Colonel Charles Marshall, Sometime Aide-de-Camp, Military Secretary, and Assistant Adjutant General on the Staff of Robert E. Lee, 1862–1865.* Boston: Little, Brown, 1927.

McClellan, George B. *McClellan's Own Story.* New York: C. L. Webster, 1887.

Nichols, George Ward. *The Story of the Great March.* New York: Harper and Brothers, 1865. Reprint, Williamstown, Mass.: Corner House, 1972.

Porter, Horace. *Campaigning with Grant.* 1897. Reprint, Secaucus, N.J.: Blue and Grey Press, 1984.

Richardson, Albert D. *Personal History of Ulysses S. Grant.* Hartford, Conn.: American Publishing, 1868.

Sears, Stephen W., ed. *The Civil War Papers of George B. McClellan: Selected Correspondence, 1860–1865.* New York: Ticknor and Fields, 1989.

Sheridan, Philip Henry. *Personal Memoirs of Philip Henry Sheridan, General, United States Army.* 2 vols. New York: Charles L. Webster. 1888. Reprint (2 vols.), New York: Appleton, 1902.

Sherman, William T. *Memoirs of General William T. Sherman.* 2 vols. New York: Charles Webster, 1891.

Simon, John Y., ed. *The Papers of Ulysses S. Grant.* 22 vols. Carbondale: Southern Illinois University Press, 1967–1995.

———, ed. *The Personal Memoirs of Julia Dent Grant.* New York: G. P. Putnam's Sons, 1975.

Smith, William Wrenshall. "Holocaust Holiday." *Civil War Times Illustrated* 18 (October 1979).

Taylor, Walter H. *Four Years with General Lee: Being a Summary of the More Important Events touching the career of Robert E. Lee in the War Between the States.* New York: D. Appleton, 1877.

———. *General Lee: His Campaigns in Virginia, 1861–1862, with Personal Reminiscences.* Norfolk, Va.: Nusbaum, 1906.

Tower, R. Lockwood, and John S. Belmont, eds. *Lee's Adjutant: The Wartime Letters of Colonel Walter Herron Taylor, 1862–1865.* Columbia: University of South Carolina Press, 1995.

Wilson, James H. *The Life of John A. Rawlins: Lawyer, Assistant Adjutant-General, Chief of Staff, Major General of Volunteers, and Secretary of War.* New York: Neale Publishing, 1916.

SECONDARY SOURCES

Books

Amann, William Frayne, ed. *Personnel of the Civil War.* New York: T. Yoseloff, 1961.

Ambrose, Stephen E. *Upton and the Army.* Baton Rouge: Louisiana State University Press, 1964.

Bartholomees, J. Boone, Jr. *Buff Facings and Gilt Buttons: Staff and Headquarters Operations in the Army of Northern Virginia, 1861–1865.* Columbia: University of South Carolina Press, 1998.

Castel, Albert. *Decision in the West: The Atlanta Campaign of 1864.* Lawrence: University of Kansas Press, 1992.

Catton, Bruce. *Bruce Catton's Civil War: Three Volumes in One,* including *Mr. Lincoln's Army, Glory Road,* and *A Stillness at Appomattox.* New York: Fairfax Press, 1984.

———. *The Coming Fury.* New York: Washington Square Press, 1961. Reprint, New York: Pocket Books, 1967.

———. *Grant Moves South.* Boston: Little, Brown, 1960.

Chandler, Alfred D., Jr. *The Visible Hand: The Managerial Revolution in American Business.* Cambridge: Harvard University Press, Belknap Press, 1977.

Chandler, David G. *The Campaigns of Napoleon.* New York: Macmillan, 1966.

Craig, Gordon A. *The Politics of the Prussian Army, 1640–1945.* Oxford: Clarendon Press, 1955.

Crute, Joseph H., Jr. *Confederate Staff Officers, 1861–1865.* Powhatan, Va.: Derwent Books, 1982.

Cullum, George W. *Biographical Register of the Officers and Graduates of the U. S. Military Academy at West Point, New York.* 8 vols. Boston: Houghton, Mifflin, 1891–1940.

Davis, Burke. *Sherman's March.* New York: Random House, 1980.

Dickinson, John. *The Building of an Army: A Detailed Account of Legislation, Administration, and Opinion in the United States, 1915–1920.* New York: Century, 1922.

Donald, David, ed. *Why the North Won the Civil War.* Baton Rouge: Louisiana State University Press, 1960.

Dornbusch, Charles E. *Regimental Publications and Personal Narratives of the Civil War.* 3 vols. New York: New York Public Library, 1961–72.

Dowdey, Clifford. *Lee*. Boston: Little, Brown, 1965.

————. *Lee's Last Campaign: The Story of Lee and His Men against Grant—1864*. Boston: Little, Brown, 1960.

Ellis, Joseph, and Robert Moore. *School for Soldiers: West Point and the Profession of Arms*. New York: Oxford University Press, 1974.

Fellman, Michael. *Citizen Sherman: A Life of William Tecumseh Sherman*. New York: Random House, 1995.

Fleming, Thomas J. *West Point: The Men and Times of the U.S. Military Academy*. New York: William Morrow, 1969.

Flexner, James Thomas. *Washington: The Indispensable Man*. New York: Little, Brown, 1969. Reprint, New York: Plume Books, 1974.

Flood, Charles Bracelen. *Lee: The Last Years*. Boston: Houghton Mifflin, 1981.

Foote, Shelby. *The Civil War: A Narrative*. 3 vols. New York: Random House, 1958–74. Reprint, New York: Vintage Books, 1986.

Foreman, Sidney. *West Point: A History of the United States Military Academy*. New York: Columbia University Press, 1950.

Freeman, Douglas Southall. *Lee's Lieutenants: A Study in Command*. 3 vols. New York: Scribner's, 1942–44.

————. *R. E. Lee: A Biography*. 4 vols. New York: Scribner's, 1934–35.

Fuller, J. F. C. *The Generalship of Ulysses S. Grant*. New York: Dodd, Mead, 1929.

————. *Grant and Lee: A Study in Personality and Generalship*. London: Eyre and Spottiswode, 1933.

Goerlitz, Walter. *History of the German General Staff*. New York: Frederick A. Praeger, 1953.

Hagerman, Edward. *The American Civil War and the Origins of Modern Warfare: Ideas, Organization, and Field Command*. Bloomington: Indiana University Press, 1988.

Hart, B. H. Liddell. *Sherman: Soldier, Realist, American*. New York: Praeger, 1958.

Hassler, Warren W., Jr. *General George B. McClellan: Shield of the Union*. Baton Rouge: Louisiana State University Press, 1957.

Hattaway, Herman, and Archer Jones. *How the North Won: A Military History of the Civil War*. Urbana: University of Illinois Press, 1983.

Hittle, James D. *The Military Staff: Its History and Development*. Harrisburg, Pa.: Military Service, 1944. Reprint, Harrisburg, Pa.: Stackpole, 1961.

Hughes, Nathaniel Cheairs, Jr. *The Battle of Belmont: Grant Strikes South*. Chapel Hill: University of North Carolina Press, 1991.

Hutton, Paul. *Phil Sheridan and His Army.* Lincoln: University of Nebraska Press, 1985.

Jones, Archer. *Civil War Command and Strategy: The Process of Victory and Defeat.* New York: Free Press, 1992.

Key, William. *The Battle of Atlanta and the Georgia Campaign.* New York: Twayne, 1958.

Lewis, Lloyd. *Sherman: Fighting Prophet.* New York: Harcourt, Brace, 1932.

Long, E. B. *The Civil War Day by Day.* Garden City, N.Y.: Doubleday, 1971.

Lowry, Don. *Dark and Cruel War: The Decisive Months of the Civil War, September–December 1864.* New York: Hippocrene Books, 1993.

Macartney, Clarence Edward. *Little Mac: The Life of General George B. McClellan.* Philadelphia: Dorrance, 1940.

Marszalek, John F. *Sherman: A Soldier's Passion for Order.* New York: Free Press, 1993.

Matter, William D. *If It Takes All Summer: The Battle of Spotsylvania.* Chapel Hill: University of North Carolina Press, 1988.

McDonough, James Lee. *Shiloh: In Hell before Night.* Knoxville: University of Tennessee Press, 1977.

McFeely, William S. *Grant: A Biography.* New York: W. W. Norton, 1981.

McPherson, James M. *Ordeal by Fire: The Civil War and Reconstruction.* New York: Knopf, 1982.

Miers, Earl Schenck. *Web of Victory: Grant at Vicksburg.* New York: Knopf, 1955.

Millett, Allan R., and Peter Maslowski. *For the Common Defense: A Military History of the United States of America.* New York: Free Press, 1984.

Millis, Walter. *American Military Thought.* Indianapolis: Bobbs-Merrill, 1966.

Nenninger, Timothy K. *The Leavenworth Schools and the Old Army: Education, Professionalism, and the Officer Corps of the United States Army, 1881–1918.* Westport, Conn.: Greenwod Press, 1978.

Nevin, David, et al., eds. *The Civil War: The Road to Shiloh.* Alexandria, Va.: Time-Life Books, 1983.

Nevins, Allan. *Ordeal of the Union.* 8 vols. New York: Scribner's, 1947–71.

O'Neal, Bill. *Fighting Men of the Indian Wars: A Biographical Encyclopedia of the Mountain Men, Soldiers, Cowboys, and Pioneers Who Took Up Arms during America's Westward Expansion.* Stillwater, Okla.: Barbed Wire Press, 1991.

Perret, Geoffrey. *Ulysses S. Grant: Soldier and President.* New York: Random House, 1997.

Royster, Charles. *The Destructive War: William Tecumseh Sherman, Stonewall Jackson, and the Americans.* New York: Knopf, 1991.

Savas, Theodore P., and David A. Woodbury, eds. *The Campaign for Atlanta and Sherman's March to the Sea: Essays on the 1864 Georgia Campaigns.* Campbell, Calif.: Savas Woodbury Publishers, 1992.

Sears, Stephen W. *George B. McClellan: The Young Napoleon.* Boston: Ticknor and Fields, 1988.

———. *Landscape Turned Red: The Battle of Antietam.* New York: Warner Books, 1983.

Shannon, Fred. *The Organization and Administration of the Union Army, 1861–1862.* 2 vols. Cleveland: Arthur H. Clark, 1928.

Simpson, Brooks D. *Let Us Have Peace: Ulysses S. Grant and the Politics of War and Reconstruction, 1861–1868.* Chapel Hill: University of North Carolina Press, 1991.

Smith, Gene. *Lee and Grant: A Dual Biography.* New York: McGraw-Hill, 1984.

Sommers, Richard J. *Richmond Redeemed: The Siege at Petersburg.* Garden City, N.Y.: Doubleday, 1981.

Spaulding, Oliver L. *The United States Army in War and Peace.* New York: G. P. Putnam's Sons, 1937.

Stackpole, Edward J. *Chancellorsville: Lee's Greatest Battle.* 2nd ed. Harrisburg, Pa.: Stackpole, 1988.

Steere, Edward. *The Wilderness Campaign.* Harrisburg, Pa.: Stackpole, 1960.

Sword, Wiley. *Shiloh: Bloody April.* New York: William Morrow, 1974.

Thomas, Emory M. *Robert E. Lee: A Biography.* New York: W. W. Norton, 1995.

Trudeau, Noah Andre. *Bloody Roads South: The Wilderness to Cold Harbor, May–June 1864.* Boston: Little, Brown, 1989.

———. *The Last Citadel: Petersburg, Virginia, June 1864–April 1865.* Baton Rouge: Louisiana State University Press, 1991.

Vetter, Charles Edmund. *Sherman: Merchant of Terror, Advocate of Peace.* Gretna, La.: Pelican Publishing, 1992.

Warner, Ezra J. *Generals in Blue.* Baton Rouge: Louisiana State University Press, 1964.

———. *Generals in Gray.* Baton Rouge: Louisiana State University Press, 1959.

Weigley, Russell F. *History of the United States Army.* New York: Macmillan, 1967.

———. *Towards an American Army: Military Thought from Washington to Marshall.* New York: Columbia University Press, 1962.

Welcher, Frank J. *The Union Army, 1861-65: Organization and Operations.* Vol. 1, *The Eastern Theater.* Bloomington: Indiana University Press, 1989.

Wheeler, Richard. *Sword over Richmond: An Eyewitness History of McClellan's Peninsula Campaign.* New York: Harper and Row, 1986.

Williams, Kenneth. *Lincoln Finds a General: A Military Study of the Civil War.* 5 vols. New York: Macmillan, 1949–59.

Williams, T. Harry. *Lincoln and His Generals.* New York: Knopf, 1952.

Journal Articles

Hagerman, Edward. "The Professionalization of George B. McClellan and Early Civil War Field Command: An Institutional Perspective." *Civil War History* 21, no. 2 (1975): 113–35.

Huett, Will. "A Man Called 'Mary Anne.'" *True West* 38 (November 1991): 42–45.

Long, E. B. "John A. Rawlins: Staff Officer Par Excellence." *Civil War Times Illustrated* 12, no. 9 (1974): 4–9, 43–46.

Neely, Mark E., Jr. "Was the Civil War a Total War?" *Civil War History* 37 (March 1991): 5–28.

Sherman, R. Joshua. "The Bugler—Unsung Hero." *True West* 40 (November 1993): 14–19.

Spiller, Roger J. "The US Army Command and General Staff College: The Beginnings of the Kindergarten (pt. 1); On the Value of the 'Leavenworth Experience' (pt. 2)." *Military Review* 61, no. 5 (1981): 2–15.

Vermillion, John M. "The Pillars of Generalship." *Parameters* 17 (summer 1987): 2–17.

Walker, Wallace E. "Emory Upton and the Army Officer's Creed." *Military Review* 61, no. 4 (1981): 65–68.

Unpublished Works

Smith, David William. "Ely Samuel Parker, 1828–1895: Military Secretary, Indian Commissioner, and Commissioner of Indian Affairs." Master's thesis, Southern Illinois University, 1973.

INDEX

Page numbers in italics refer to illustrations.